# Yuri Bear Storm

## 1

Author: Ikunigomakinako

Illustrator: Akiko Morishima

TOKYOPOP®

# Contents

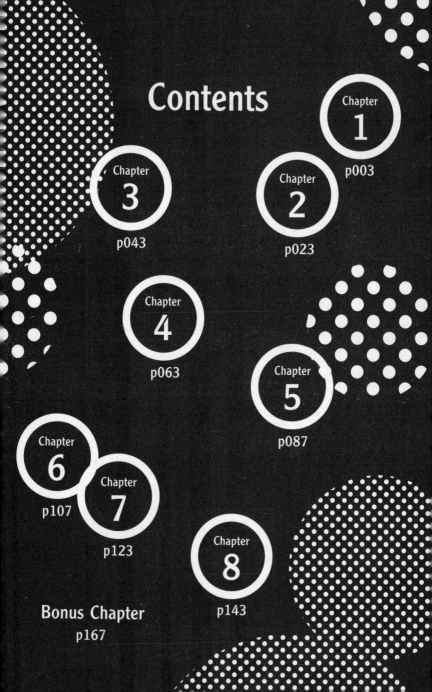

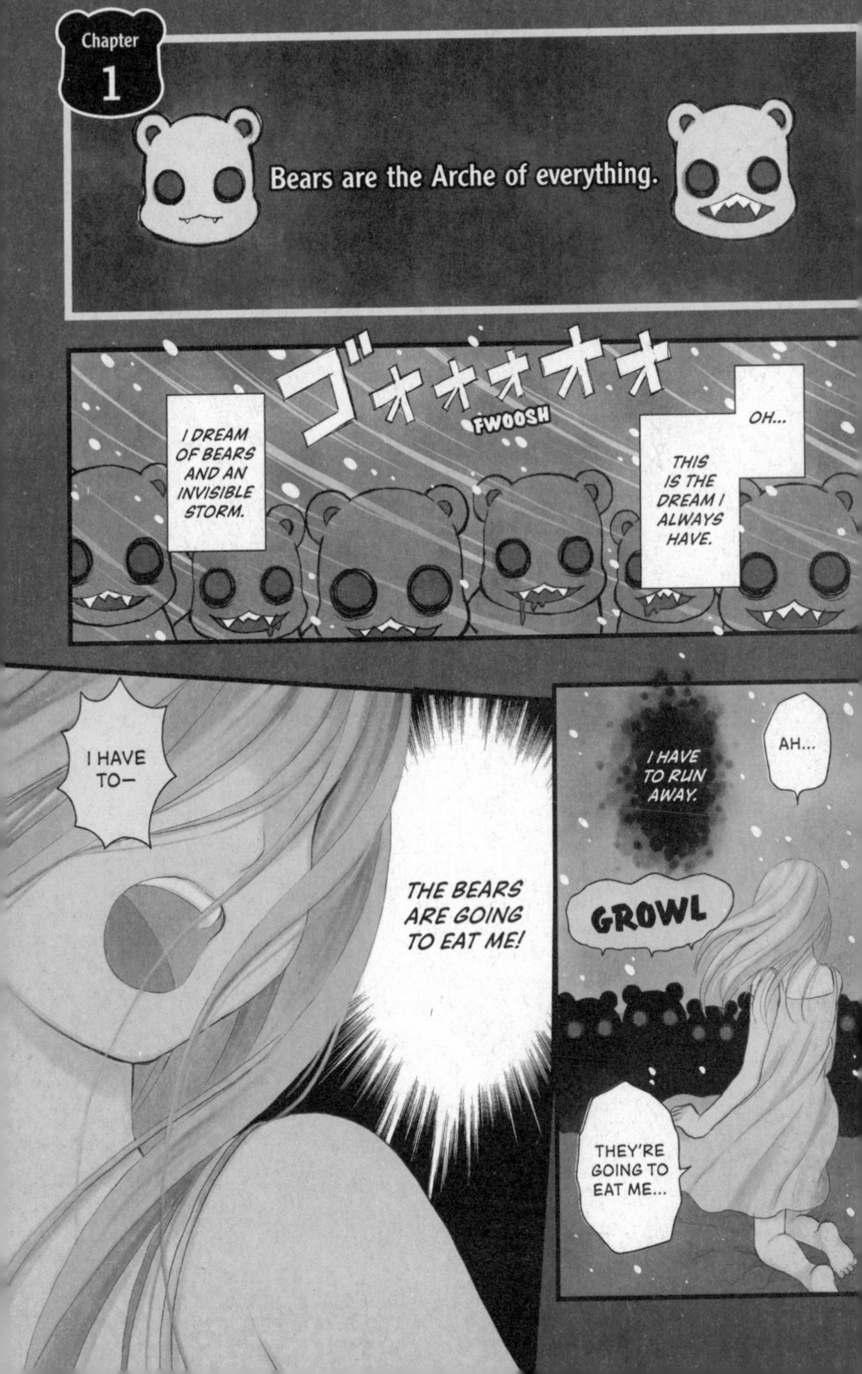
Chapter
1
Bears are the Arche of everything.
OH...
THIS IS THE DREAM I ALWAYS HAVE.
ゴォォォオオ
FWOOSH
I DREAM OF BEARS AND AN INVISIBLE STORM.
AH...
I HAVE TO RUN AWAY.
GROWL
THEY'RE GOING TO EAT ME...
I HAVE TO—
THE BEARS ARE GOING TO EAT ME!

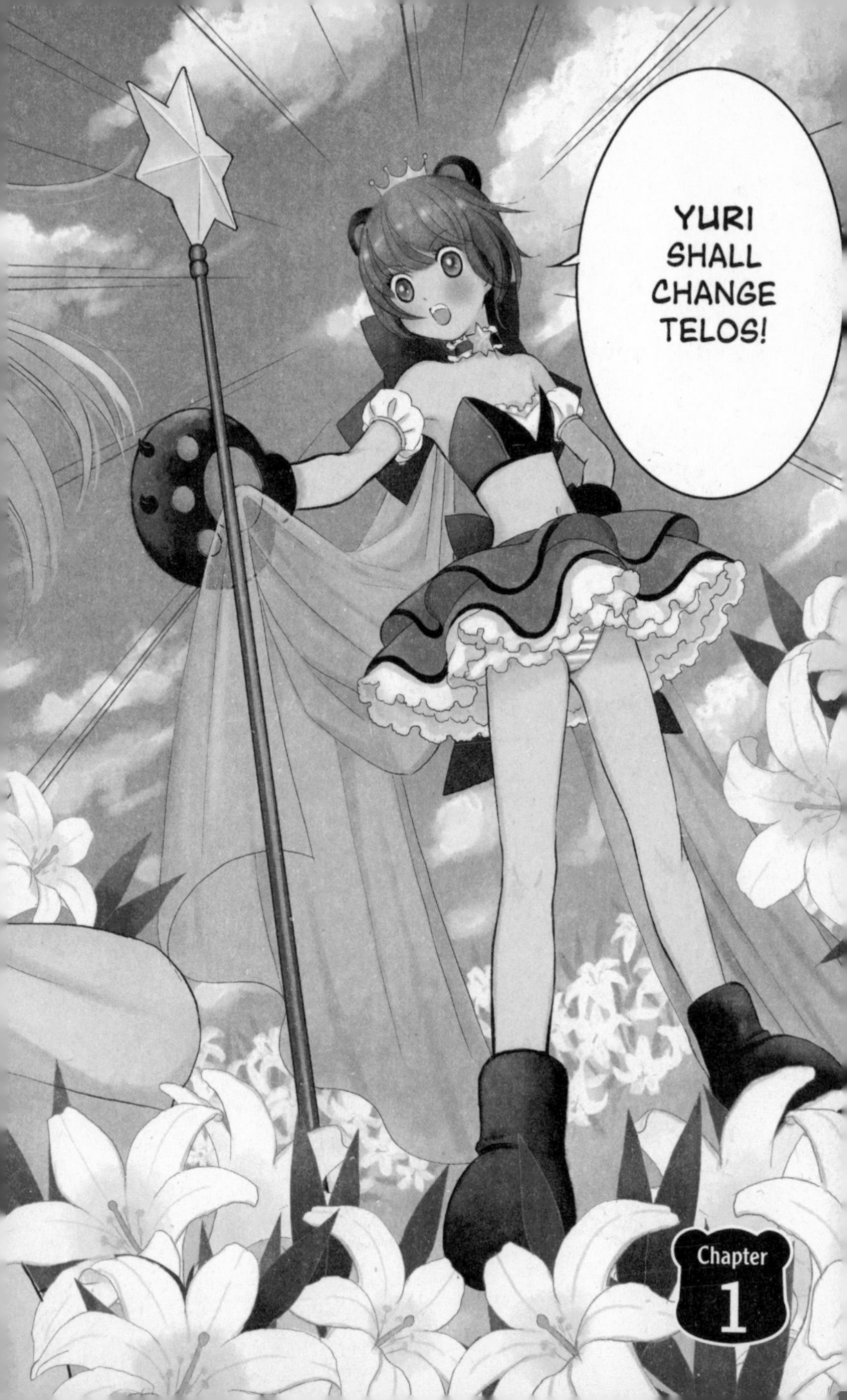
YURI SHALL CHANGE TELOS!
Chapter 1

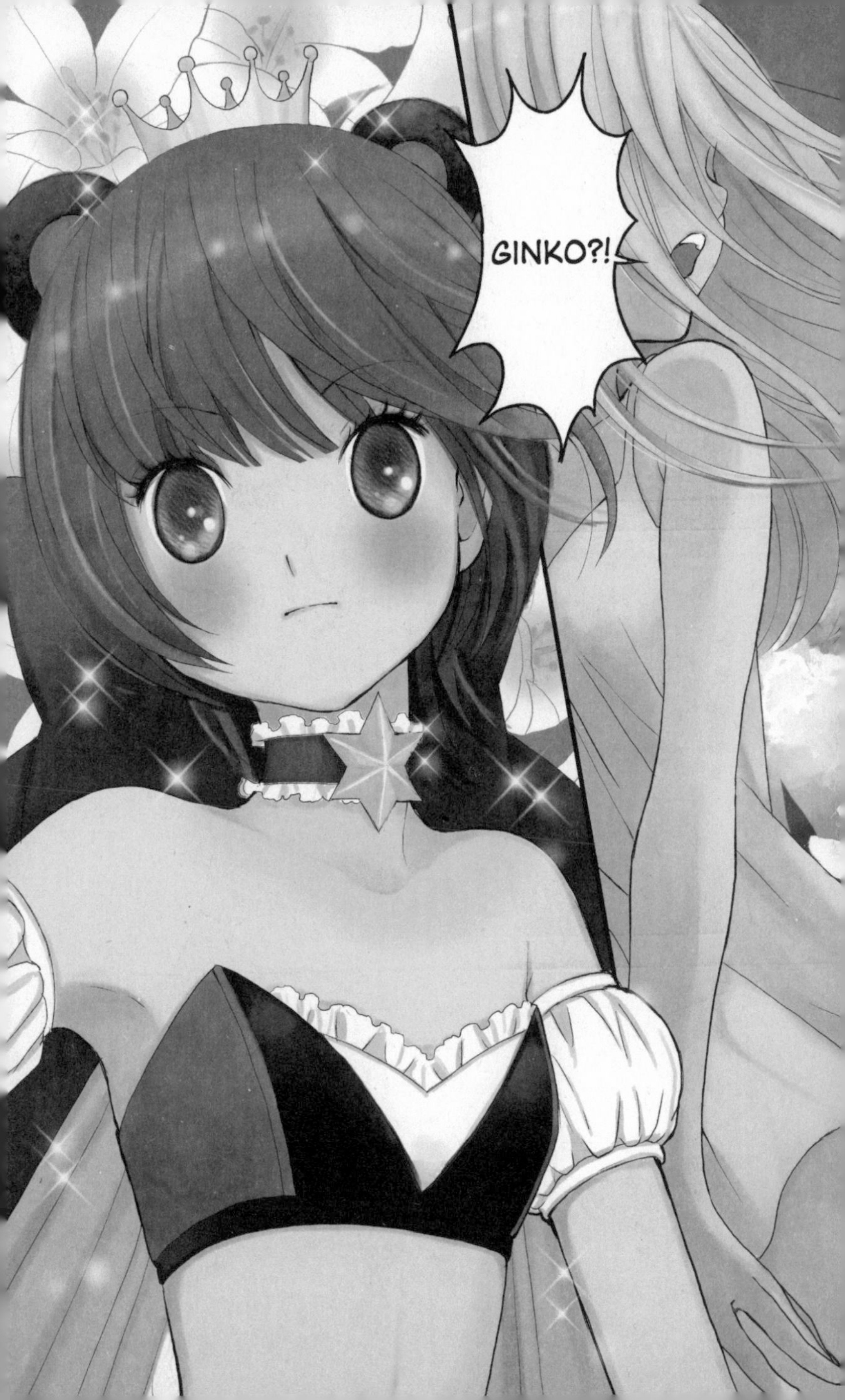
GINKO?!

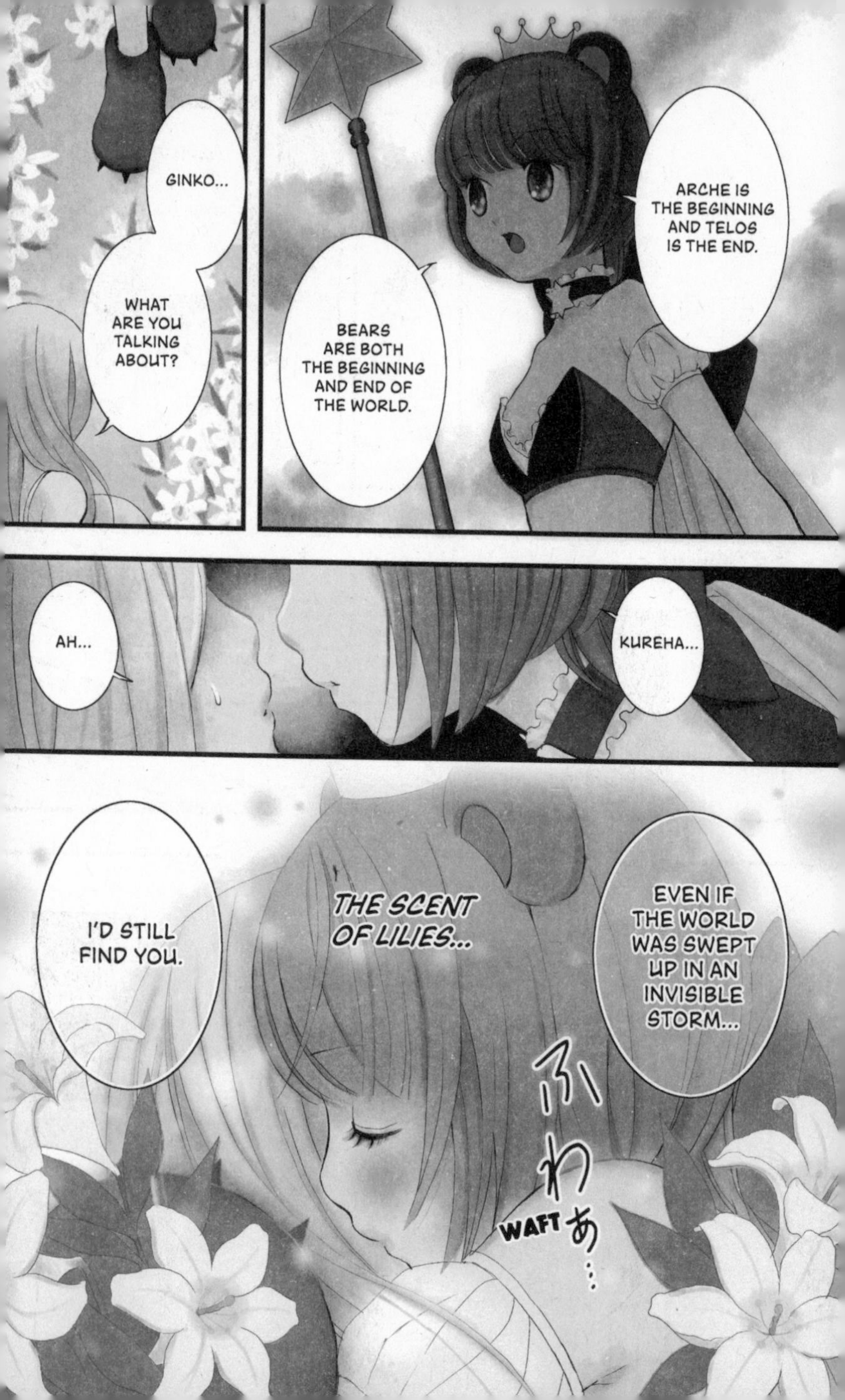
ARCHE IS THE BEGINNING AND TELOS IS THE END.
BEARS ARE BOTH THE BEGINNING AND END OF THE WORLD.
GINKO...
WHAT ARE YOU TALKING ABOUT?
KUREHA...
AH...
EVEN IF THE WORLD WAS SWEPT UP IN AN INVISIBLE STORM...
THE SCENT OF LILIES...
I'D STILL FIND YOU.
ふわぁ…
WAFT

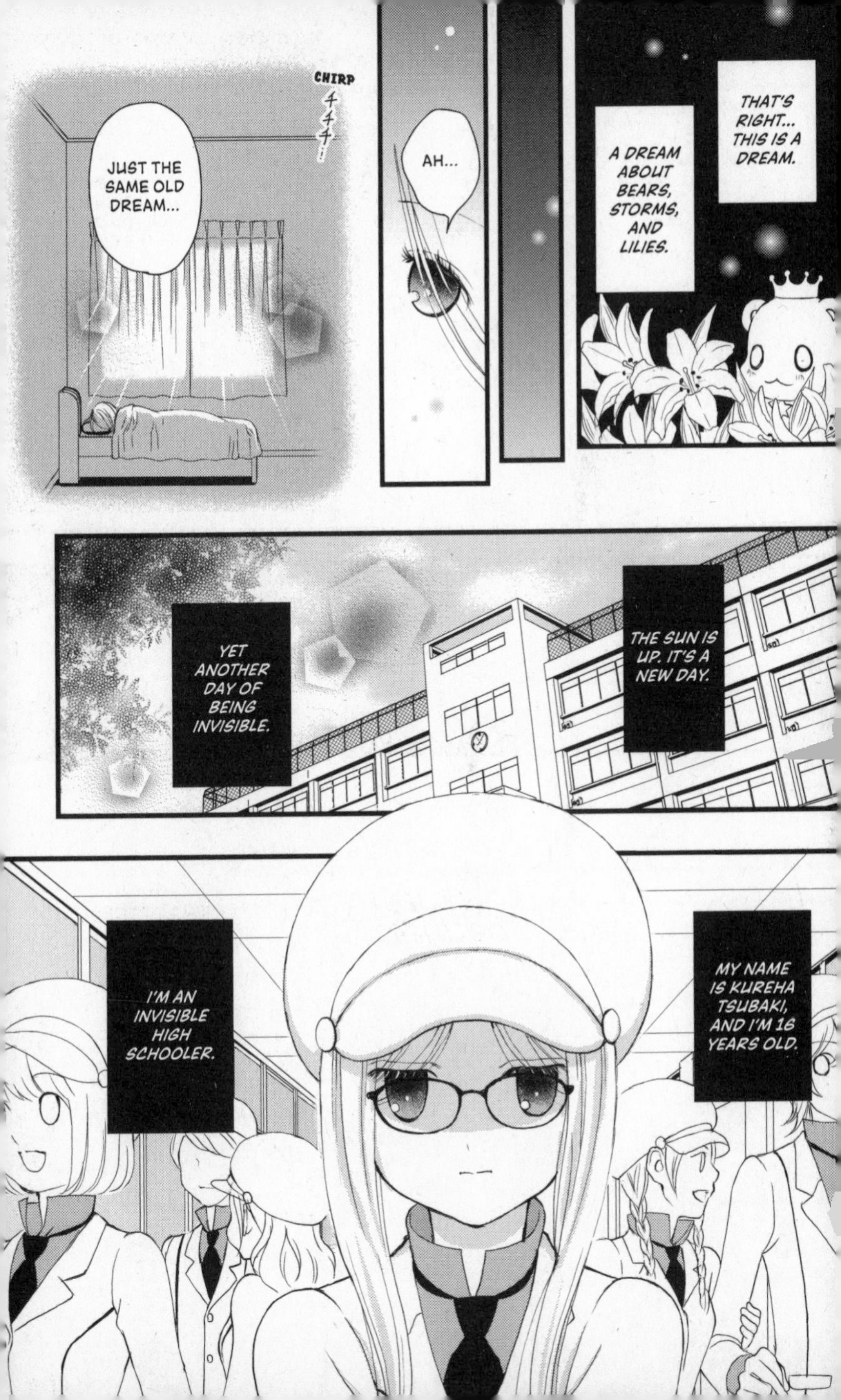
THAT'S RIGHT... THIS IS A DREAM.
A DREAM ABOUT BEARS, STORMS, AND LILIES.
AH...
CHIRP
JUST THE SAME OLD DREAM...
THE SUN IS UP. IT'S A NEW DAY.
YET ANOTHER DAY OF BEING INVISIBLE.
MY NAME IS KUREHA TSUBAKI, AND I'M 16 YEARS OLD.
I'M AN INVISIBLE HIGH SCHOOLER.

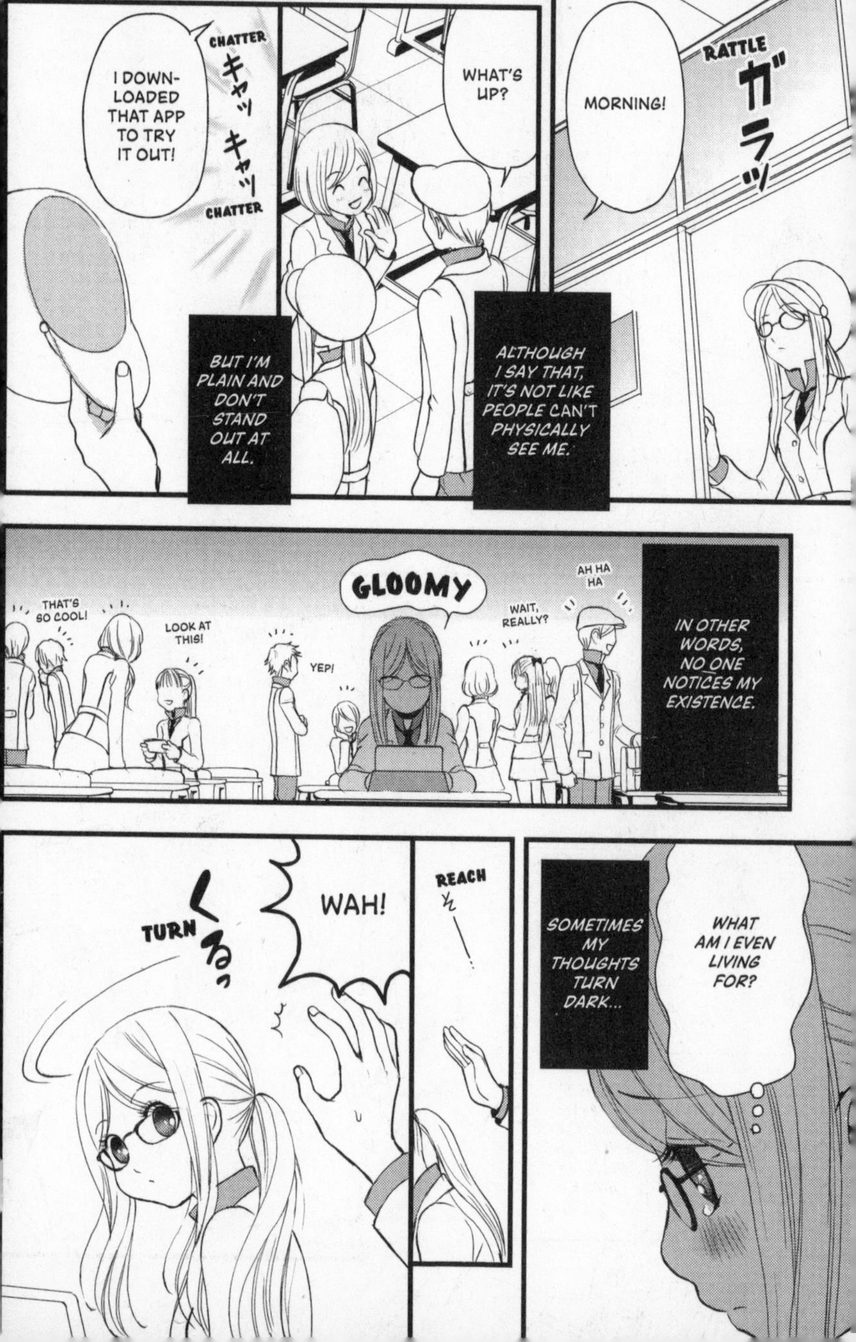
RATTLE
ガラッ
MORNING!
WHAT'S UP?
ALTHOUGH I SAY THAT, IT'S NOT LIKE PEOPLE CAN'T PHYSICALLY SEE ME.
CHATTER
キャッ キャッ
CHATTER
I DOWN-LOADED THAT APP TO TRY IT OUT!
BUT I'M PLAIN AND DON'T STAND OUT AT ALL.
IN OTHER WORDS, NO ONE NOTICES MY EXISTENCE.
AH HA HA
WAIT, REALLY?
GLOOMY
YEP!
LOOK AT THIS!
THAT'S SO COOL!
WHAT AM I EVEN LIVING FOR?
SOMETIMES MY THOUGHTS TURN DARK...
REACH
WAH!
TURN
くるっ

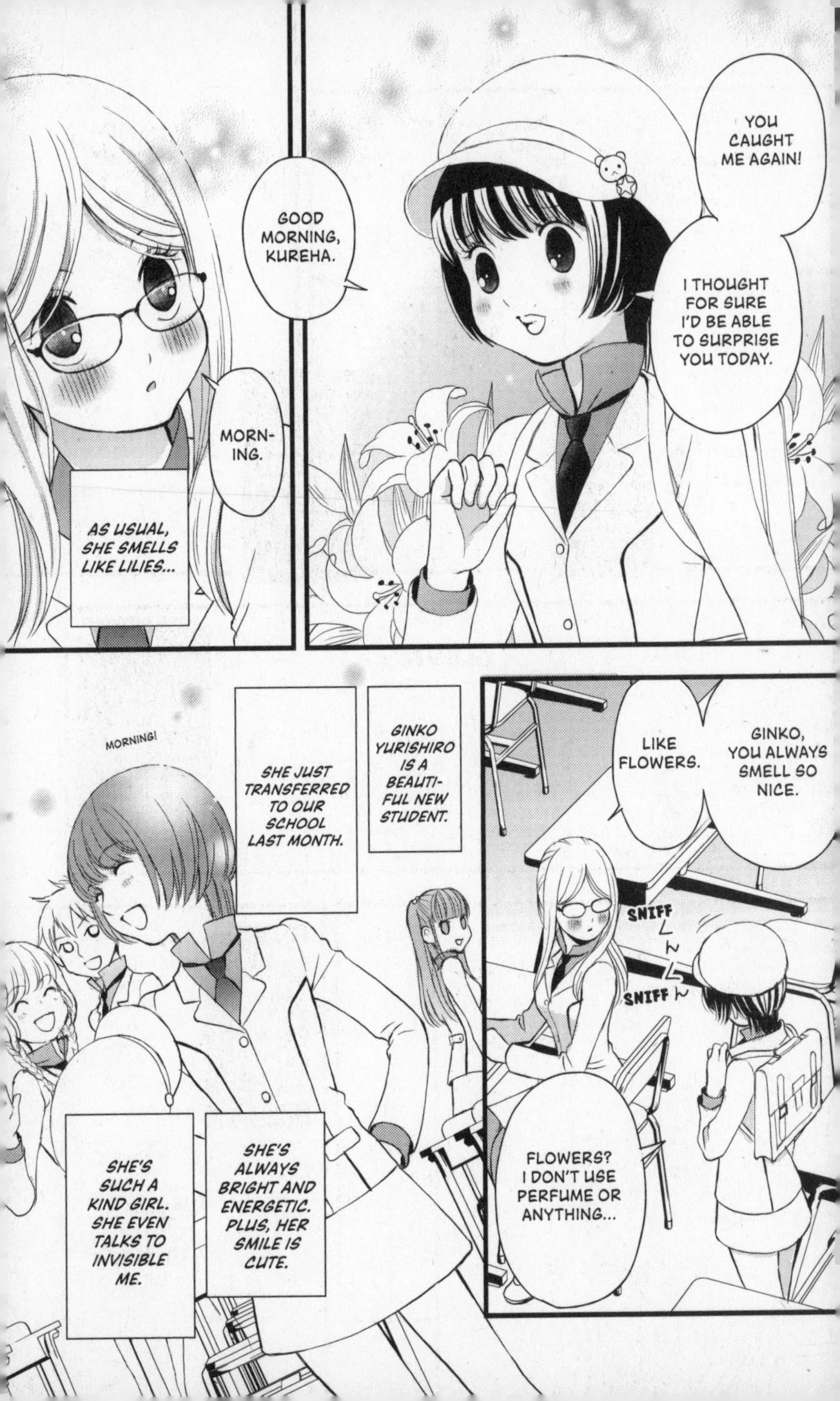

YOU CAUGHT ME AGAIN!
I THOUGHT FOR SURE I'D BE ABLE TO SURPRISE YOU TODAY.
GOOD MORNING, KUREHA.
MORN-ING.
AS USUAL, SHE SMELLS LIKE LILIES...
GINKO, YOU ALWAYS SMELL SO NICE.
LIKE FLOWERS.
SNIFF
SNIFF
FLOWERS? I DON'T USE PERFUME OR ANYTHING...
GINKO YURISHIRO IS A BEAUTI-FUL NEW STUDENT.
SHE JUST TRANSFERRED TO OUR SCHOOL LAST MONTH.
MORNING!
SHE'S ALWAYS BRIGHT AND ENERGETIC. PLUS, HER SMILE IS CUTE.
SHE'S SUCH A KIND GIRL. SHE EVEN TALKS TO INVISIBLE ME.

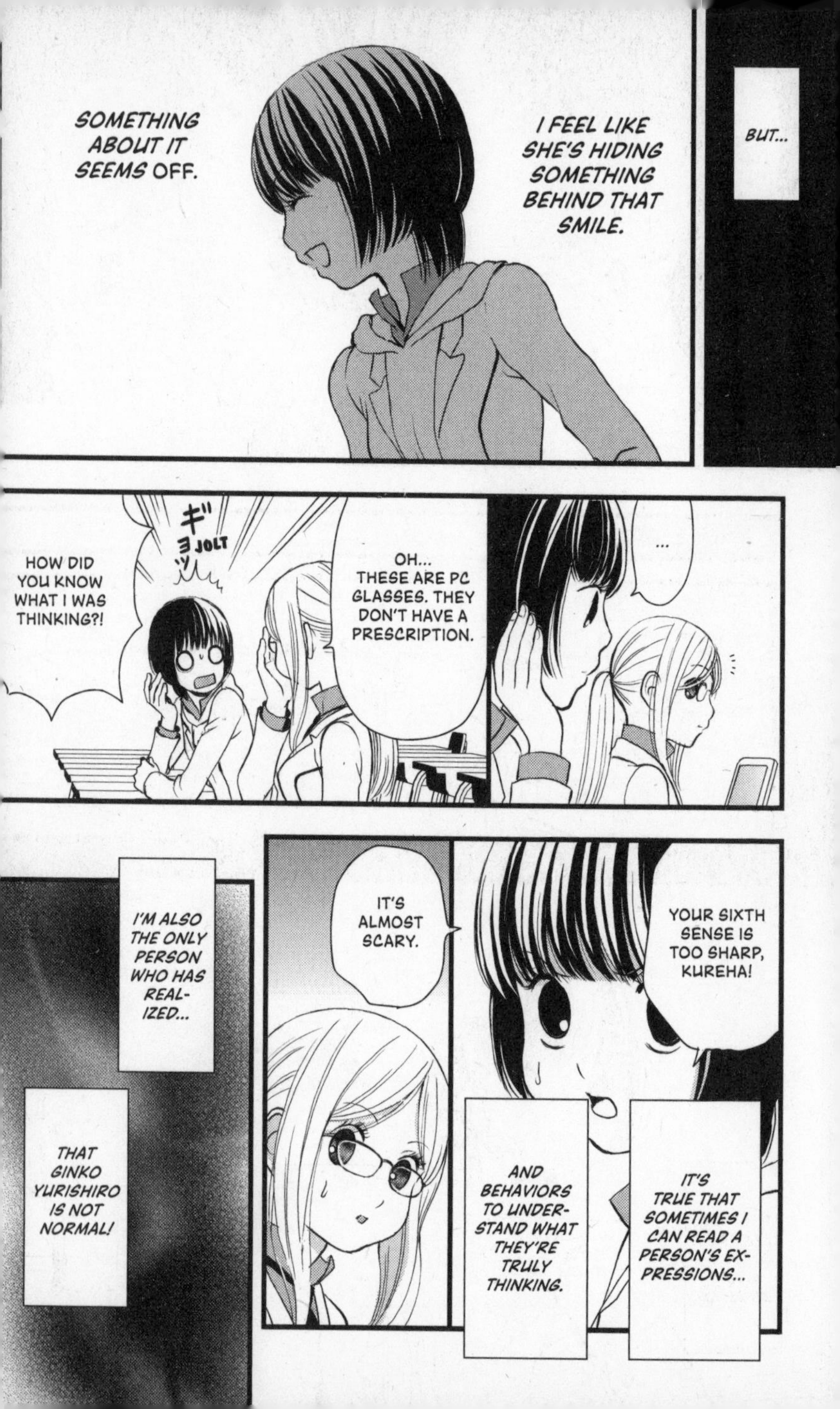

BUT...
I FEEL LIKE SHE'S HIDING SOMETHING BEHIND THAT SMILE.
SOMETHING ABOUT IT SEEMS OFF.
...
OH... THESE ARE PC GLASSES. THEY DON'T HAVE A PRESCRIPTION.
ギヨッ JOLT
HOW DID YOU KNOW WHAT I WAS THINKING?!
YOUR SIXTH SENSE IS TOO SHARP, KUREHA!
IT'S ALMOST SCARY.
IT'S TRUE THAT SOMETIMES I CAN READ A PERSON'S EXPRESSIONS...
AND BEHAVIORS TO UNDERSTAND WHAT THEY'RE TRULY THINKING.
I'M ALSO THE ONLY PERSON WHO HAS REALIZED...
THAT GINKO YURISHIRO IS NOT NORMAL!

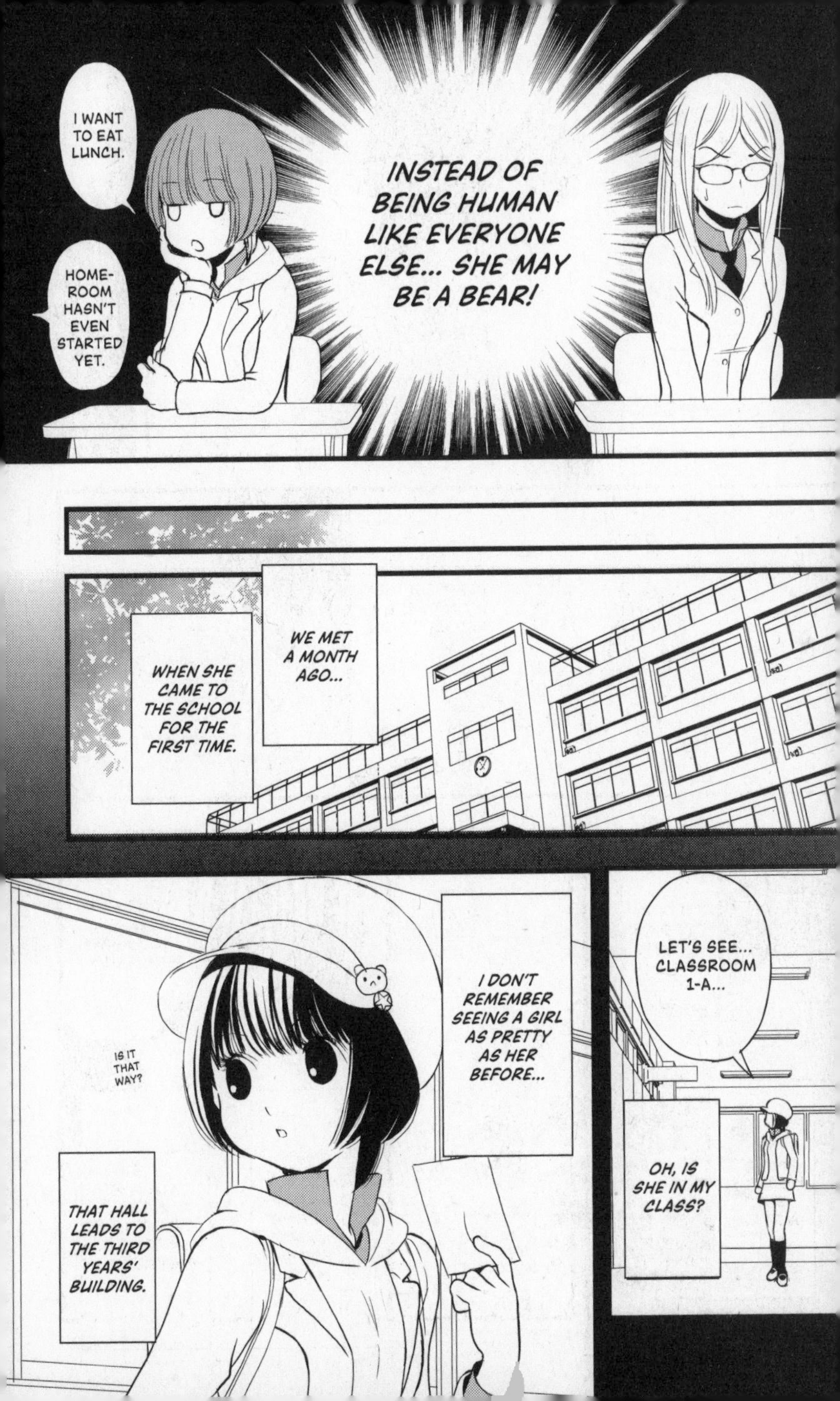
INSTEAD OF BEING HUMAN LIKE EVERYONE ELSE... SHE MAY BE A BEAR!
I WANT TO EAT LUNCH.
HOME-ROOM HASN'T EVEN STARTED YET.
WE MET A MONTH AGO...
WHEN SHE CAME TO THE SCHOOL FOR THE FIRST TIME.
LET'S SEE... CLASSROOM 1-A...
OH, IS SHE IN MY CLASS?
I DON'T REMEMBER SEEING A GIRL AS PRETTY AS HER BEFORE...
IS IT THAT WAY?
THAT HALL LEADS TO THE THIRD YEARS' BUILDING.

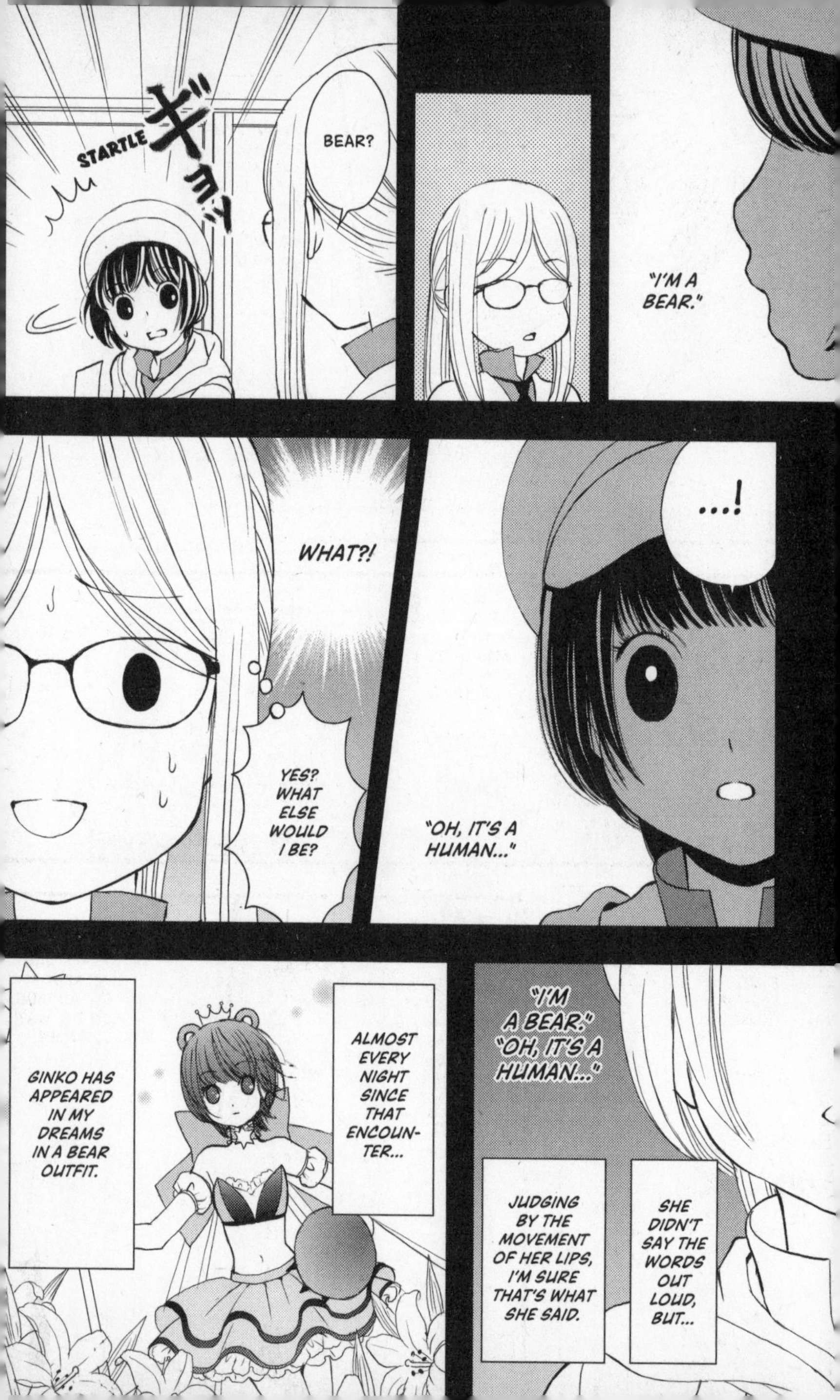
"I'M A BEAR."
BEAR?
STARTLE
ギョッ
...!
"OH, IT'S A HUMAN..."
WHAT?!
YES? WHAT ELSE WOULD I BE?
"I'M A BEAR." "OH, IT'S A HUMAN..."
SHE DIDN'T SAY THE WORDS OUT LOUD, BUT...
JUDGING BY THE MOVEMENT OF HER LIPS, I'M SURE THAT'S WHAT SHE SAID.
ALMOST EVERY NIGHT SINCE THAT ENCOUNTER...
GINKO HAS APPEARED IN MY DREAMS IN A BEAR OUTFIT.

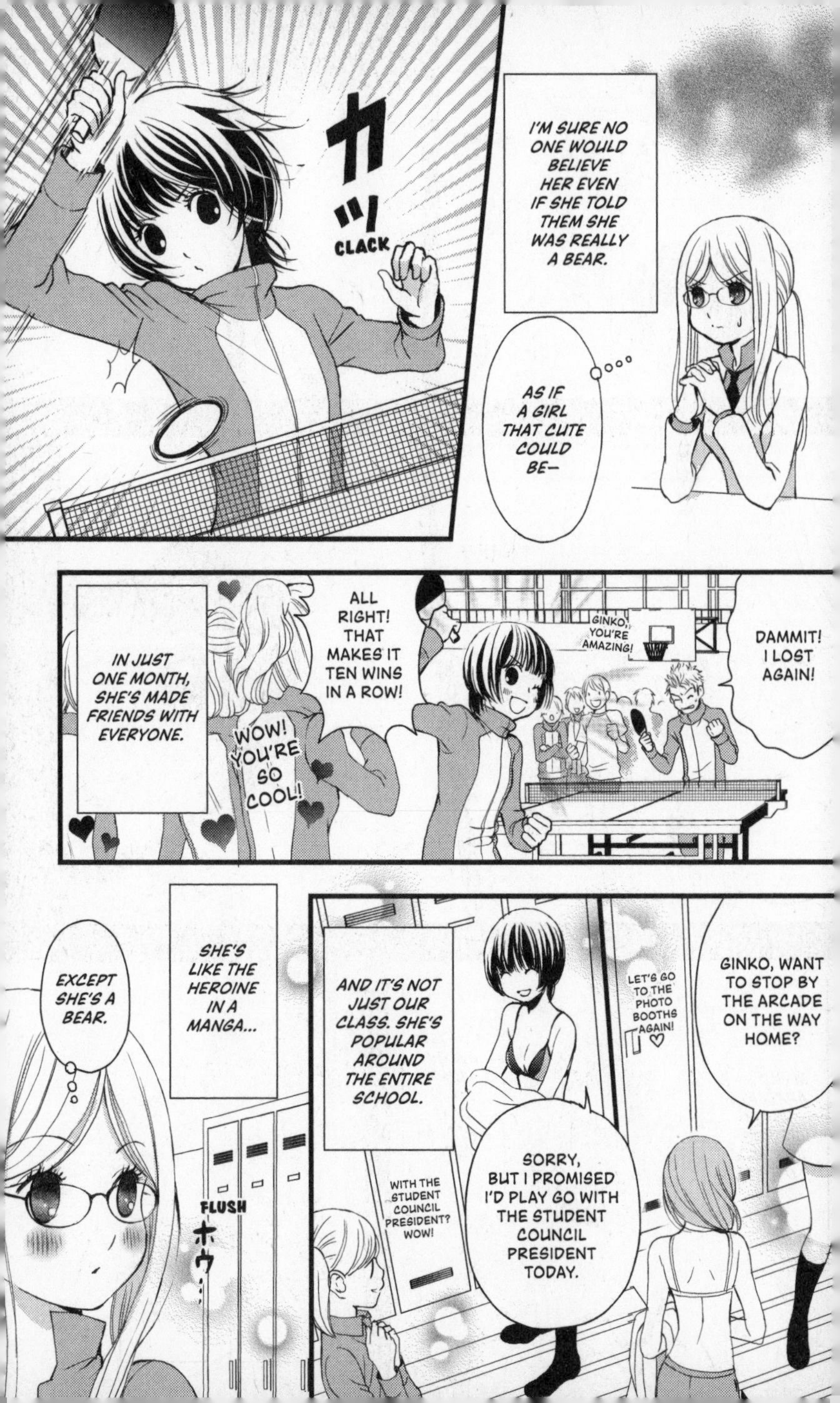
I'M SURE NO ONE WOULD BELIEVE HER EVEN IF SHE TOLD THEM SHE WAS REALLY A BEAR.
AS IF A GIRL THAT CUTE COULD BE—
カッ
CLACK
DAMMIT! I LOST AGAIN!
GINKO, YOU'RE AMAZING!
ALL RIGHT! THAT MAKES IT TEN WINS IN A ROW!
WOW! YOU'RE SO COOL!
IN JUST ONE MONTH, SHE'S MADE FRIENDS WITH EVERYONE.
GINKO, WANT TO STOP BY THE ARCADE ON THE WAY HOME?
LET'S GO TO THE PHOTO BOOTHS AGAIN! ♡
AND IT'S NOT JUST OUR CLASS. SHE'S POPULAR AROUND THE ENTIRE SCHOOL.
SORRY, BUT I PROMISED I'D PLAY GO WITH THE STUDENT COUNCIL PRESIDENT TODAY.
WITH THE STUDENT COUNCIL PRESIDENT? WOW!
SHE'S LIKE THE HEROINE IN A MANGA...
EXCEPT SHE'S A BEAR.
FLUSH
ホウ…

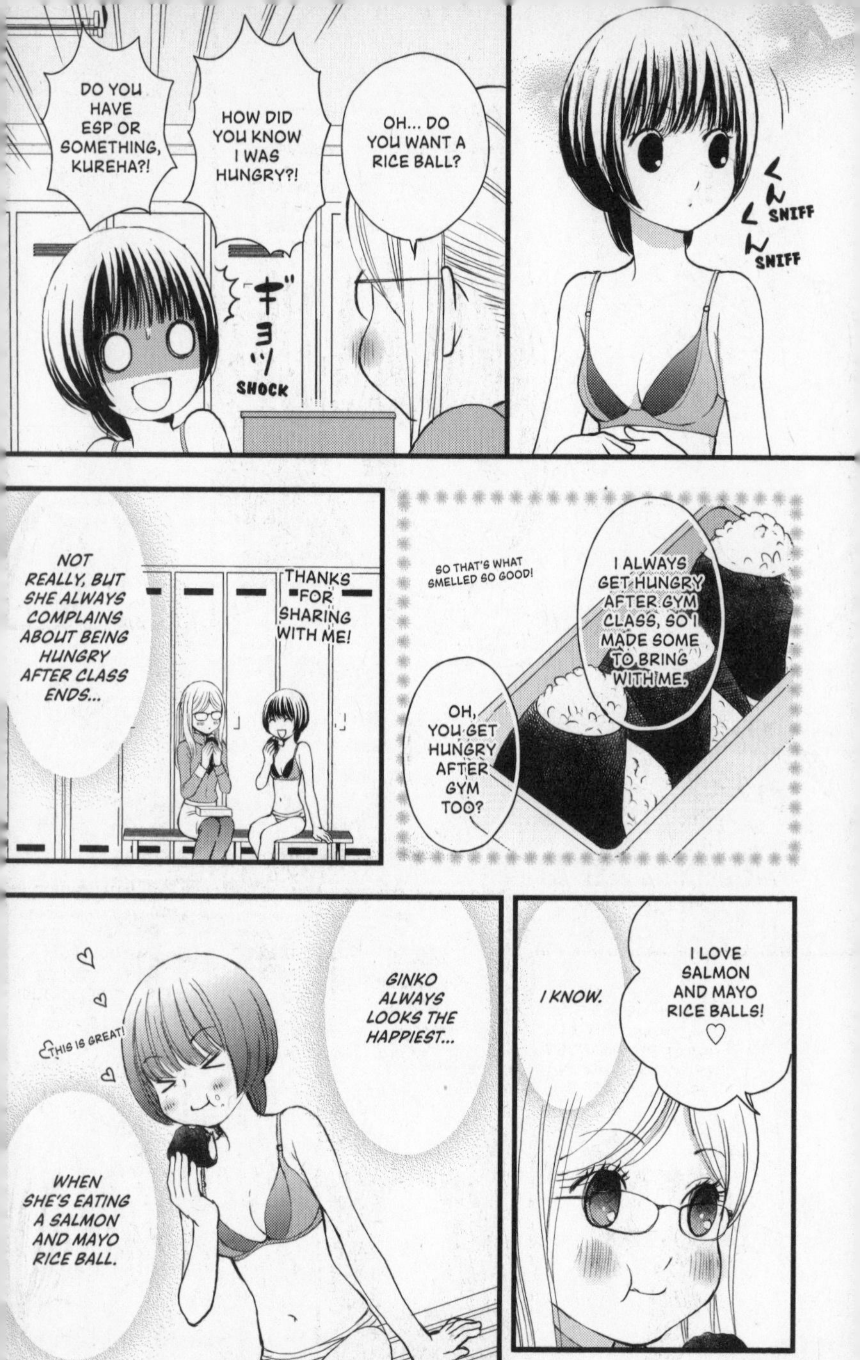
くんくん
SNIFF
SNIFF
OH... DO YOU WANT A RICE BALL?
HOW DID YOU KNOW I WAS HUNGRY?!
DO YOU HAVE ESP OR SOMETHING, KUREHA?!
ギョッ
SHOCK
I ALWAYS GET HUNGRY AFTER GYM CLASS, SO I MADE SOME TO BRING WITH ME.
SO THAT'S WHAT SMELLED SO GOOD!
OH, YOU GET HUNGRY AFTER GYM TOO?
THANKS FOR SHARING WITH ME!
NOT REALLY, BUT SHE ALWAYS COMPLAINS ABOUT BEING HUNGRY AFTER CLASS ENDS...
I LOVE SALMON AND MAYO RICE BALLS! ♡
I KNOW.
GINKO ALWAYS LOOKS THE HAPPIEST...
♡THIS IS GREAT!
WHEN SHE'S EATING A SALMON AND MAYO RICE BALL.

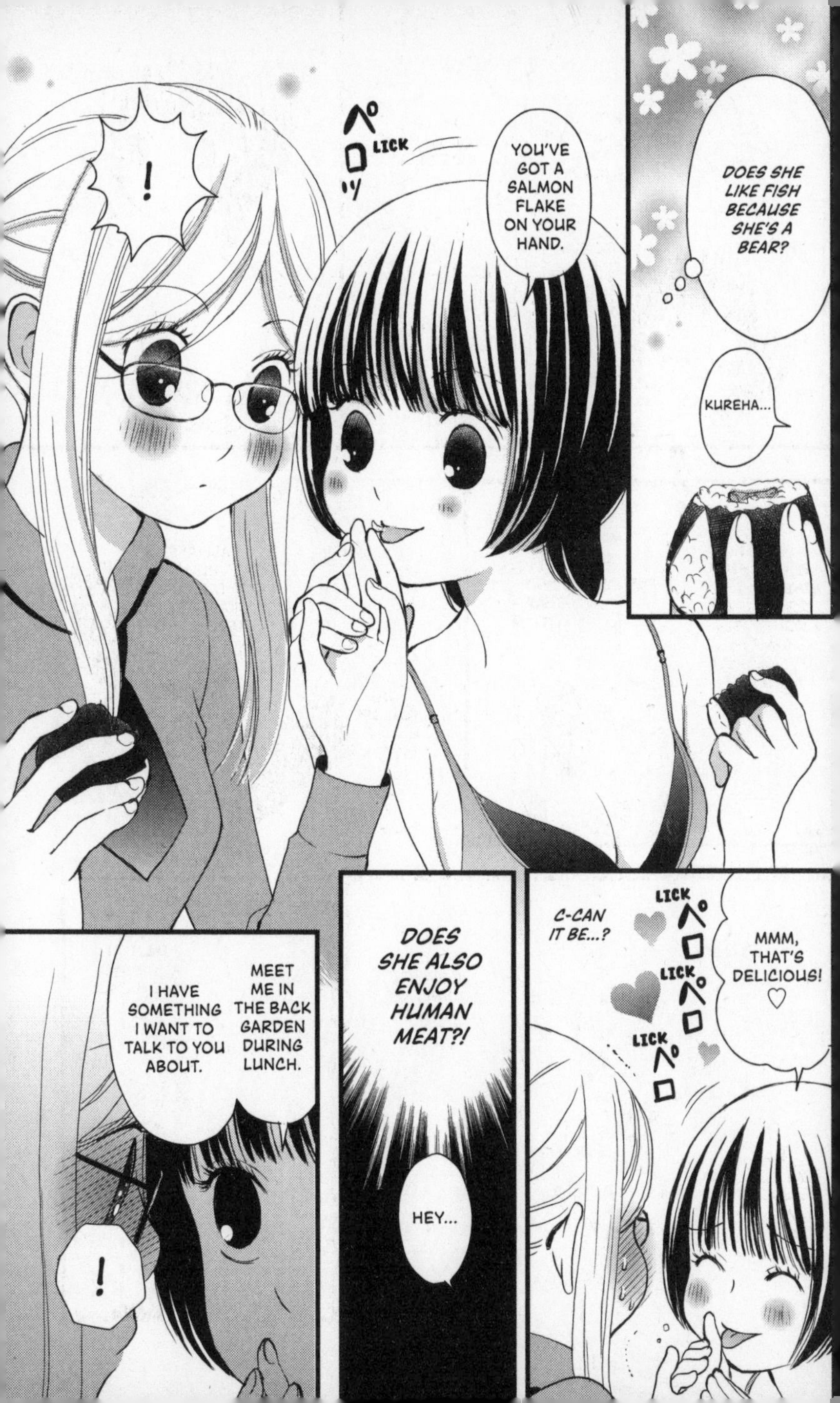
DOES SHE LIKE FISH BECAUSE SHE'S A BEAR?
KUREHA...
YOU'VE GOT A SALMON FLAKE ON YOUR HAND.
ペロッ LICK
!
MMM, THAT'S DELICIOUS! ♡
LICK ペロ
LICK ペロ
LICK ペロ
C-CAN IT BE...?
DOES SHE ALSO ENJOY HUMAN MEAT?!
HEY...
MEET ME IN THE BACK GARDEN DURING LUNCH.
I HAVE SOMETHING I WANT TO TALK TO YOU ABOUT.
!

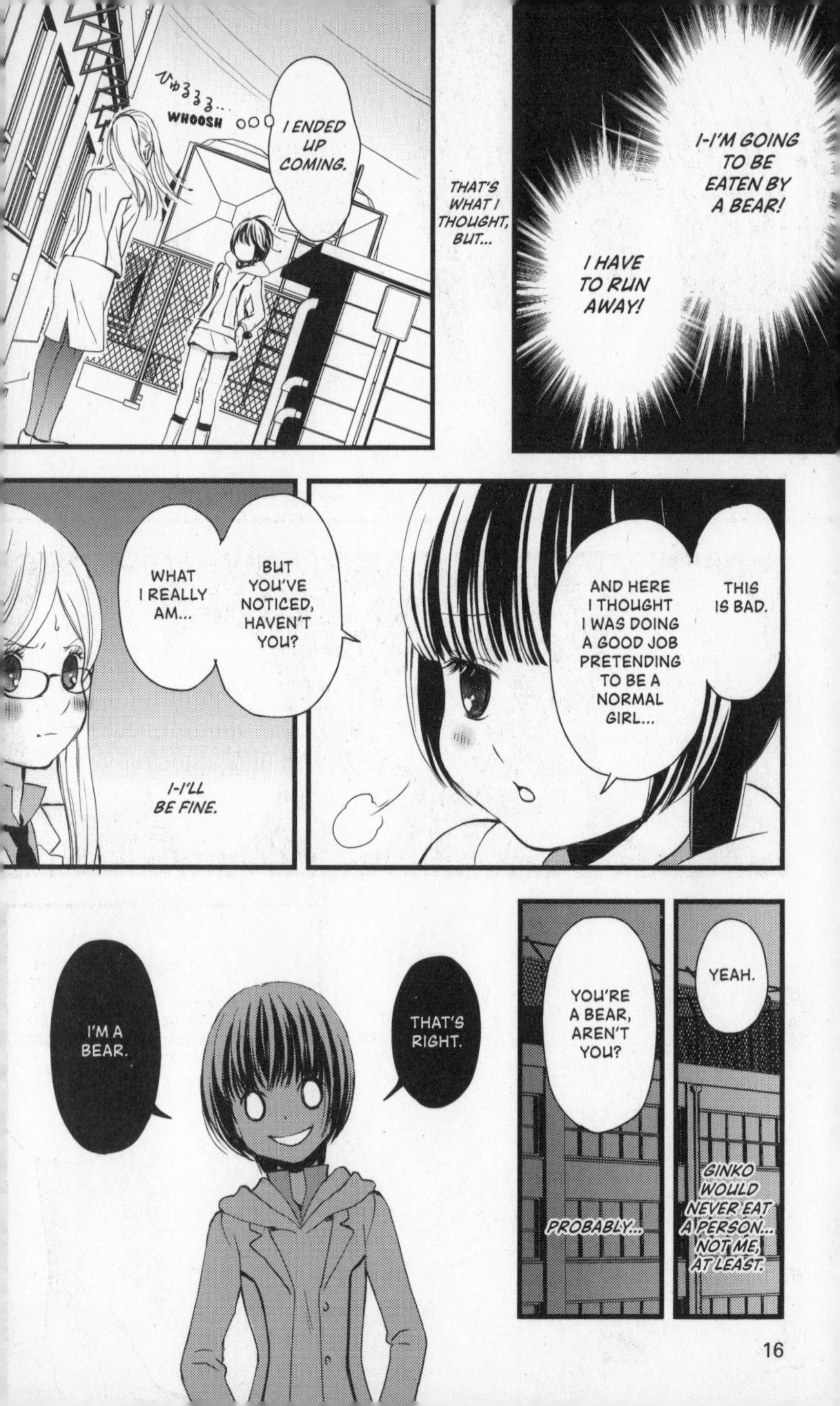
I-I'M GOING TO BE EATEN BY A BEAR!
I HAVE TO RUN AWAY!
THAT'S WHAT I THOUGHT, BUT...
I ENDED UP COMING.
ひゅるるる...
WHOOSH
THIS IS BAD.
AND HERE I THOUGHT I WAS DOING A GOOD JOB PRETENDING TO BE A NORMAL GIRL...
BUT YOU'VE NOTICED, HAVEN'T YOU?
WHAT I REALLY AM...
I-I'LL BE FINE.
YEAH.
GINKO WOULD NEVER EAT A PERSON... NOT ME, AT LEAST.
YOU'RE A BEAR, AREN'T YOU?
PROBABLY...
THAT'S RIGHT.
I'M A BEAR.

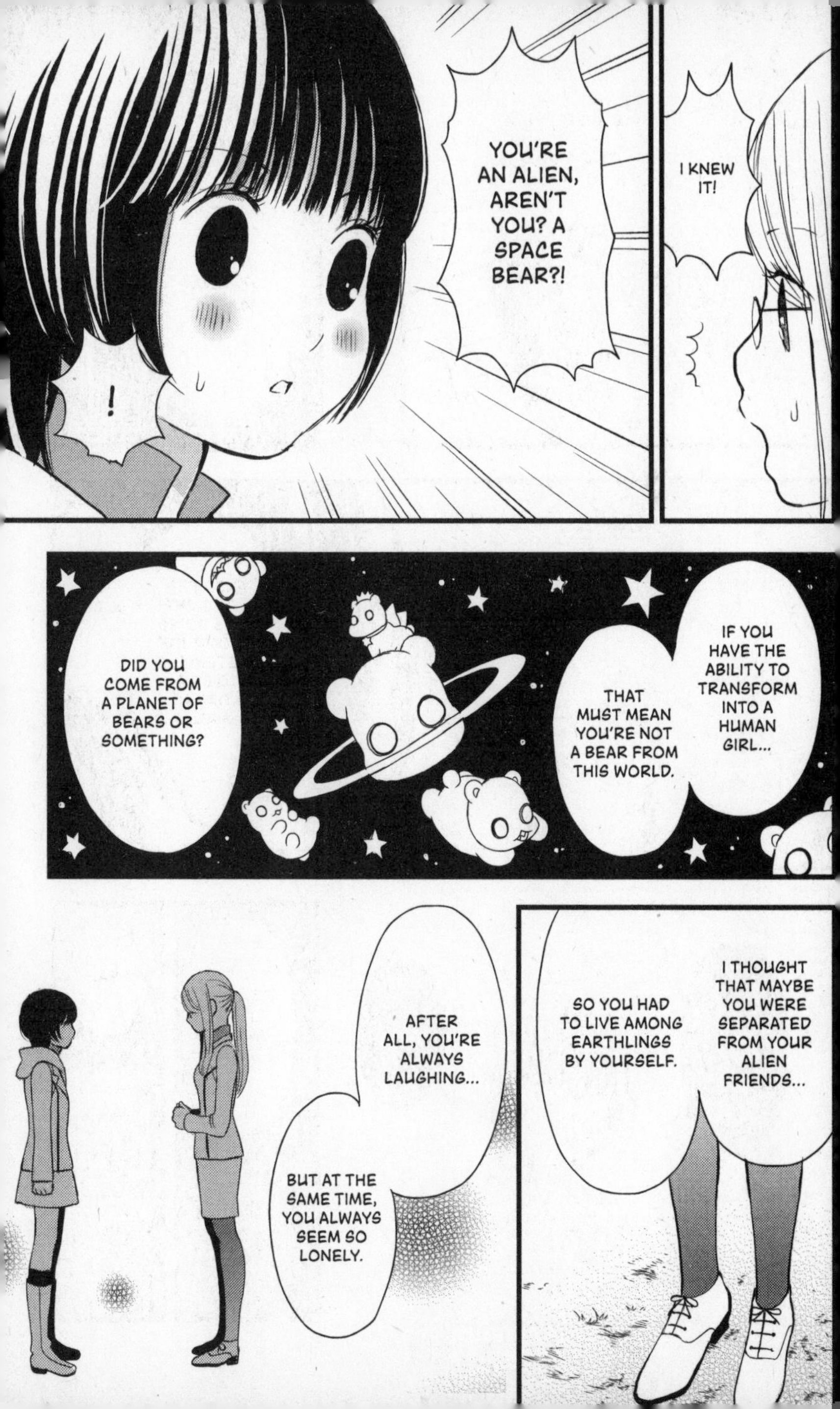
I KNEW IT!
YOU'RE AN ALIEN, AREN'T YOU? A SPACE BEAR?!
!
IF YOU HAVE THE ABILITY TO TRANSFORM INTO A HUMAN GIRL...
THAT MUST MEAN YOU'RE NOT A BEAR FROM THIS WORLD.
DID YOU COME FROM A PLANET OF BEARS OR SOMETHING?
I THOUGHT THAT MAYBE YOU WERE SEPARATED FROM YOUR ALIEN FRIENDS...
SO YOU HAD TO LIVE AMONG EARTHLINGS BY YOURSELF.
AFTER ALL, YOU'RE ALWAYS LAUGHING...
BUT AT THE SAME TIME, YOU ALWAYS SEEM SO LONELY.

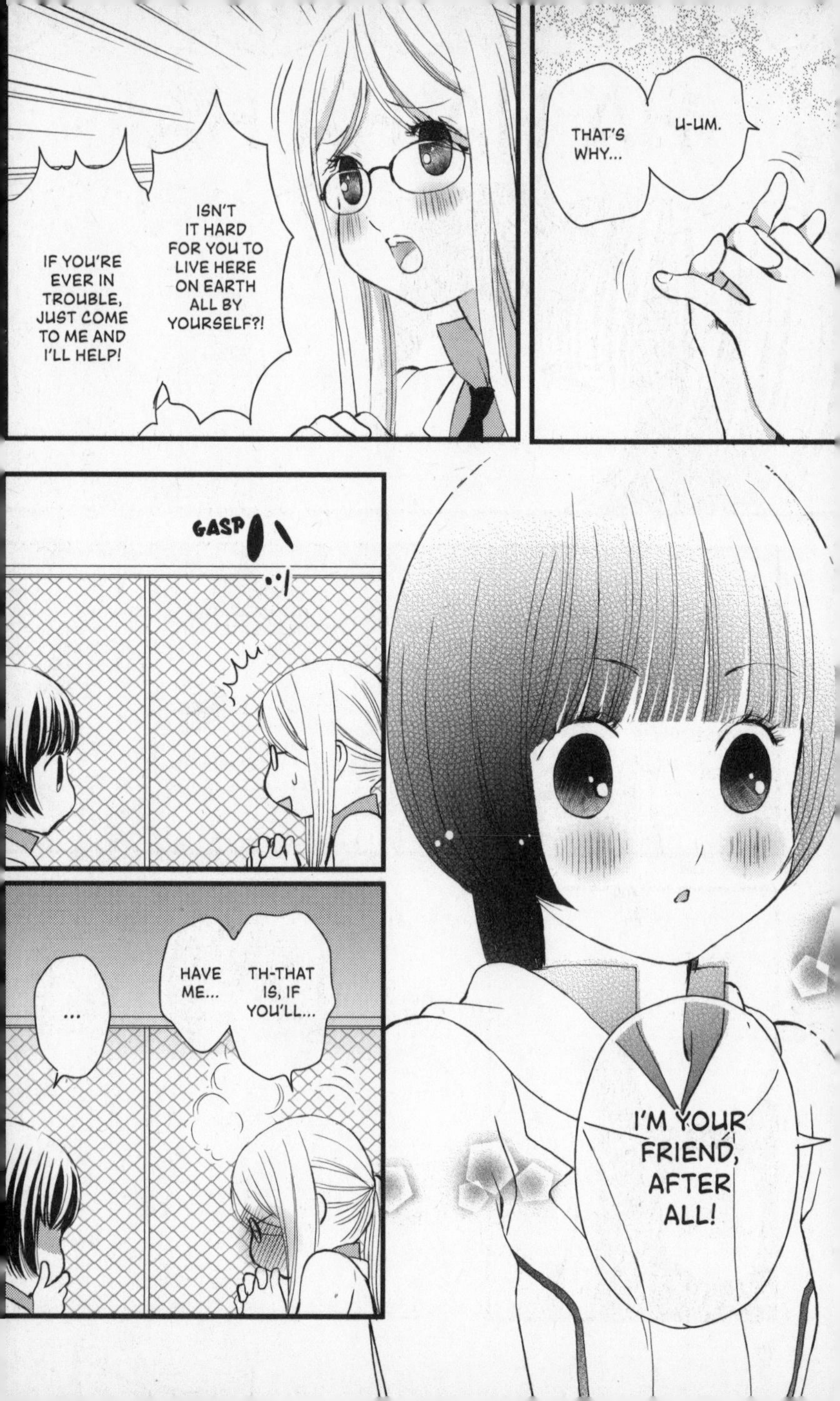
U-UM.
THAT'S WHY...
ISN'T IT HARD FOR YOU TO LIVE HERE ON EARTH ALL BY YOURSELF?!
IF YOU'RE EVER IN TROUBLE, JUST COME TO ME AND I'LL HELP!
I'M YOUR FRIEND, AFTER ALL!
GASP
TH-THAT IS, IF YOU'LL...
HAVE ME...
...

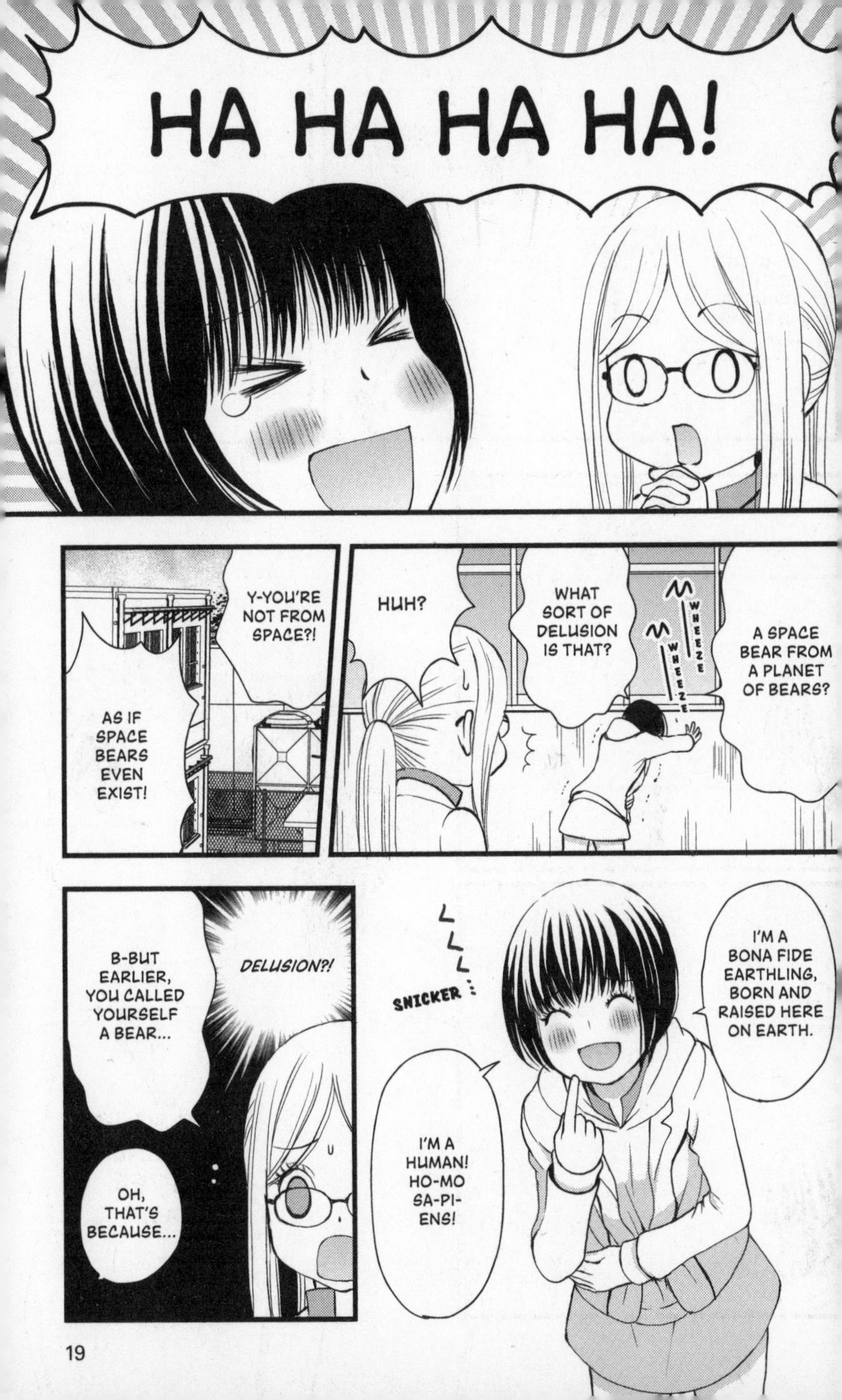
HA HA HA HA HA!
A SPACE BEAR FROM A PLANET OF BEARS?
WHEEZE WHEEZE
WHAT SORT OF DELUSION IS THAT?
HUH?
Y-YOU'RE NOT FROM SPACE?!
AS IF SPACE BEARS EVEN EXIST!
I'M A BONA FIDE EARTHLING, BORN AND RAISED HERE ON EARTH.
SNICKER
I'M A HUMAN! HO-MO SA-PI-ENS!
DELUSION?!
B-BUT EARLIER, YOU CALLED YOURSELF A BEAR...
OH, THAT'S BECAUSE...

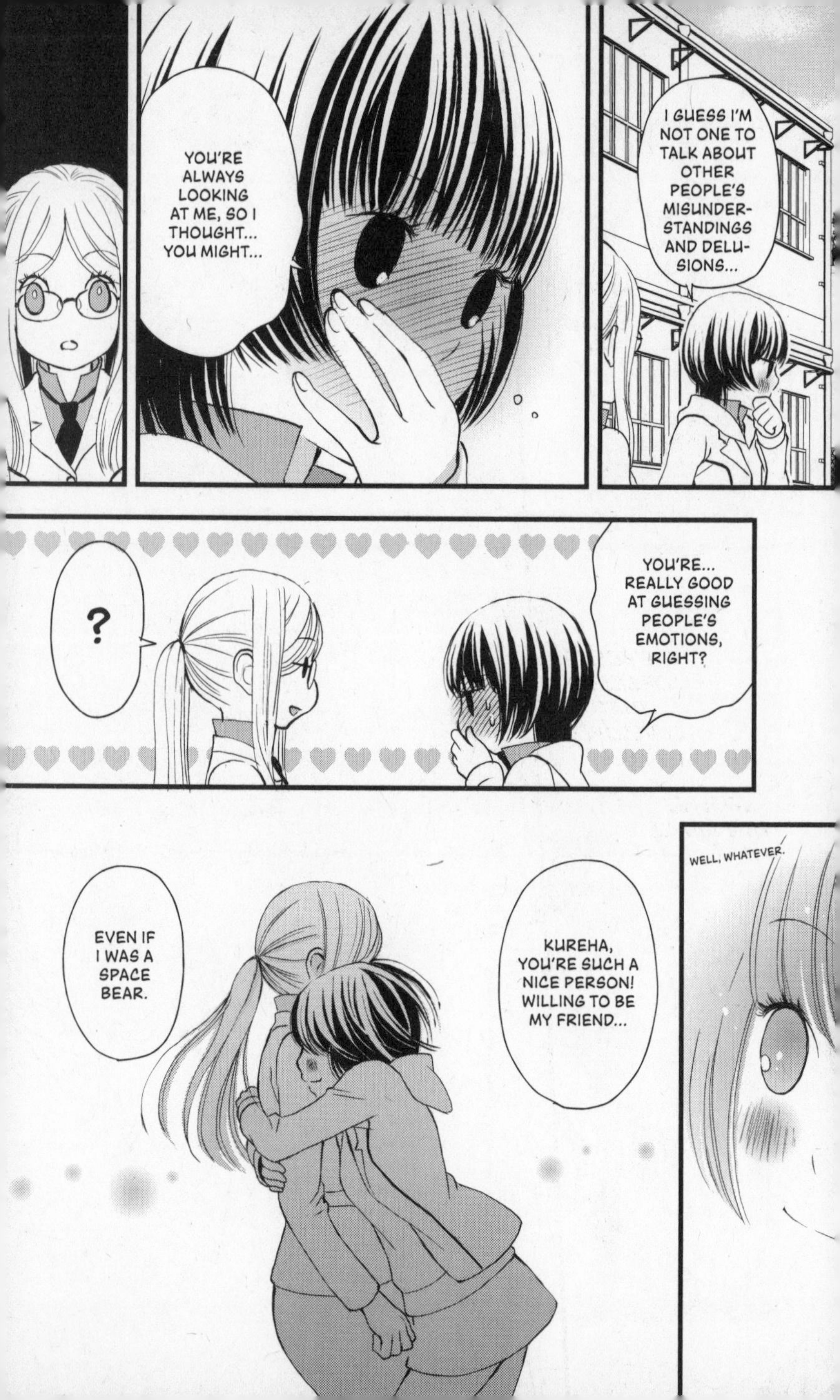
I GUESS I'M NOT ONE TO TALK ABOUT OTHER PEOPLE'S MISUNDER-STANDINGS AND DELU-SIONS...
YOU'RE ALWAYS LOOKING AT ME, SO I THOUGHT... YOU MIGHT...
YOU'RE... REALLY GOOD AT GUESSING PEOPLE'S EMOTIONS, RIGHT?
?
WELL, WHATEVER.
KUREHA, YOU'RE SUCH A NICE PERSON! WILLING TO BE MY FRIEND...
EVEN IF I WAS A SPACE BEAR.

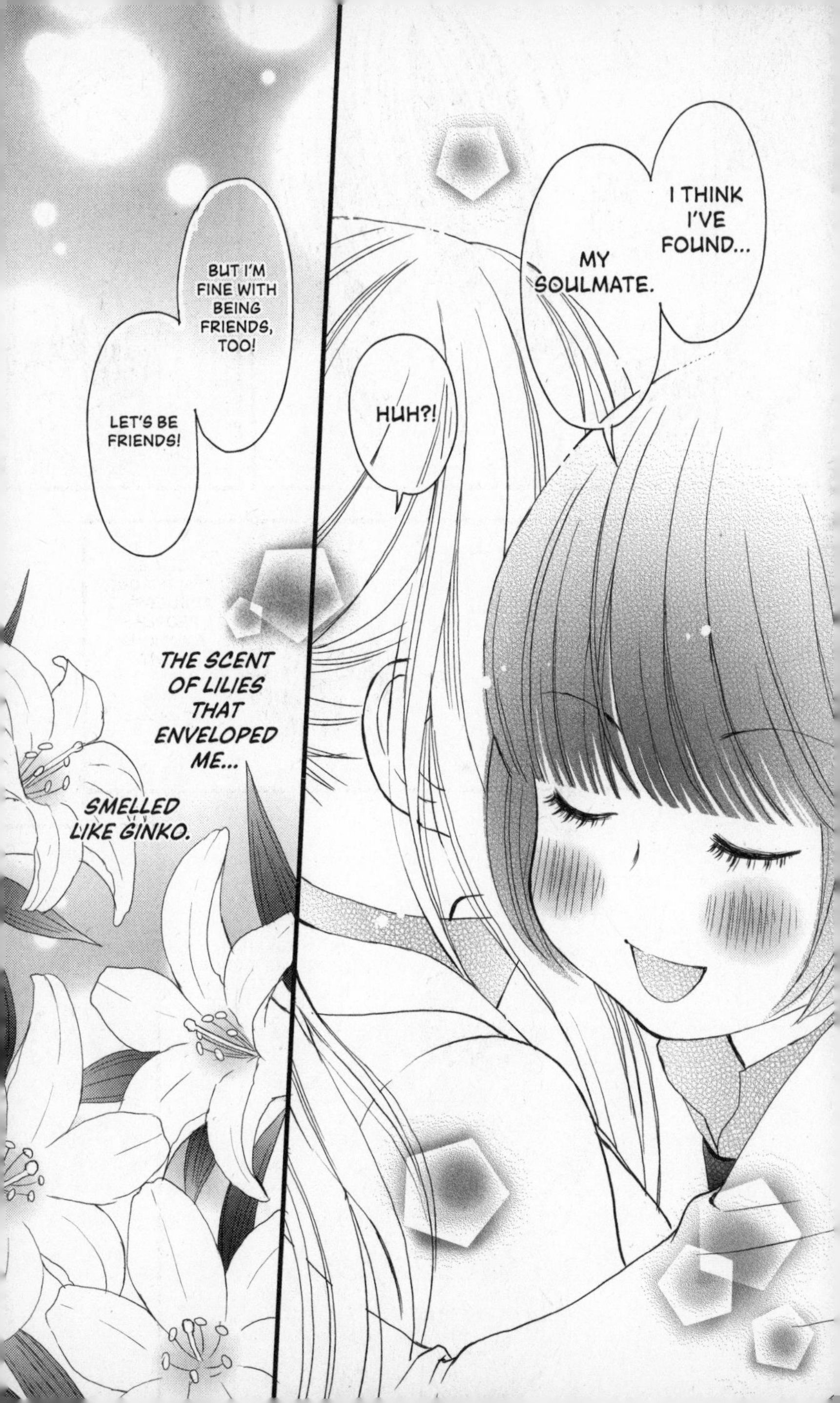
I THINK I'VE FOUND...
MY SOULMATE.
HUH?!
BUT I'M FINE WITH BEING FRIENDS, TOO!
LET'S BE FRIENDS!
THE SCENT OF LILIES THAT ENVELOPED ME...
SMELLED LIKE GINKO.

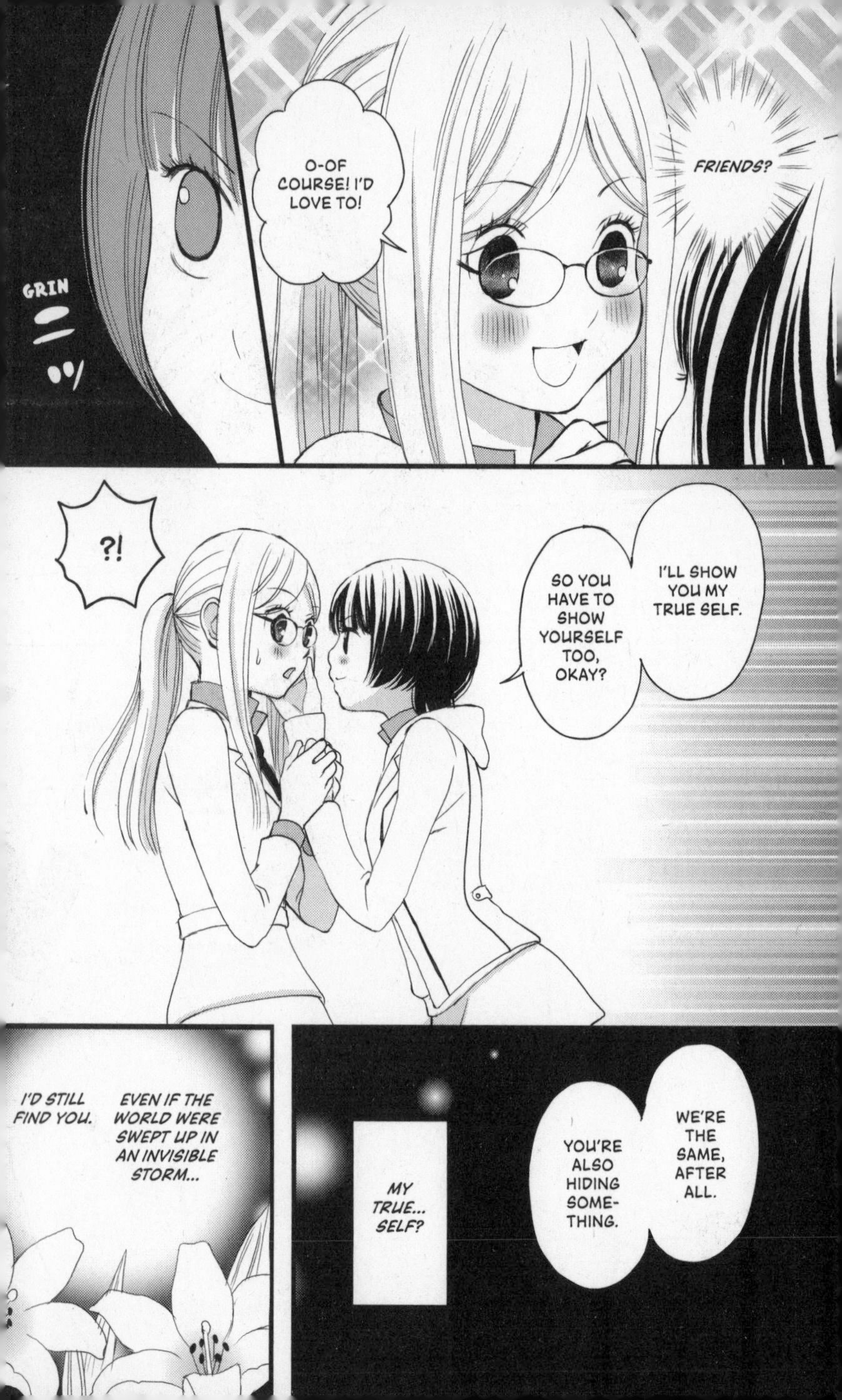
FRIENDS?
O-OF COURSE! I'D LOVE TO!
GRIN
I'LL SHOW YOU MY TRUE SELF.
SO YOU HAVE TO SHOW YOURSELF TOO, OKAY?
?!
WE'RE THE SAME, AFTER ALL.
YOU'RE ALSO HIDING SOME-THING.
MY TRUE... SELF?
EVEN IF THE WORLD WERE SWEPT UP IN AN INVISIBLE STORM...
I'D STILL FIND YOU.

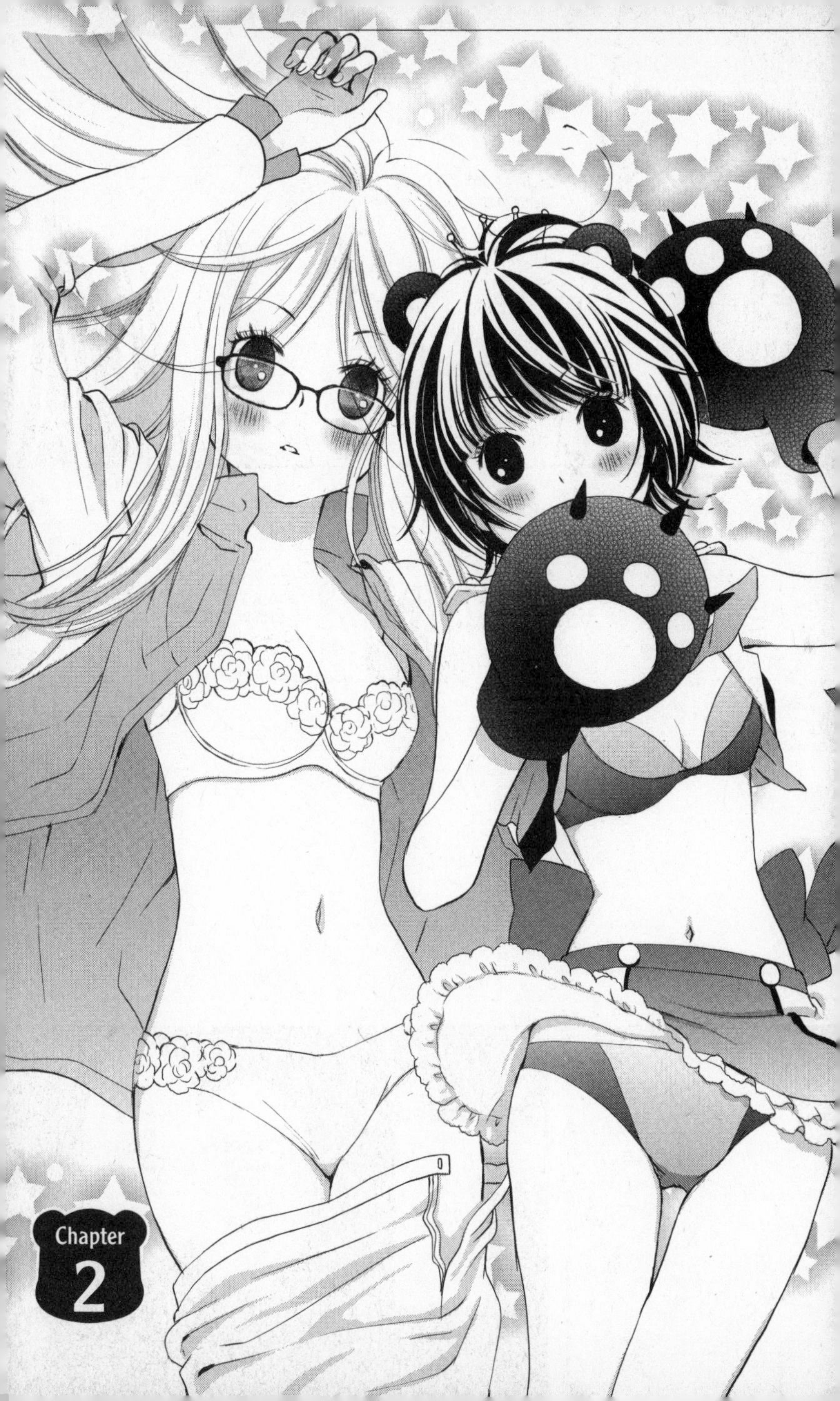
Chapter
2

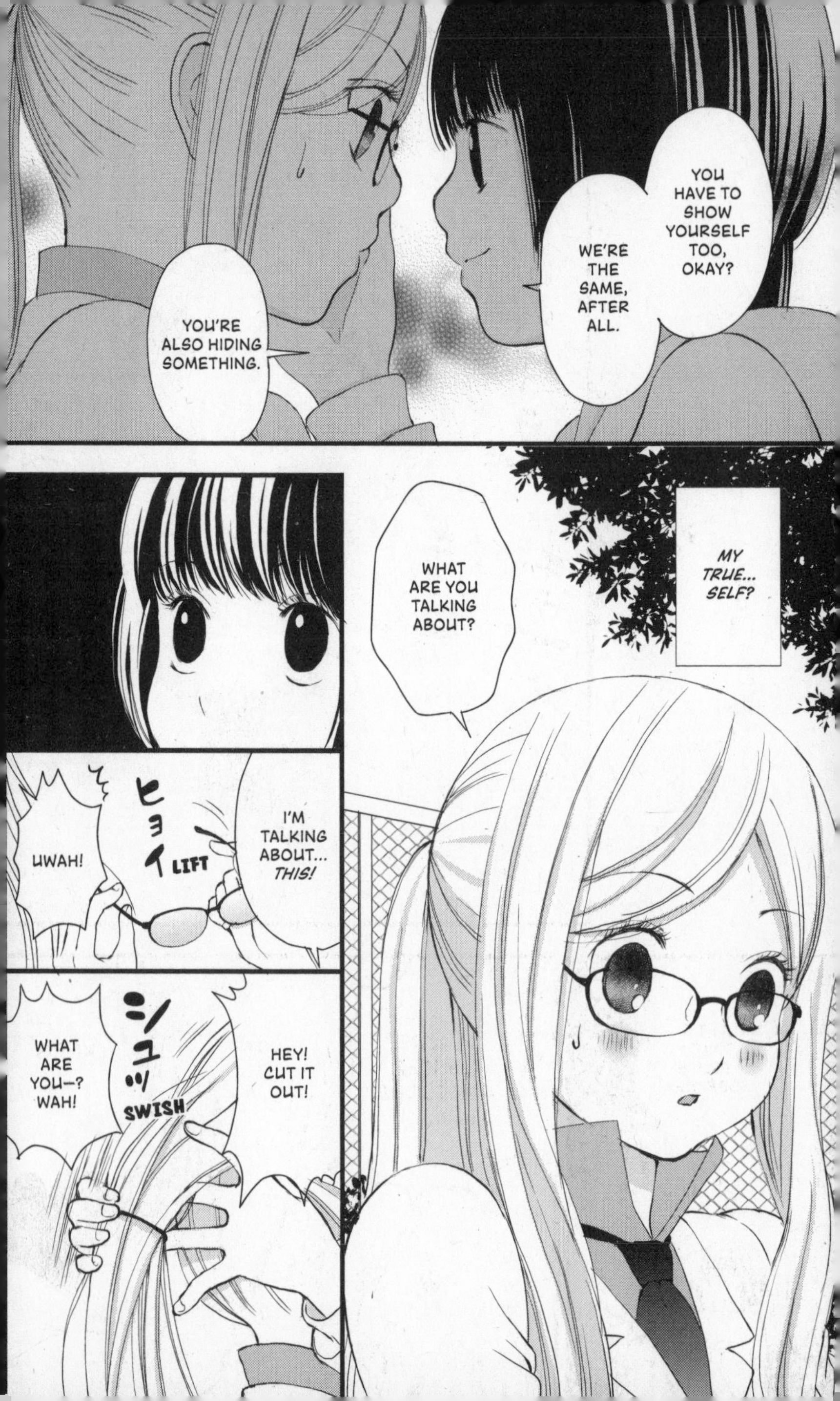

YOU HAVE TO SHOW YOURSELF TOO, OKAY?
WE'RE THE SAME, AFTER ALL.
YOU'RE ALSO HIDING SOMETHING.
MY TRUE... SELF?
WHAT ARE YOU TALKING ABOUT?
I'M TALKING ABOUT... *THIS!*
ヒョイ
LIFT
UWAH!
HEY! CUT IT OUT!
シュッ
SWISH
WHAT ARE YOU—? WAH!

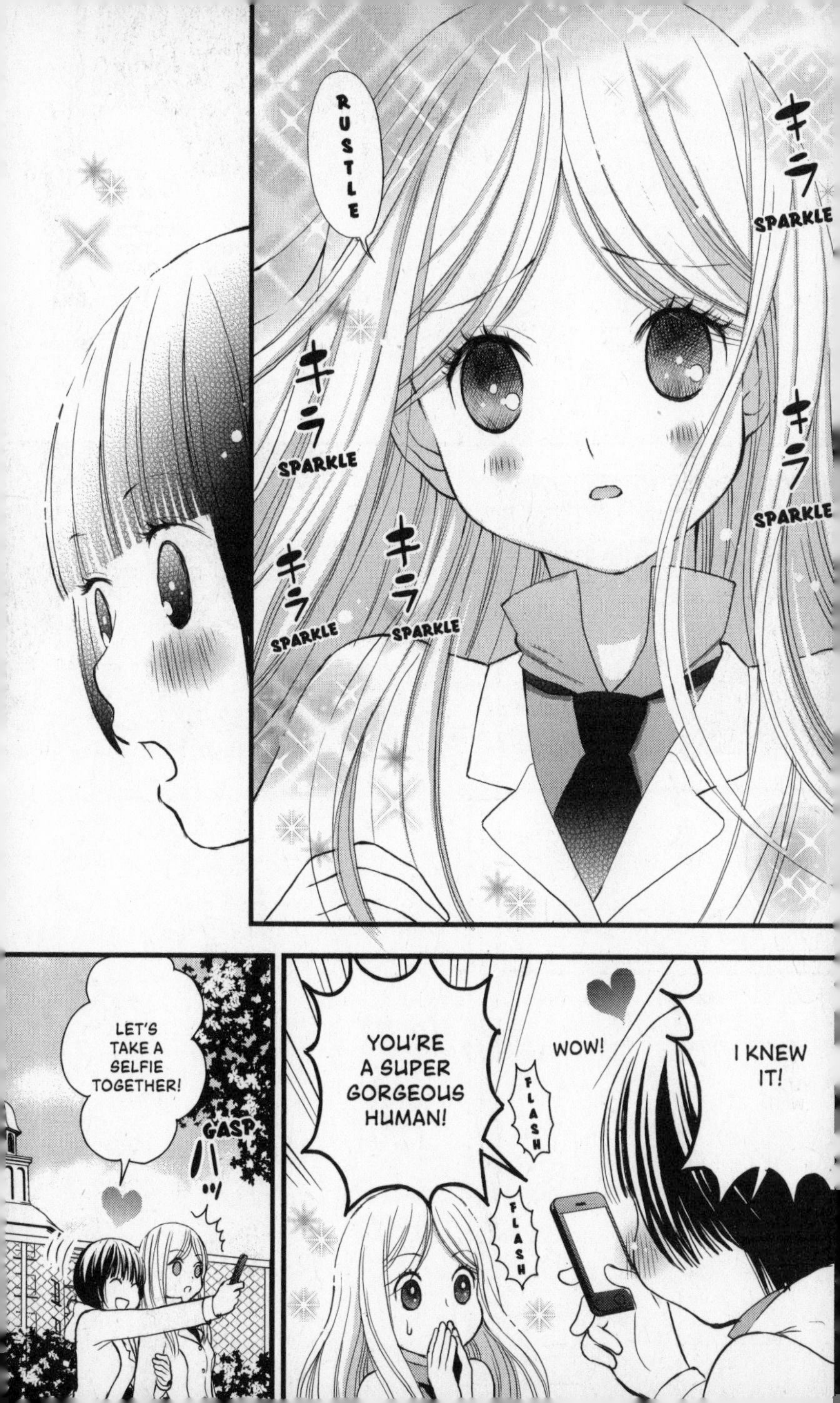
キラ
SPARKLE
キラ
SPARKLE
RUSTLE
キラ
SPARKLE
キラ
SPARKLE
キラ
SPARKLE
I KNEW IT!
WOW!
YOU'RE A SUPER GORGEOUS HUMAN!
FLASH
FLASH
GASP
LET'S TAKE A SELFIE TOGETHER!

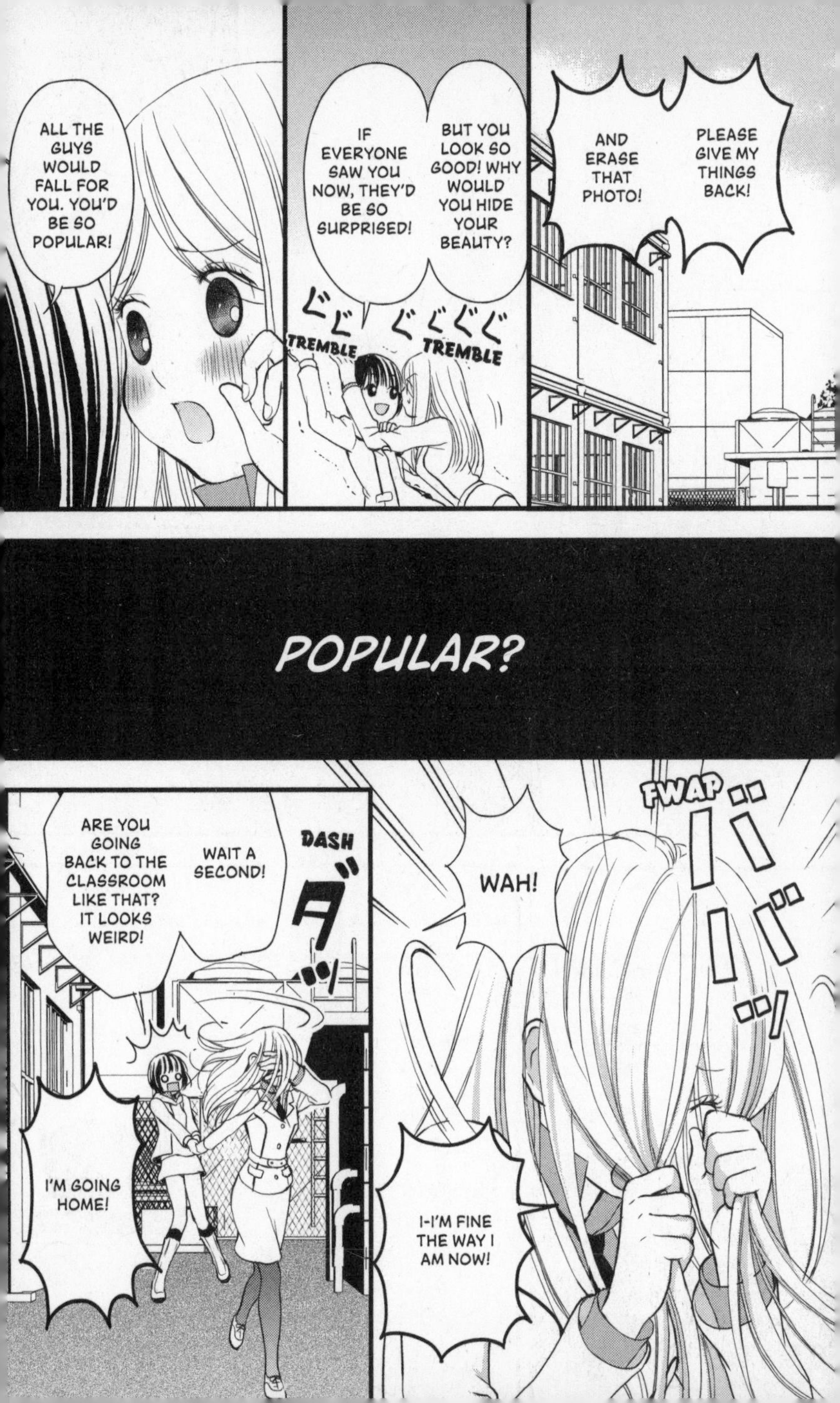
PLEASE GIVE MY THINGS BACK!
AND ERASE THAT PHOTO!
BUT YOU LOOK SO GOOD! WHY WOULD YOU HIDE YOUR BEAUTY?
IF EVERYONE SAW YOU NOW, THEY'D BE SO SURPRISED!
ぐぐぐぐ
TREMBLE
ぐぐ
TREMBLE
ALL THE GUYS WOULD FALL FOR YOU. YOU'D BE SO POPULAR!
POPULAR?
FWAP
WAH!
I-I'M FINE THE WAY I AM NOW!
DASH
ダッ
WAIT A SECOND!
ARE YOU GOING BACK TO THE CLASSROOM LIKE THAT? IT LOOKS WEIRD!
I'M GOING HOME!

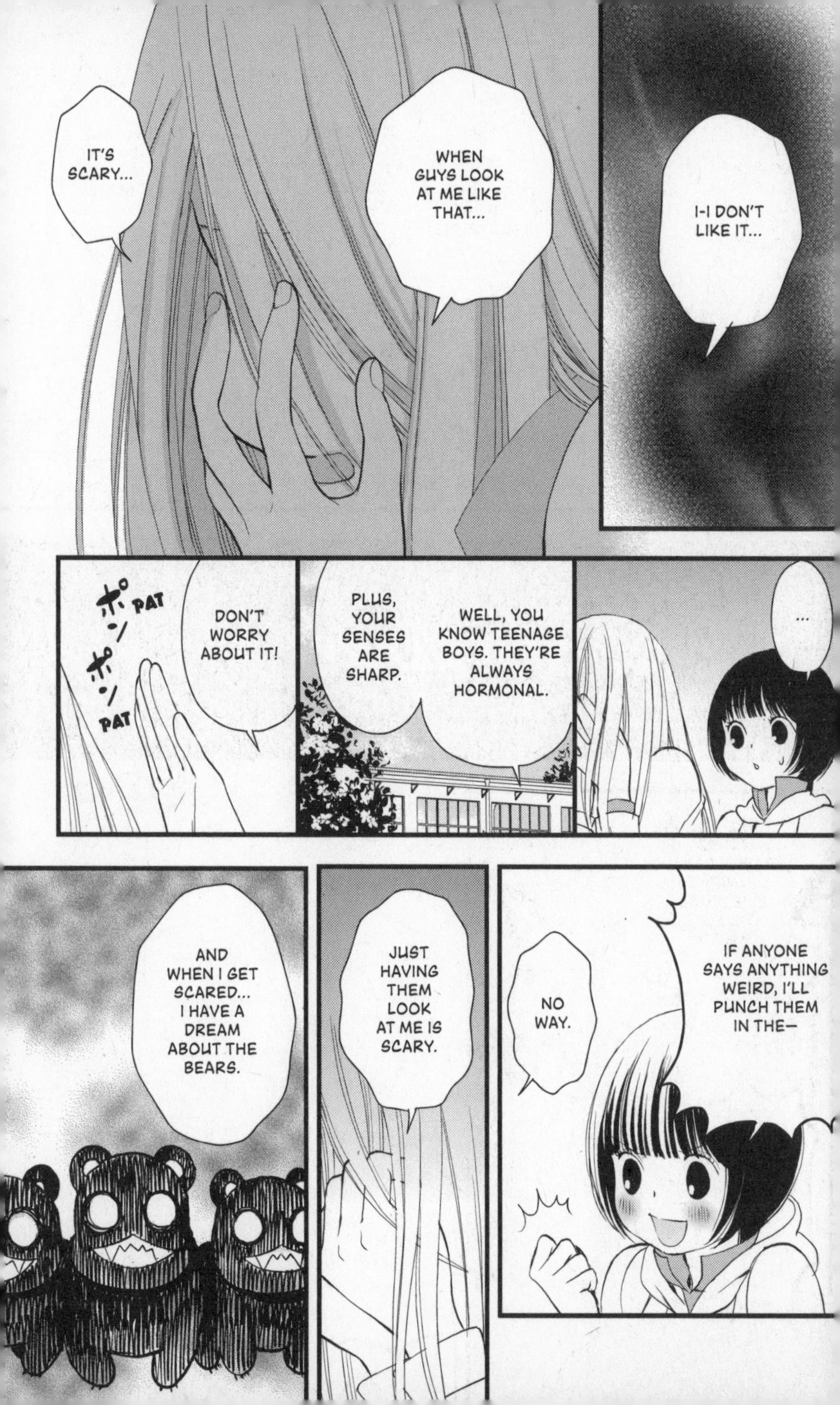
I-I DON'T LIKE IT...
WHEN GUYS LOOK AT ME LIKE THAT...
IT'S SCARY...
...
WELL, YOU KNOW TEENAGE BOYS. THEY'RE ALWAYS HORMONAL.
PLUS, YOUR SENSES ARE SHARP.
DON'T WORRY ABOUT IT!
ポン PAT
ポン PAT
IF ANYONE SAYS ANYTHING WEIRD, I'LL PUNCH THEM IN THE—
NO WAY.
JUST HAVING THEM LOOK AT ME IS SCARY.
AND WHEN I GET SCARED... I HAVE A DREAM ABOUT THE BEARS.

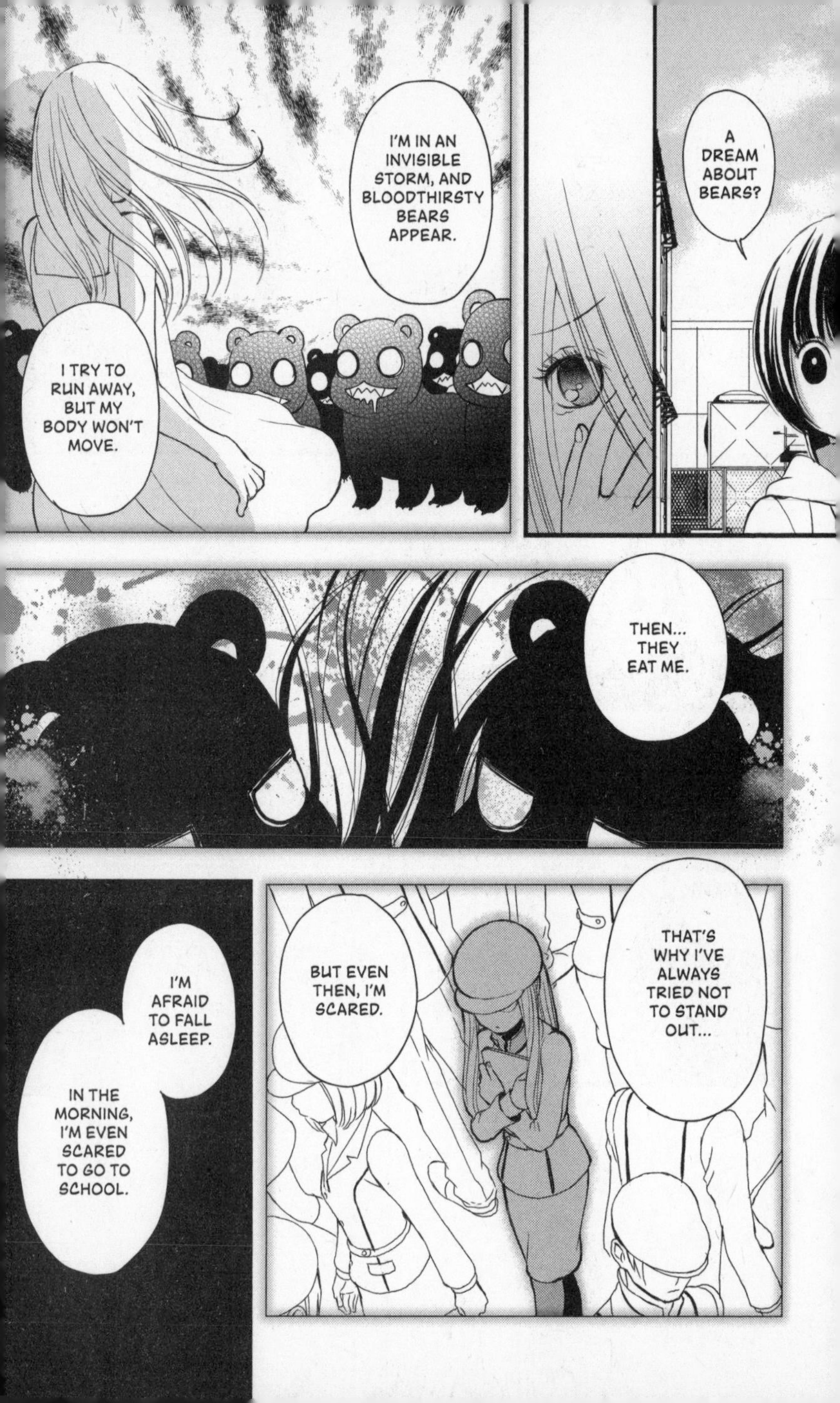
A DREAM ABOUT BEARS?
I'M IN AN INVISIBLE STORM, AND BLOODTHIRSTY BEARS APPEAR.
I TRY TO RUN AWAY, BUT MY BODY WON'T MOVE.
THEN... THEY EAT ME.
THAT'S WHY I'VE ALWAYS TRIED NOT TO STAND OUT...
BUT EVEN THEN, I'M SCARED.
I'M AFRAID TO FALL ASLEEP.
IN THE MORNING, I'M EVEN SCARED TO GO TO SCHOOL.

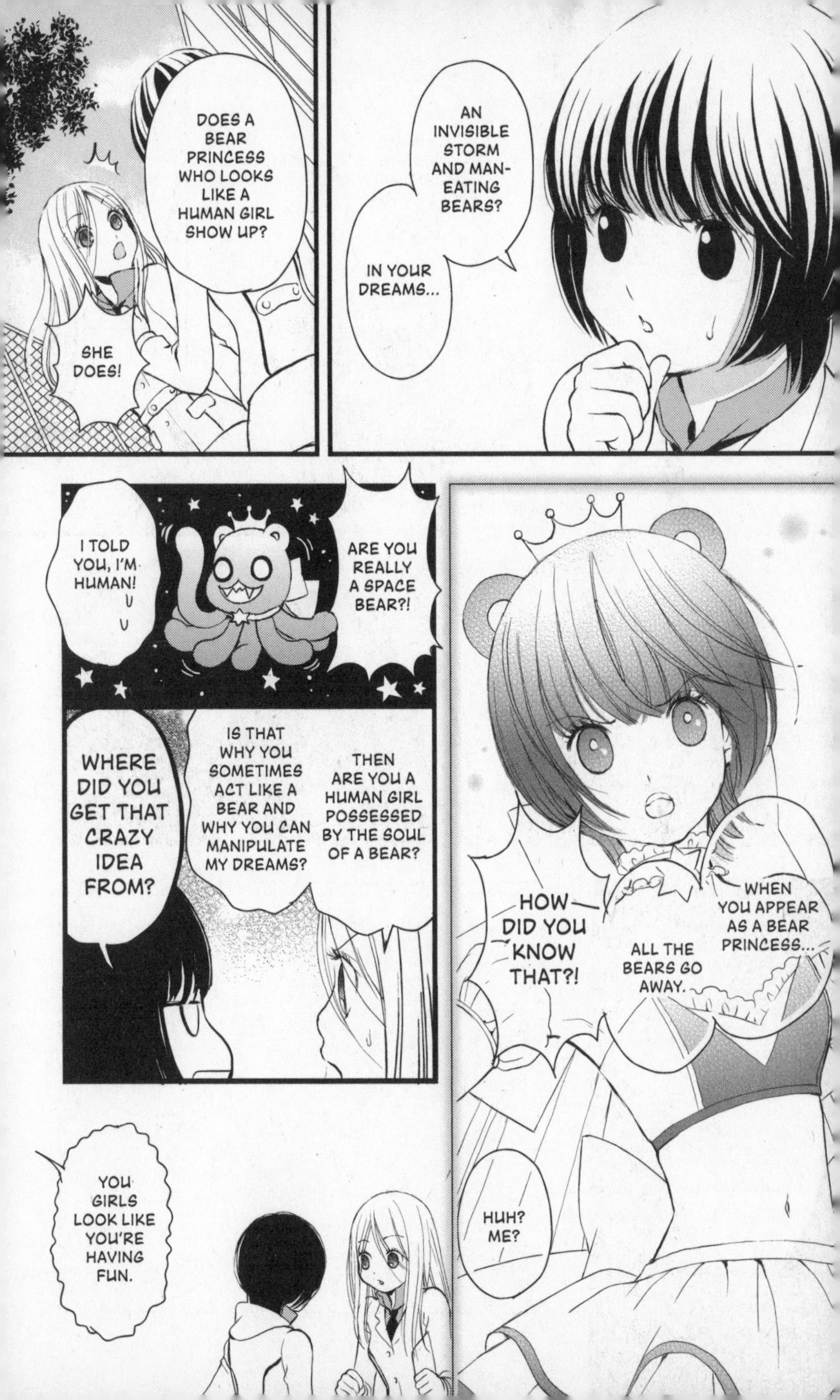

AN INVISIBLE STORM AND MAN-EATING BEARS?
IN YOUR DREAMS...
DOES A BEAR PRINCESS WHO LOOKS LIKE A HUMAN GIRL SHOW UP?
SHE DOES!
WHEN YOU APPEAR AS A BEAR PRINCESS...
ALL THE BEARS GO AWAY.
HOW DID YOU KNOW THAT?!
HUH? ME?
ARE YOU REALLY A SPACE BEAR?!
I TOLD YOU, I'M HUMAN!
THEN ARE YOU A HUMAN GIRL POSSESSED BY THE SOUL OF A BEAR?
IS THAT WHY YOU SOMETIMES ACT LIKE A BEAR AND WHY YOU CAN MANIPULATE MY DREAMS?
WHERE DID YOU GET THAT CRAZY IDEA FROM?
YOU GIRLS LOOK LIKE YOU'RE HAVING FUN.

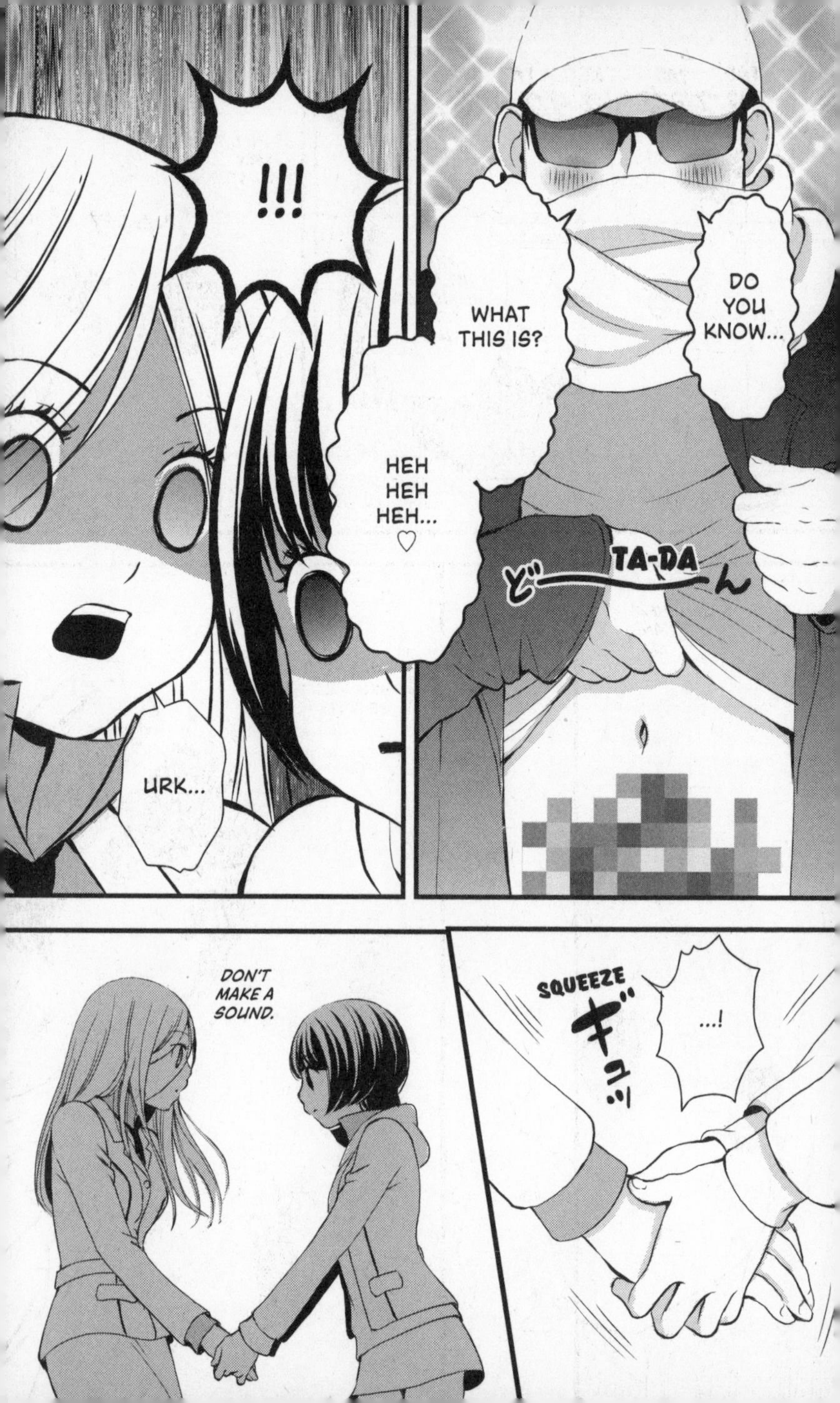

DO YOU KNOW...
WHAT THIS IS?
HEH HEH HEH... ♡
TA-DA
ど——ん
!!!
URK...
SQUEEZE
ギュッ
...!
DON'T MAKE A SOUND.

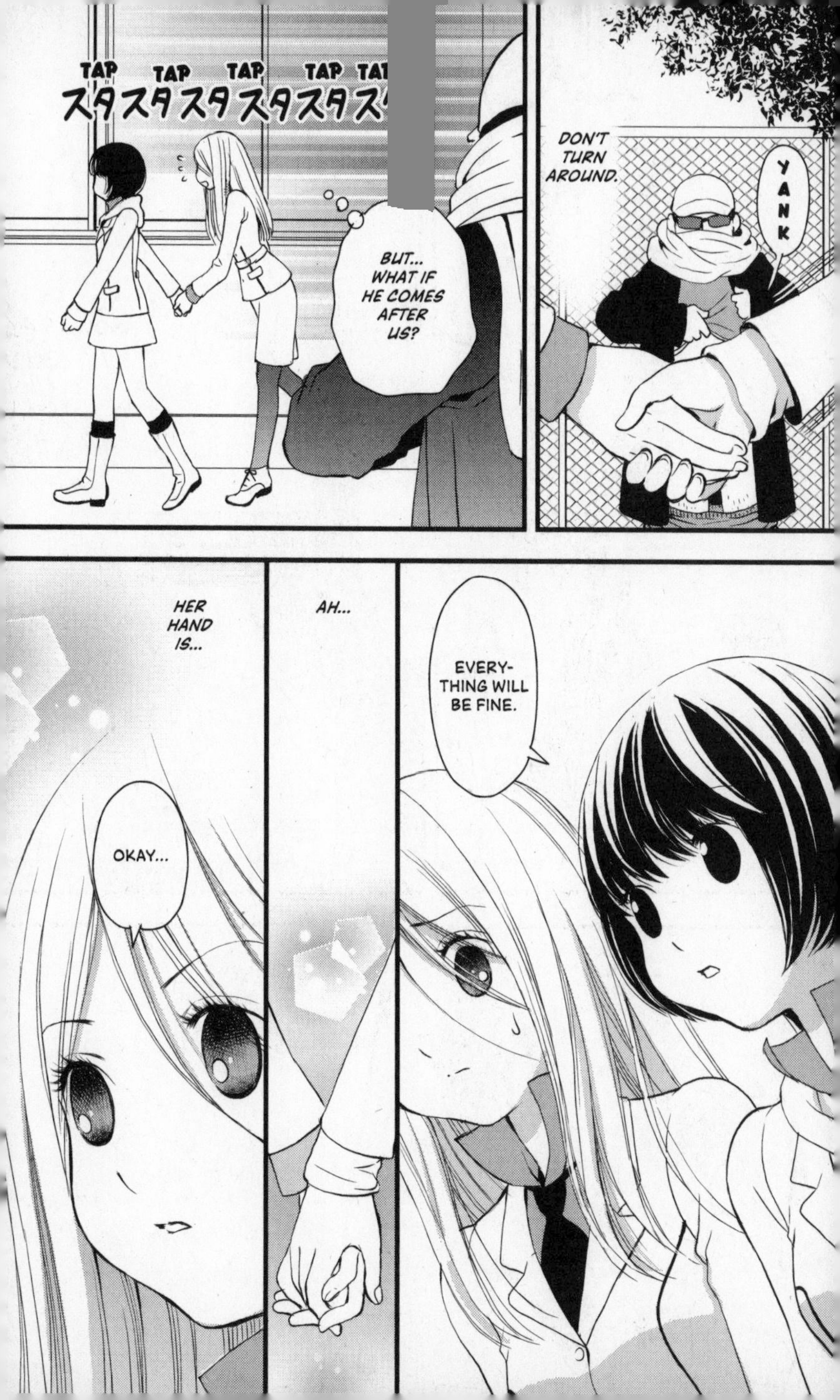

DON'T TURN AROUND.
YANK
TAP TAP TAP TAP TAP
スタスタスタスタスタス
BUT... WHAT IF HE COMES AFTER US?
EVERY-THING WILL BE FINE.
AH...
HER HAND IS...
OKAY...

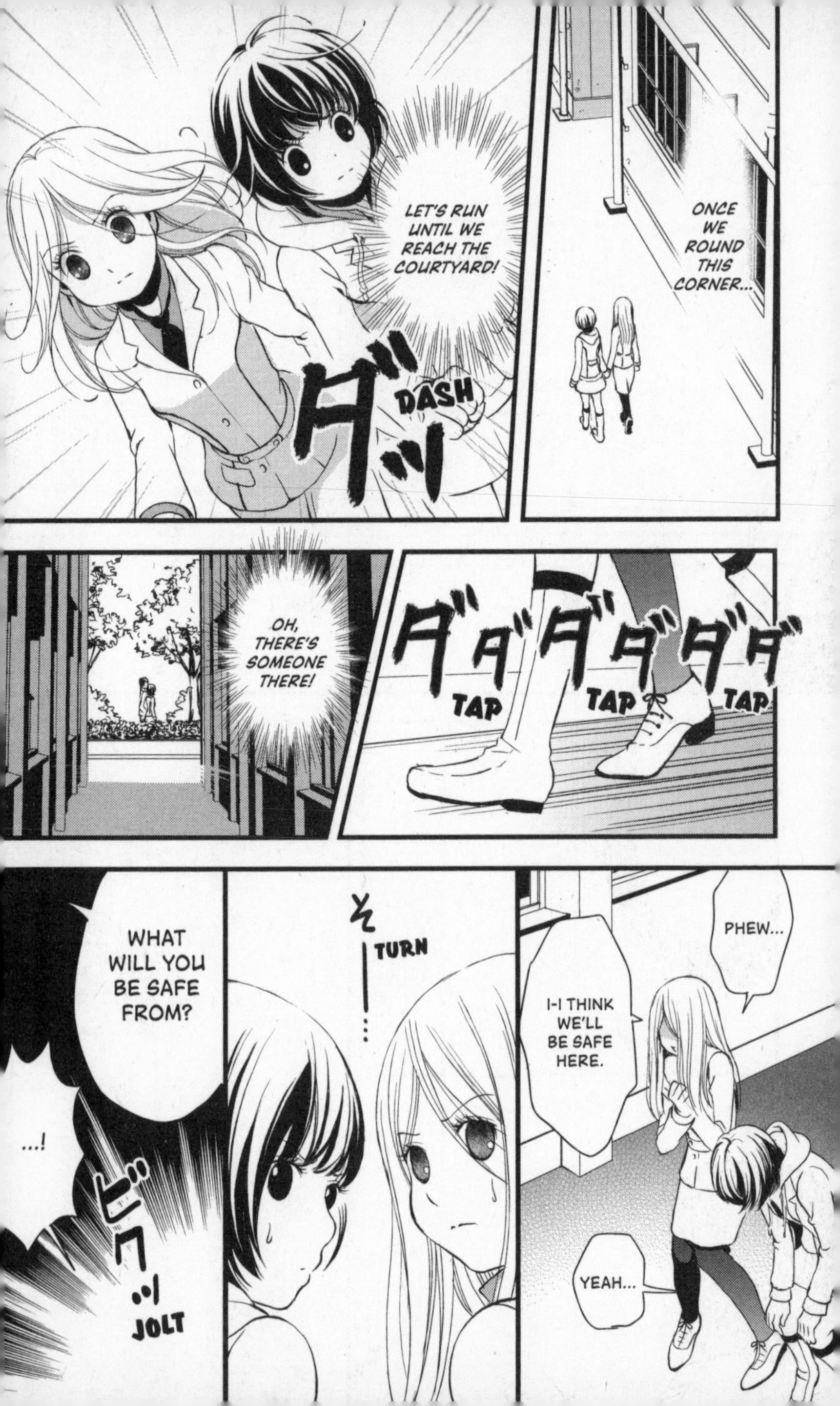
ONCE WE ROUND THIS CORNER...
LET'S RUN UNTIL WE REACH THE COURTYARD!
ダッ
DASH
ダダダダダダ
TAP
TAP
TAP
OH, THERE'S SOMEONE THERE!
PHEW...
I-I THINK WE'LL BE SAFE HERE.
YEAH...
TURN
WHAT WILL YOU BE SAFE FROM?
...!
ビクッ
JOLT

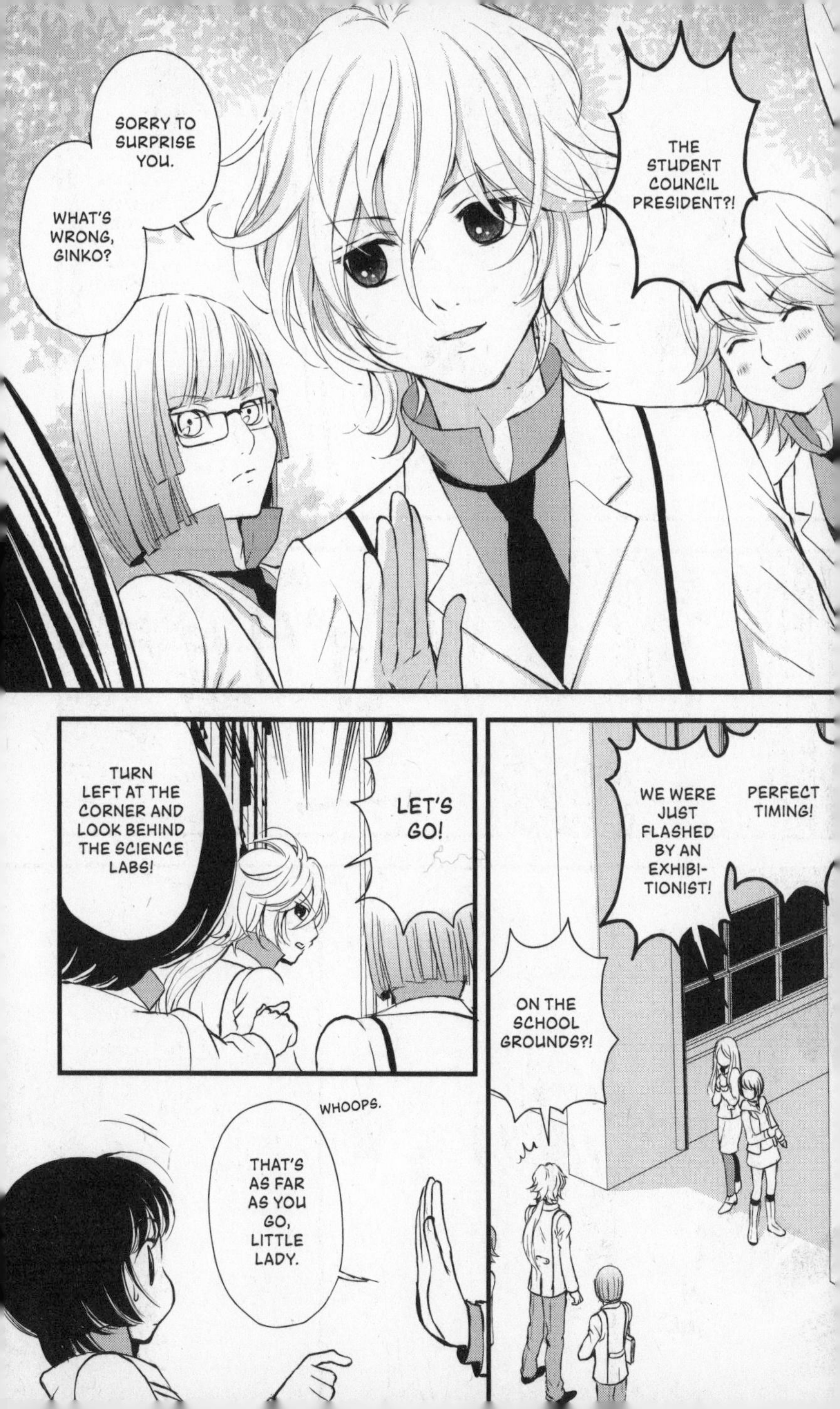
THE STUDENT COUNCIL PRESIDENT?!
SORRY TO SURPRISE YOU.
WHAT'S WRONG, GINKO?
PERFECT TIMING!
WE WERE JUST FLASHED BY AN EXHIBITIONIST!
ON THE SCHOOL GROUNDS?!
LET'S GO!
TURN LEFT AT THE CORNER AND LOOK BEHIND THE SCIENCE LABS!
WHOOPS.
THAT'S AS FAR AS YOU GO, LITTLE LADY.

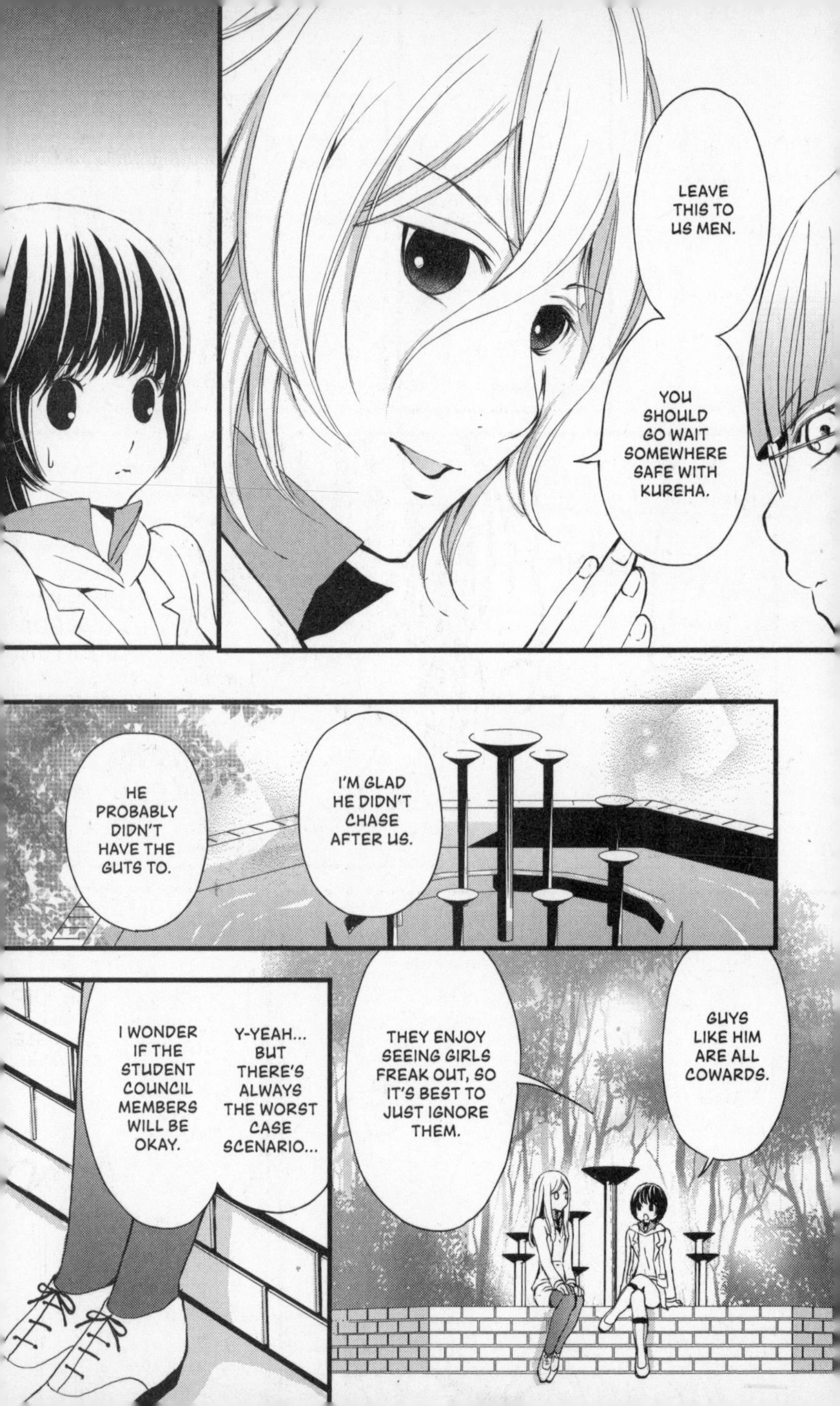
LEAVE THIS TO US MEN.
YOU SHOULD GO WAIT SOMEWHERE SAFE WITH KUREHA.
I'M GLAD HE DIDN'T CHASE AFTER US.
HE PROBABLY DIDN'T HAVE THE GUTS TO.
GUYS LIKE HIM ARE ALL COWARDS.
THEY ENJOY SEEING GIRLS FREAK OUT, SO IT'S BEST TO JUST IGNORE THEM.
Y-YEAH... BUT THERE'S ALWAYS THE WORST CASE SCENARIO...
I WONDER IF THE STUDENT COUNCIL MEMBERS WILL BE OKAY.

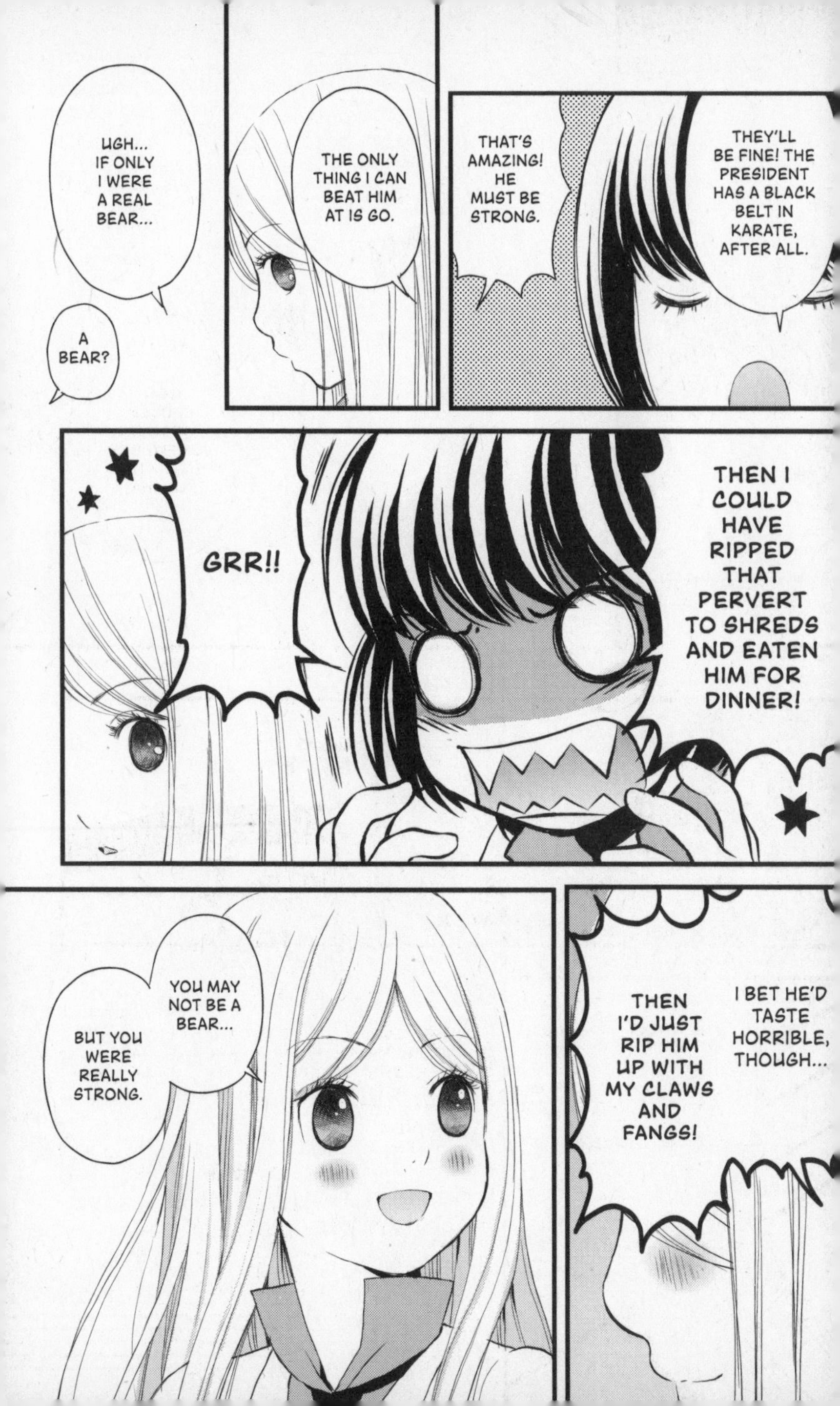
THEY'LL BE FINE! THE PRESIDENT HAS A BLACK BELT IN KARATE, AFTER ALL.
THAT'S AMAZING! HE MUST BE STRONG.
THE ONLY THING I CAN BEAT HIM AT IS GO.
UGH... IF ONLY I WERE A REAL BEAR...
A BEAR?
THEN I COULD HAVE RIPPED THAT PERVERT TO SHREDS AND EATEN HIM FOR DINNER!
GRR!!
THEN I'D JUST RIP HIM UP WITH MY CLAWS AND FANGS!
I BET HE'D TASTE HORRIBLE, THOUGH...
YOU MAY NOT BE A BEAR...
BUT YOU WERE REALLY STRONG.

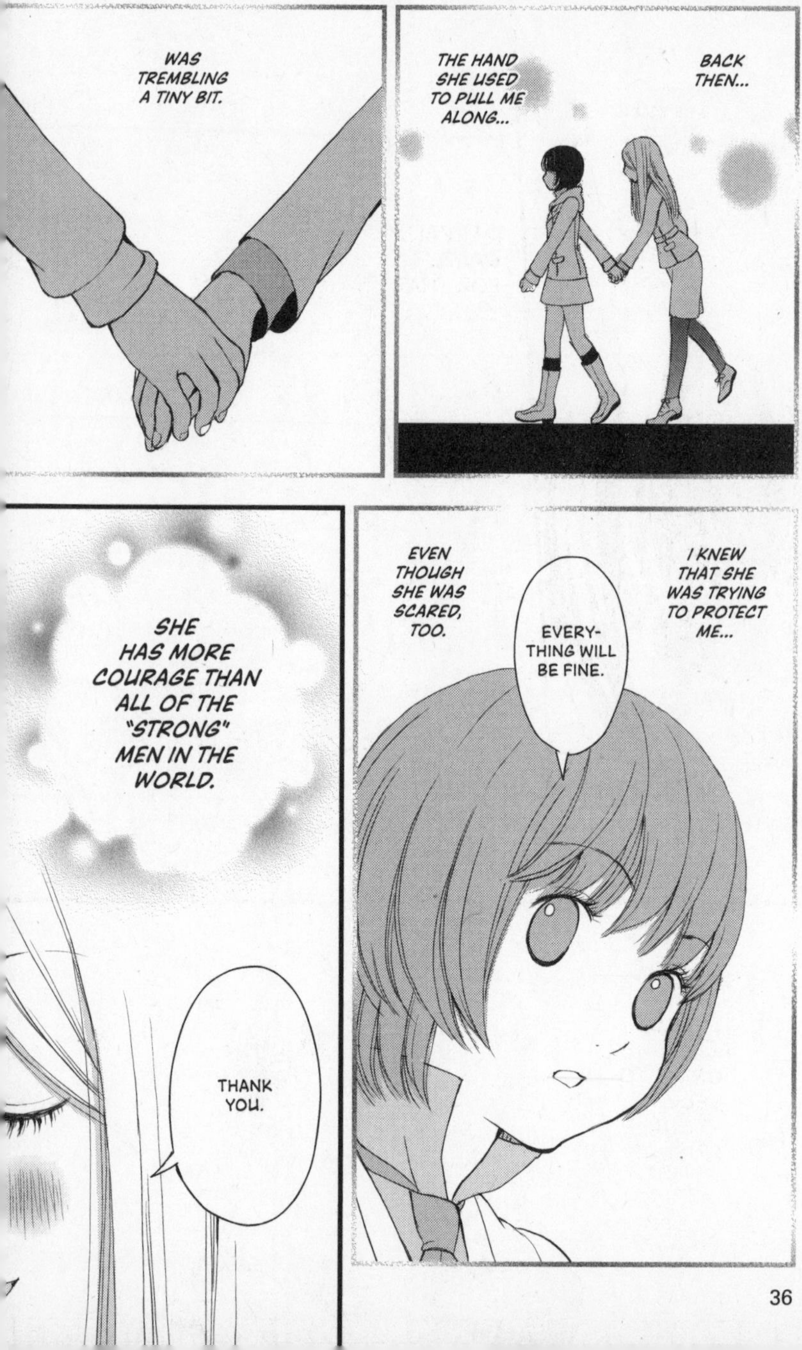
BACK THEN...
THE HAND SHE USED TO PULL ME ALONG...
WAS TREMBLING A TINY BIT.
I KNEW THAT SHE WAS TRYING TO PROTECT ME...
EVEN THOUGH SHE WAS SCARED, TOO.
EVERY-THING WILL BE FINE.
SHE HAS MORE COURAGE THAN ALL OF THE "STRONG" MEN IN THE WORLD.
THANK YOU.

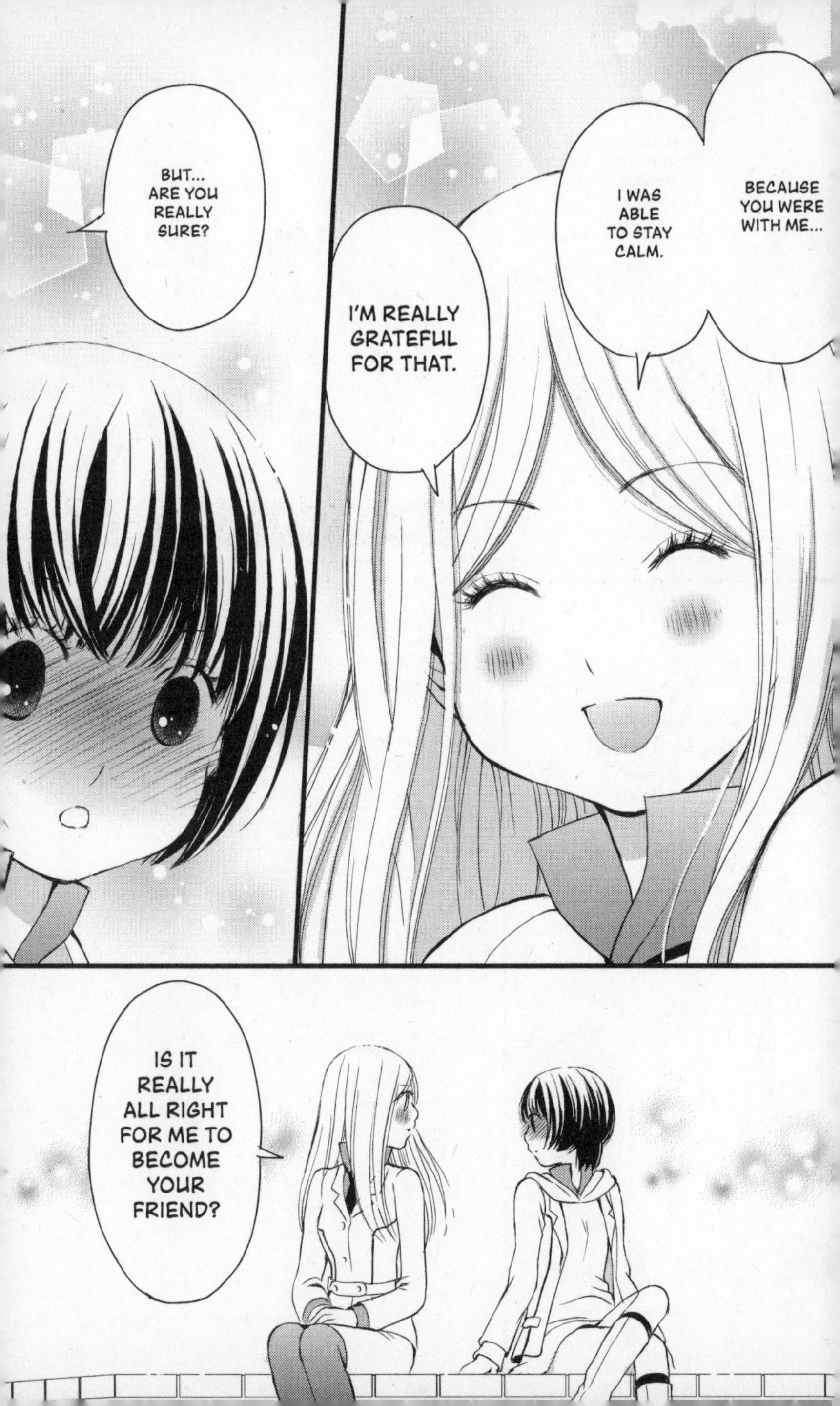
BECAUSE YOU WERE WITH ME...
I WAS ABLE TO STAY CALM.
I'M REALLY GRATEFUL FOR THAT.
BUT... ARE YOU REALLY SURE?
IS IT REALLY ALL RIGHT FOR ME TO BECOME YOUR FRIEND?

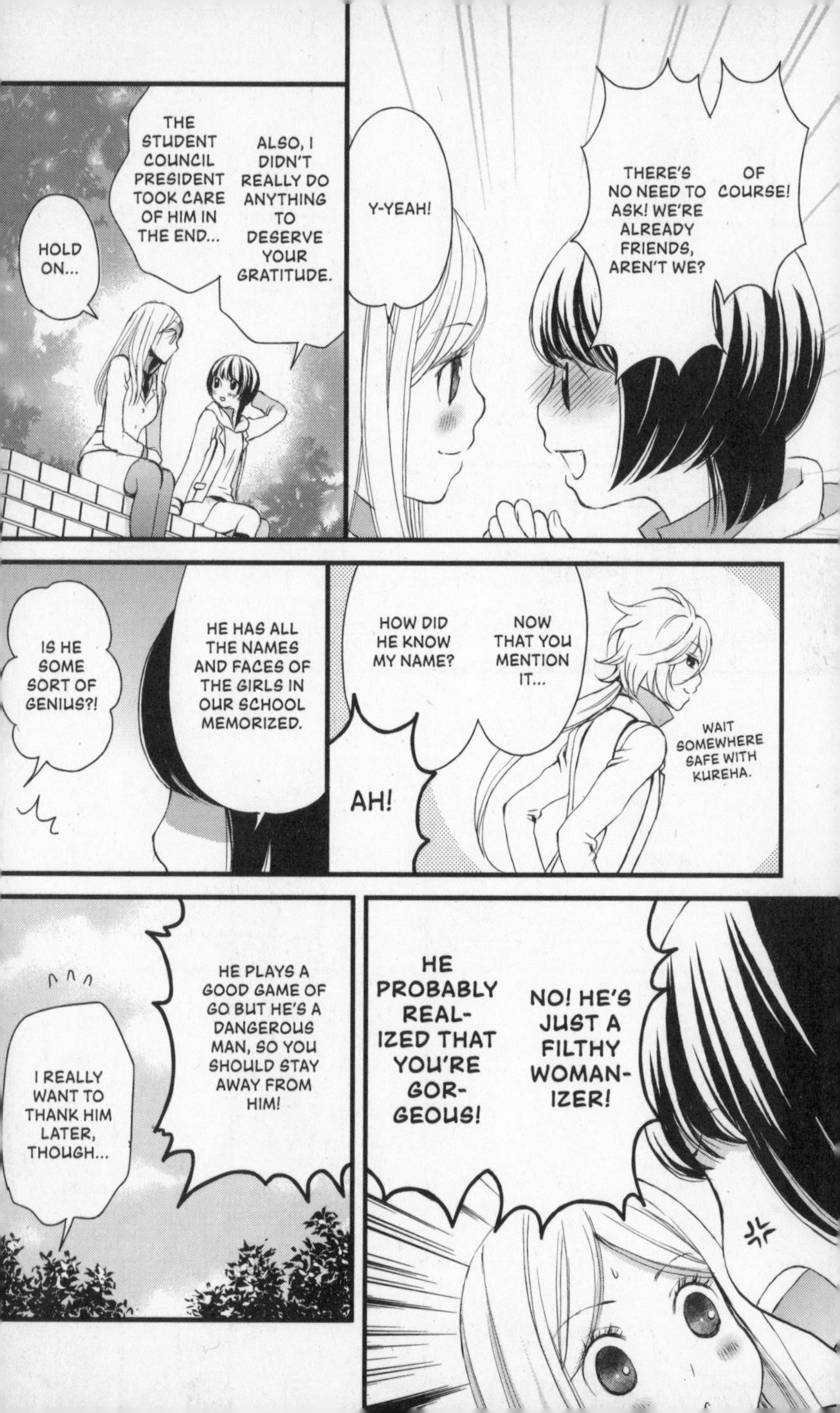
OF COURSE!
THERE'S NO NEED TO ASK! WE'RE ALREADY FRIENDS, AREN'T WE?
Y-YEAH!
ALSO, I DIDN'T REALLY DO ANYTHING TO DESERVE YOUR GRATITUDE.
THE STUDENT COUNCIL PRESIDENT TOOK CARE OF HIM IN THE END...
HOLD ON...
WAIT SOMEWHERE SAFE WITH KUREHA.
NOW THAT YOU MENTION IT...
HOW DID HE KNOW MY NAME?
AH!
HE HAS ALL THE NAMES AND FACES OF THE GIRLS IN OUR SCHOOL MEMORIZED.
IS HE SOME SORT OF GENIUS?!
NO! HE'S JUST A FILTHY WOMAN-IZER!
HE PROBABLY REAL-IZED THAT YOU'RE GOR-GEOUS!
HE PLAYS A GOOD GAME OF GO BUT HE'S A DANGEROUS MAN, SO YOU SHOULD STAY AWAY FROM HIM!
I REALLY WANT TO THANK HIM LATER, THOUGH...

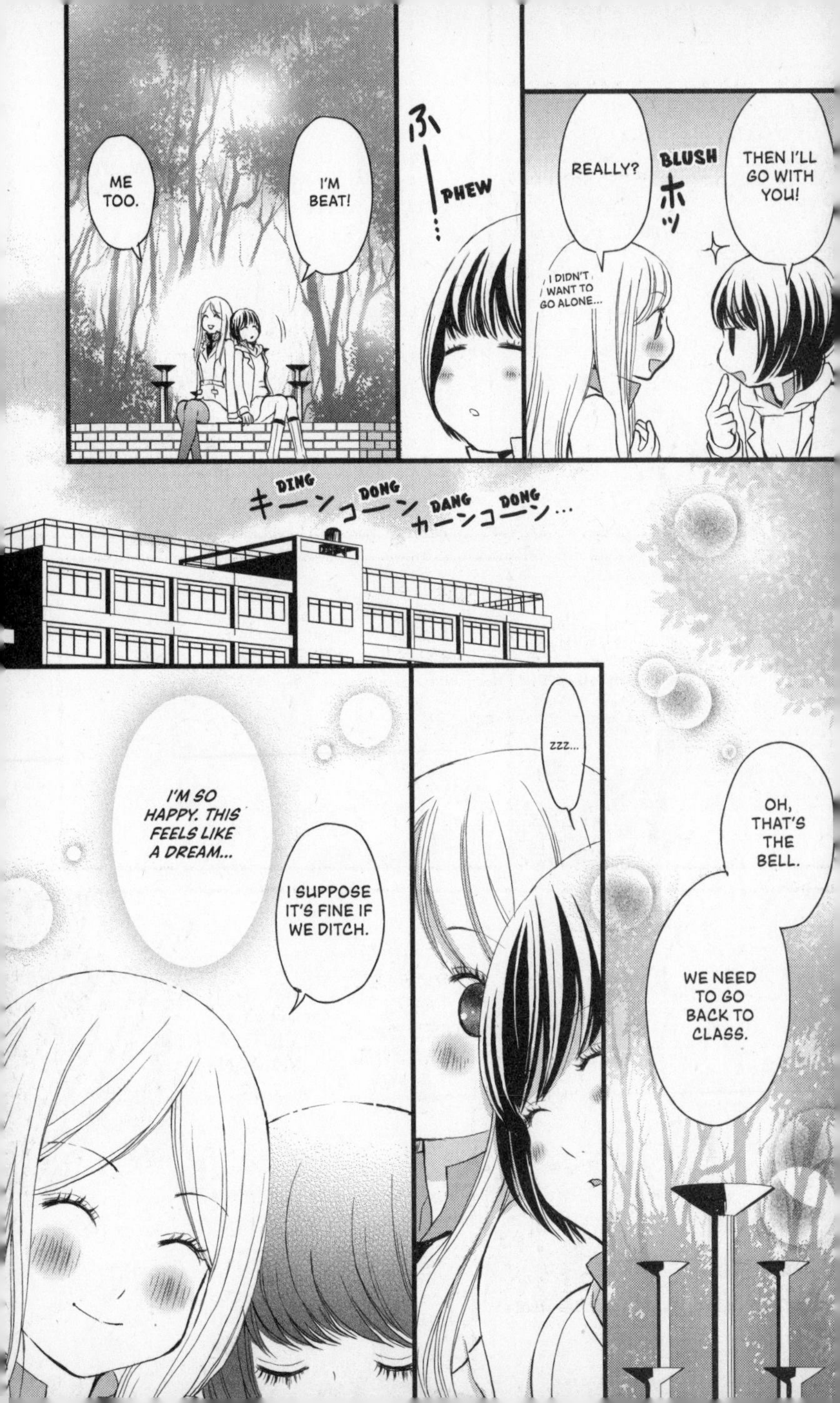
THEN I'LL GO WITH YOU!
BLUSH
ホッ
REALLY?
I DIDN'T WANT TO GO ALONE...
ふー…
PHEW
I'M BEAT!
ME TOO.
キーンコーン
DING DONG
カーンコーン…
DANG DONG
OH, THAT'S THE BELL.
WE NEED TO GO BACK TO CLASS.
zzz...
I'M SO HAPPY. THIS FEELS LIKE A DREAM...
I SUPPOSE IT'S FINE IF WE DITCH.

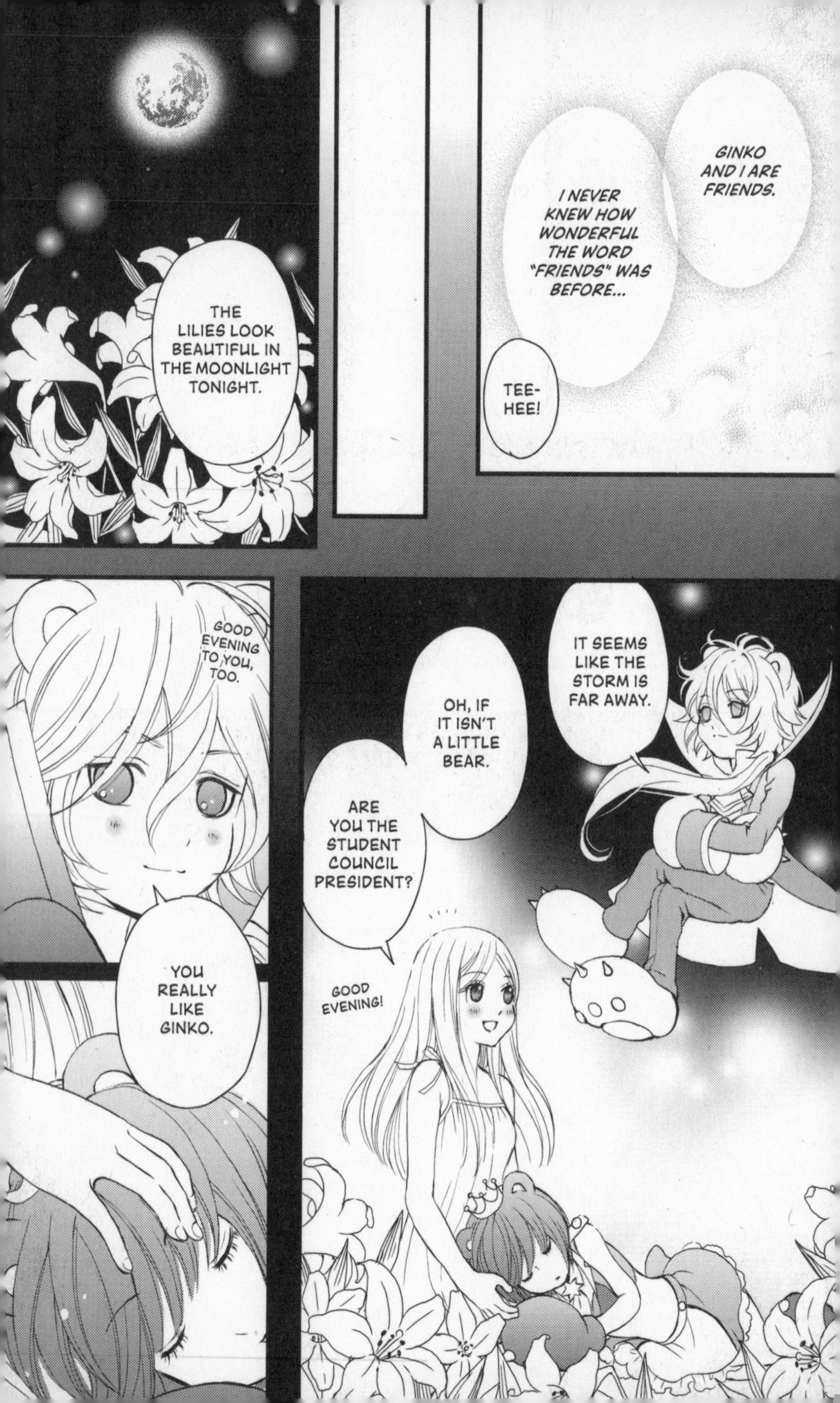
GINKO AND I ARE FRIENDS.
I NEVER KNEW HOW WONDERFUL THE WORD "FRIENDS" WAS BEFORE...
TEE-HEE!
THE LILIES LOOK BEAUTIFUL IN THE MOONLIGHT TONIGHT.
IT SEEMS LIKE THE STORM IS FAR AWAY.
OH, IF IT ISN'T A LITTLE BEAR.
ARE YOU THE STUDENT COUNCIL PRESIDENT?
GOOD EVENING!
GOOD EVENING TO YOU, TOO.
YOU REALLY LIKE GINKO.

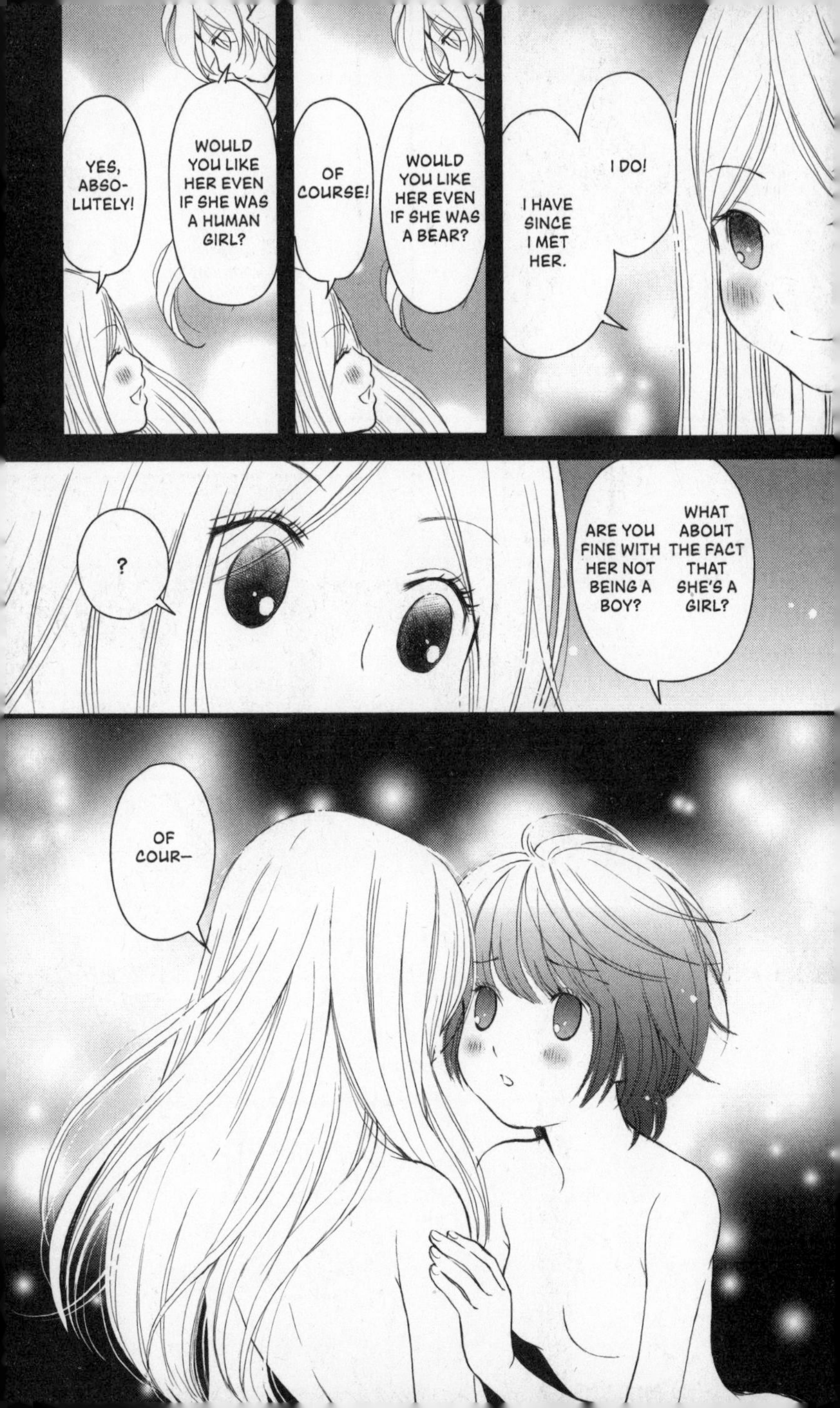
I DO!
I HAVE SINCE I MET HER.
WOULD YOU LIKE HER EVEN IF SHE WAS A BEAR?
OF COURSE!
WOULD YOU LIKE HER EVEN IF SHE WAS A HUMAN GIRL?
YES, ABSO-LUTELY!
WHAT ABOUT THE FACT THAT SHE'S A GIRL?
ARE YOU FINE WITH HER NOT BEING A BOY?
?
OF COUR—

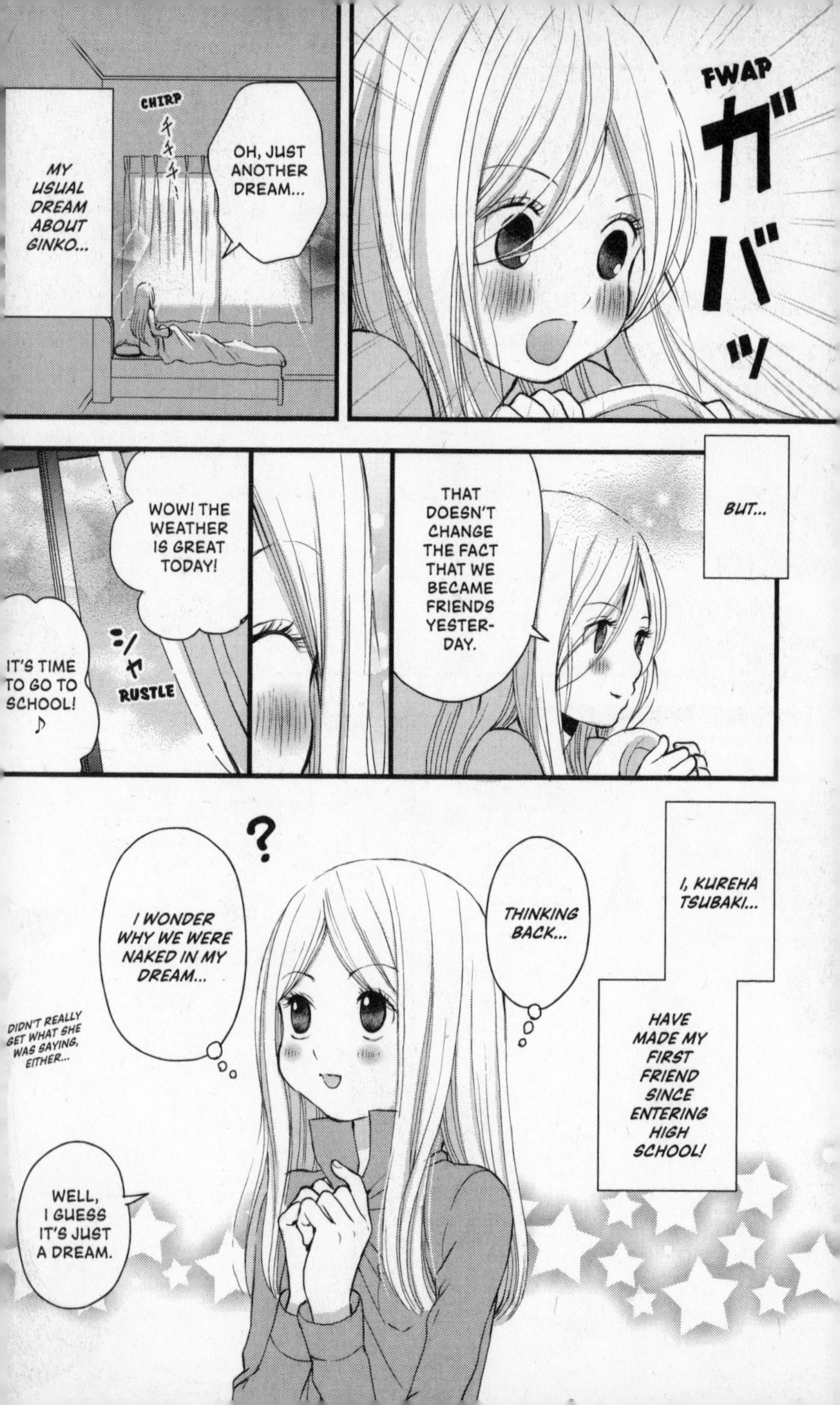
FWAP
ガバッ
CHIRP
チチチ…
OH, JUST ANOTHER DREAM...
MY USUAL DREAM ABOUT GINKO...
BUT...
THAT DOESN'T CHANGE THE FACT THAT WE BECAME FRIENDS YESTER-DAY.
WOW! THE WEATHER IS GREAT TODAY!
シャ
RUSTLE
IT'S TIME TO GO TO SCHOOL! ♪
I, KUREHA TSUBAKI...
HAVE MADE MY FIRST FRIEND SINCE ENTERING HIGH SCHOOL!
THINKING BACK...
?
I WONDER WHY WE WERE NAKED IN MY DREAM...
DIDN'T REALLY GET WHAT SHE WAS SAYING, EITHER...
WELL, I GUESS IT'S JUST A DREAM.

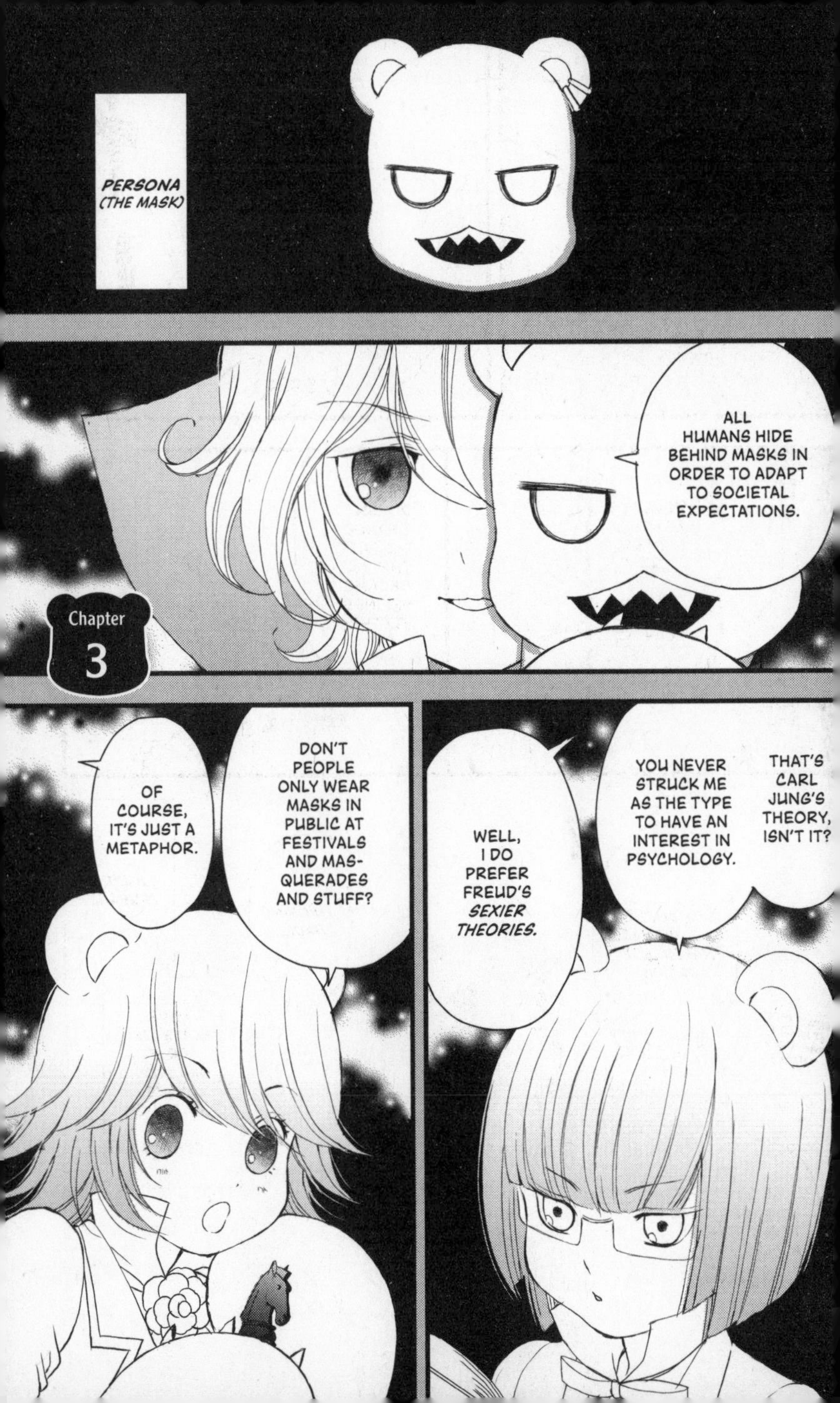
PERSONA (THE MASK)
ALL HUMANS HIDE BEHIND MASKS IN ORDER TO ADAPT TO SOCIETAL EXPECTATIONS.
Chapter 3
THAT'S CARL JUNG'S THEORY, ISN'T IT?
YOU NEVER STRUCK ME AS THE TYPE TO HAVE AN INTEREST IN PSYCHOLOGY.
WELL, I DO PREFER FREUD'S *SEXIER THEORIES.*
DON'T PEOPLE ONLY WEAR MASKS IN PUBLIC AT FESTIVALS AND MAS-QUERADES AND STUFF?
OF COURSE, IT'S JUST A METAPHOR.

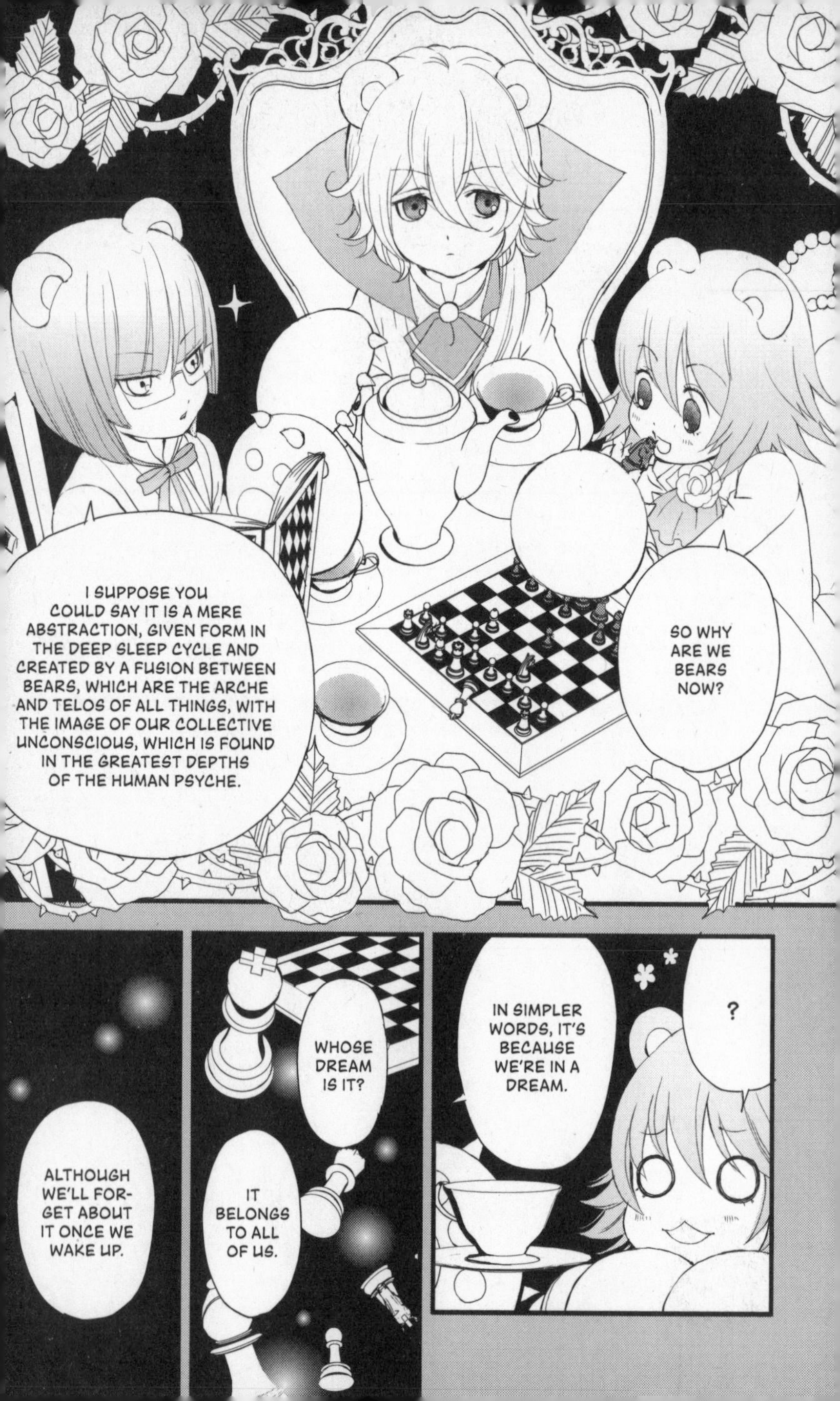
SO WHY ARE WE BEARS NOW?
I SUPPOSE YOU COULD SAY IT IS A MERE ABSTRACTION, GIVEN FORM IN THE DEEP SLEEP CYCLE AND CREATED BY A FUSION BETWEEN BEARS, WHICH ARE THE ARCHE AND TELOS OF ALL THINGS, WITH THE IMAGE OF OUR COLLECTIVE UNCONSCIOUS, WHICH IS FOUND IN THE GREATEST DEPTHS OF THE HUMAN PSYCHE.
?
IN SIMPLER WORDS, IT'S BECAUSE WE'RE IN A DREAM.
WHOSE DREAM IS IT?
IT BELONGS TO ALL OF US.
ALTHOUGH WE'LL FOR-GET ABOUT IT ONCE WE WAKE UP.

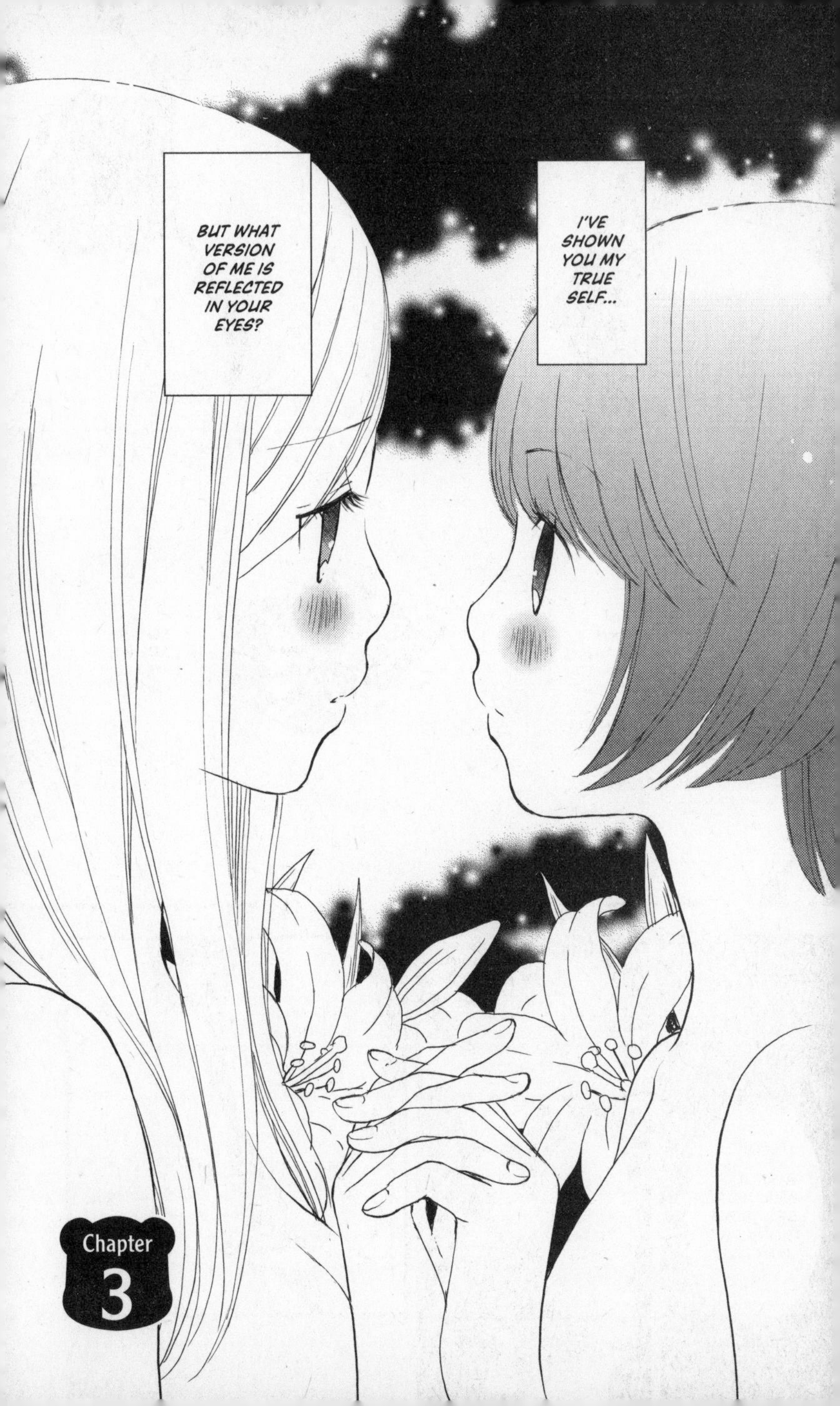
I'VE SHOWN YOU MY TRUE SELF...
BUT WHAT VERSION OF ME IS REFLECTED IN YOUR EYES?
Chapter 3

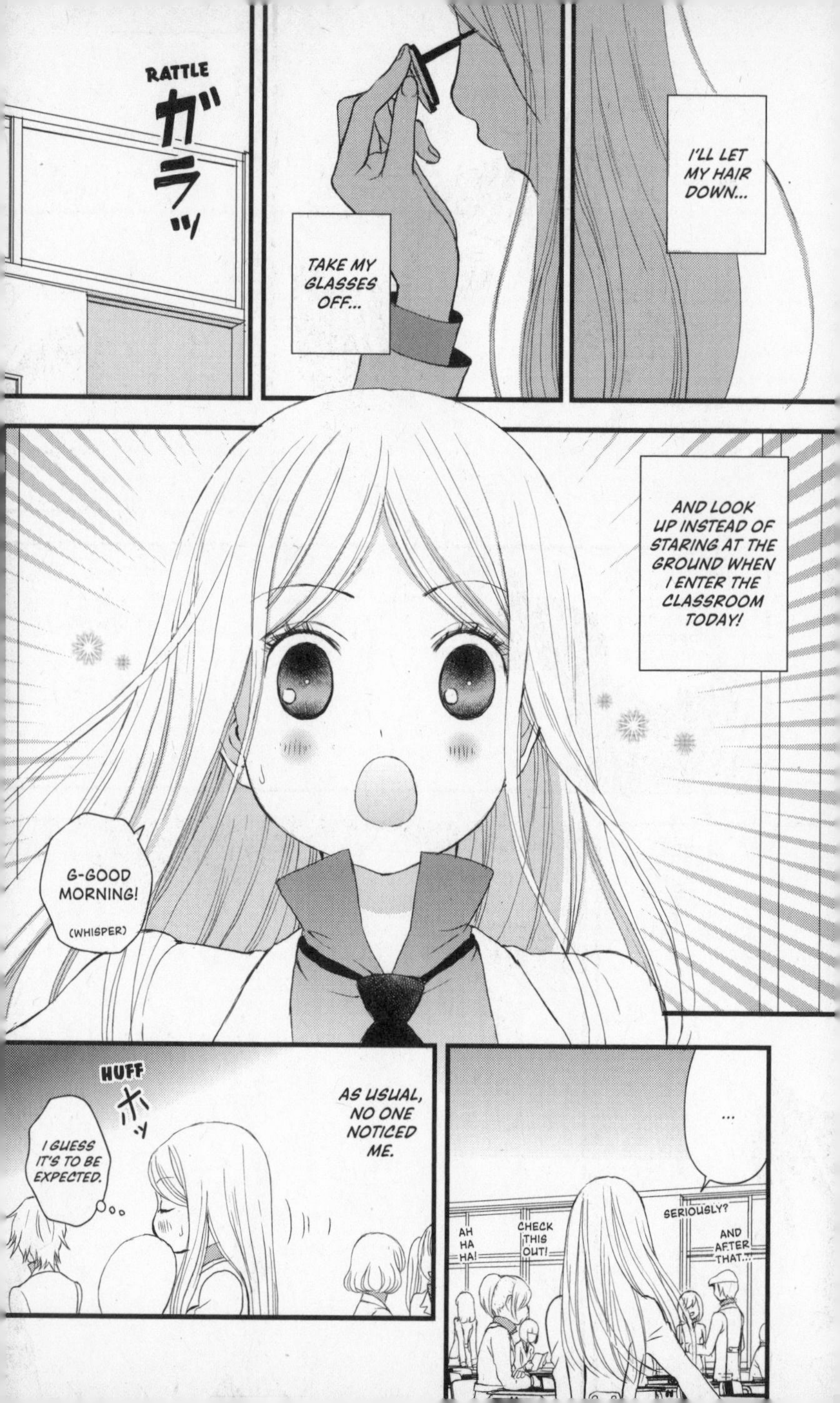
I'LL LET MY HAIR DOWN...
TAKE MY GLASSES OFF...
RATTLE
ガラッ
AND LOOK UP INSTEAD OF STARING AT THE GROUND WHEN I ENTER THE CLASSROOM TODAY!
G-GOOD MORNING!
(WHISPER)
...
SERIOUSLY?
AND AFTER THAT...
CHECK THIS OUT!
AH HA HA!
AS USUAL, NO ONE NOTICED ME.
HUFF
ホッ
I GUESS IT'S TO BE EXPECTED.

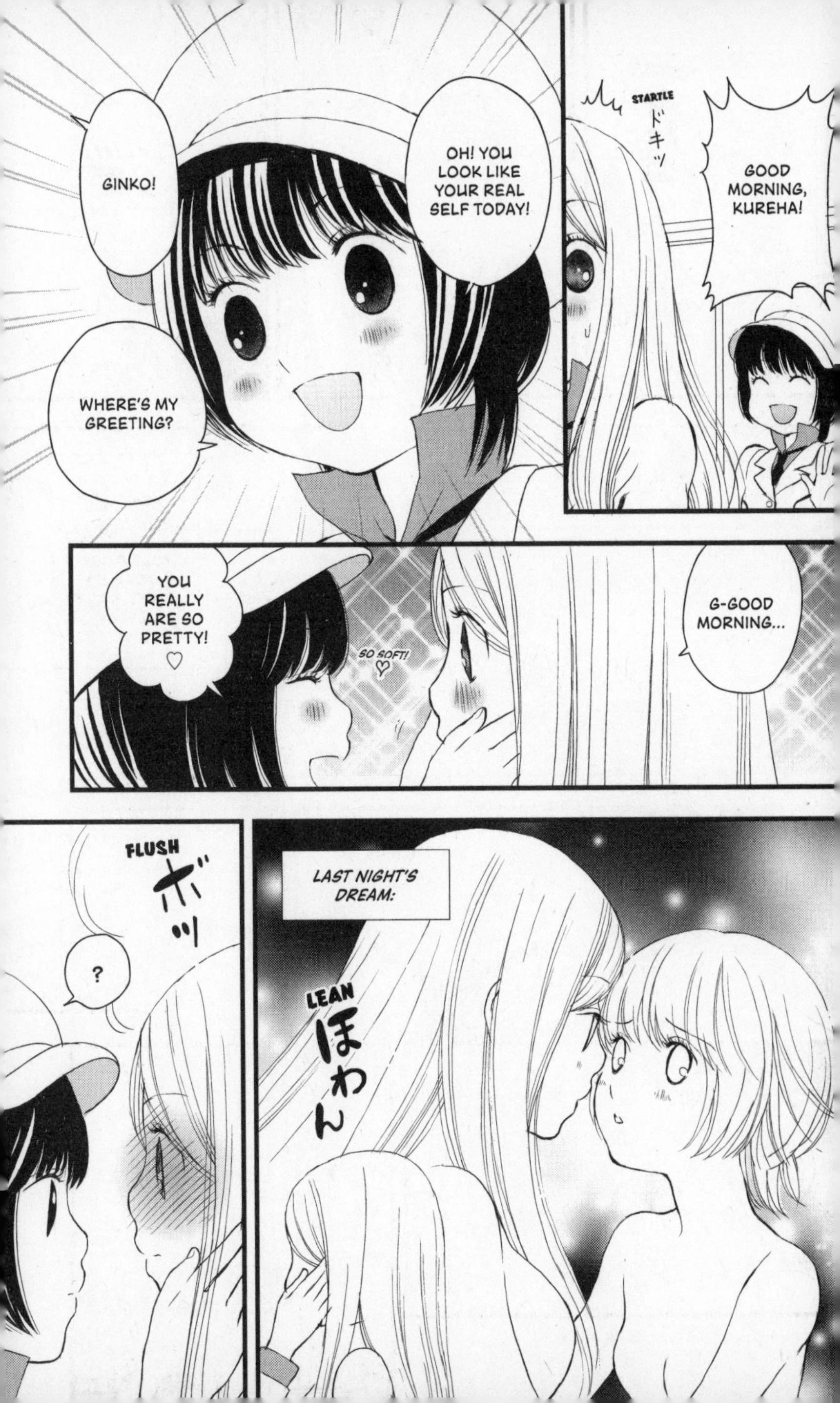
STARTLE
ドキッ
GOOD MORNING, KUREHA!
OH! YOU LOOK LIKE YOUR REAL SELF TODAY!
GINKO!
WHERE'S MY GREETING?
G-GOOD MORNING...
SO SOFT! ♡
YOU REALLY ARE SO PRETTY! ♡
LAST NIGHT'S DREAM:
LEAN
ほわん
FLUSH
ボッ
?

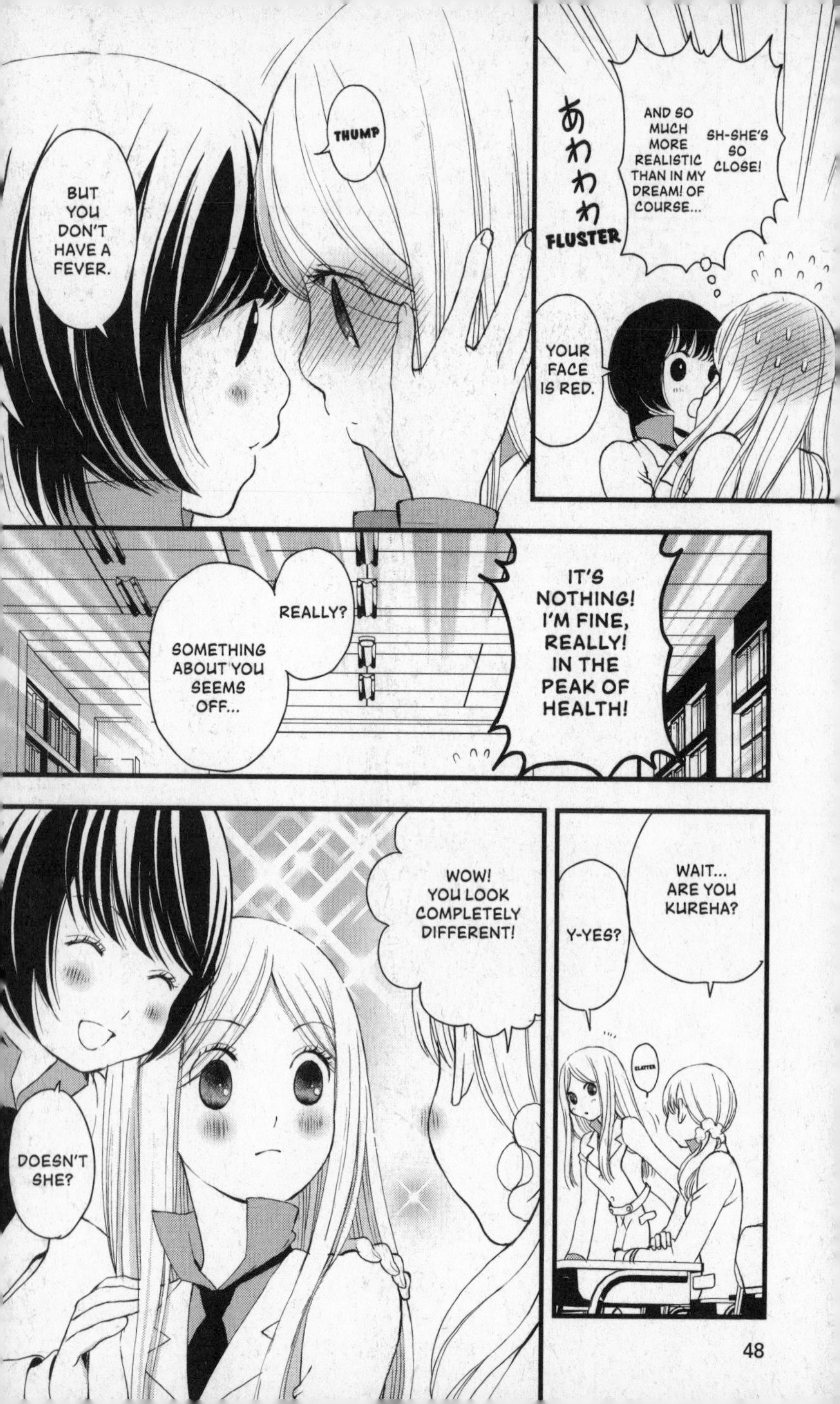
SH-SHE'S SO CLOSE!
AND SO MUCH MORE REALISTIC THAN IN MY DREAM! OF COURSE...
あわわわ
FLUSTER
YOUR FACE IS RED.
THUMP
BUT YOU DON'T HAVE A FEVER.
IT'S NOTHING! I'M FINE, REALLY! IN THE PEAK OF HEALTH!
REALLY?
SOMETHING ABOUT YOU SEEMS OFF...
WAIT... ARE YOU KUREHA?
Y-YES?
CLATTER
WOW! YOU LOOK COMPLETELY DIFFERENT!
DOESN'T SHE?

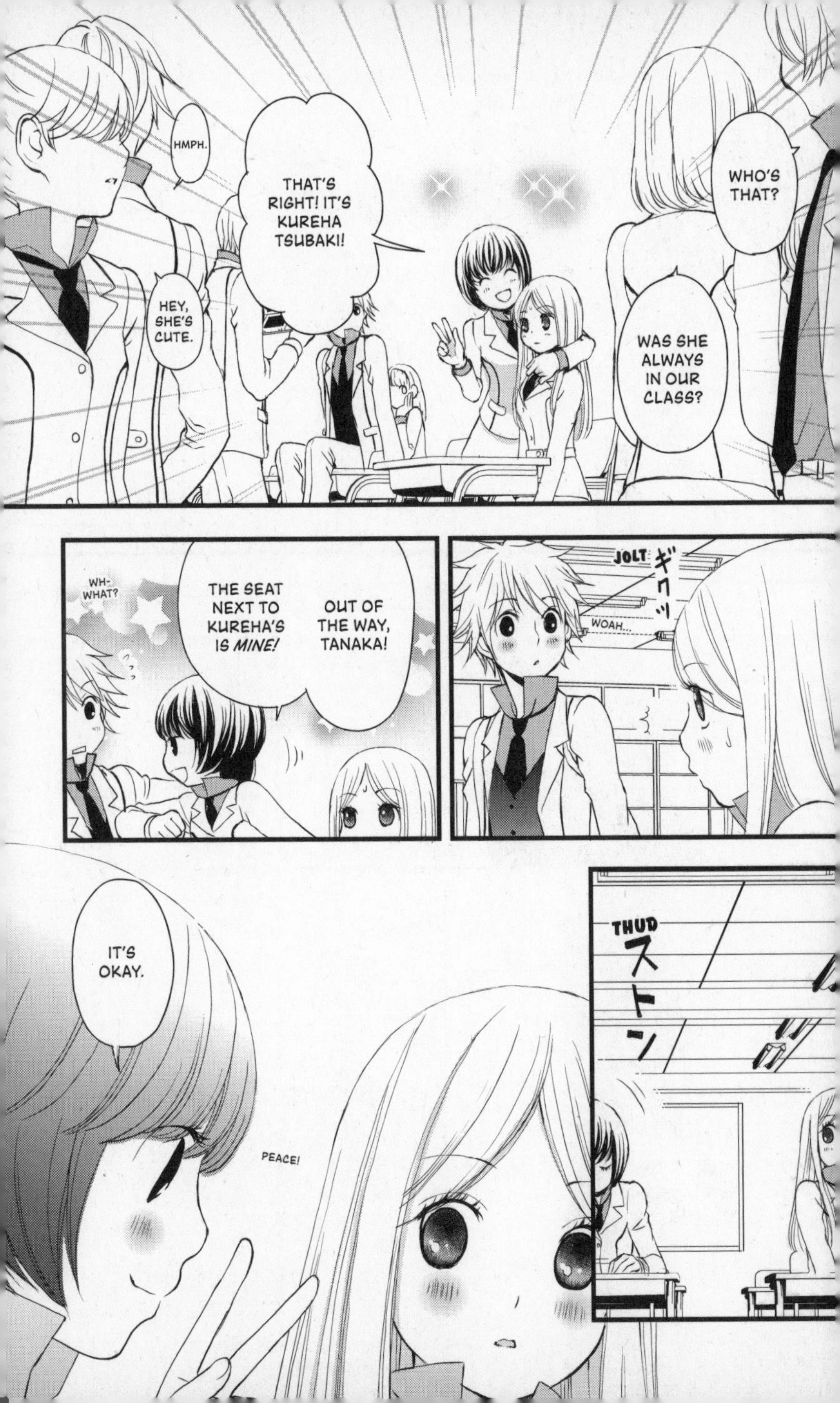
WHO'S THAT?
WAS SHE ALWAYS IN OUR CLASS?
THAT'S RIGHT! IT'S KUREHA TSUBAKI!
HMPH.
HEY, SHE'S CUTE.
JOLT
ギクッ
WOAH...
OUT OF THE WAY, TANAKA!
THE SEAT NEXT TO KUREHA'S IS *MINE!*
WH-WHAT?
THUD
ストン
PEACE!
IT'S OKAY.

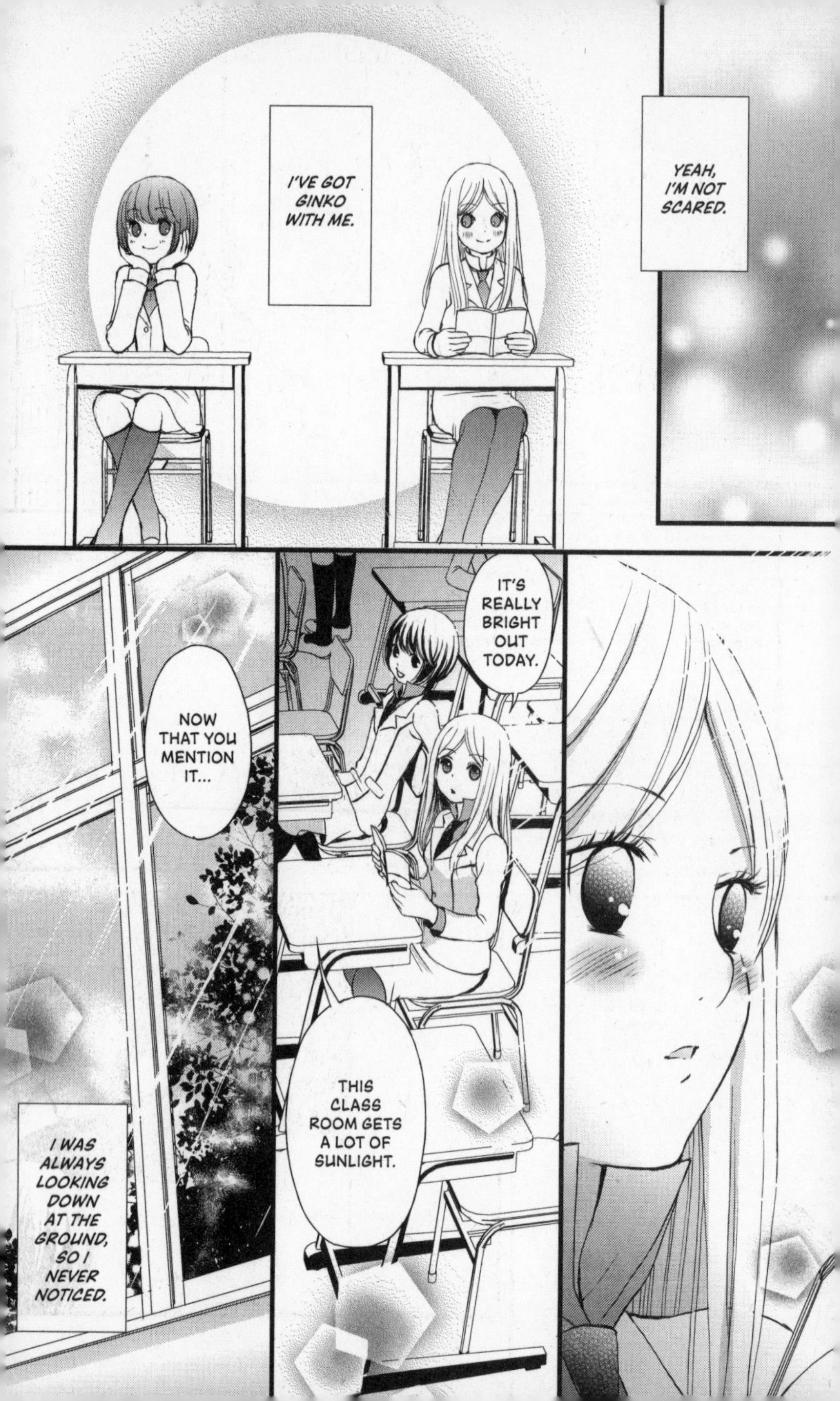
YEAH, I'M NOT SCARED.
I'VE GOT GINKO WITH ME.
IT'S REALLY BRIGHT OUT TODAY.
THIS CLASS ROOM GETS A LOT OF SUNLIGHT.
NOW THAT YOU MENTION IT...
I WAS ALWAYS LOOKING DOWN AT THE GROUND, SO I NEVER NOTICED.

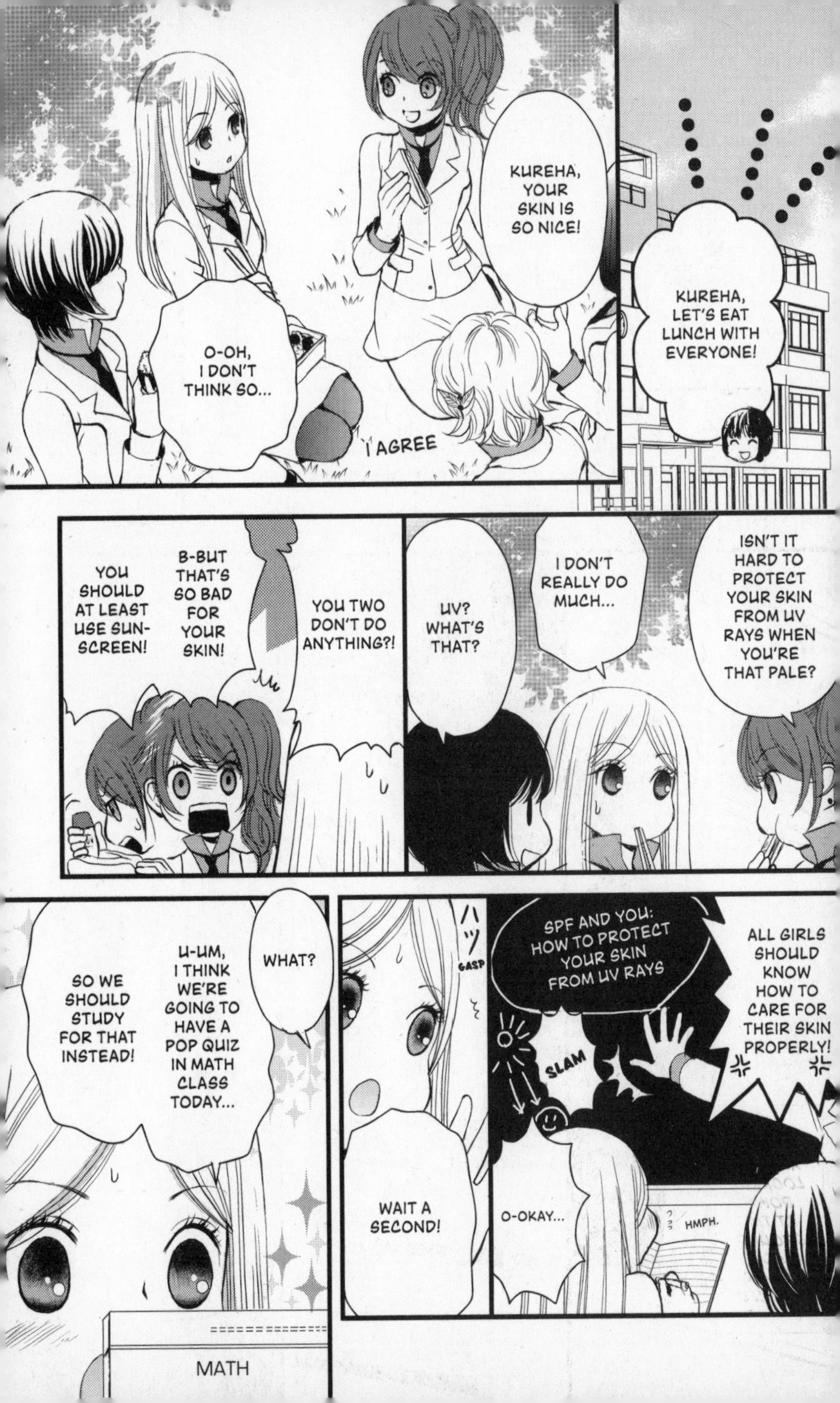
KUREHA, LET'S EAT LUNCH WITH EVERYONE!
KUREHA, YOUR SKIN IS SO NICE!
I AGREE
O-OH, I DON'T THINK SO...
ISN'T IT HARD TO PROTECT YOUR SKIN FROM UV RAYS WHEN YOU'RE THAT PALE?
I DON'T REALLY DO MUCH...
UV? WHAT'S THAT?
YOU TWO DON'T DO ANYTHING?!
B-BUT THAT'S SO BAD FOR YOUR SKIN!
YOU SHOULD AT LEAST USE SUN-SCREEN!
ALL GIRLS SHOULD KNOW HOW TO CARE FOR THEIR SKIN PROPERLY!
SPF AND YOU: HOW TO PROTECT YOUR SKIN FROM UV RAYS
SLAM
ハッ
GASP
HMPH.
O-OKAY...
WAIT A SECOND!
WHAT?
U-UM, I THINK WE'RE GOING TO HAVE A POP QUIZ IN MATH CLASS TODAY...
SO WE SHOULD STUDY FOR THAT INSTEAD!
MATH

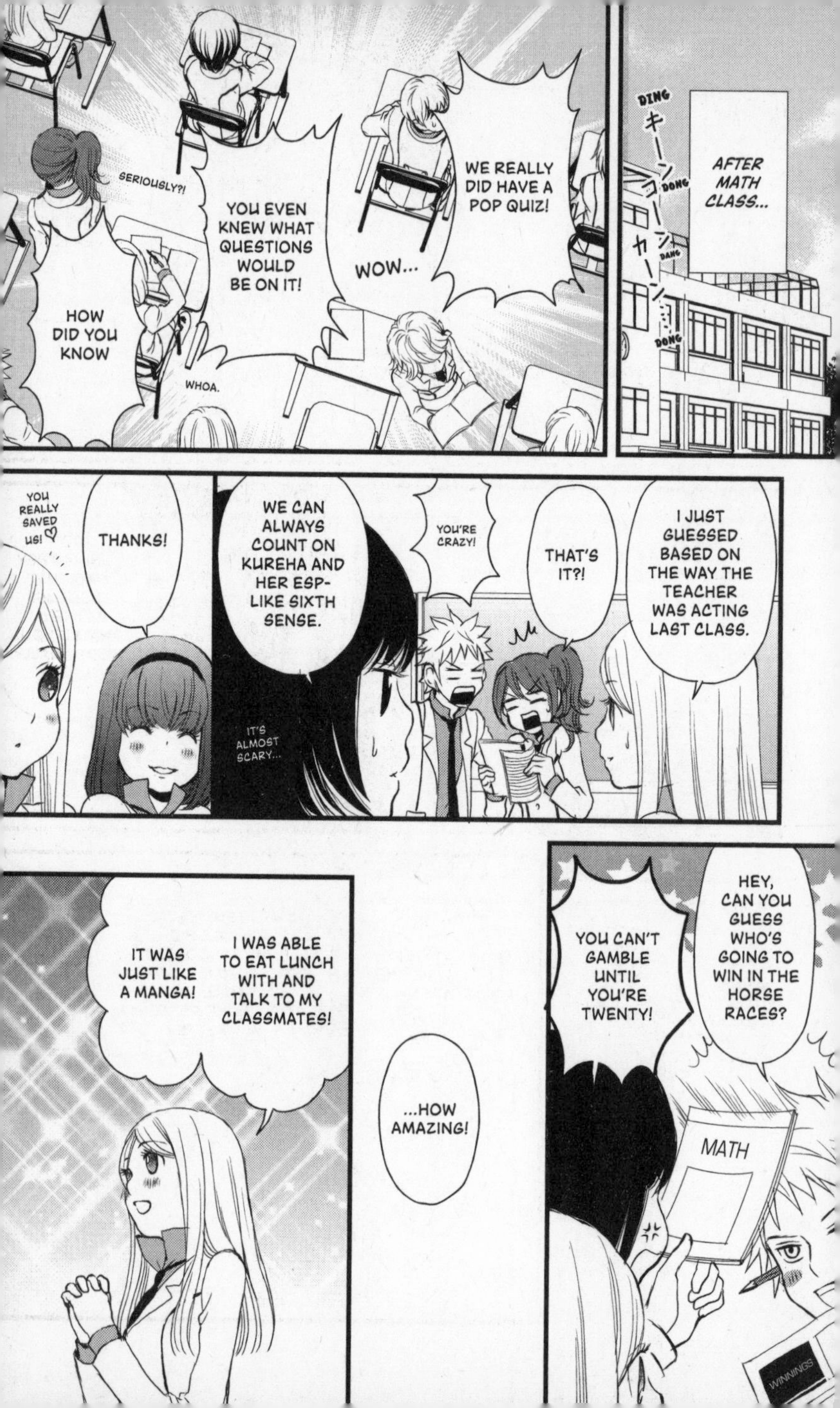
DING
キーン
DONG
コーン
DANG
カーン
DONG
AFTER MATH CLASS...
WE REALLY DID HAVE A POP QUIZ!
WOW...
YOU EVEN KNEW WHAT QUESTIONS WOULD BE ON IT!
SERIOUSLY?!
HOW DID YOU KNOW
WHOA.
I JUST GUESSED BASED ON THE WAY THE TEACHER WAS ACTING LAST CLASS.
THAT'S IT?!
YOU'RE CRAZY!
WE CAN ALWAYS COUNT ON KUREHA AND HER ESP-LIKE SIXTH SENSE.
IT'S ALMOST SCARY...
THANKS!
YOU REALLY SAVED US! ♡
HEY, CAN YOU GUESS WHO'S GOING TO WIN IN THE HORSE RACES?
YOU CAN'T GAMBLE UNTIL YOU'RE TWENTY!
MATH
WINNINGS
...HOW AMAZING!
I WAS ABLE TO EAT LUNCH WITH AND TALK TO MY CLASSMATES!
IT WAS JUST LIKE A MANGA!

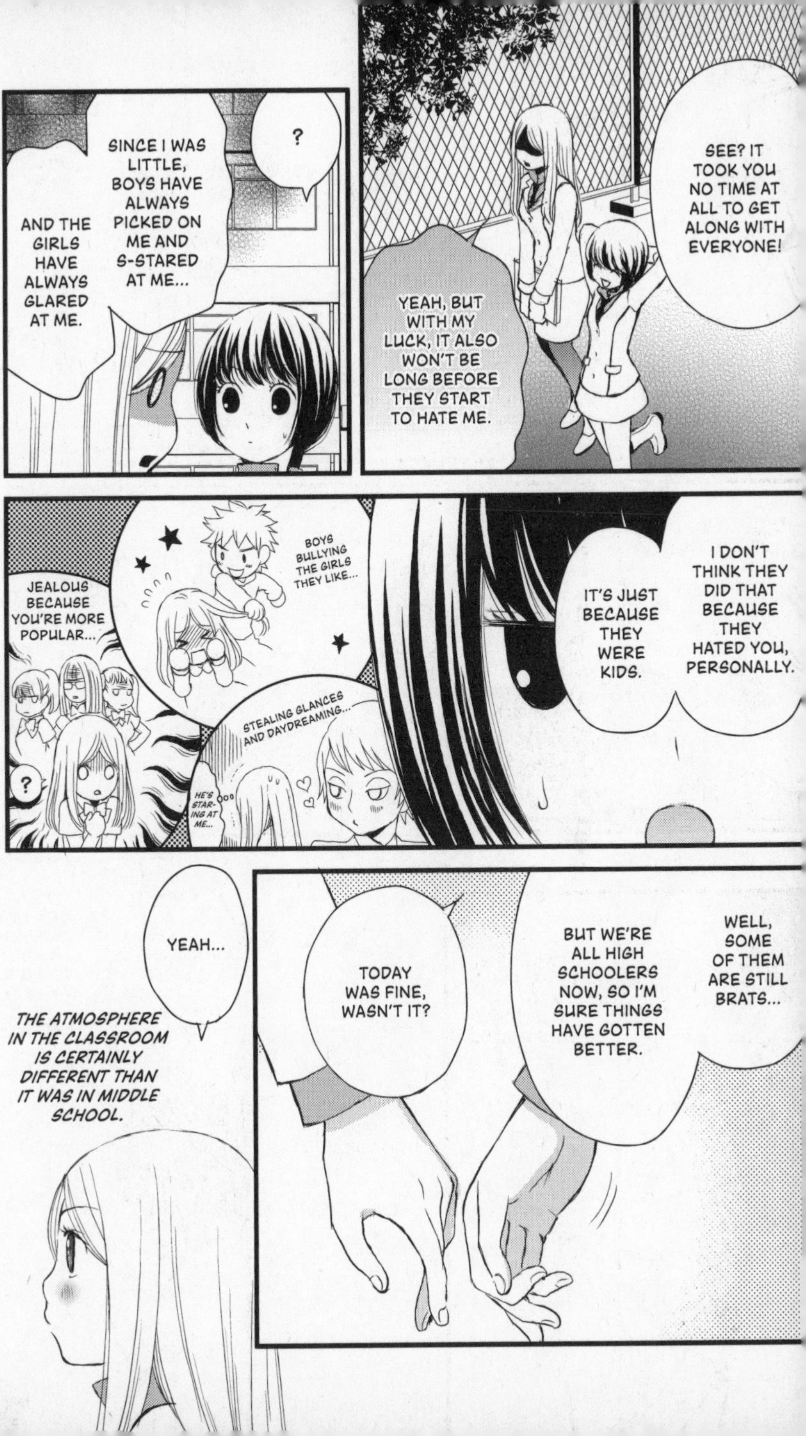
SEE? IT TOOK YOU NO TIME AT ALL TO GET ALONG WITH EVERYONE!
YEAH, BUT WITH MY LUCK, IT ALSO WON'T BE LONG BEFORE THEY START TO HATE ME.
?
SINCE I WAS LITTLE, BOYS HAVE ALWAYS PICKED ON ME AND S-STARED AT ME...
AND THE GIRLS HAVE ALWAYS GLARED AT ME.
I DON'T THINK THEY DID THAT BECAUSE THEY HATED YOU, PERSONALLY.
IT'S JUST BECAUSE THEY WERE KIDS.
BOYS BULLYING THE GIRLS THEY LIKE...
JEALOUS BECAUSE YOU'RE MORE POPULAR...
STEALING GLANCES AND DAYDREAMING...
HE'S STARING AT ME...
?
WELL, SOME OF THEM ARE STILL BRATS...
BUT WE'RE ALL HIGH SCHOOLERS NOW, SO I'M SURE THINGS HAVE GOTTEN BETTER.
TODAY WAS FINE, WASN'T IT?
YEAH...
THE ATMOSPHERE IN THE CLASSROOM IS CERTAINLY DIFFERENT THAN IT WAS IN MIDDLE SCHOOL.

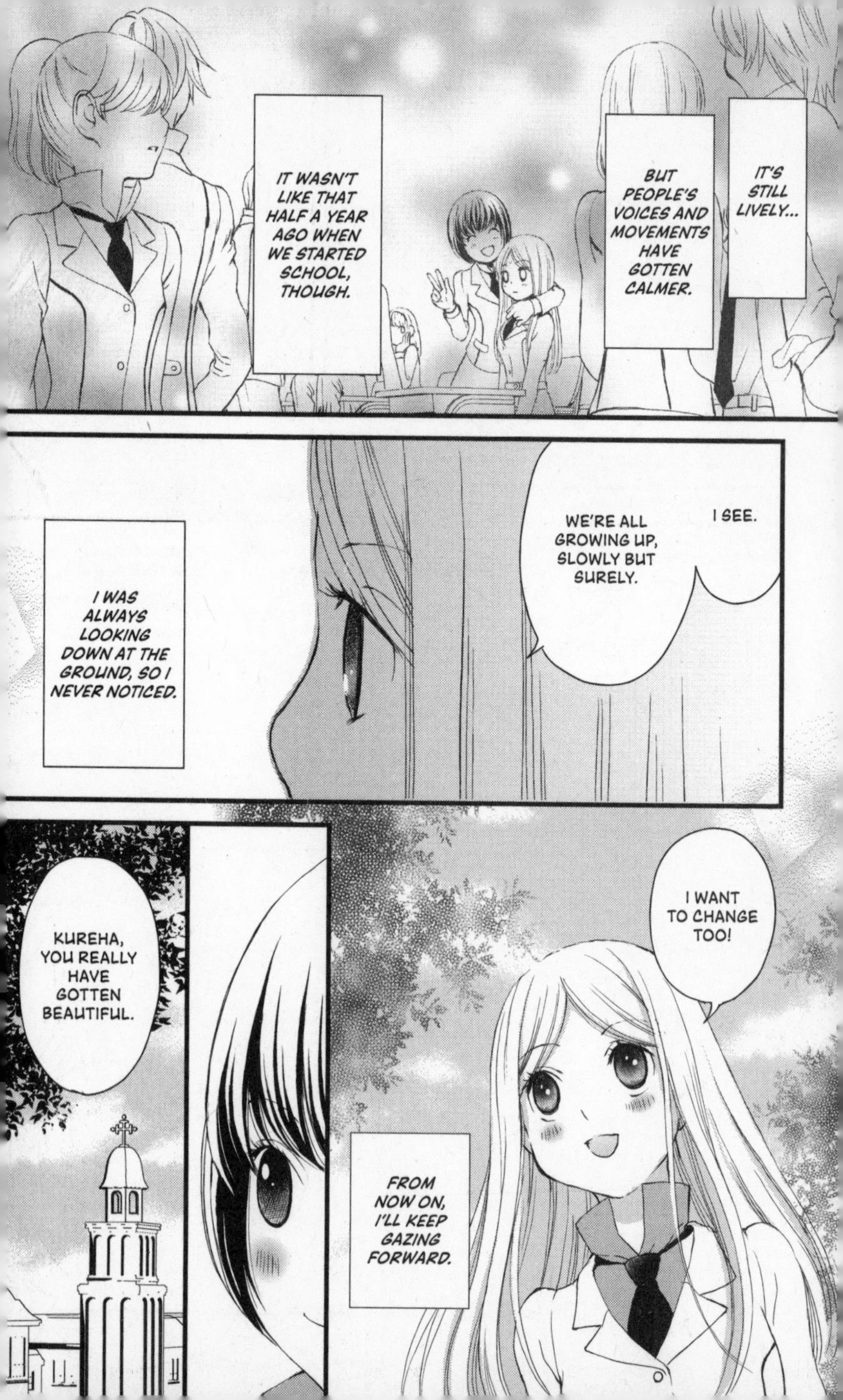
IT'S STILL LIVELY...
BUT PEOPLE'S VOICES AND MOVEMENTS HAVE GOTTEN CALMER.
IT WASN'T LIKE THAT HALF A YEAR AGO WHEN WE STARTED SCHOOL, THOUGH.
I SEE.
WE'RE ALL GROWING UP, SLOWLY BUT SURELY.
I WAS ALWAYS LOOKING DOWN AT THE GROUND, SO I NEVER NOTICED.
I WANT TO CHANGE TOO!
FROM NOW ON, I'LL KEEP GAZING FORWARD.
KUREHA, YOU REALLY HAVE GOTTEN BEAUTIFUL.

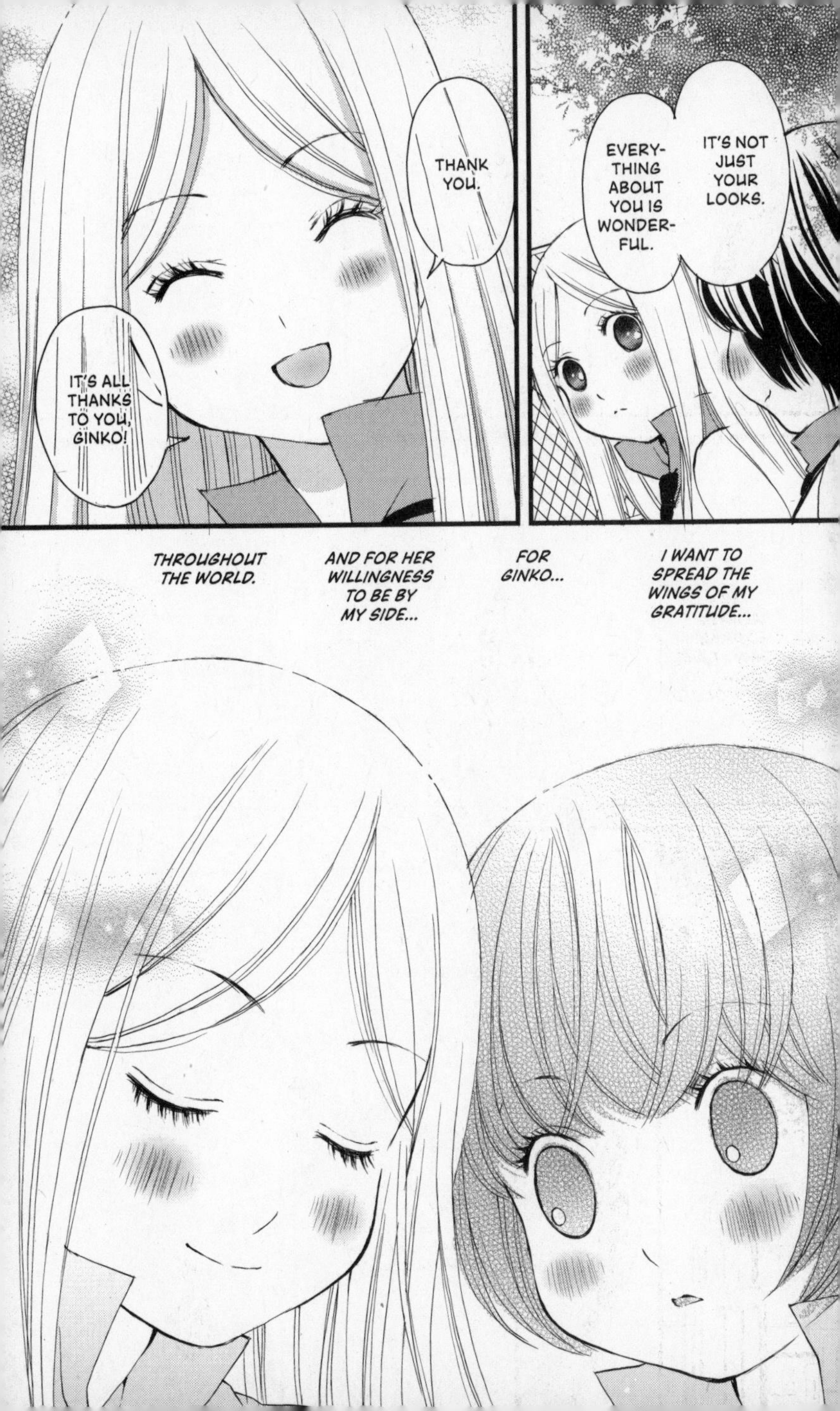
IT'S NOT JUST YOUR LOOKS.
EVERY-THING ABOUT YOU IS WONDER-FUL.
THANK YOU.
IT'S ALL THANKS TO YOU, GINKO!
I WANT TO SPREAD THE WINGS OF MY GRATITUDE...
FOR GINKO...
AND FOR HER WILLINGNESS TO BE BY MY SIDE...
THROUGHOUT THE WORLD.

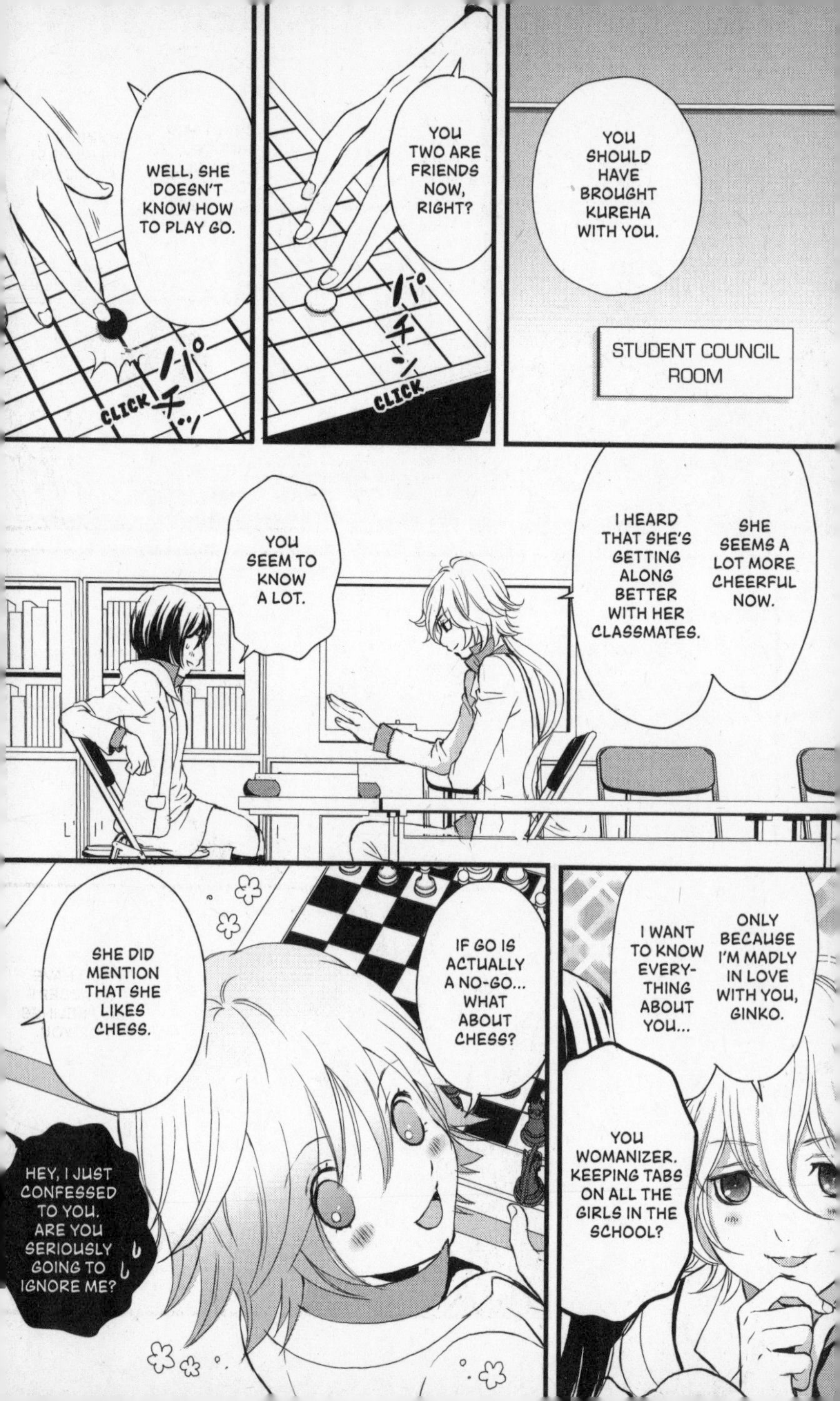
YOU SHOULD HAVE BROUGHT KUREHA WITH YOU.
STUDENT COUNCIL ROOM
YOU TWO ARE FRIENDS NOW, RIGHT?
パチン
CLICK
WELL, SHE DOESN'T KNOW HOW TO PLAY GO.
パチッ
CLICK
SHE SEEMS A LOT MORE CHEERFUL NOW.
I HEARD THAT SHE'S GETTING ALONG BETTER WITH HER CLASSMATES.
YOU SEEM TO KNOW A LOT.
ONLY BECAUSE I'M MADLY IN LOVE WITH YOU, GINKO.
I WANT TO KNOW EVERY-THING ABOUT YOU...
YOU WOMANIZER. KEEPING TABS ON ALL THE GIRLS IN THE SCHOOL?
IF GO IS ACTUALLY A NO-GO... WHAT ABOUT CHESS?
SHE DID MENTION THAT SHE LIKES CHESS.
HEY, I JUST CONFESSED TO YOU. ARE YOU SERIOUSLY GOING TO IGNORE ME?

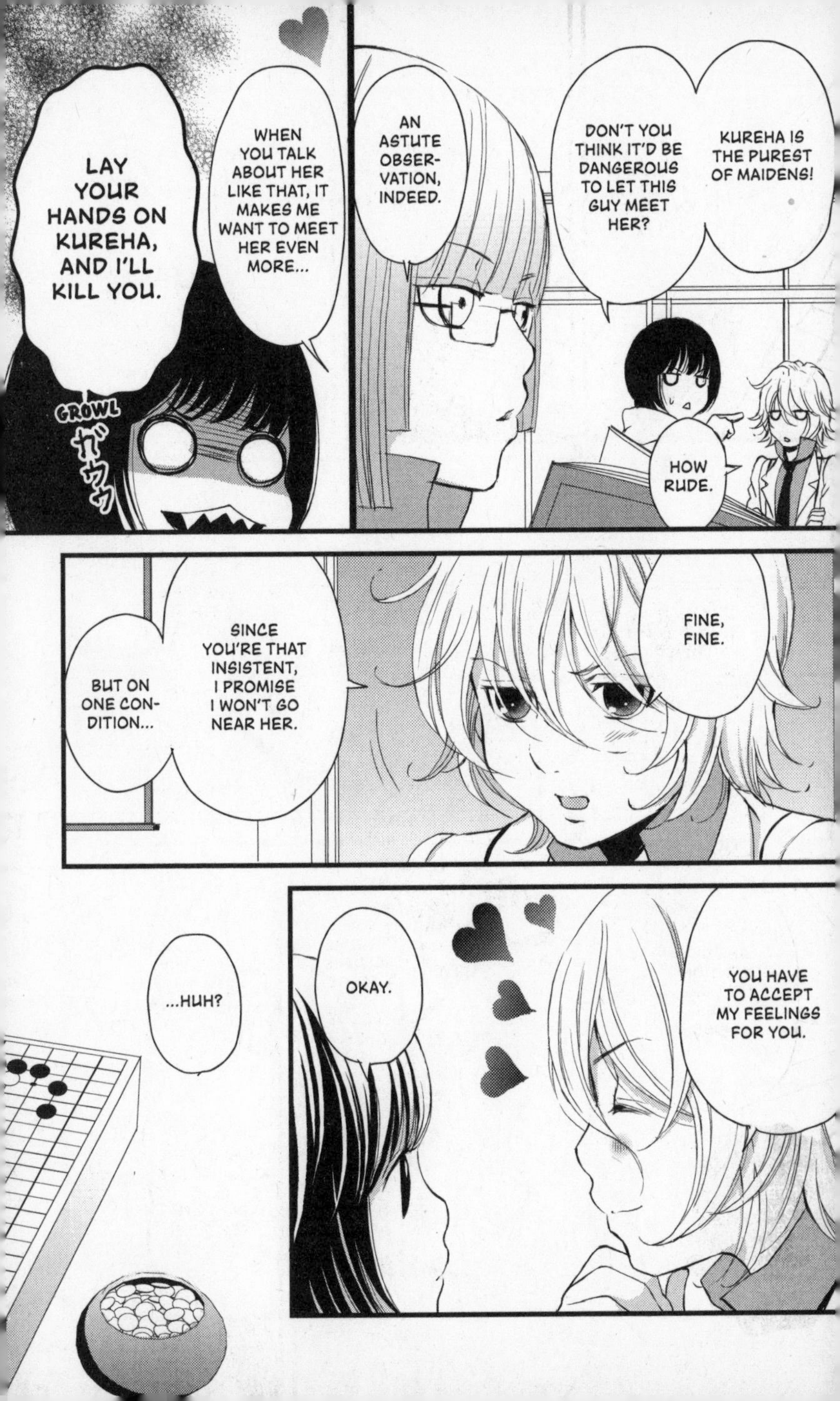
KUREHA IS THE PUREST OF MAIDENS!
DON'T YOU THINK IT'D BE DANGEROUS TO LET THIS GUY MEET HER?
AN ASTUTE OBSERVATION, INDEED.
HOW RUDE.
WHEN YOU TALK ABOUT HER LIKE THAT, IT MAKES ME WANT TO MEET HER EVEN MORE...
LAY YOUR HANDS ON KUREHA, AND I'LL KILL YOU.
GROWL
ガウウ
FINE, FINE.
SINCE YOU'RE THAT INSISTENT, I PROMISE I WON'T GO NEAR HER.
BUT ON ONE CONDITION...
YOU HAVE TO ACCEPT MY FEELINGS FOR YOU.
OKAY.
...HUH?

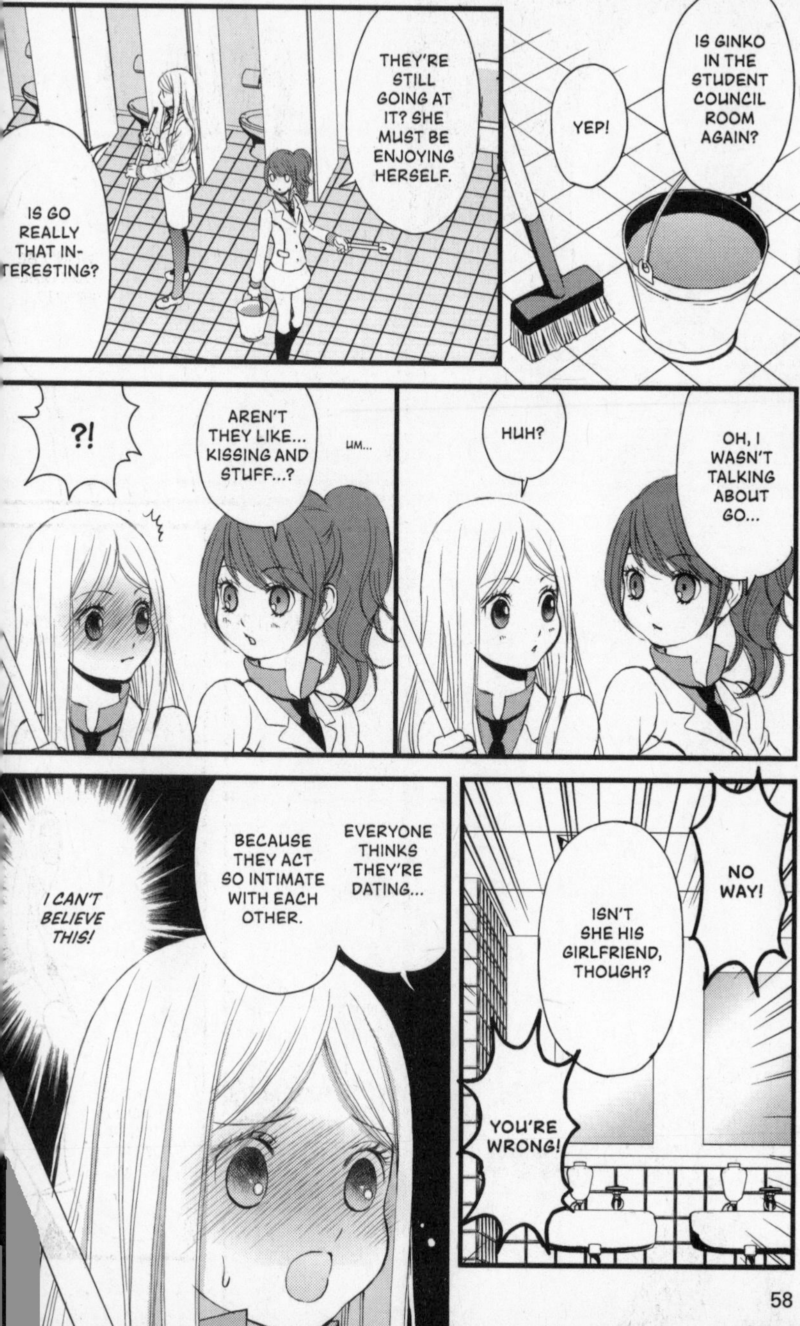
IS GINKO IN THE STUDENT COUNCIL ROOM AGAIN?
YEP!
THEY'RE STILL GOING AT IT? SHE MUST BE ENJOYING HERSELF.
IS GO REALLY THAT IN-TERESTING?
HUH?
OH, I WASN'T TALKING ABOUT GO...
UM...
AREN'T THEY LIKE... KISSING AND STUFF...?
?!
ISN'T SHE HIS GIRLFRIEND, THOUGH?
NO WAY!
YOU'RE WRONG!
EVERYONE THINKS THEY'RE DATING...
BECAUSE THEY ACT SO INTIMATE WITH EACH OTHER.
I CAN'T BELIEVE THIS!

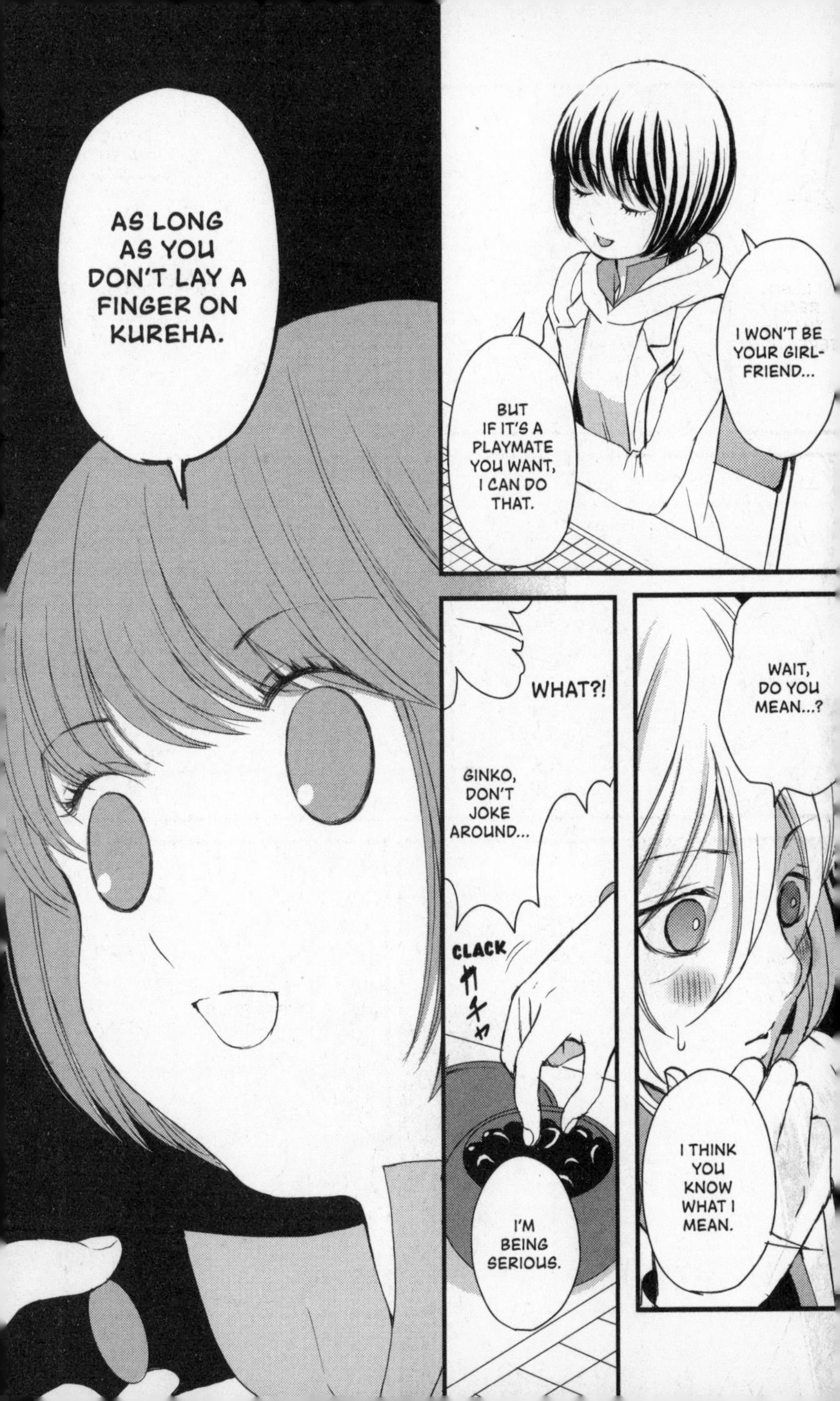
I WON'T BE YOUR GIRL-FRIEND...
BUT IF IT'S A PLAYMATE YOU WANT, I CAN DO THAT.
WAIT, DO YOU MEAN...?
I THINK YOU KNOW WHAT I MEAN.
WHAT?!
GINKO, DON'T JOKE AROUND...
CLACK
カチャ
I'M BEING SERIOUS.
AS LONG AS YOU DON'T LAY A FINGER ON KUREHA.

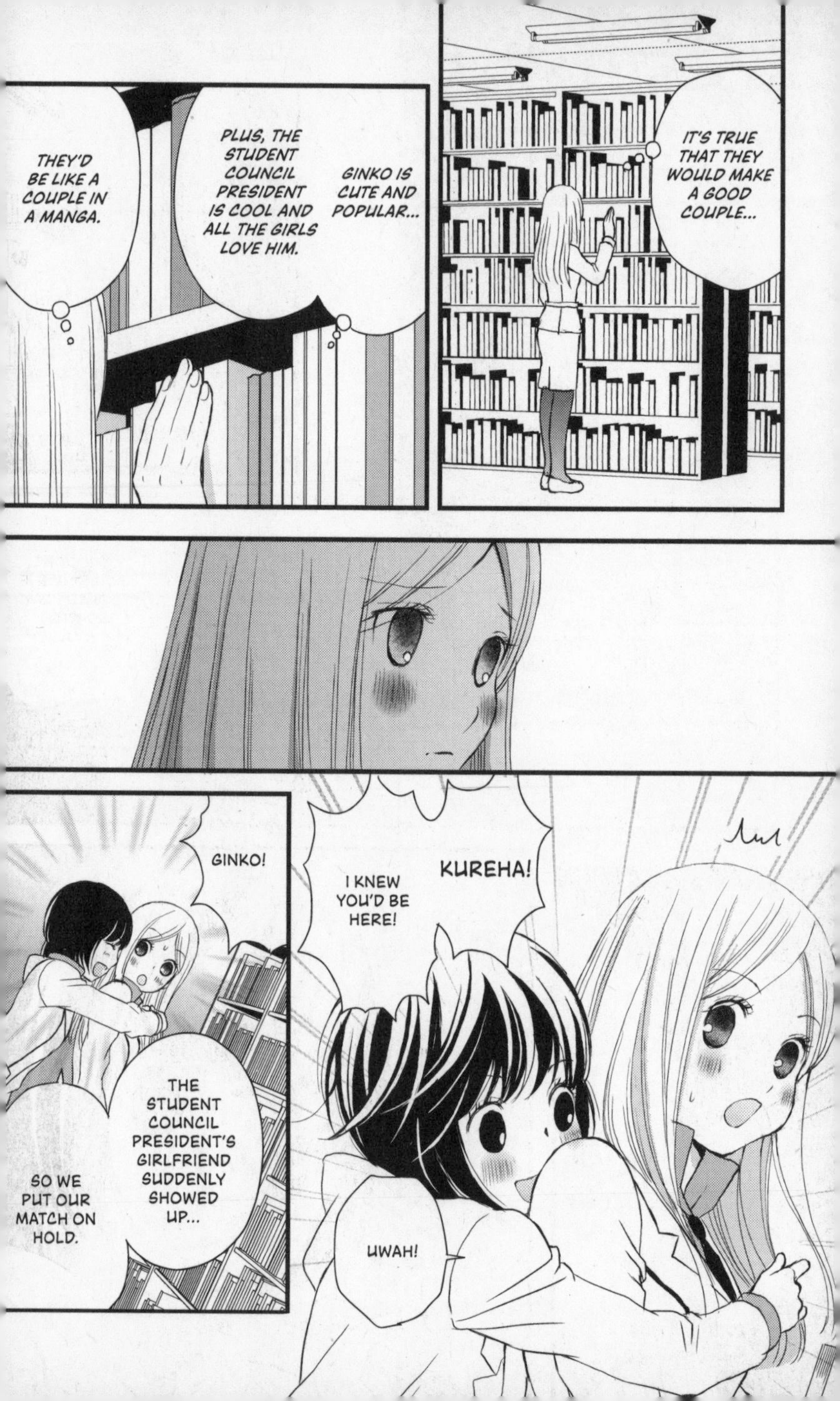
IT'S TRUE THAT THEY WOULD MAKE A GOOD COUPLE...
GINKO IS CUTE AND POPULAR...
PLUS, THE STUDENT COUNCIL PRESIDENT IS COOL AND ALL THE GIRLS LOVE HIM.
THEY'D BE LIKE A COUPLE IN A MANGA.
KUREHA!
I KNEW YOU'D BE HERE!
UWAH!
GINKO!
THE STUDENT COUNCIL PRESIDENT'S GIRLFRIEND SUDDENLY SHOWED UP...
SO WE PUT OUR MATCH ON HOLD.

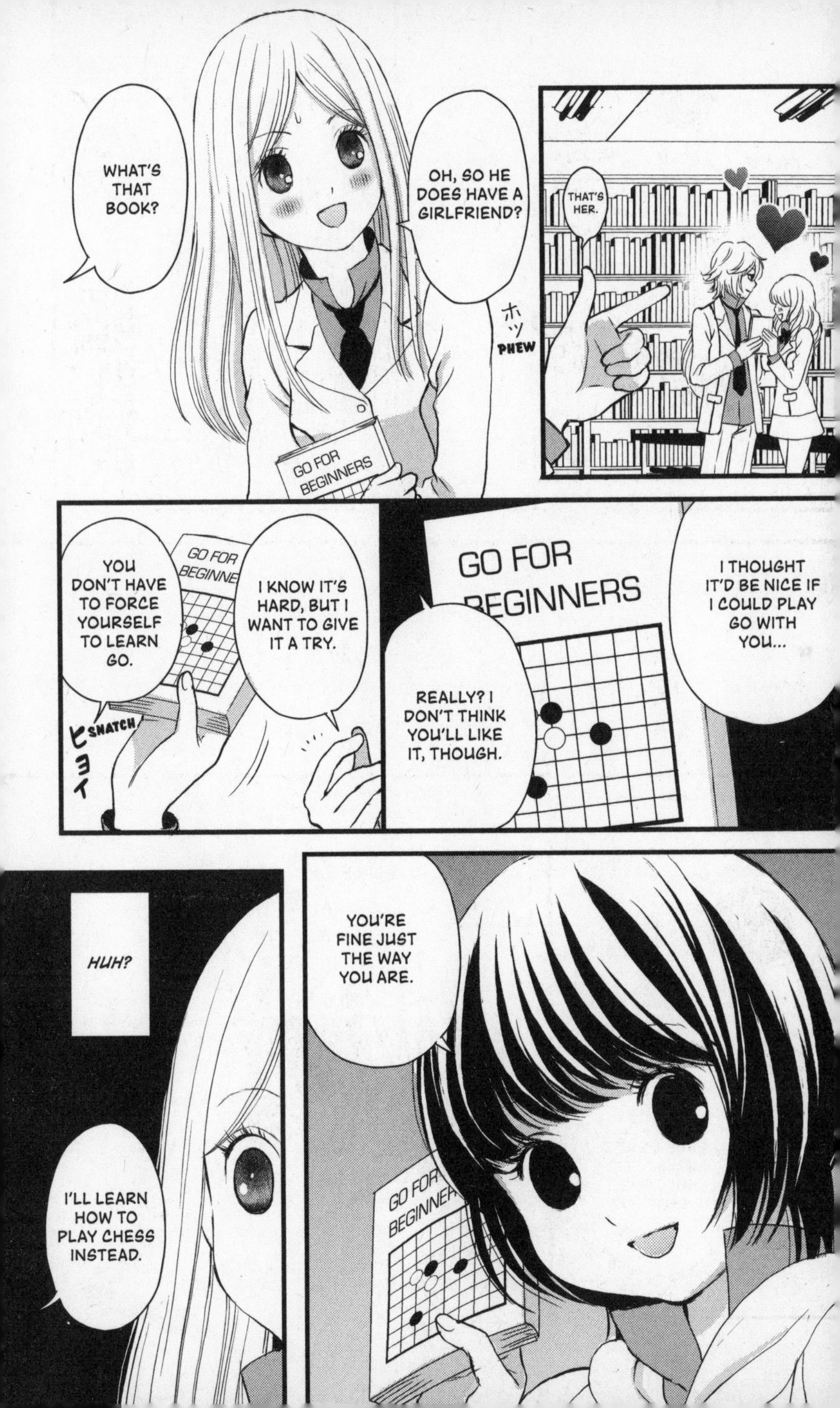
THAT'S HER.
OH, SO HE DOES HAVE A GIRLFRIEND?
ホッ PHEW
WHAT'S THAT BOOK?
GO FOR BEGINNERS
I THOUGHT IT'D BE NICE IF I COULD PLAY GO WITH YOU...
GO FOR BEGINNERS
REALLY? I DON'T THINK YOU'LL LIKE IT, THOUGH.
I KNOW IT'S HARD, BUT I WANT TO GIVE IT A TRY.
YOU DON'T HAVE TO FORCE YOURSELF TO LEARN GO.
ヒョイ SNATCH
YOU'RE FINE JUST THE WAY YOU ARE.
HUH?
I'LL LEARN HOW TO PLAY CHESS INSTEAD.

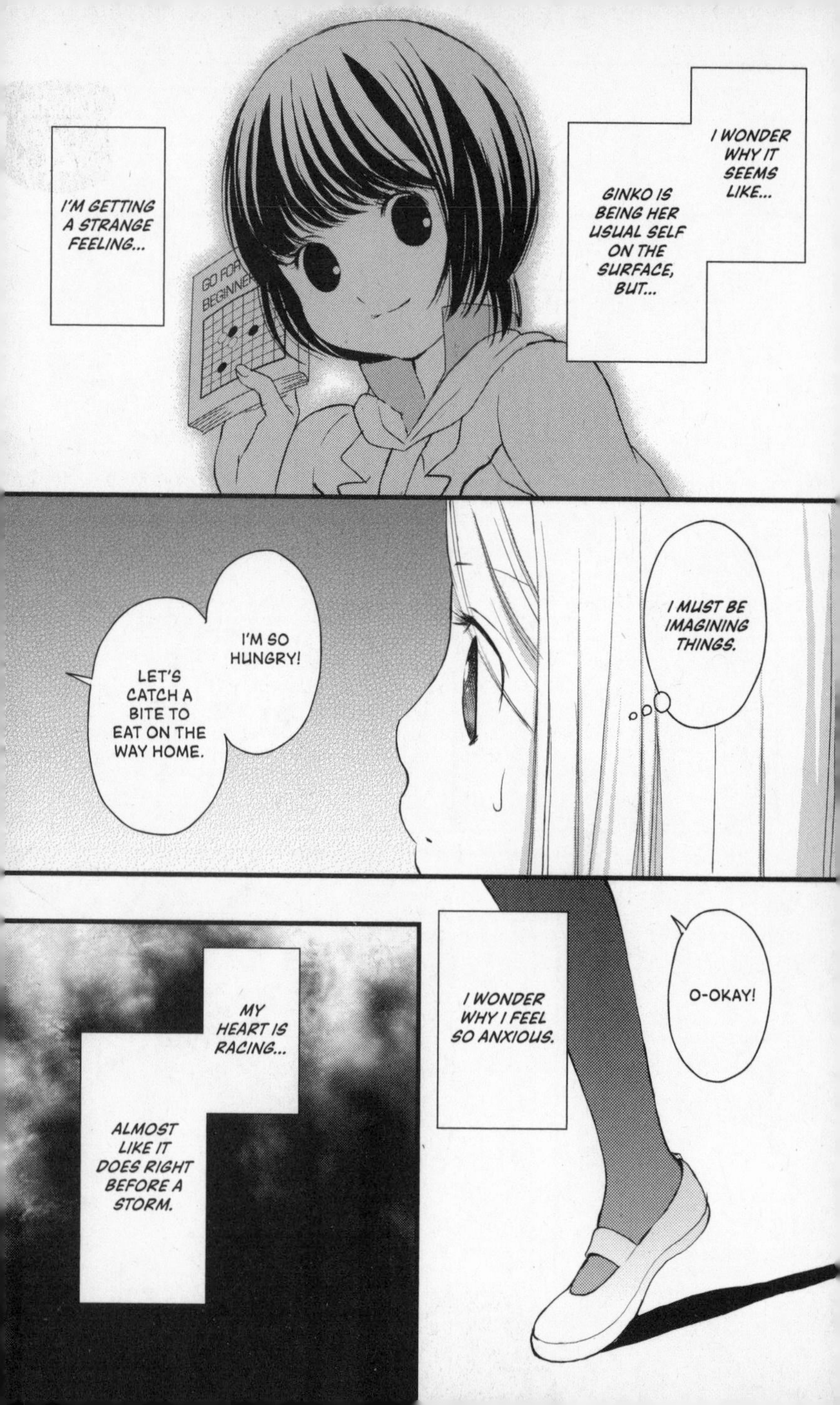
I WONDER WHY IT SEEMS LIKE...
GINKO IS BEING HER USUAL SELF ON THE SURFACE, BUT...
I'M GETTING A STRANGE FEELING...
I MUST BE IMAGINING THINGS.
I'M SO HUNGRY! LET'S CATCH A BITE TO EAT ON THE WAY HOME.
O-OKAY!
I WONDER WHY I FEEL SO ANXIOUS.
MY HEART IS RACING...
ALMOST LIKE IT DOES RIGHT BEFORE A STORM.

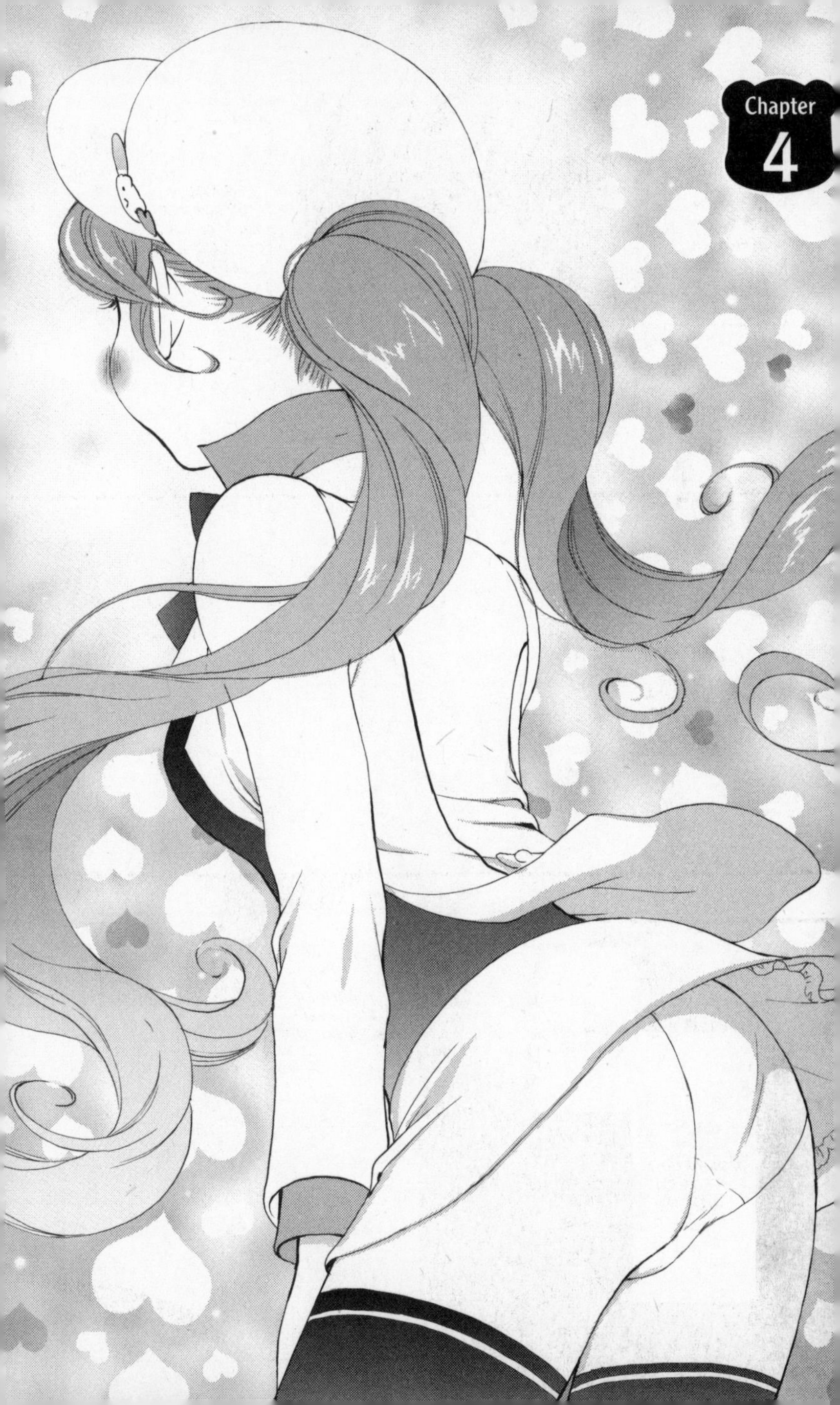
Chapter
4

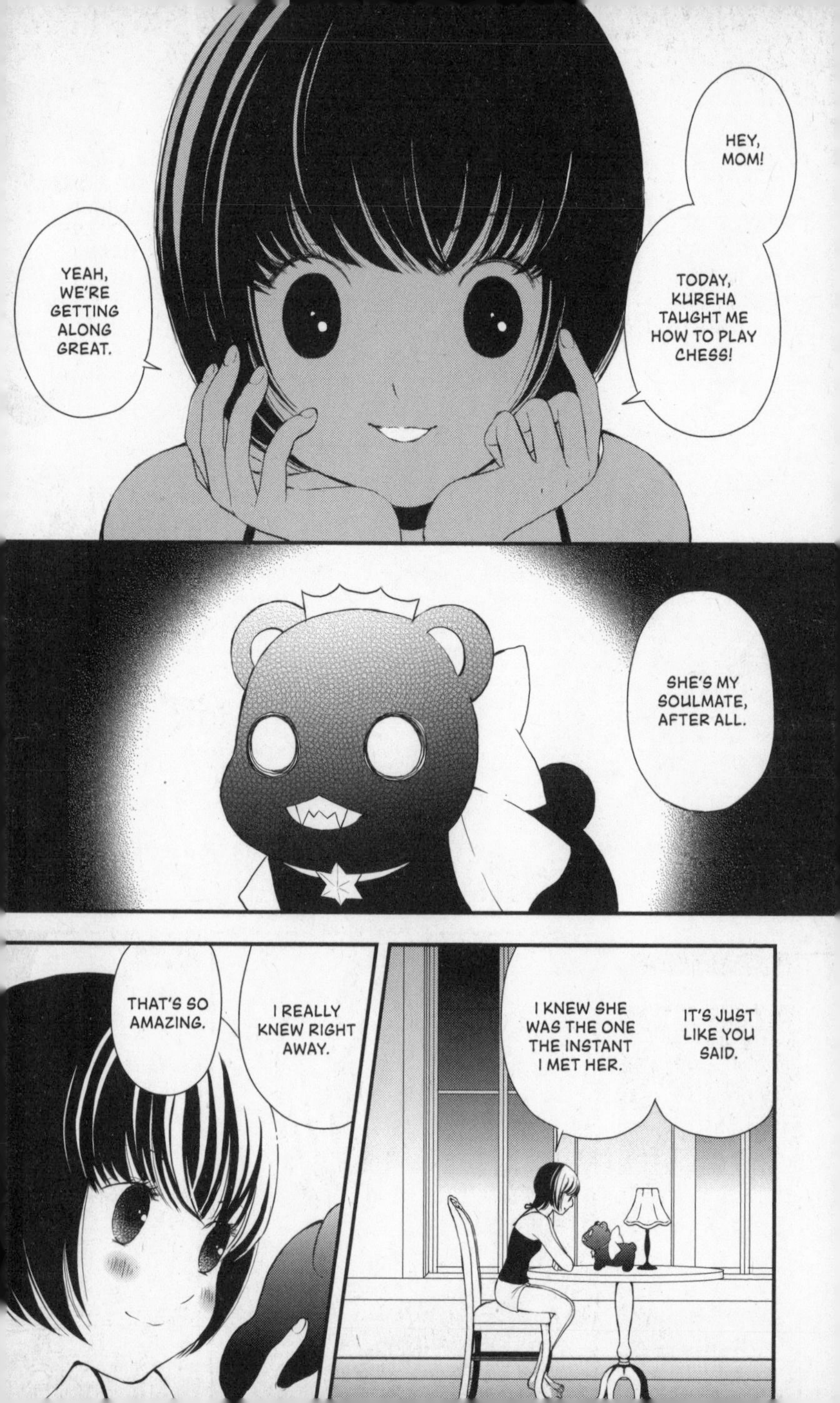
HEY, MOM!
TODAY, KUREHA TAUGHT ME HOW TO PLAY CHESS!
YEAH, WE'RE GETTING ALONG GREAT.
SHE'S MY SOULMATE, AFTER ALL.
IT'S JUST LIKE YOU SAID.
I KNEW SHE WAS THE ONE THE INSTANT I MET HER.
I REALLY KNEW RIGHT AWAY.
THAT'S SO AMAZING.

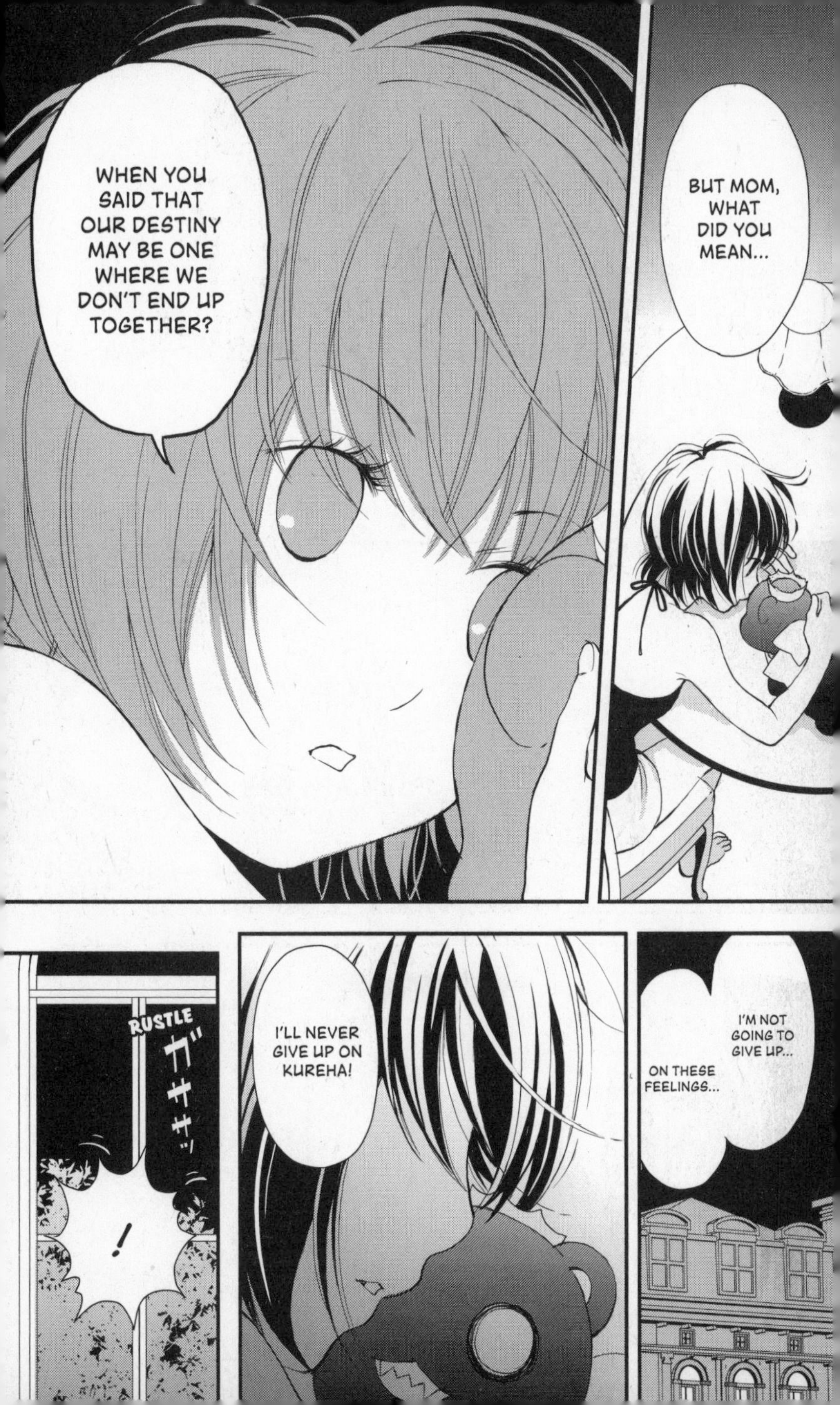
BUT MOM, WHAT DID YOU MEAN...
WHEN YOU SAID THAT OUR DESTINY MAY BE ONE WHERE WE DON'T END UP TOGETHER?
I'M NOT GOING TO GIVE UP...
ON THESE FEELINGS...
I'LL NEVER GIVE UP ON KUREHA!
RUSTLE
!

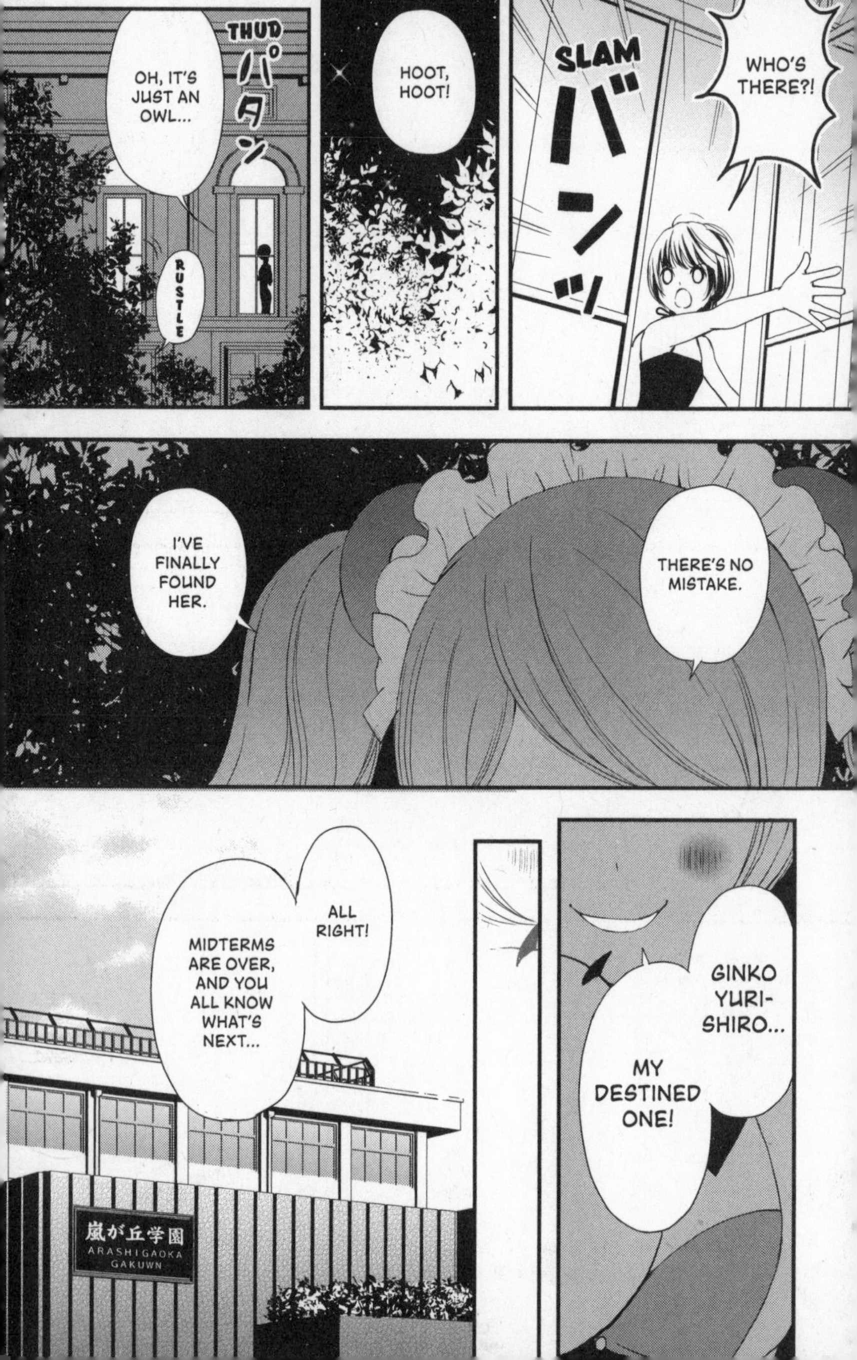
SLAM
バン
WHO'S THERE?!
HOOT, HOOT!
THUD
パタン
OH, IT'S JUST AN OWL...
RUSTLE
THERE'S NO MISTAKE.
I'VE FINALLY FOUND HER.
GINKO YURI-SHIRO...
MY DESTINED ONE!
ALL RIGHT!
MIDTERMS ARE OVER, AND YOU ALL KNOW WHAT'S NEXT...
嵐が丘学園
ARASHIGAOKA GAKUWN

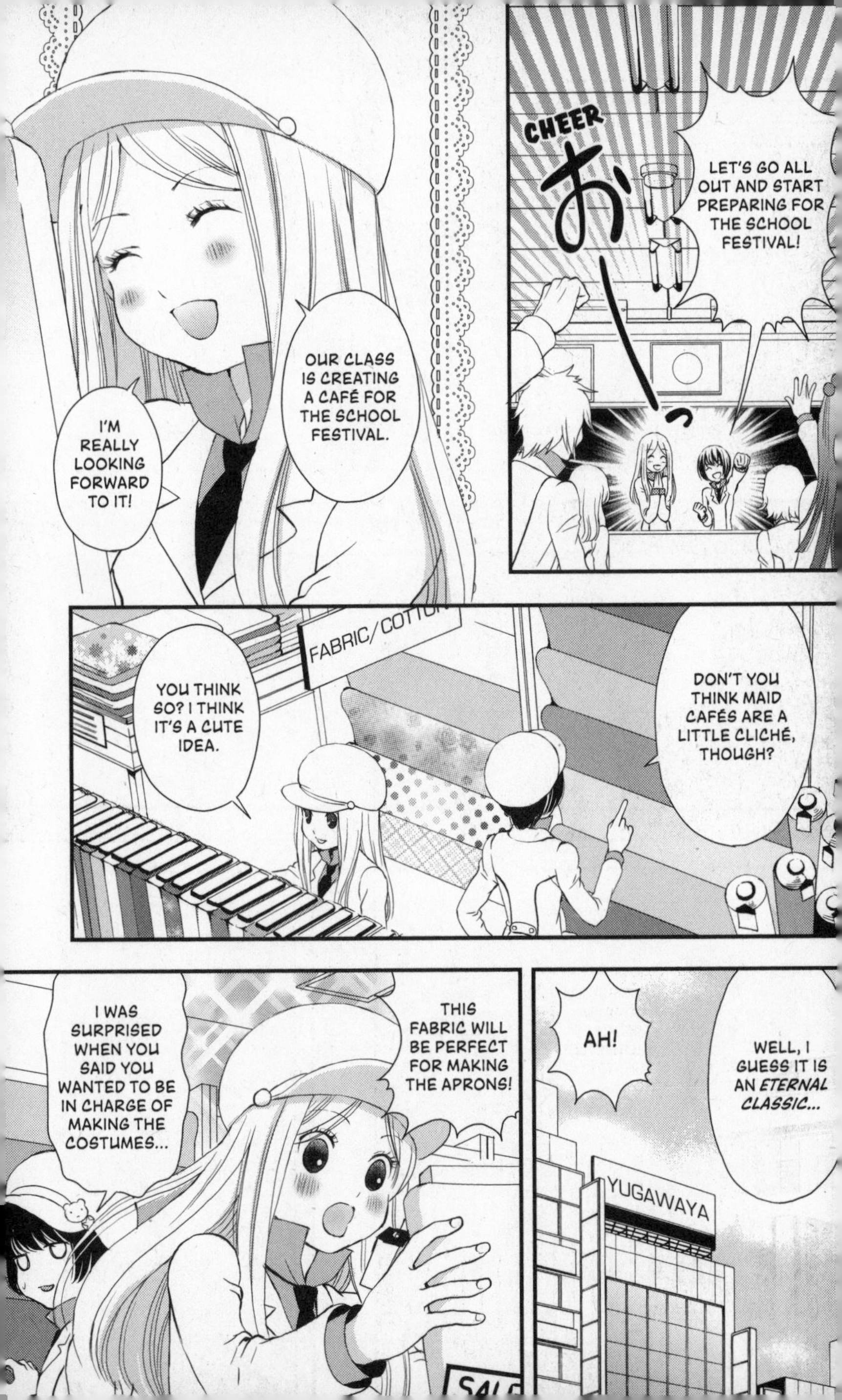
LET'S GO ALL OUT AND START PREPARING FOR THE SCHOOL FESTIVAL!
CHEER
おーっ
OUR CLASS IS CREATING A CAFÉ FOR THE SCHOOL FESTIVAL.
I'M REALLY LOOKING FORWARD TO IT!
DON'T YOU THINK MAID CAFÉS ARE A LITTLE CLICHÉ, THOUGH?
FABRIC/COTTO
YOU THINK SO? I THINK IT'S A CUTE IDEA.
WELL, I GUESS IT IS AN *ETERNAL CLASSIC*...
AH!
YUGAWAYA
THIS FABRIC WILL BE PERFECT FOR MAKING THE APRONS!
I WAS SURPRISED WHEN YOU SAID YOU WANTED TO BE IN CHARGE OF MAKING THE COSTUMES...

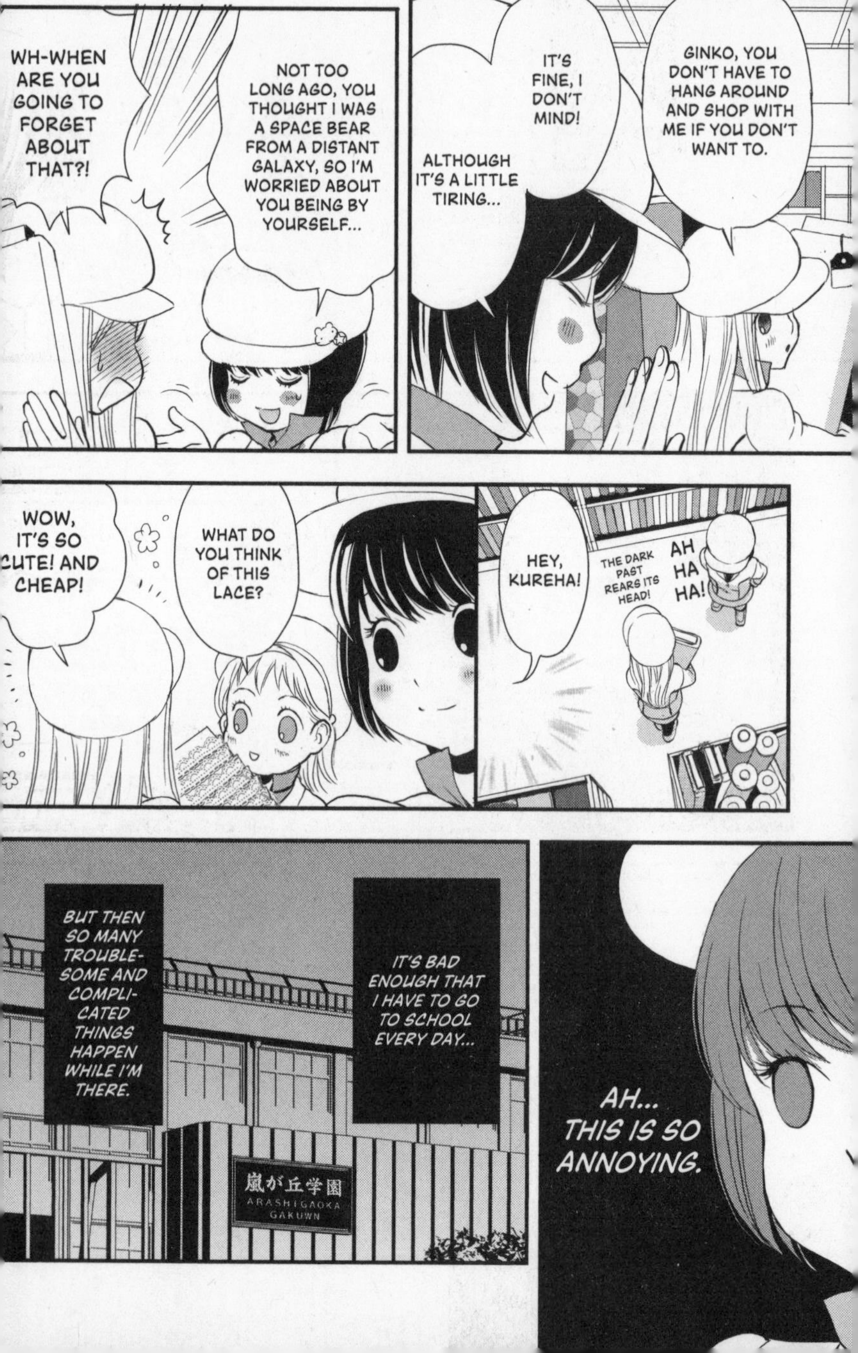
GINKO, YOU DON'T HAVE TO HANG AROUND AND SHOP WITH ME IF YOU DON'T WANT TO.
IT'S FINE, I DON'T MIND!
ALTHOUGH IT'S A LITTLE TIRING...
NOT TOO LONG AGO, YOU THOUGHT I WAS A SPACE BEAR FROM A DISTANT GALAXY, SO I'M WORRIED ABOUT YOU BEING BY YOURSELF...
WH-WHEN ARE YOU GOING TO FORGET ABOUT THAT?!
AH HA HA!
THE DARK PAST REARS ITS HEAD!
HEY, KUREHA!
WHAT DO YOU THINK OF THIS LACE?
WOW, IT'S SO CUTE! AND CHEAP!
AH... THIS IS SO ANNOYING.
IT'S BAD ENOUGH THAT I HAVE TO GO TO SCHOOL EVERY DAY...
BUT THEN SO MANY TROUBLE-SOME AND COMPLI-CATED THINGS HAPPEN WHILE I'M THERE.
嵐が丘学園
ARASHIGAOKA GAKUWN

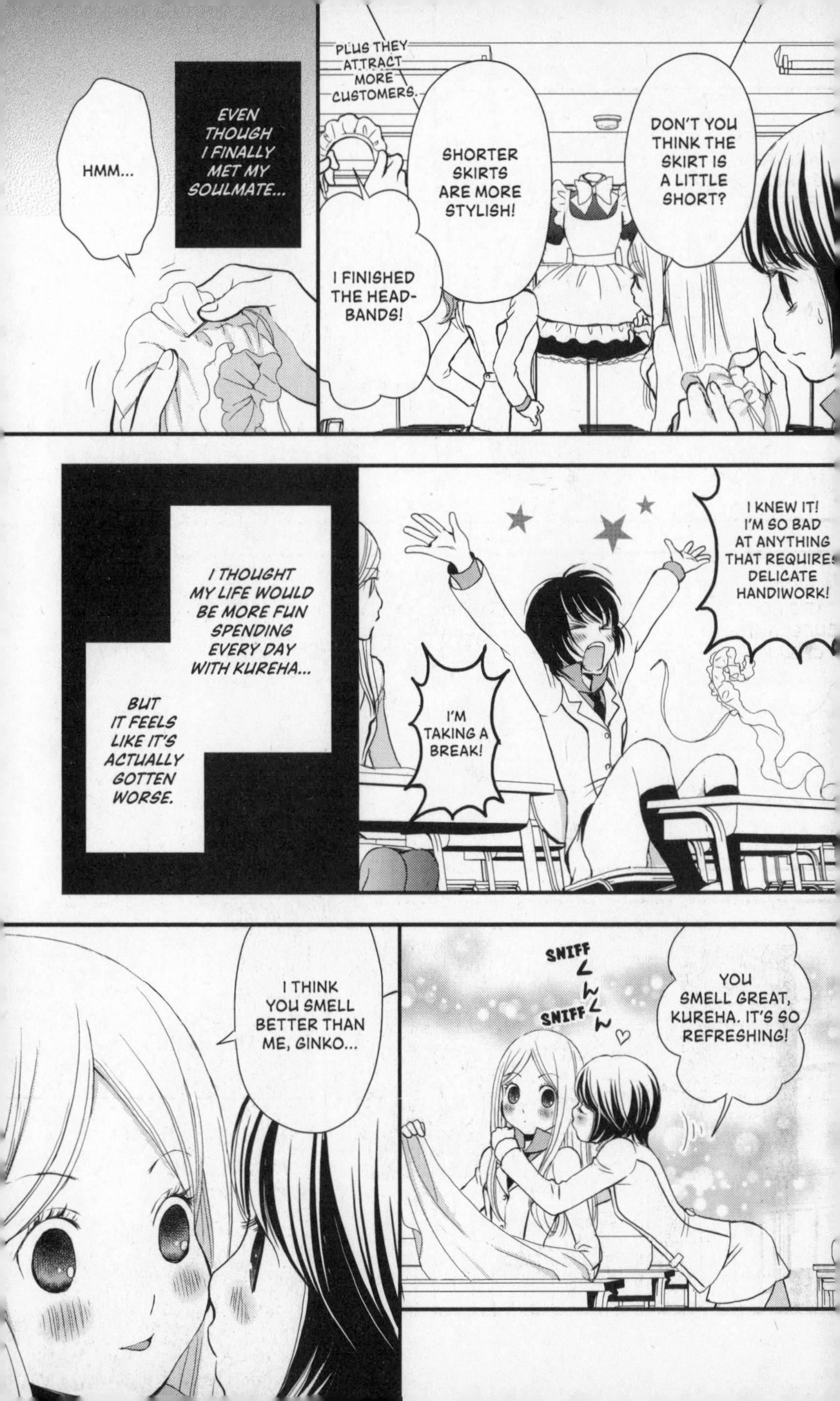
DON'T YOU THINK THE SKIRT IS A LITTLE SHORT?
SHORTER SKIRTS ARE MORE STYLISH!
PLUS THEY ATTRACT MORE CUSTOMERS.
I FINISHED THE HEAD-BANDS!
EVEN THOUGH I FINALLY MET MY SOULMATE...
HMM...
I KNEW IT! I'M SO BAD AT ANYTHING THAT REQUIRES DELICATE HANDIWORK!
I'M TAKING A BREAK!
I THOUGHT MY LIFE WOULD BE MORE FUN SPENDING EVERY DAY WITH KUREHA...
BUT IT FEELS LIKE IT'S ACTUALLY GOTTEN WORSE.
YOU SMELL GREAT, KUREHA. IT'S SO REFRESHING!
SNIFF
SNIFF
I THINK YOU SMELL BETTER THAN ME, GINKO...

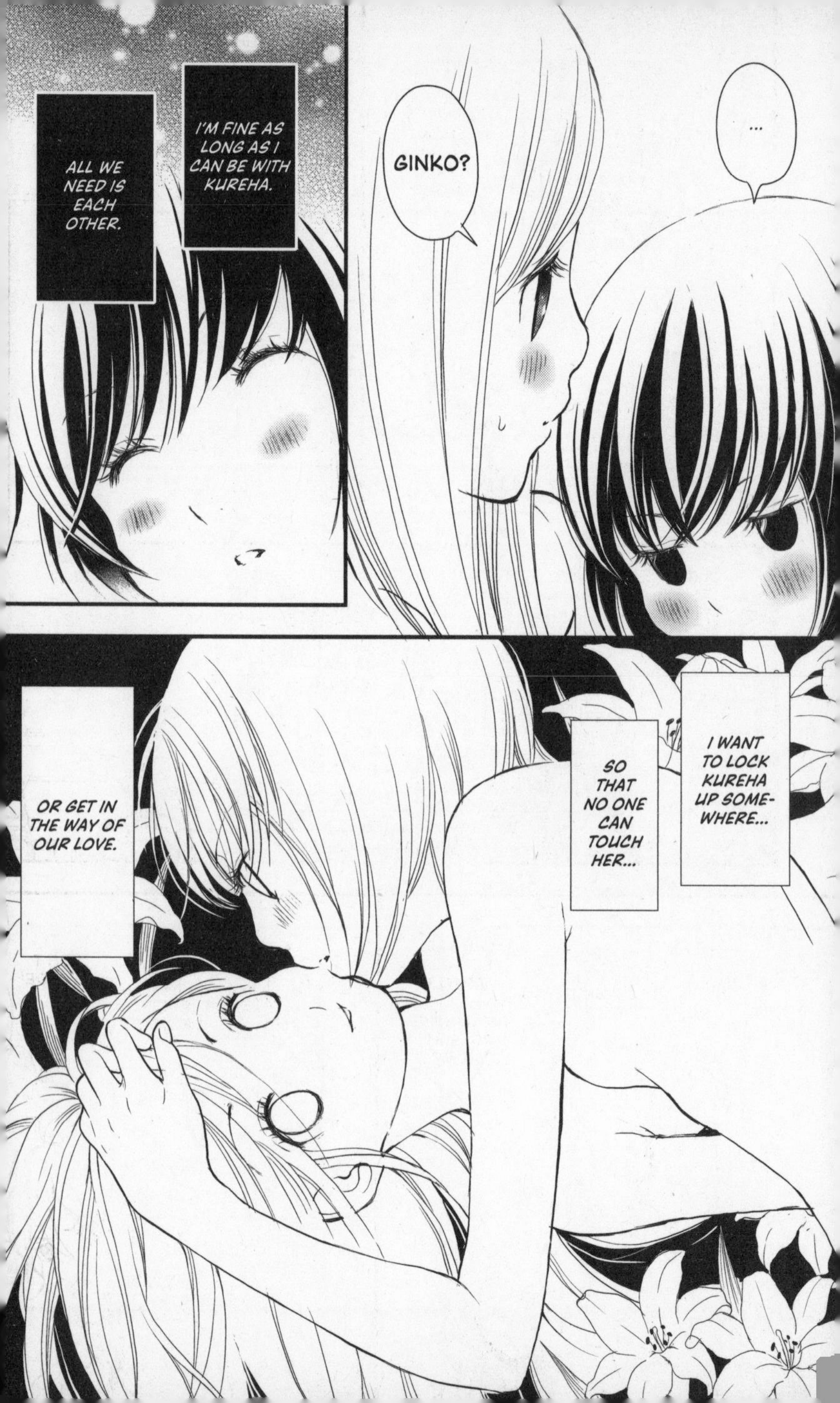
...
GINKO?
I'M FINE AS LONG AS I CAN BE WITH KUREHA.
ALL WE NEED IS EACH OTHER.
I WANT TO LOCK KUREHA UP SOME-WHERE...
SO THAT NO ONE CAN TOUCH HER...
OR GET IN THE WAY OF OUR LOVE.

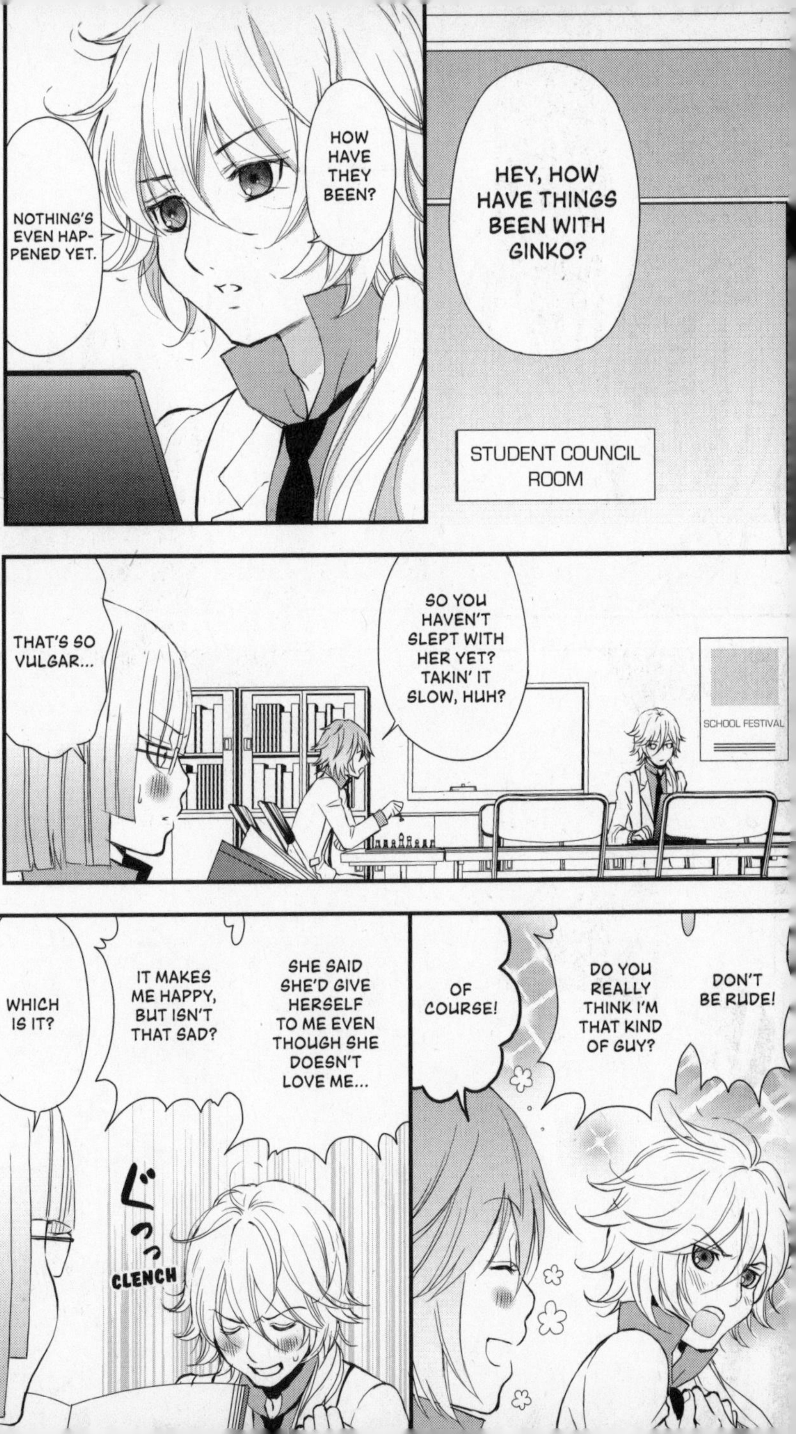
HEY, HOW HAVE THINGS BEEN WITH GINKO?
STUDENT COUNCIL ROOM
HOW HAVE THEY BEEN?
NOTHING'S EVEN HAPPENED YET.
SCHOOL FESTIVAL
SO YOU HAVEN'T SLEPT WITH HER YET? TAKIN' IT SLOW, HUH?
THAT'S SO VULGAR...
DON'T BE RUDE!
DO YOU REALLY THINK I'M THAT KIND OF GUY?
OF COURSE!
SHE SAID SHE'D GIVE HERSELF TO ME EVEN THOUGH SHE DOESN'T LOVE ME...
IT MAKES ME HAPPY, BUT ISN'T THAT SAD?
WHICH IS IT?
ぐっ
CLENCH

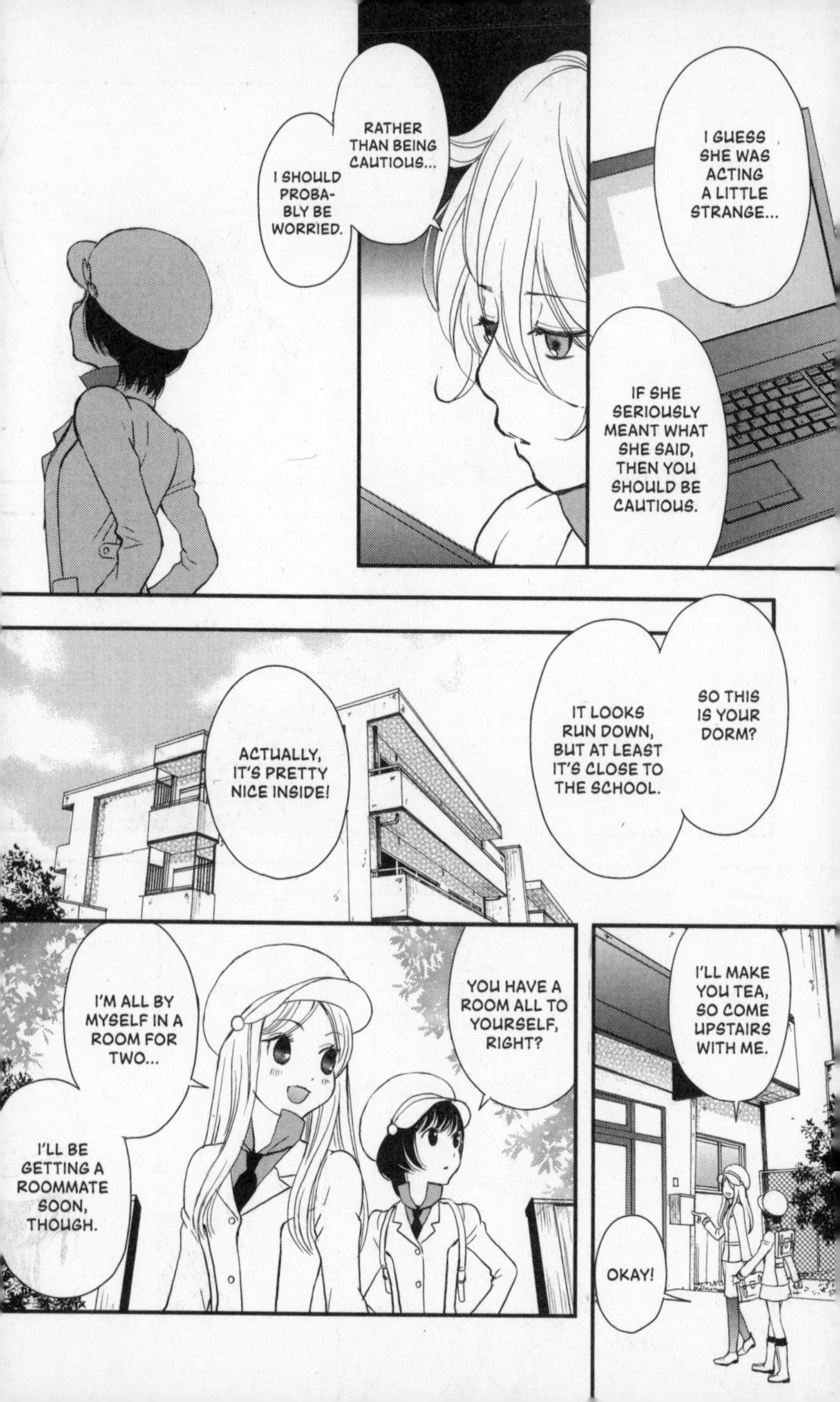
I GUESS SHE WAS ACTING A LITTLE STRANGE...
IF SHE SERIOUSLY MEANT WHAT SHE SAID, THEN YOU SHOULD BE CAUTIOUS.
RATHER THAN BEING CAUTIOUS...
I SHOULD PROBA-BLY BE WORRIED.
SO THIS IS YOUR DORM?
IT LOOKS RUN DOWN, BUT AT LEAST IT'S CLOSE TO THE SCHOOL.
ACTUALLY, IT'S PRETTY NICE INSIDE!
I'LL MAKE YOU TEA, SO COME UPSTAIRS WITH ME.
OKAY!
YOU HAVE A ROOM ALL TO YOURSELF, RIGHT?
I'M ALL BY MYSELF IN A ROOM FOR TWO...
I'LL BE GETTING A ROOMMATE SOON, THOUGH.

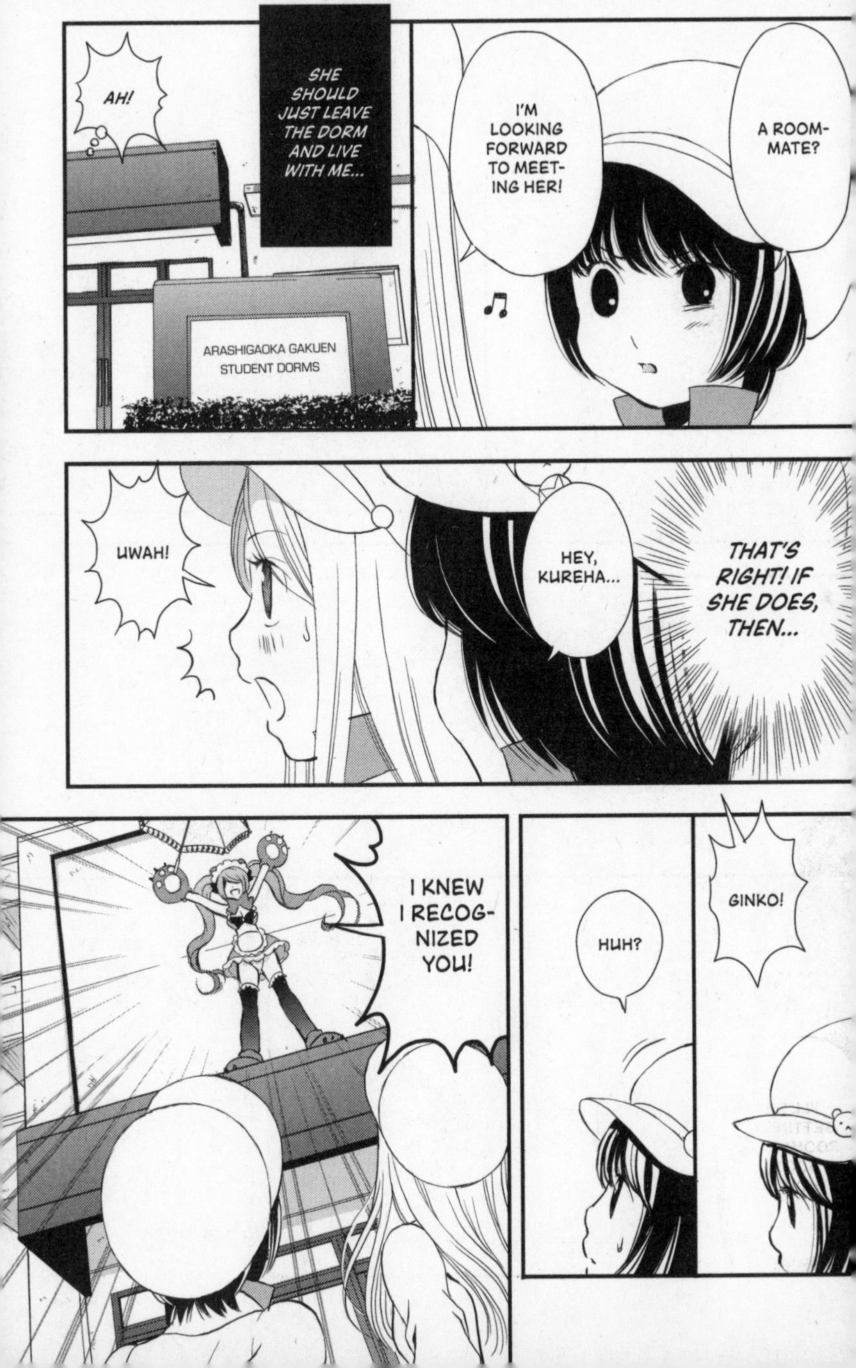
A ROOM-MATE?
I'M LOOKING FORWARD TO MEET-ING HER!
SHE SHOULD JUST LEAVE THE DORM AND LIVE WITH ME...
AH!
ARASHIGAOKA GAKUEN STUDENT DORMS
THAT'S RIGHT! IF SHE DOES, THEN...
HEY, KUREHA...
UWAH!
GINKO!
HUH?
I KNEW I RECOG-NIZED YOU!

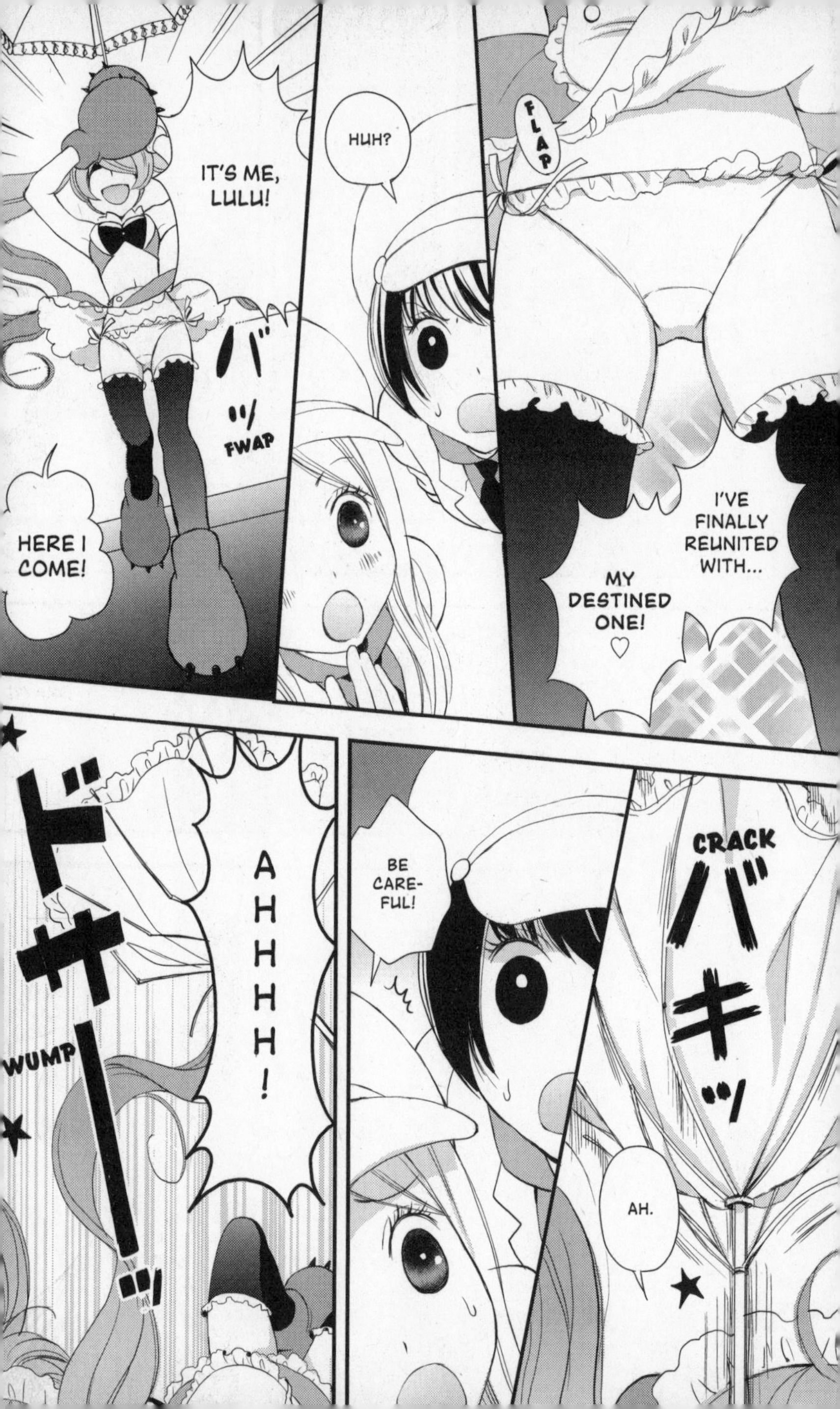
FLAP
I'VE FINALLY REUNITED WITH...
MY DESTINED ONE! ♡
HUH?
IT'S ME, LULU!
バッ
FWAP
HERE I COME!
CRACK
バキッ
AH.
BE CAREFUL!
AHHHHH!
ドザーッ
WUMP

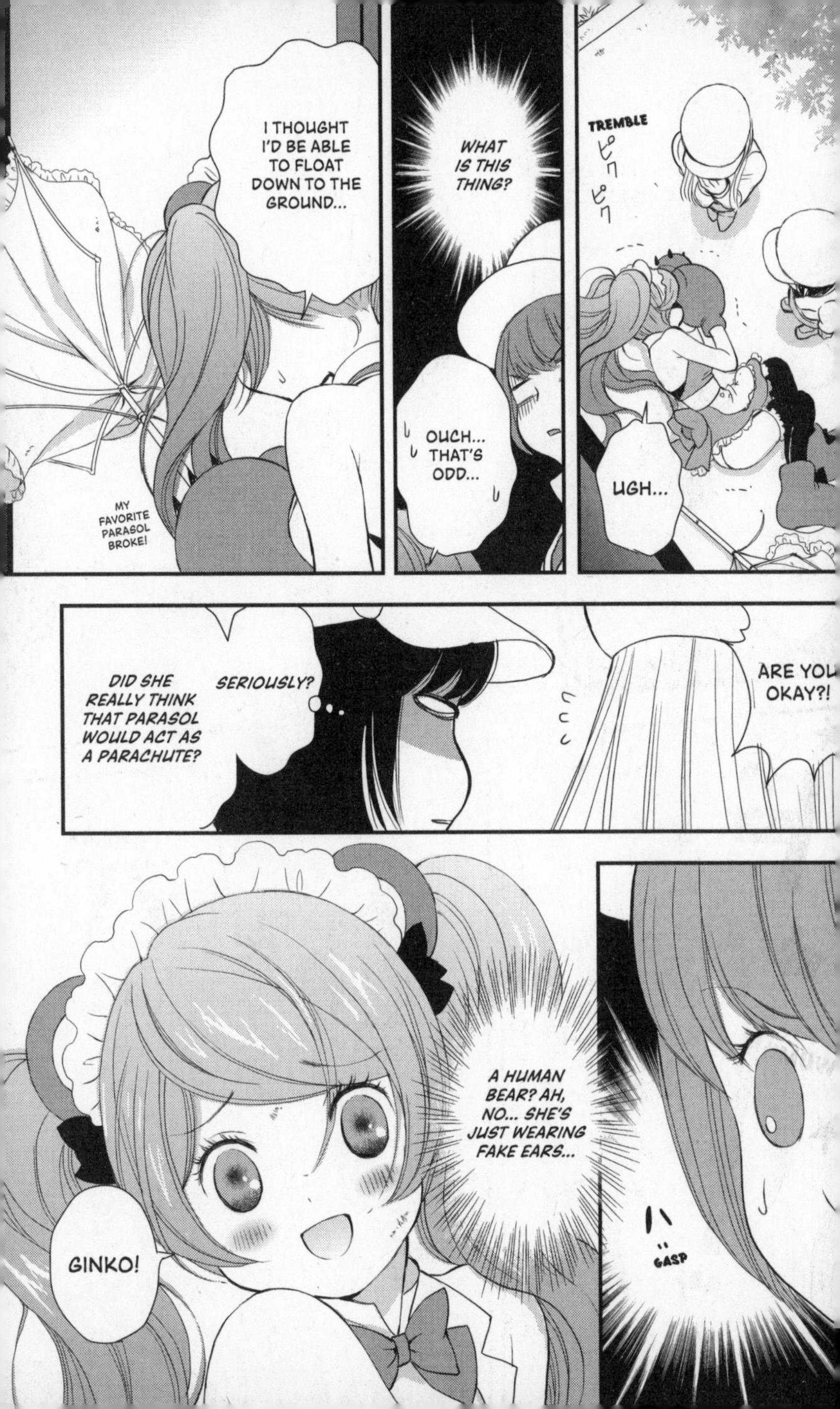
TREMBLE
ピク ピク
UGH...
WHAT IS THIS THING?
OUCH... THAT'S ODD...
I THOUGHT I'D BE ABLE TO FLOAT DOWN TO THE GROUND...
MY FAVORITE PARASOL BROKE!
ARE YOU OKAY?!
SERIOUSLY?
DID SHE REALLY THINK THAT PARASOL WOULD ACT AS A PARACHUTE?
ハッ
GASP
A HUMAN BEAR? AH, NO... SHE'S JUST WEARING FAKE EARS...
GINKO!

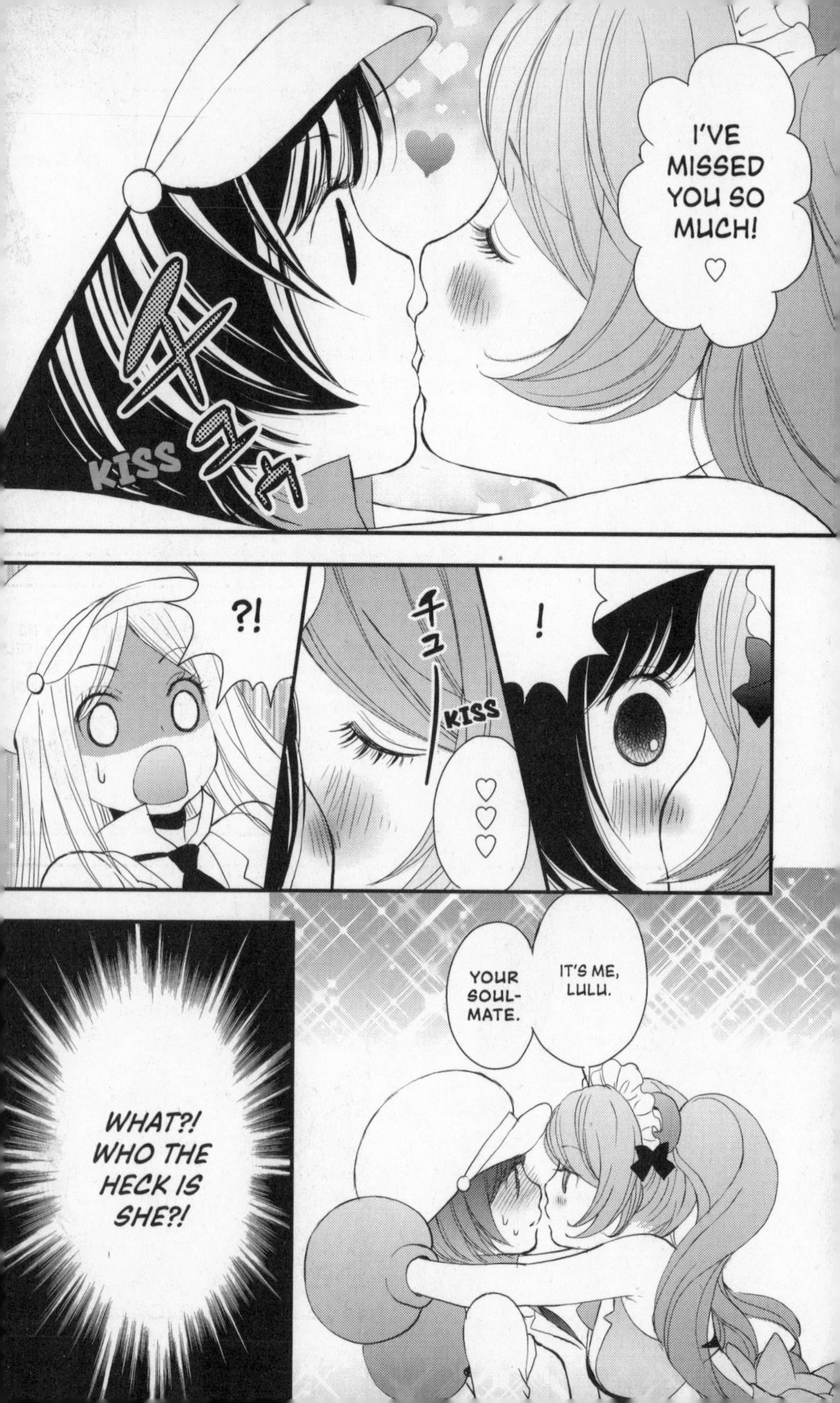
I'VE MISSED YOU SO MUCH! ♡
KISS
!
チュー
KISS
♡♡♡
?!
IT'S ME, LULU.
YOUR SOULMATE.
WHAT?! WHO THE HECK IS SHE?!

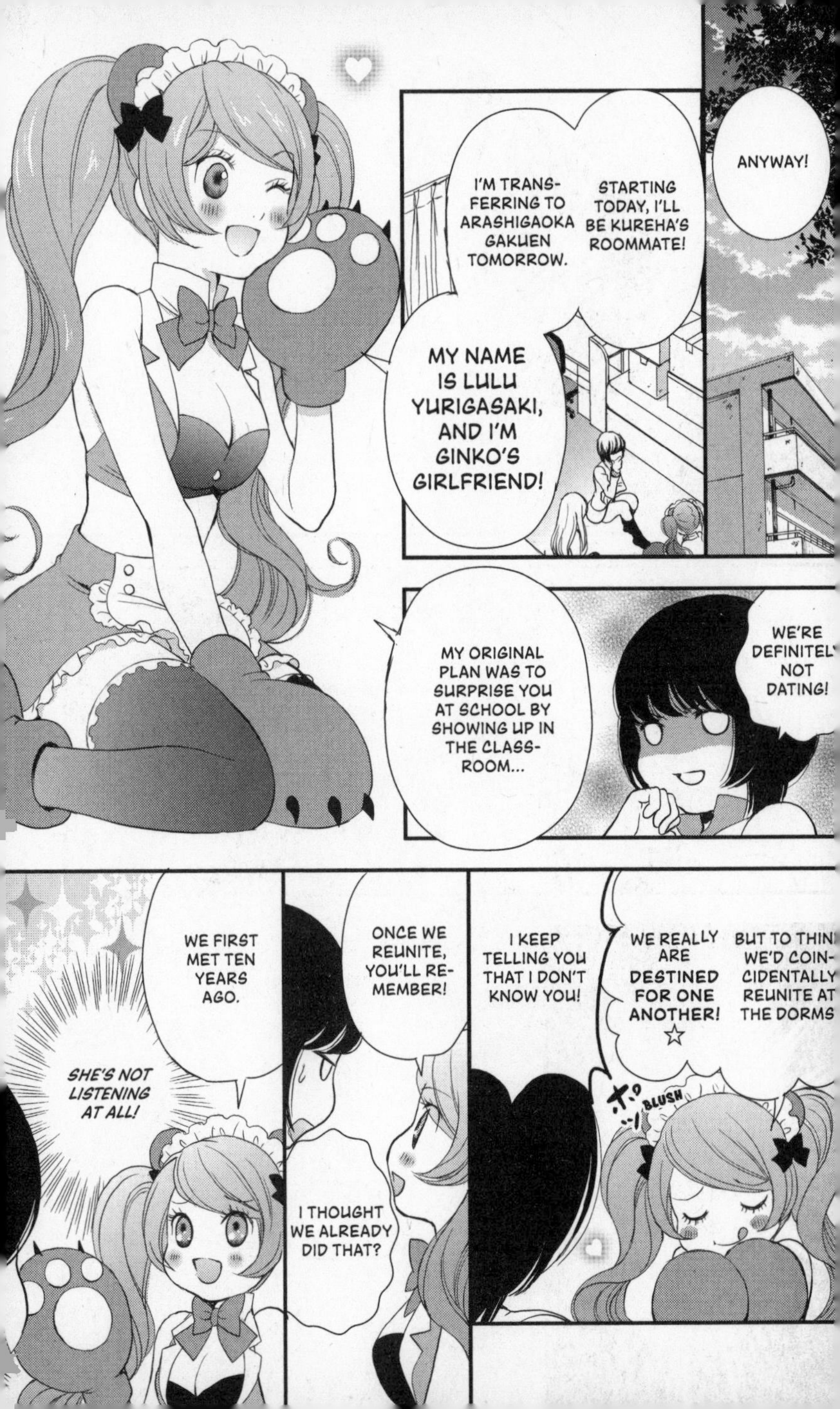
ANYWAY!
STARTING TODAY, I'LL BE KUREHA'S ROOMMATE!
I'M TRANS-FERRING TO ARASHIGAOKA GAKUEN TOMORROW.
MY NAME IS LULU YURIGASAKI, AND I'M GINKO'S GIRLFRIEND!
WE'RE DEFINITEL NOT DATING!
MY ORIGINAL PLAN WAS TO SURPRISE YOU AT SCHOOL BY SHOWING UP IN THE CLASS-ROOM...
BUT TO THIN WE'D COIN-CIDENTALLY REUNITE AT THE DORMS
WE REALLY ARE DESTINED FOR ONE ANOTHER! ☆
I KEEP TELLING YOU THAT I DON'T KNOW YOU!
BLUSH
ONCE WE REUNITE, YOU'LL RE-MEMBER!
I THOUGHT WE ALREADY DID THAT?
WE FIRST MET TEN YEARS AGO.
SHE'S NOT LISTENING AT ALL!

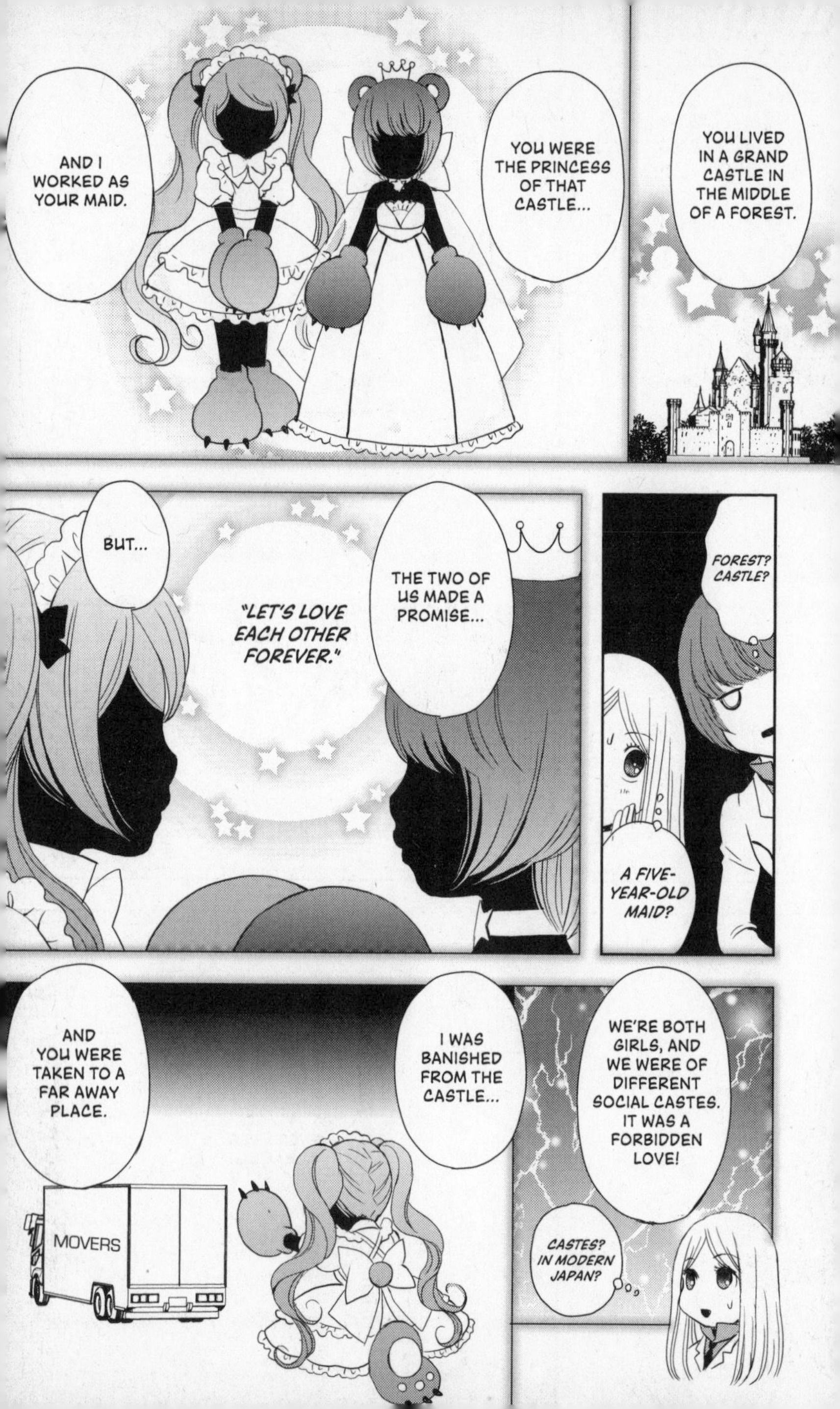
YOU LIVED IN A GRAND CASTLE IN THE MIDDLE OF A FOREST.
YOU WERE THE PRINCESS OF THAT CASTLE...
AND I WORKED AS YOUR MAID.
FOREST? CASTLE?
A FIVE-YEAR-OLD MAID?
THE TWO OF US MADE A PROMISE...
"LET'S LOVE EACH OTHER FOREVER."
BUT...
WE'RE BOTH GIRLS, AND WE WERE OF DIFFERENT SOCIAL CASTES. IT WAS A FORBIDDEN LOVE!
CASTES? IN MODERN JAPAN?
I WAS BANISHED FROM THE CASTLE...
AND YOU WERE TAKEN TO A FAR AWAY PLACE.
MOVERS

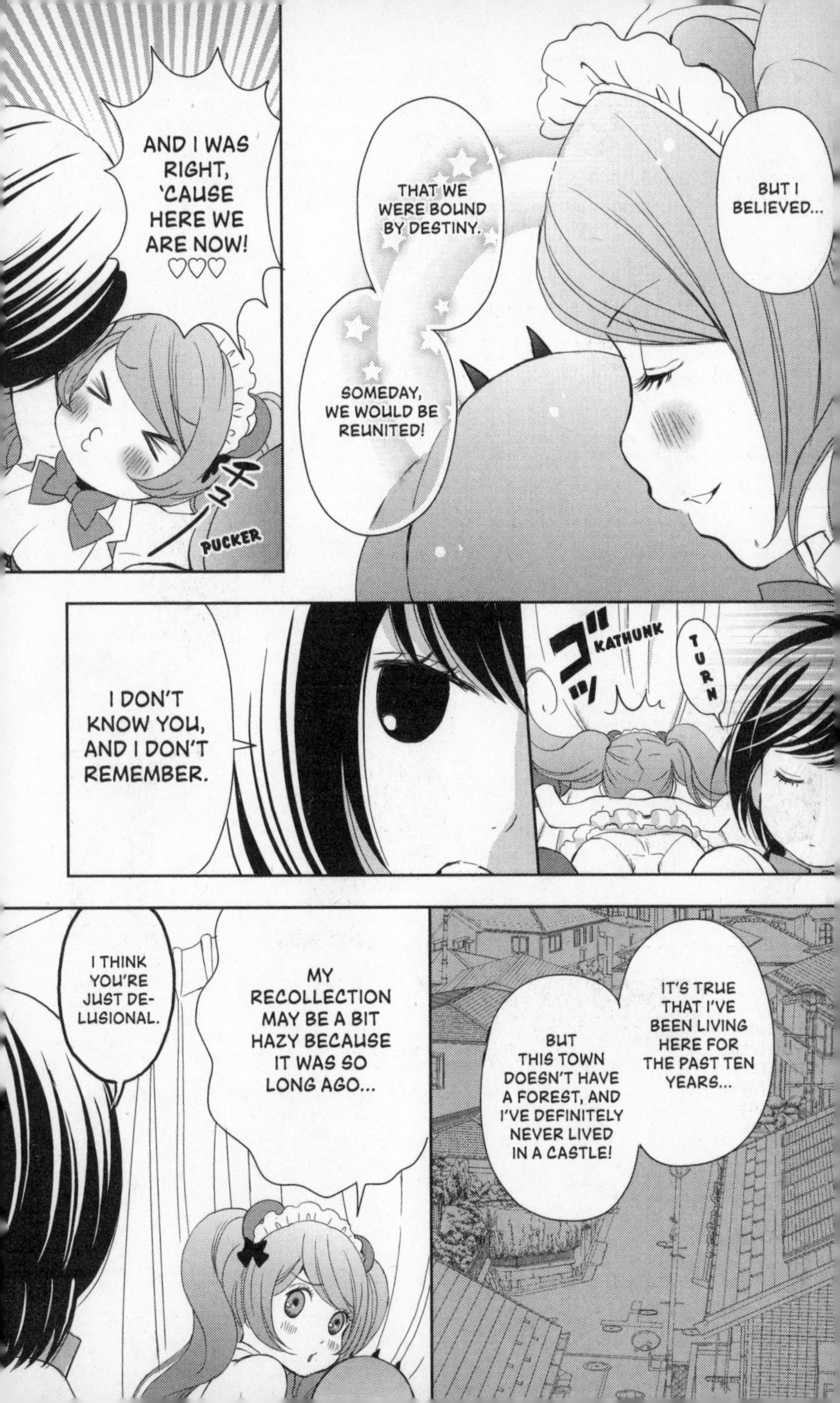
BUT I BELIEVED...
THAT WE WERE BOUND BY DESTINY.
SOMEDAY, WE WOULD BE REUNITED!
AND I WAS RIGHT, 'CAUSE HERE WE ARE NOW! ♡♡♡
PUCKER
TURN
KATHUNK
I DON'T KNOW YOU, AND I DON'T REMEMBER.
IT'S TRUE THAT I'VE BEEN LIVING HERE FOR THE PAST TEN YEARS...
BUT THIS TOWN DOESN'T HAVE A FOREST, AND I'VE DEFINITELY NEVER LIVED IN A CASTLE!
MY RECOLLECTION MAY BE A BIT HAZY BECAUSE IT WAS SO LONG AGO...
I THINK YOU'RE JUST DE-LUSIONAL.

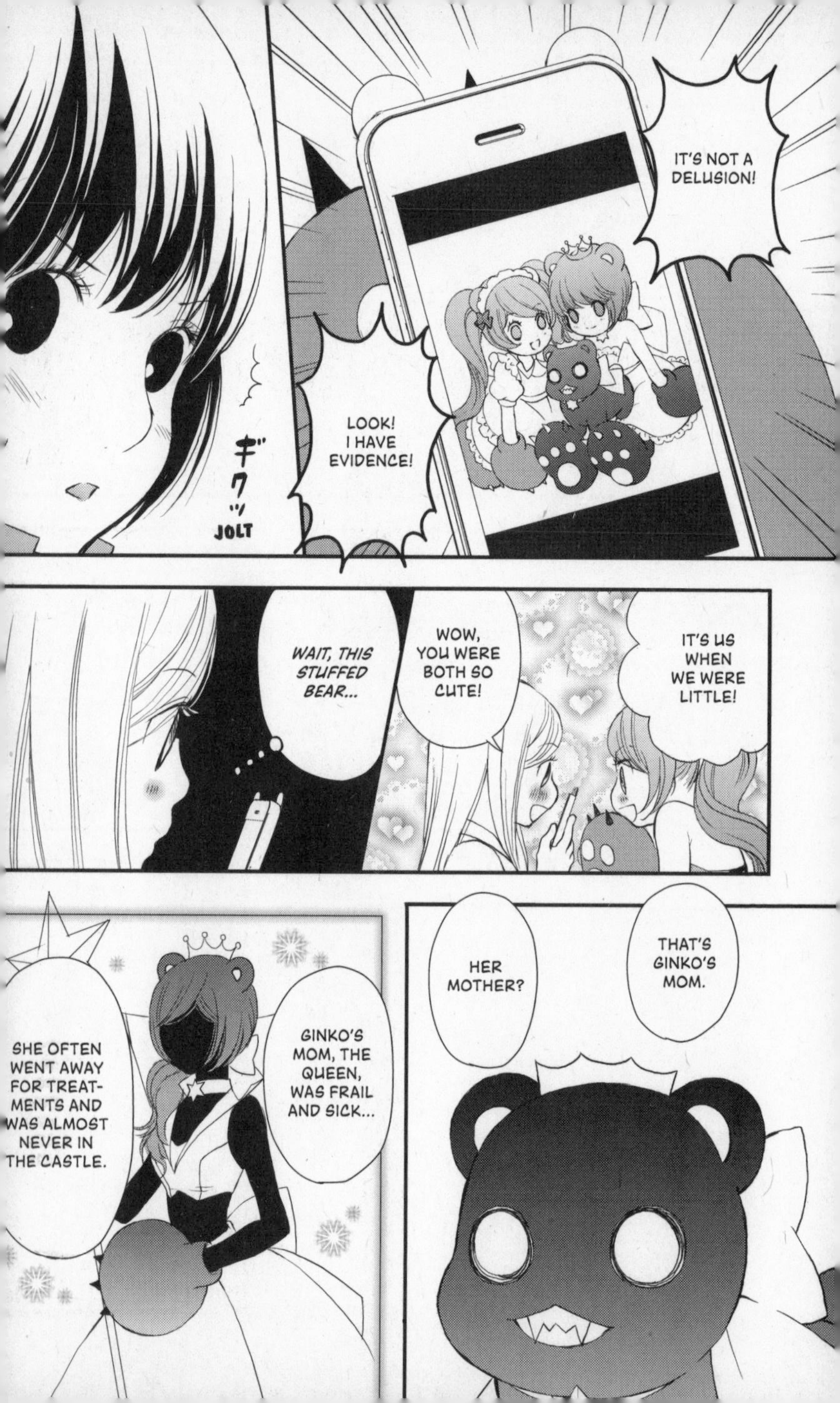
IT'S NOT A DELUSION!
LOOK! I HAVE EVIDENCE!
ギクッ
JOLT
IT'S US WHEN WE WERE LITTLE!
WOW, YOU WERE BOTH SO CUTE!
*WAIT, THIS STUFFED BEAR...*
...
THAT'S GINKO'S MOM.
HER MOTHER?
GINKO'S MOM, THE QUEEN, WAS FRAIL AND SICK...
SHE OFTEN WENT AWAY FOR TREAT-MENTS AND WAS ALMOST NEVER IN THE CASTLE.

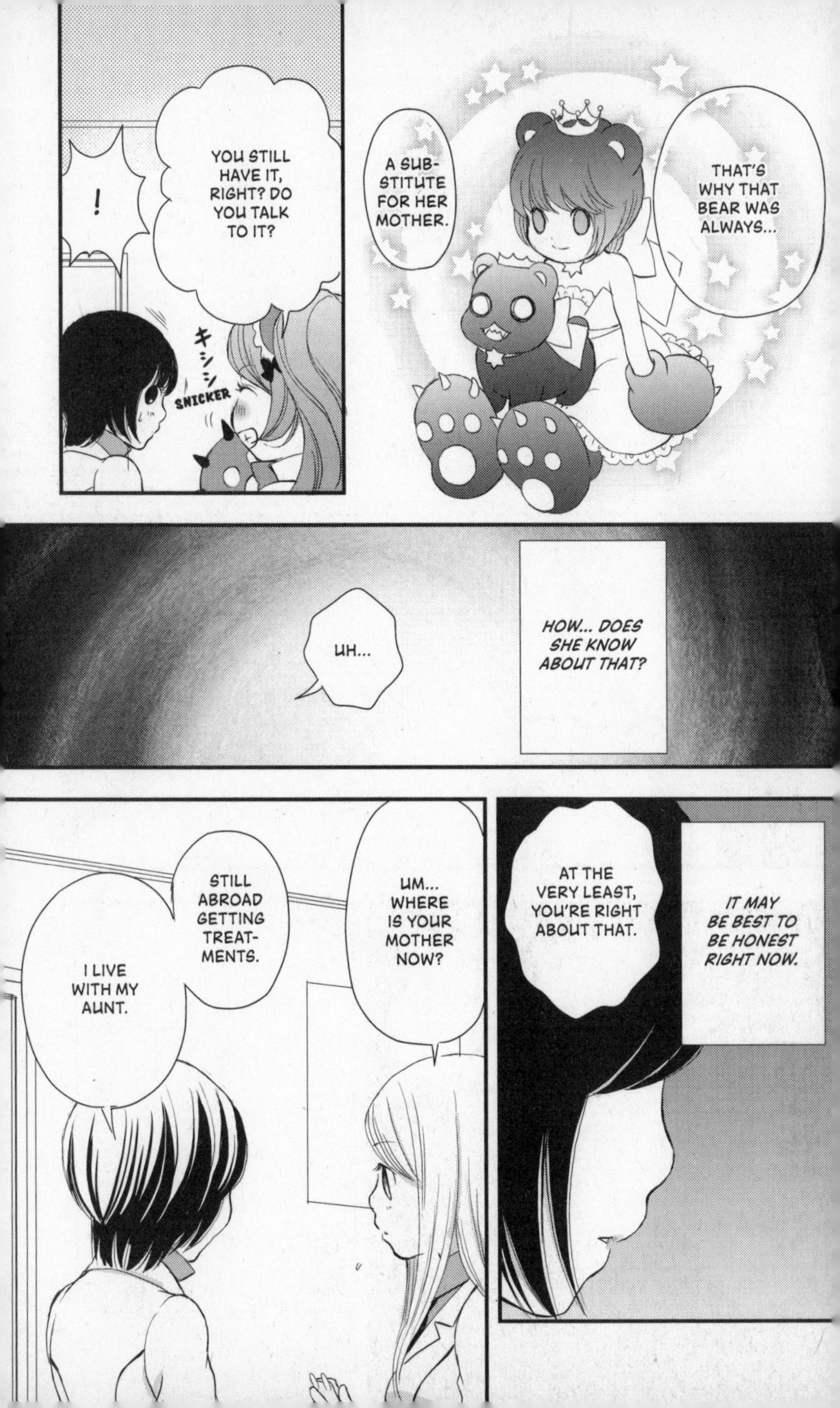
THAT'S WHY THAT BEAR WAS ALWAYS...
A SUB-STITUTE FOR HER MOTHER.
YOU STILL HAVE IT, RIGHT? DO YOU TALK TO IT?
!
キシシ
SNICKER
HOW... DOES SHE KNOW ABOUT THAT?
UH...
IT MAY BE BEST TO BE HONEST RIGHT NOW.
AT THE VERY LEAST, YOU'RE RIGHT ABOUT THAT.
UM... WHERE IS YOUR MOTHER NOW?
STILL ABROAD GETTING TREAT-MENTS.
I LIVE WITH MY AUNT.

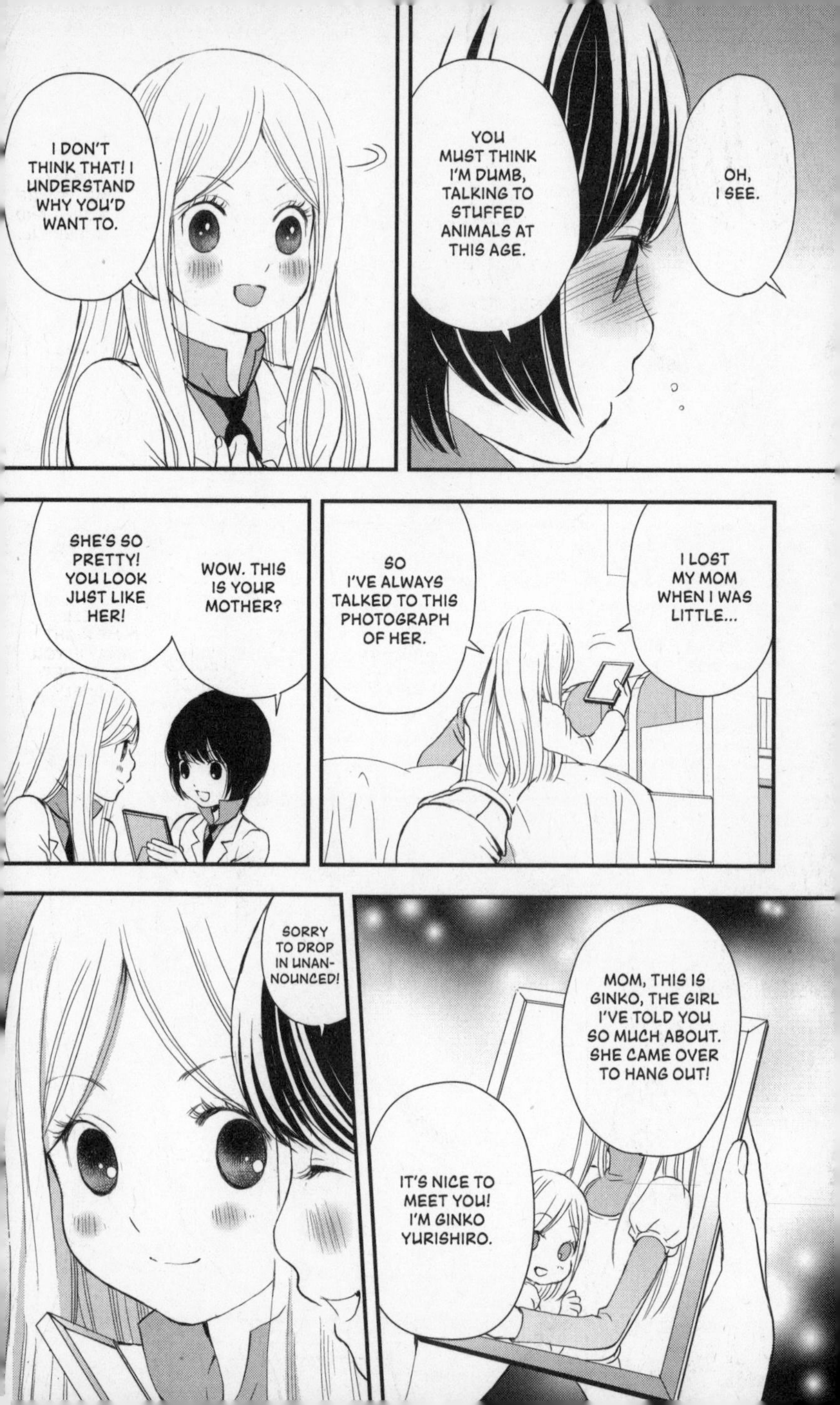
OH, I SEE.
YOU MUST THINK I'M DUMB, TALKING TO STUFFED ANIMALS AT THIS AGE.
I DON'T THINK THAT! I UNDERSTAND WHY YOU'D WANT TO.
I LOST MY MOM WHEN I WAS LITTLE...
SO I'VE ALWAYS TALKED TO THIS PHOTOGRAPH OF HER.
WOW. THIS IS YOUR MOTHER?
SHE'S SO PRETTY! YOU LOOK JUST LIKE HER!
MOM, THIS IS GINKO, THE GIRL I'VE TOLD YOU SO MUCH ABOUT. SHE CAME OVER TO HANG OUT!
IT'S NICE TO MEET YOU! I'M GINKO YURISHIRO.
SORRY TO DROP IN UNAN-NOUNCED!

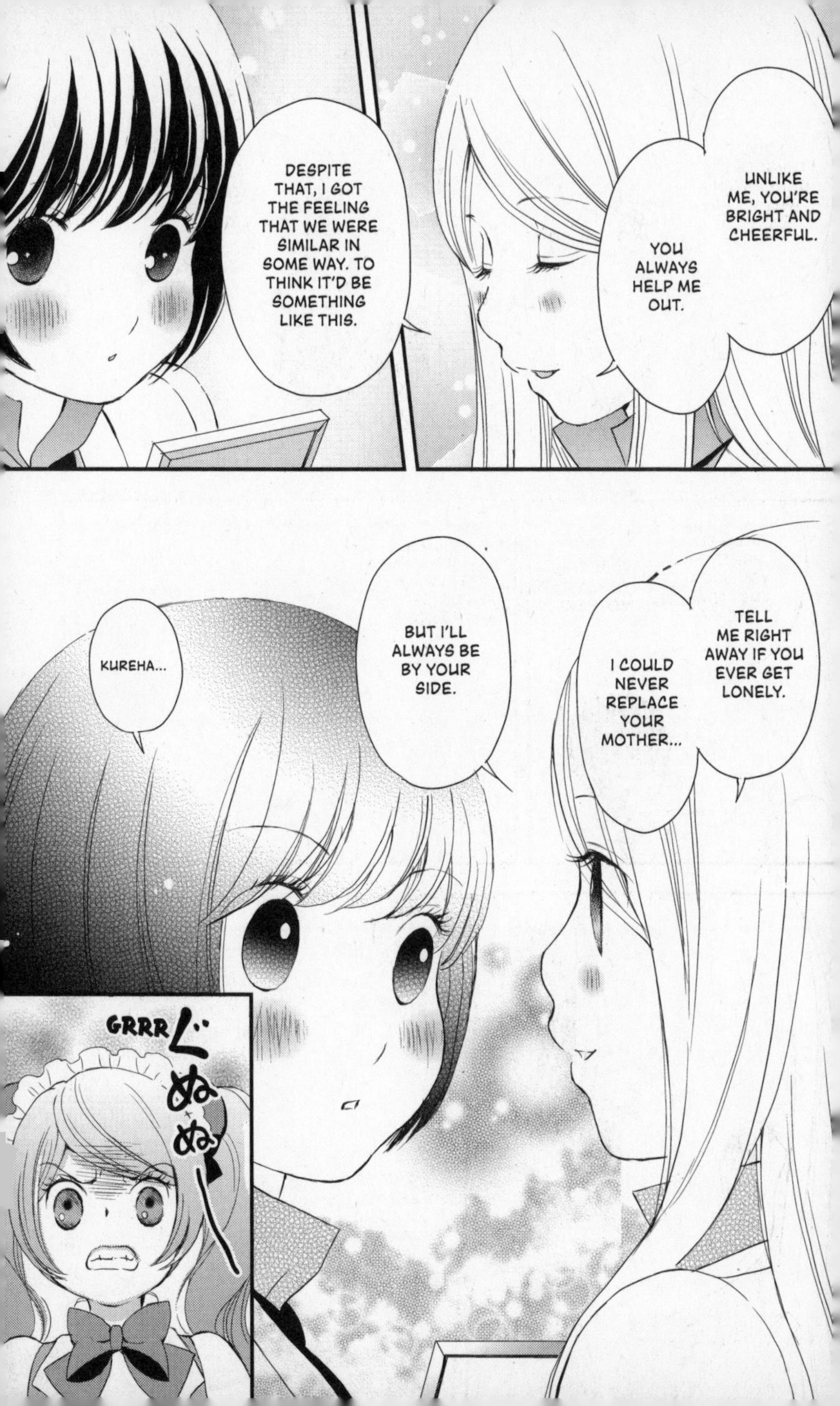
UNLIKE ME, YOU'RE BRIGHT AND CHEERFUL.
YOU ALWAYS HELP ME OUT.
DESPITE THAT, I GOT THE FEELING THAT WE WERE SIMILAR IN SOME WAY. TO THINK IT'D BE SOMETHING LIKE THIS.
TELL ME RIGHT AWAY IF YOU EVER GET LONELY.
I COULD NEVER REPLACE YOUR MOTHER...
BUT I'LL ALWAYS BE BY YOUR SIDE.
KUREHA...
GRRR
ぐぬぬ

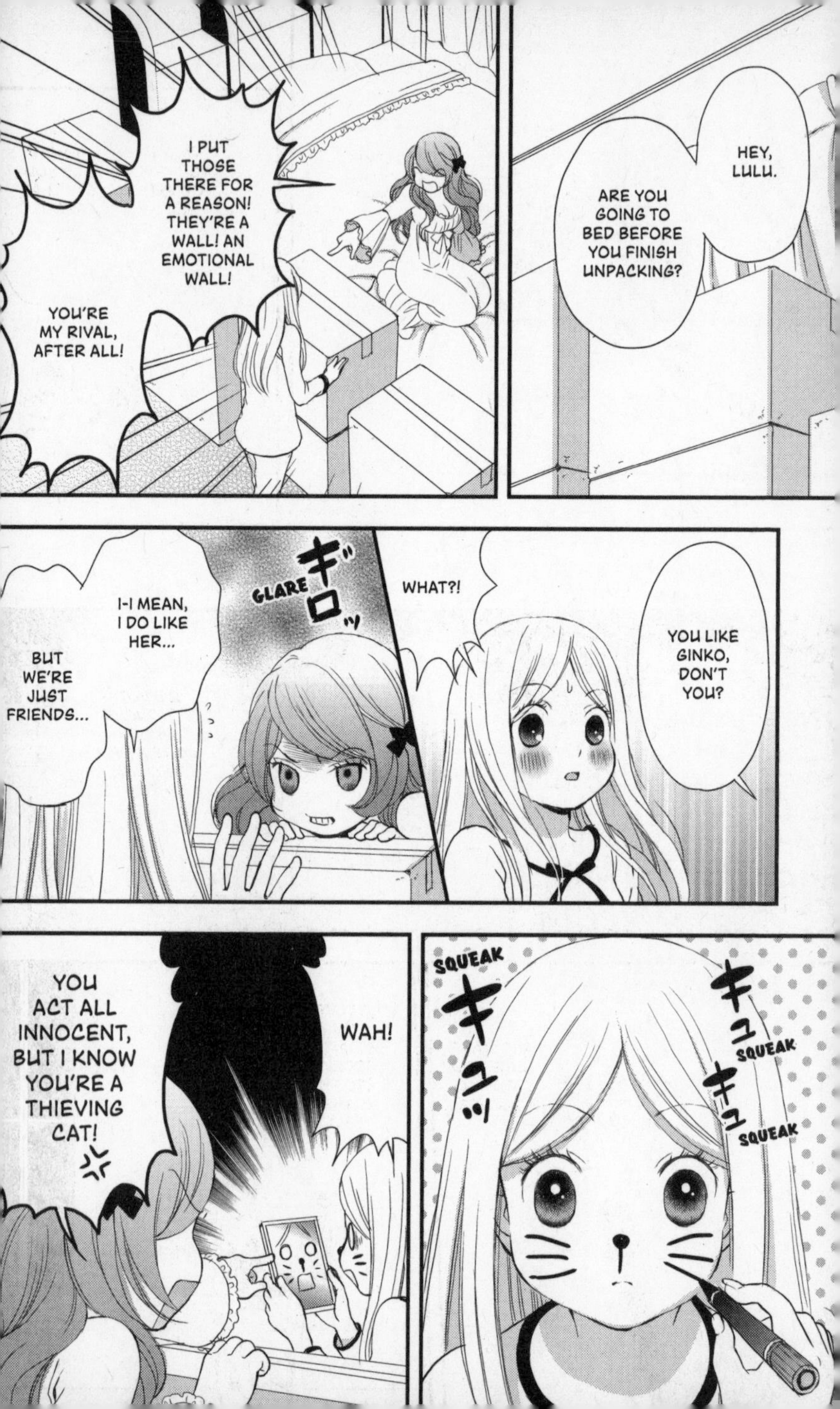
HEY, LULU.
ARE YOU GOING TO BED BEFORE YOU FINISH UNPACKING?
I PUT THOSE THERE FOR A REASON! THEY'RE A WALL! AN EMOTIONAL WALL!
YOU'RE MY RIVAL, AFTER ALL!
YOU LIKE GINKO, DON'T YOU?
WHAT?!
GLARE
I-I MEAN, I DO LIKE HER...
BUT WE'RE JUST FRIENDS...
SQUEAK
SQUEAK
SQUEAK
WAH!
YOU ACT ALL INNOCENT, BUT I KNOW YOU'RE A THIEVING CAT!

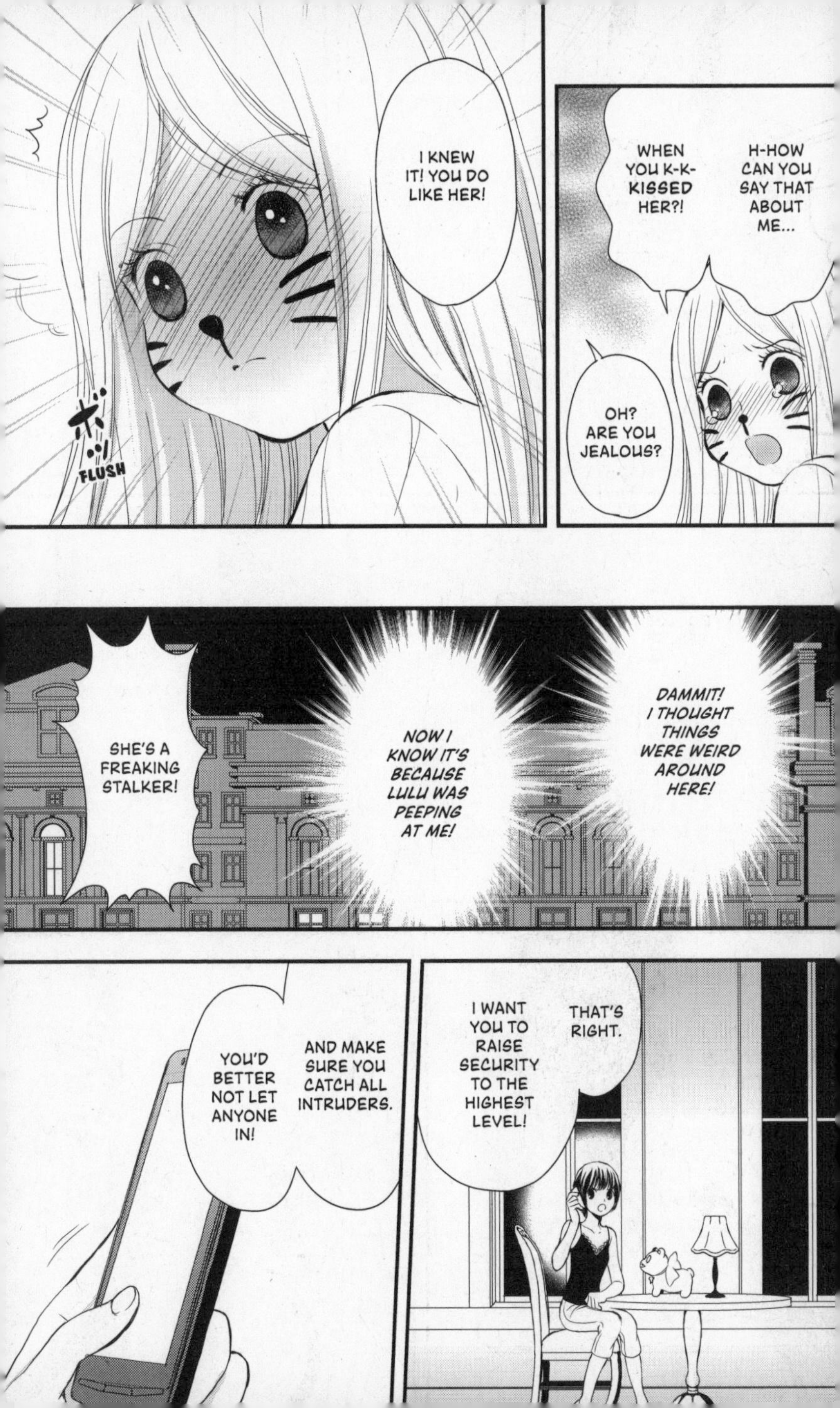
H-HOW CAN YOU SAY THAT ABOUT ME...
WHEN YOU K-K-KISSED HER?!
OH? ARE YOU JEALOUS?
I KNEW IT! YOU DO LIKE HER!
ボッ
FLUSH
DAMMIT! I THOUGHT THINGS WERE WEIRD AROUND HERE!
NOW I KNOW IT'S BECAUSE LULU WAS PEEPING AT ME!
SHE'S A FREAKING STALKER!
THAT'S RIGHT.
I WANT YOU TO RAISE SECURITY TO THE HIGHEST LEVEL!
AND MAKE SURE YOU CATCH ALL INTRUDERS.
YOU'D BETTER NOT LET ANYONE IN!

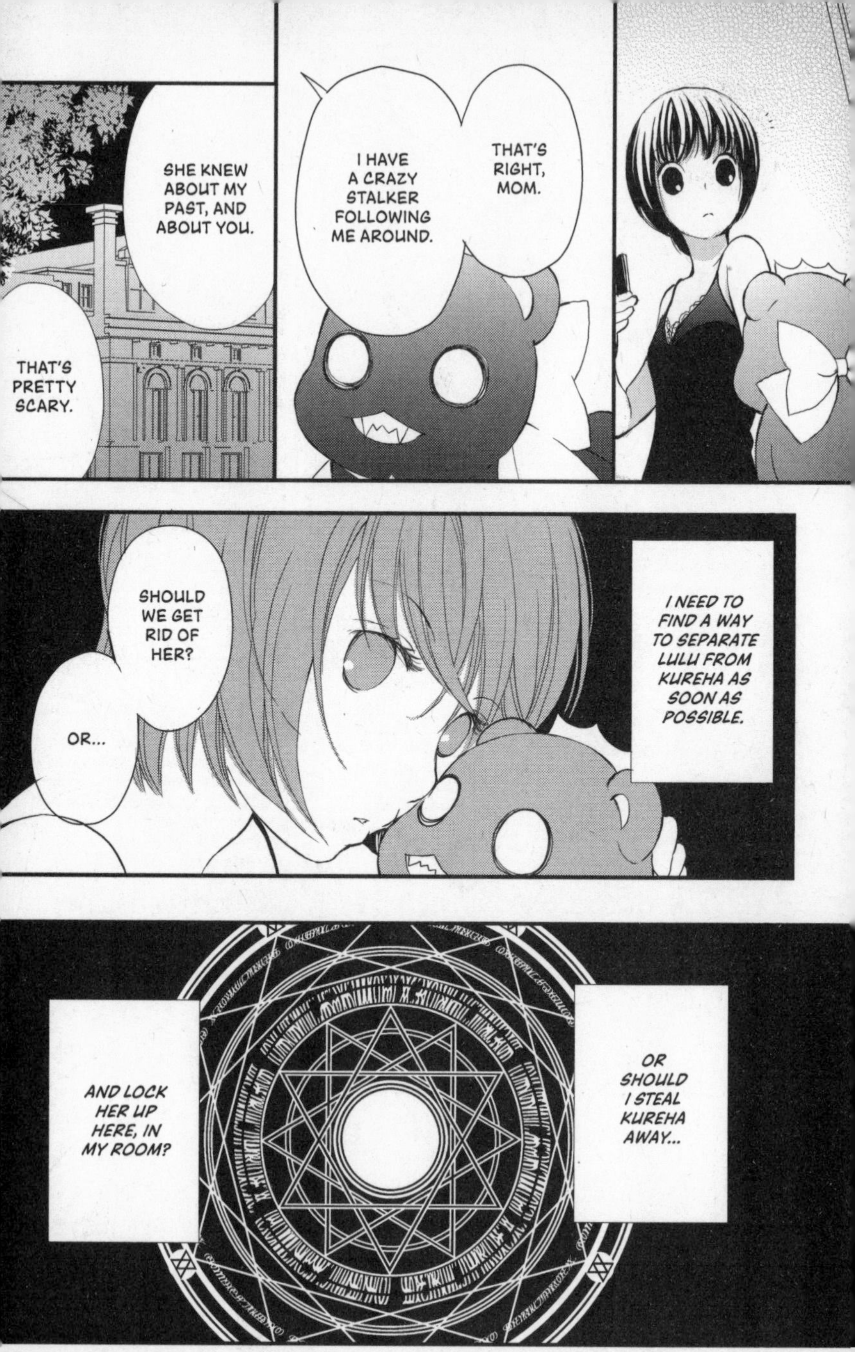
THAT'S RIGHT, MOM.
I HAVE A CRAZY STALKER FOLLOWING ME AROUND.
SHE KNEW ABOUT MY PAST, AND ABOUT YOU.
THAT'S PRETTY SCARY.
I NEED TO FIND A WAY TO SEPARATE LULU FROM KUREHA AS SOON AS POSSIBLE.
SHOULD WE GET RID OF HER?
OR...
OR SHOULD I STEAL KUREHA AWAY...
AND LOCK HER UP HERE, IN MY ROOM?

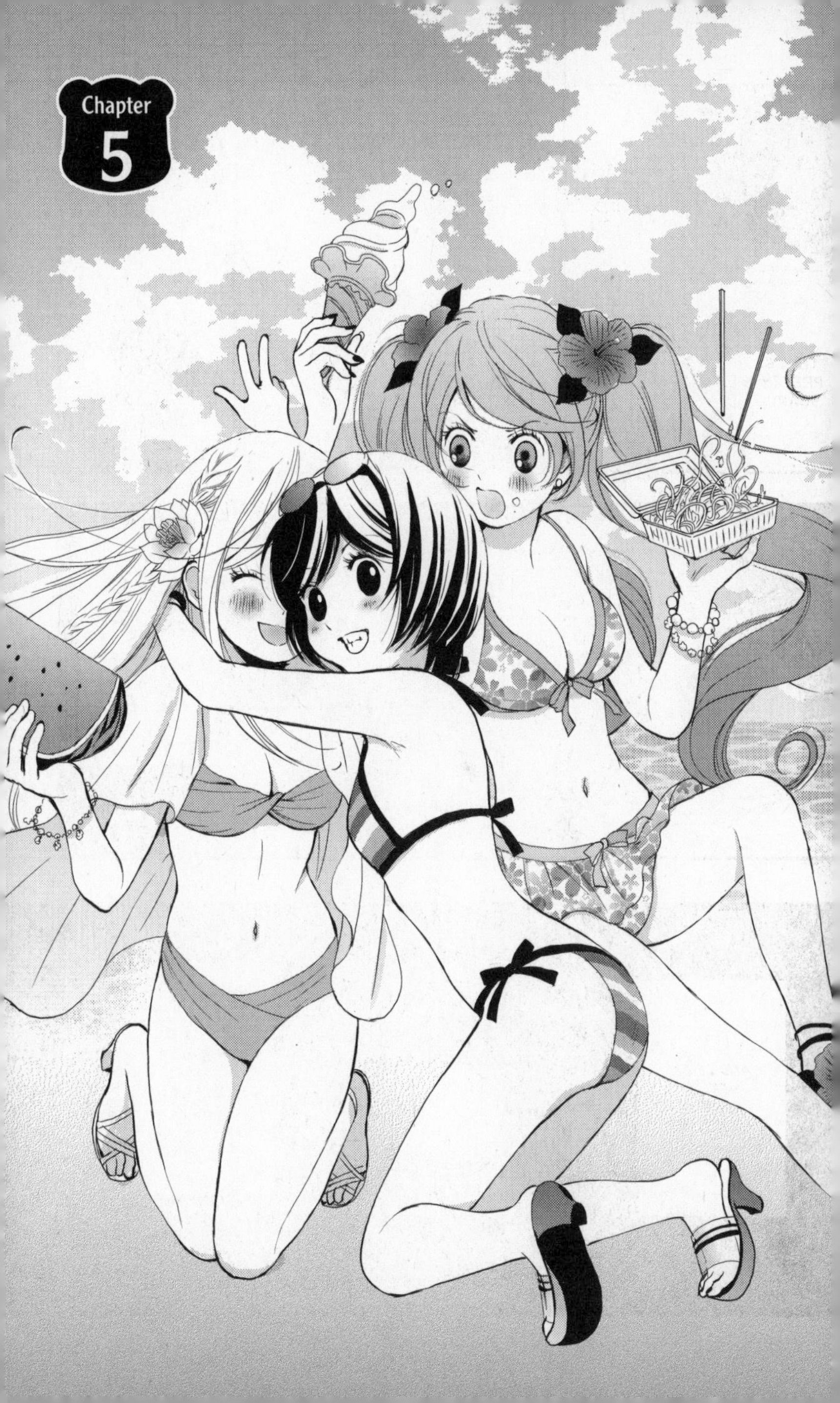
Chapter
5

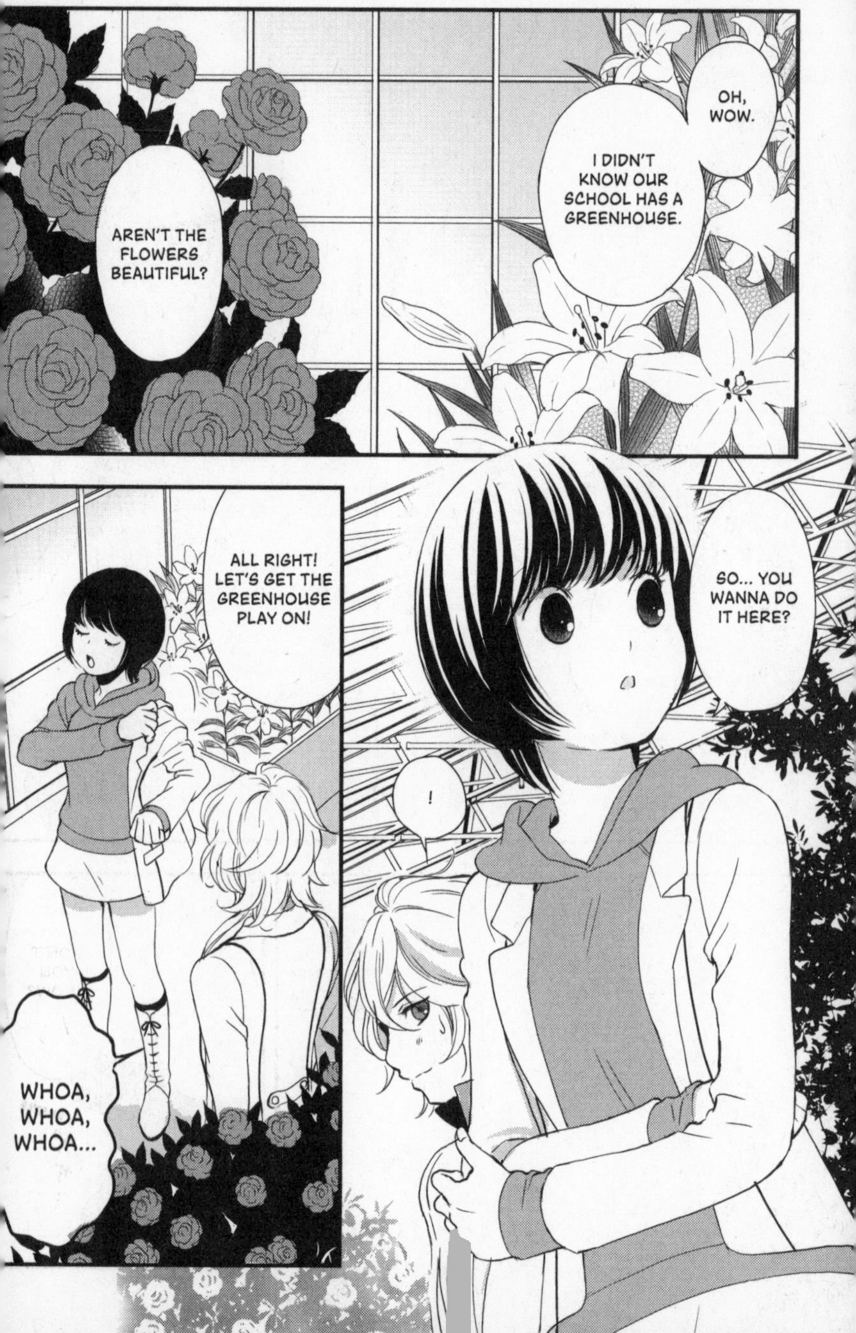
OH, WOW.
I DIDN'T KNOW OUR SCHOOL HAS A GREENHOUSE.
AREN'T THE FLOWERS BEAUTIFUL?
SO... YOU WANNA DO IT HERE?
!
ALL RIGHT! LET'S GET THE GREENHOUSE PLAY ON!
WHOA, WHOA, WHOA...

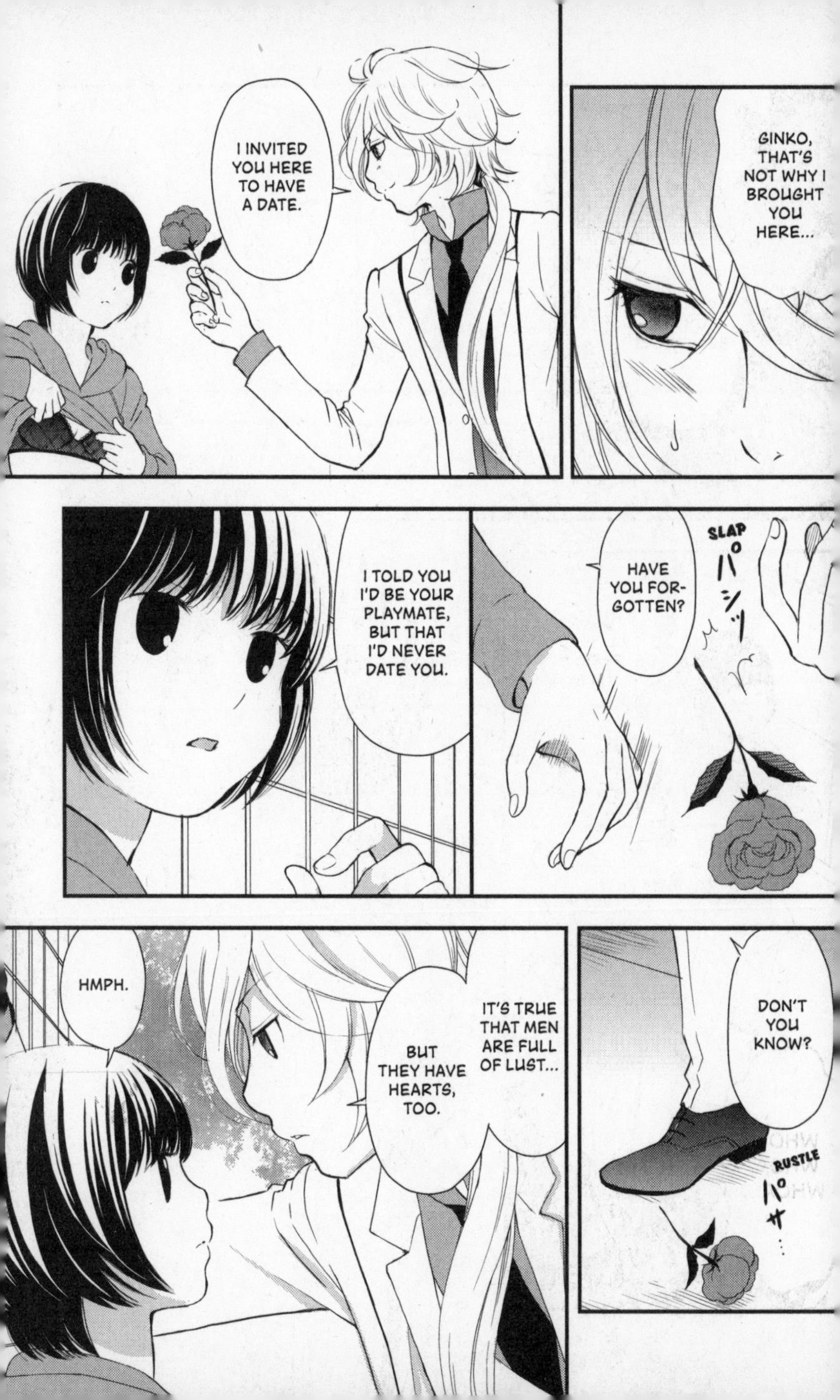
GINKO, THAT'S NOT WHY I BROUGHT YOU HERE...
I INVITED YOU HERE TO HAVE A DATE.
HAVE YOU FORGOTTEN?
SLAP
パシッ
I TOLD YOU I'D BE YOUR PLAYMATE, BUT THAT I'D NEVER DATE YOU.
DON'T YOU KNOW?
RUSTLE
IT'S TRUE THAT MEN ARE FULL OF LUST...
BUT THEY HAVE HEARTS, TOO.
HMPH.

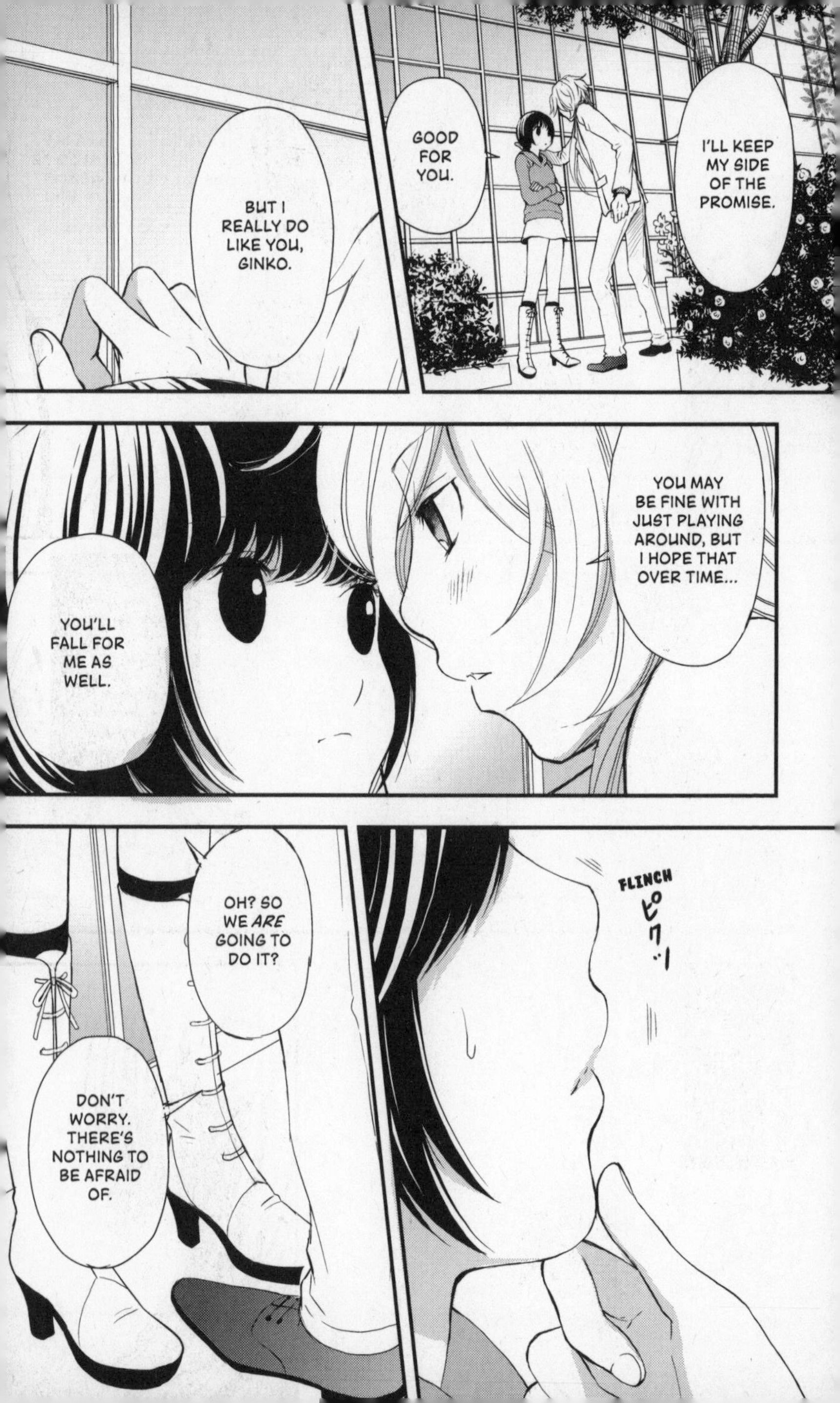
I'LL KEEP MY SIDE OF THE PROMISE.
GOOD FOR YOU.
BUT I REALLY DO LIKE YOU, GINKO.
YOU MAY BE FINE WITH JUST PLAYING AROUND, BUT I HOPE THAT OVER TIME...
YOU'LL FALL FOR ME AS WELL.
FLINCH
ピクッ
OH? SO WE *ARE* GOING TO DO IT?
DON'T WORRY. THERE'S NOTHING TO BE AFRAID OF.

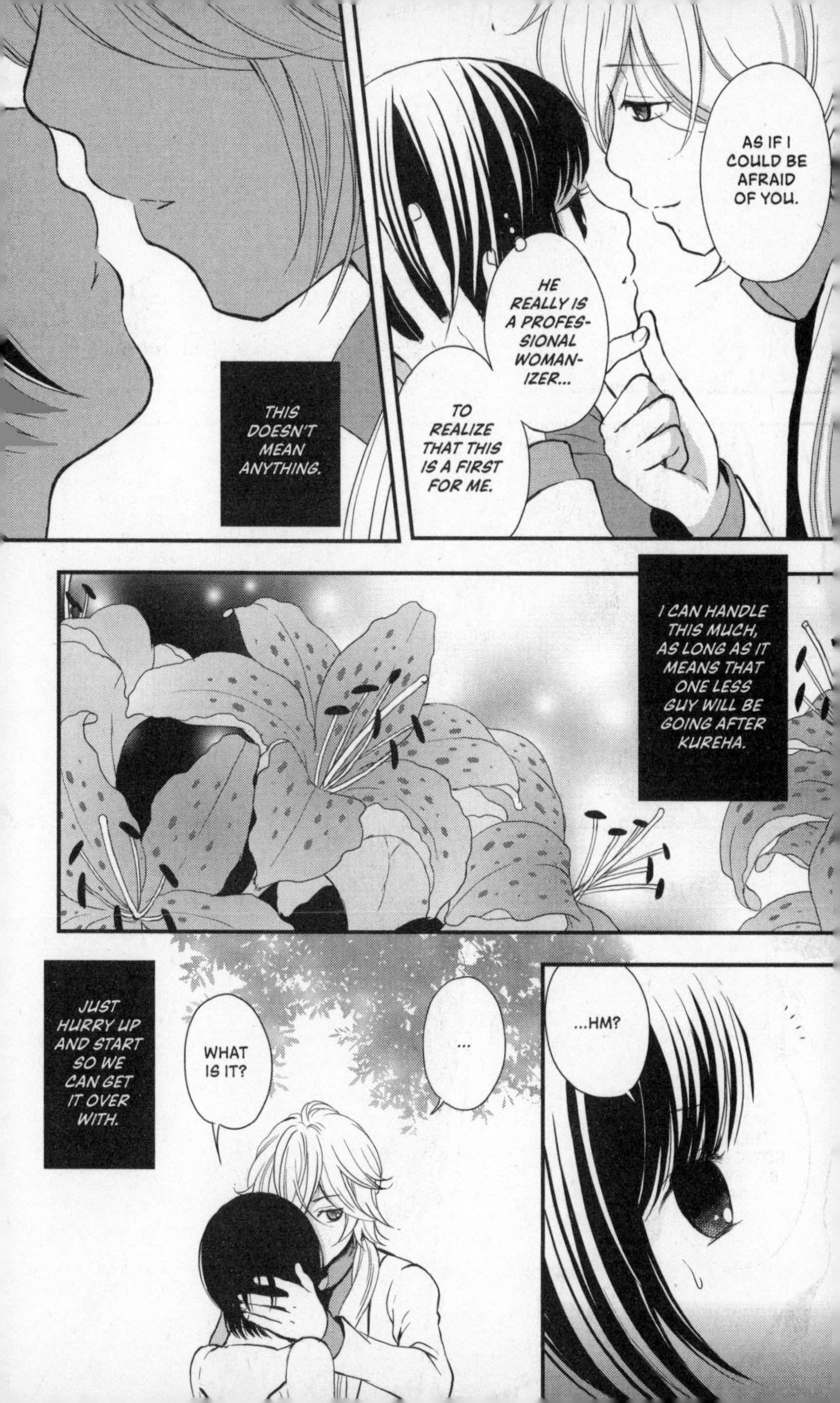
AS IF I COULD BE AFRAID OF YOU.
HE REALLY IS A PROFESSIONAL WOMANIZER...
TO REALIZE THAT THIS IS A FIRST FOR ME.
THIS DOESN'T MEAN ANYTHING.
I CAN HANDLE THIS MUCH, AS LONG AS IT MEANS THAT ONE LESS GUY WILL BE GOING AFTER KUREHA.
...HM?
...
WHAT IS IT?
JUST HURRY UP AND START SO WE CAN GET IT OVER WITH.

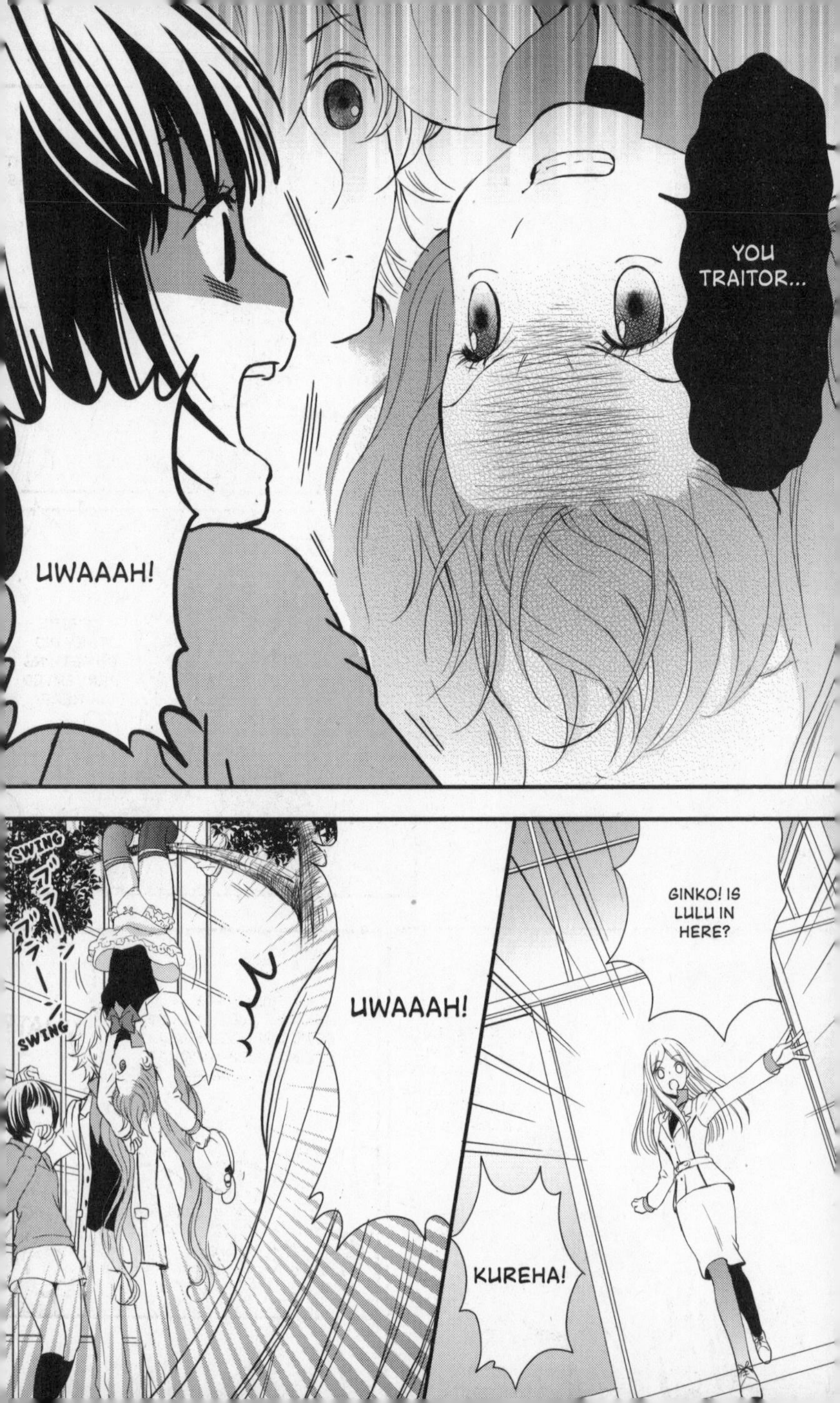
YOU TRAITOR...
UWAAAH!
GINKO! IS LULU IN HERE?
KUREHA!
UWAAAH!
SWING
SWING

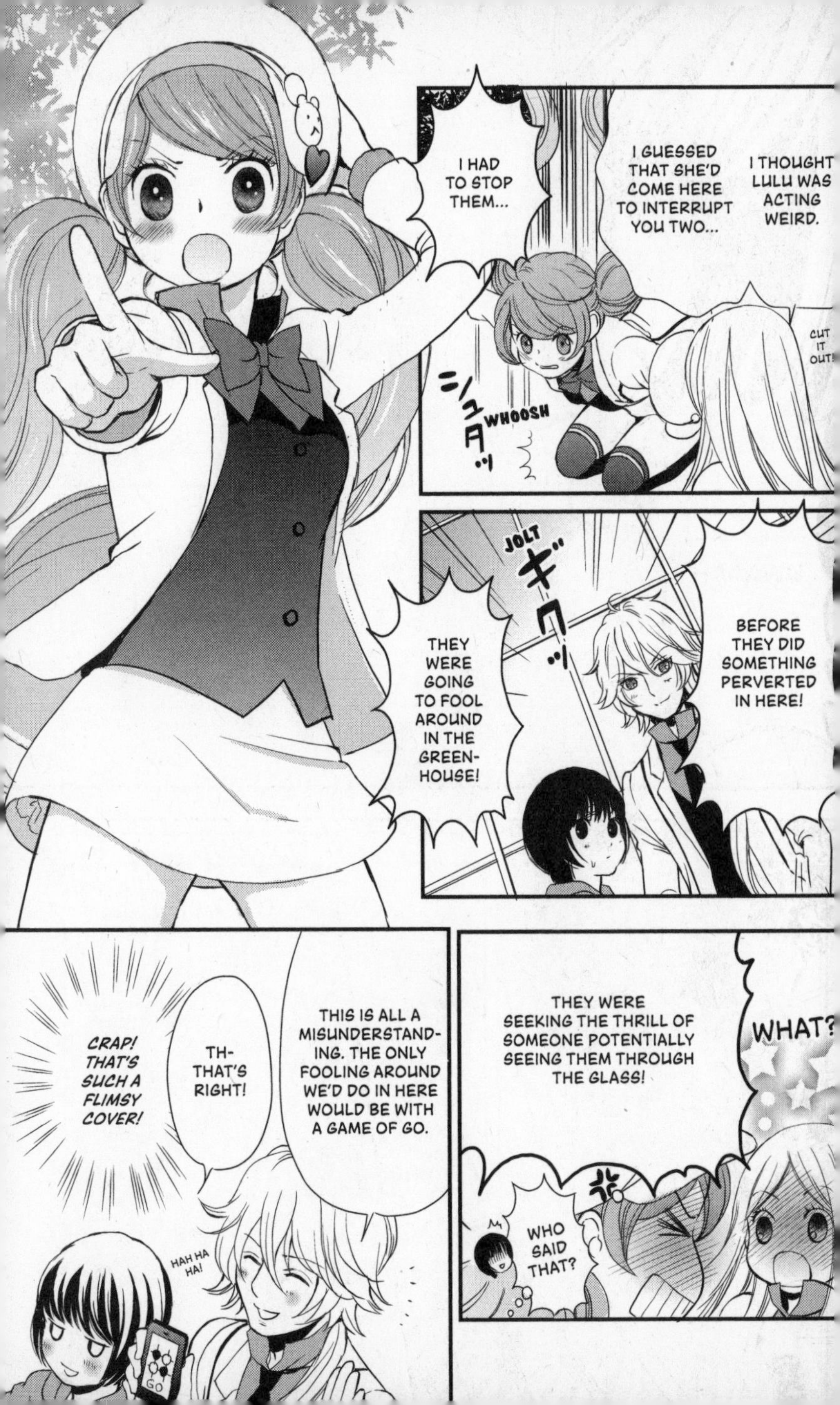

I THOUGHT LULU WAS ACTING WEIRD.
I GUESSED THAT SHE'D COME HERE TO INTERRUPT YOU TWO...
I HAD TO STOP THEM...
CUT IT OUT!
シュタッ
WHOOSH
BEFORE THEY DID SOMETHING PERVERTED IN HERE!
ギクッ
JOLT
THEY WERE GOING TO FOOL AROUND IN THE GREEN-HOUSE!
WHAT?
THEY WERE SEEKING THE THRILL OF SOMEONE POTENTIALLY SEEING THEM THROUGH THE GLASS!
WHO SAID THAT?
THIS IS ALL A MISUNDERSTAND-ING. THE ONLY FOOLING AROUND WE'D DO IN HERE WOULD BE WITH A GAME OF GO.
TH-THAT'S RIGHT!
CRAP! THAT'S SUCH A FLIMSY COVER!
HAH HA HA!
GO

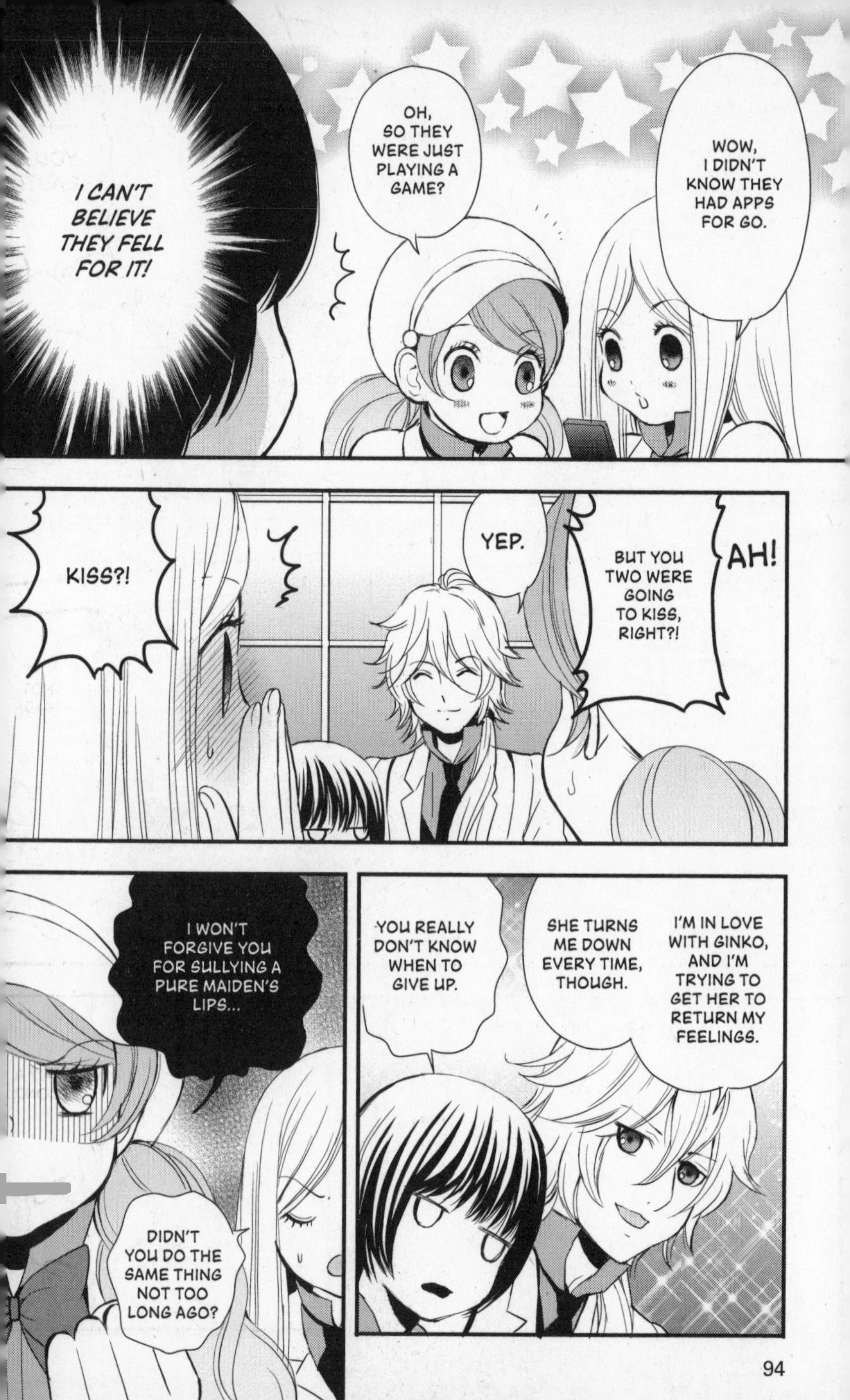
WOW, I DIDN'T KNOW THEY HAD APPS FOR GO.
OH, SO THEY WERE JUST PLAYING A GAME?
I CAN'T BELIEVE THEY FELL FOR IT!
AH!
BUT YOU TWO WERE GOING TO KISS, RIGHT?!
YEP.
KISS?!
I'M IN LOVE WITH GINKO, AND I'M TRYING TO GET HER TO RETURN MY FEELINGS.
SHE TURNS ME DOWN EVERY TIME, THOUGH.
YOU REALLY DON'T KNOW WHEN TO GIVE UP.
I WON'T FORGIVE YOU FOR SULLYING A PURE MAIDEN'S LIPS...
DIDN'T YOU DO THE SAME THING NOT TOO LONG AGO?

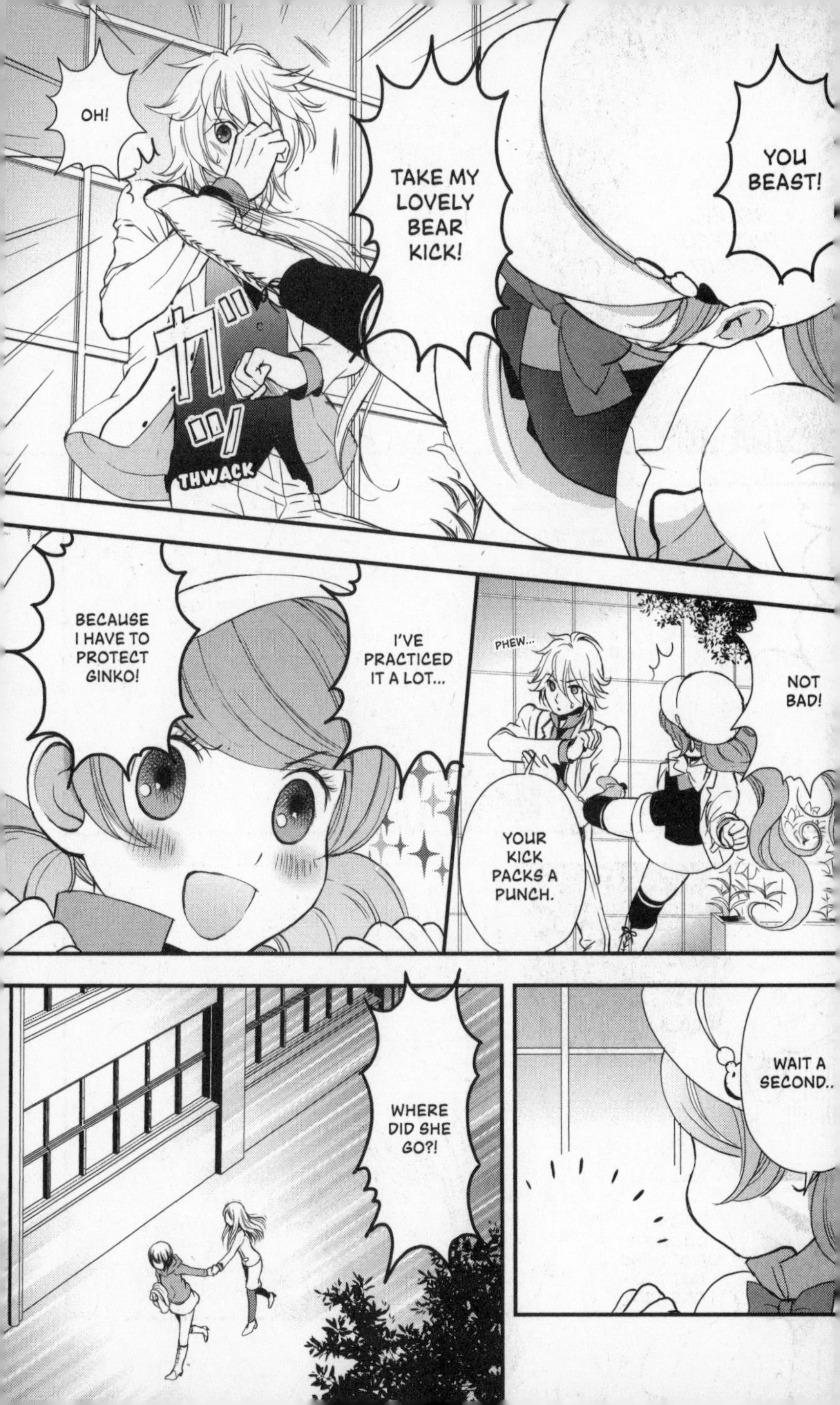
YOU BEAST!
TAKE MY LOVELY BEAR KICK!
THWACK
OH!
NOT BAD!
PHEW...
YOUR KICK PACKS A PUNCH.
I'VE PRACTICED IT A LOT...
BECAUSE I HAVE TO PROTECT GINKO!
WAIT A SECOND..
WHERE DID SHE GO?!

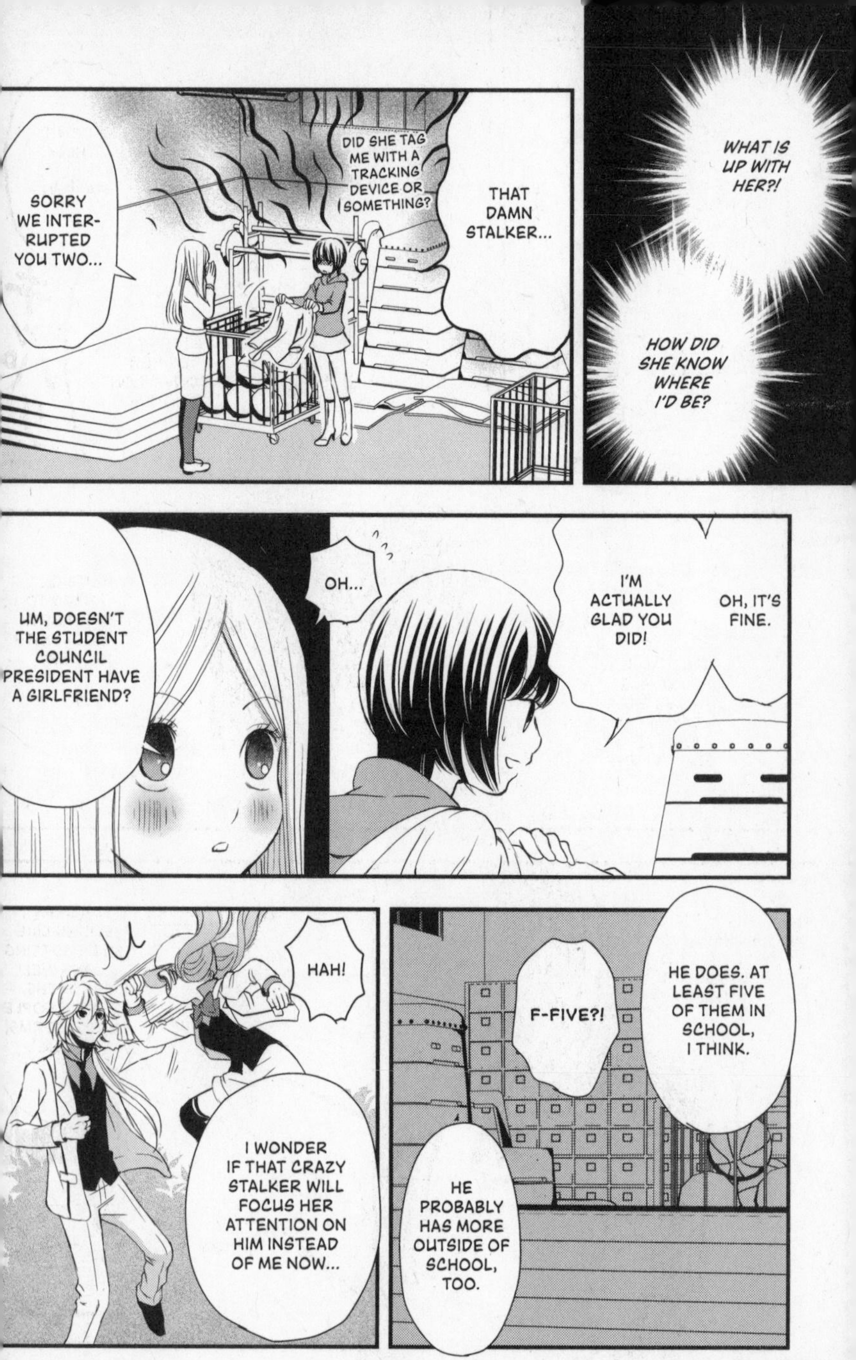
WHAT IS UP WITH HER?!
HOW DID SHE KNOW WHERE I'D BE?
THAT DAMN STALKER...
DID SHE TAG ME WITH A TRACKING DEVICE OR SOMETHING?
SORRY WE INTER-RUPTED YOU TWO...
OH, IT'S FINE.
I'M ACTUALLY GLAD YOU DID!
OH...
UM, DOESN'T THE STUDENT COUNCIL PRESIDENT HAVE A GIRLFRIEND?
HE DOES. AT LEAST FIVE OF THEM IN SCHOOL, I THINK.
F-FIVE?!
HE PROBABLY HAS MORE OUTSIDE OF SCHOOL, TOO.
HAH!
I WONDER IF THAT CRAZY STALKER WILL FOCUS HER ATTENTION ON HIM INSTEAD OF ME NOW...

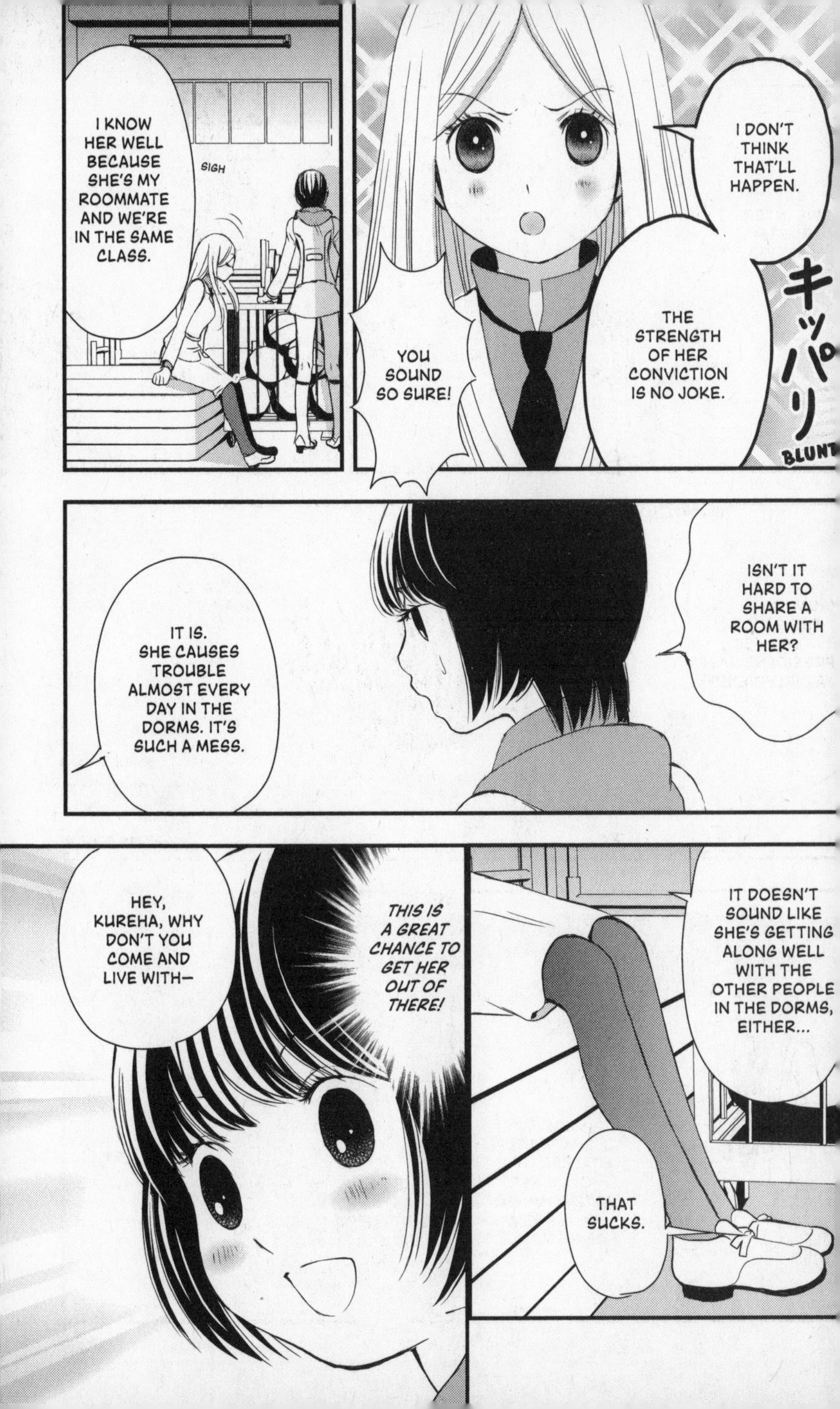
I DON'T THINK THAT'LL HAPPEN.
キッパリ
BLUNT
THE STRENGTH OF HER CONVICTION IS NO JOKE.
YOU SOUND SO SURE!
I KNOW HER WELL BECAUSE SHE'S MY ROOMMATE AND WE'RE IN THE SAME CLASS.
SIGH
ISN'T IT HARD TO SHARE A ROOM WITH HER?
IT IS. SHE CAUSES TROUBLE ALMOST EVERY DAY IN THE DORMS. IT'S SUCH A MESS.
IT DOESN'T SOUND LIKE SHE'S GETTING ALONG WELL WITH THE OTHER PEOPLE IN THE DORMS, EITHER...
THAT SUCKS.
THIS IS A GREAT CHANCE TO GET HER OUT OF THERE!
HEY, KUREHA, WHY DON'T YOU COME AND LIVE WITH—

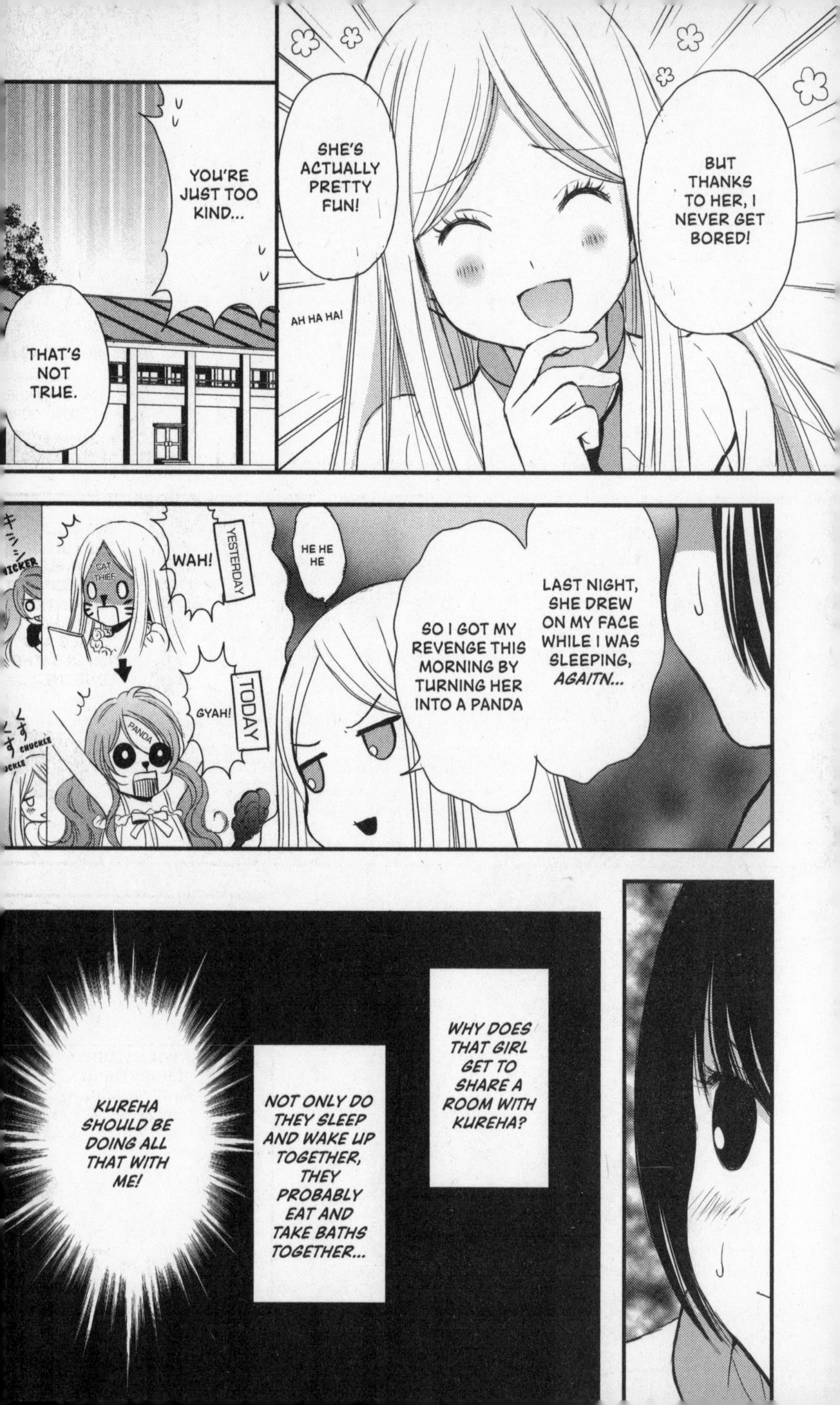
BUT THANKS TO HER, I NEVER GET BORED!
SHE'S ACTUALLY PRETTY FUN!
AH HA HA!
YOU'RE JUST TOO KIND...
THAT'S NOT TRUE.
LAST NIGHT, SHE DREW ON MY FACE WHILE I WAS SLEEPING, *AGAITN*...
SO I GOT MY REVENGE THIS MORNING BY TURNING HER INTO A PANDA
HE HE HE
YESTERDAY
WAH!
CAT THIEF
TODAY
GYAH!
PANDA
CHUCKLE
WHY DOES THAT GIRL GET TO SHARE A ROOM WITH KUREHA?
NOT ONLY DO THEY SLEEP AND WAKE UP TOGETHER, THEY PROBABLY EAT AND TAKE BATHS TOGETHER...
KUREHA SHOULD BE DOING ALL THAT WITH ME!

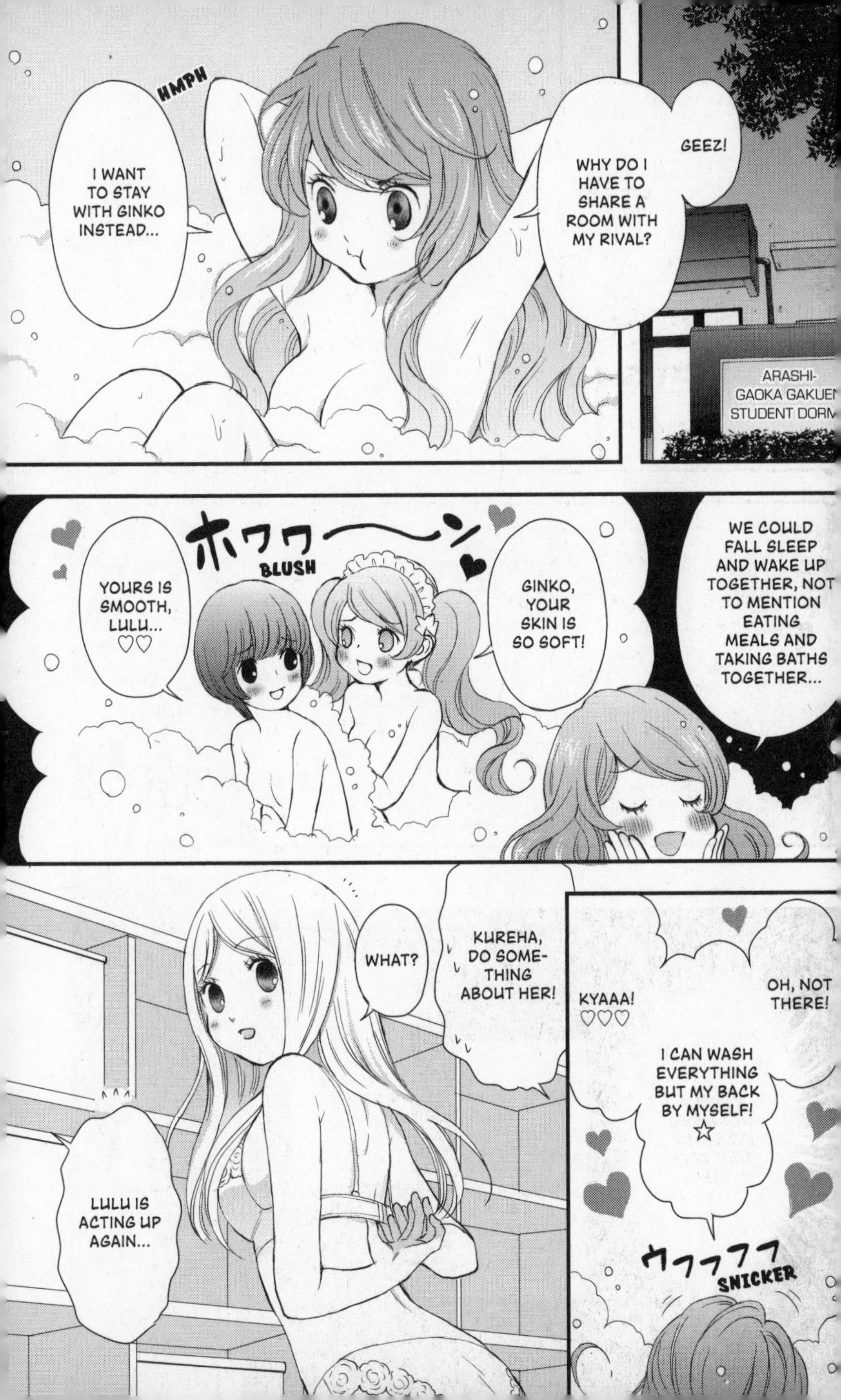
ARASHI-GAOKA GAKUEN STUDENT DORM
GEEZ!
WHY DO I HAVE TO SHARE A ROOM WITH MY RIVAL?
HMPH
I WANT TO STAY WITH GINKO INSTEAD...
WE COULD FALL SLEEP AND WAKE UP TOGETHER, NOT TO MENTION EATING MEALS AND TAKING BATHS TOGETHER...
GINKO, YOUR SKIN IS SO SOFT!
ホワワーーン
BLUSH
YOURS IS SMOOTH, LULU... ♡♡
OH, NOT THERE!
KYAAA! ♡♡♡
I CAN WASH EVERYTHING BUT MY BACK BY MYSELF! ☆
ウフフフフ
SNICKER
KUREHA, DO SOMETHING ABOUT HER!
WHAT?
LULU IS ACTING UP AGAIN...

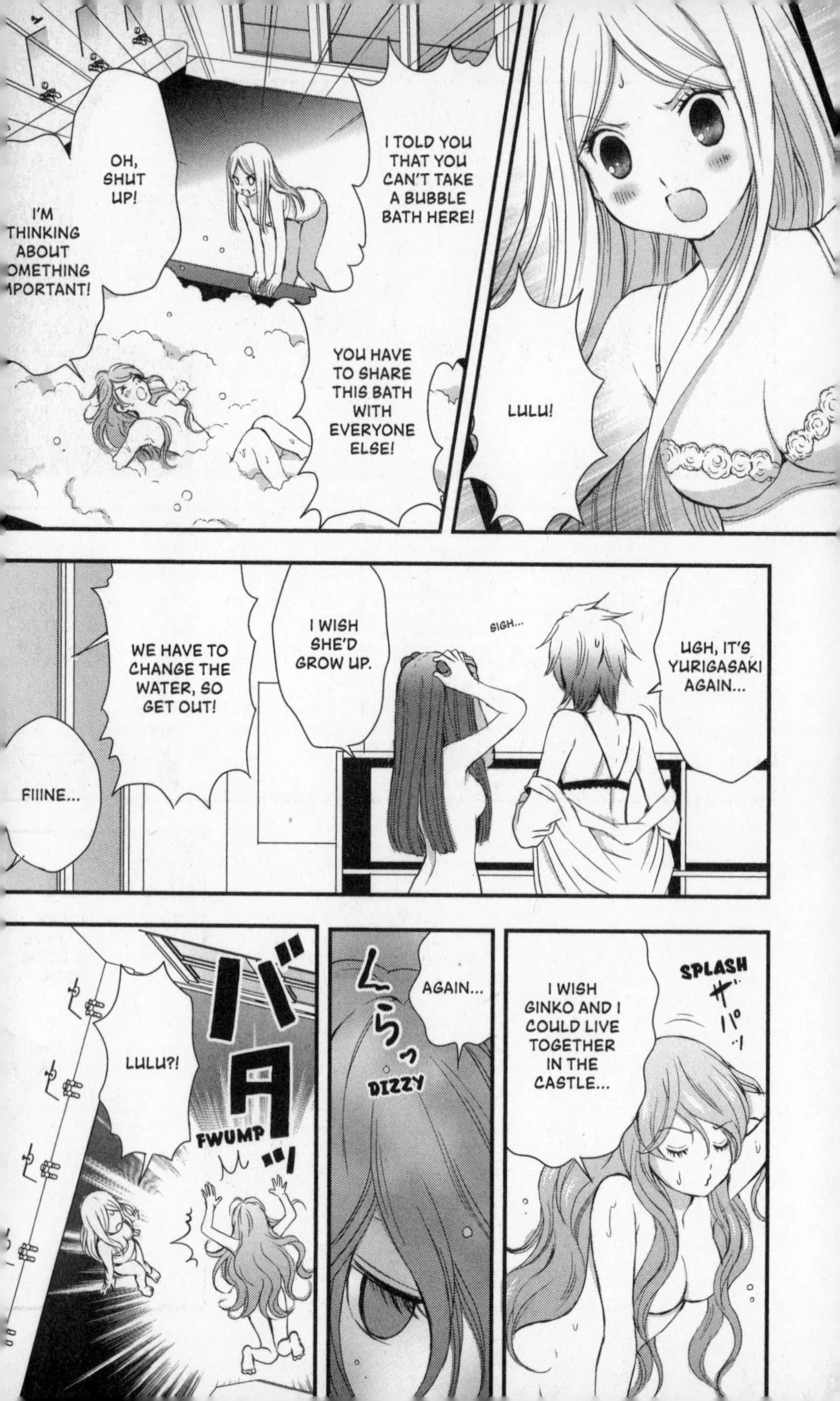
LULU!
I TOLD YOU THAT YOU CAN'T TAKE A BUBBLE BATH HERE!
YOU HAVE TO SHARE THIS BATH WITH EVERYONE ELSE!
OH, SHUT UP!
I'M THINKING ABOUT OMETHING MPORTANT!
UGH, IT'S YURIGASAKI AGAIN...
SIGH...
I WISH SHE'D GROW UP.
WE HAVE TO CHANGE THE WATER, SO GET OUT!
FIIINE...
SPLASH
I WISH GINKO AND I COULD LIVE TOGETHER IN THE CASTLE...
AGAIN...
DIZZY
LULU?!
FWUMP

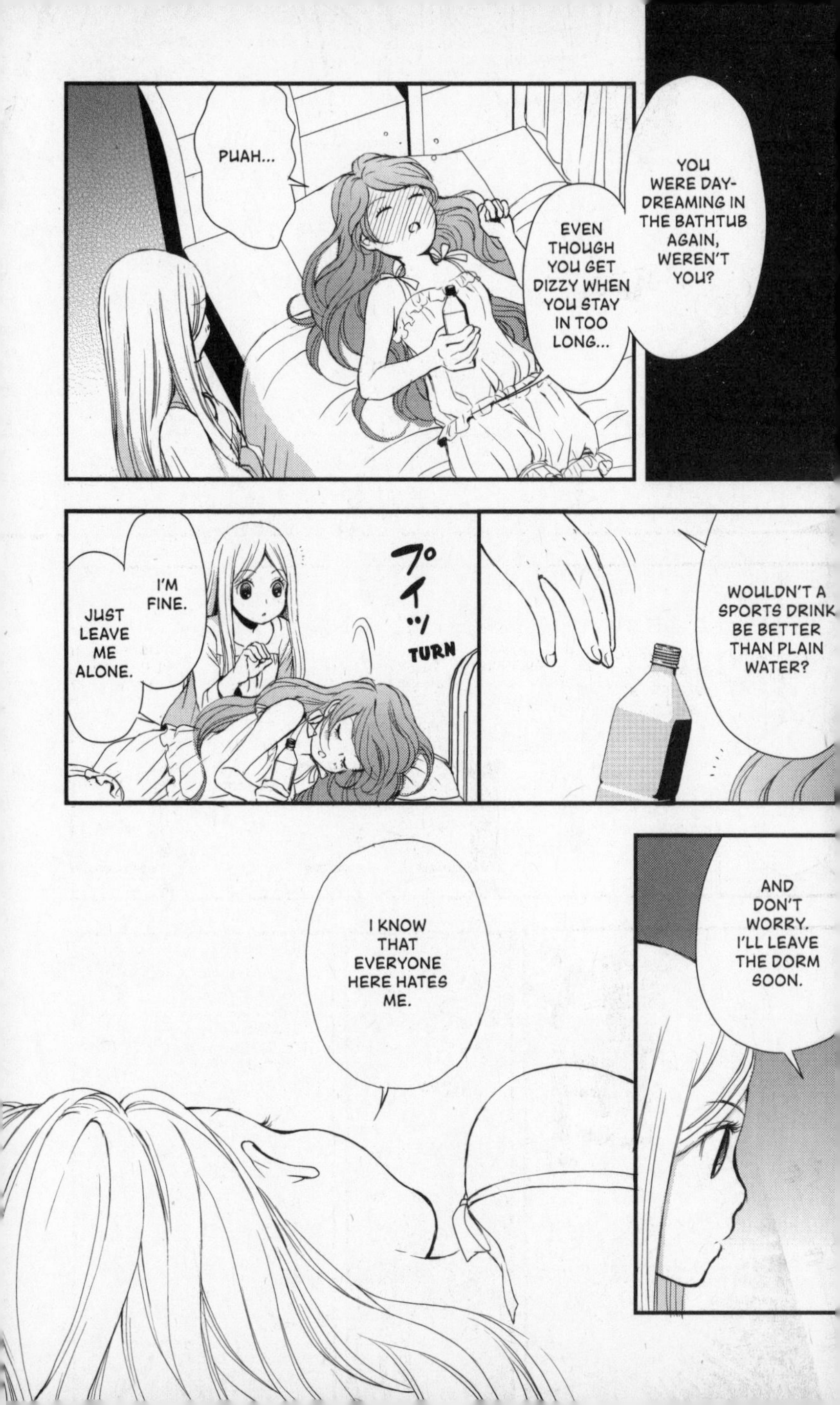
YOU WERE DAY-DREAMING IN THE BATHTUB AGAIN, WEREN'T YOU?
EVEN THOUGH YOU GET DIZZY WHEN YOU STAY IN TOO LONG...
PUAH...
WOULDN'T A SPORTS DRINK BE BETTER THAN PLAIN WATER?
プイッ
TURN
I'M FINE.
JUST LEAVE ME ALONE.
AND DON'T WORRY. I'LL LEAVE THE DORM SOON.
I KNOW THAT EVERYONE HERE HATES ME.

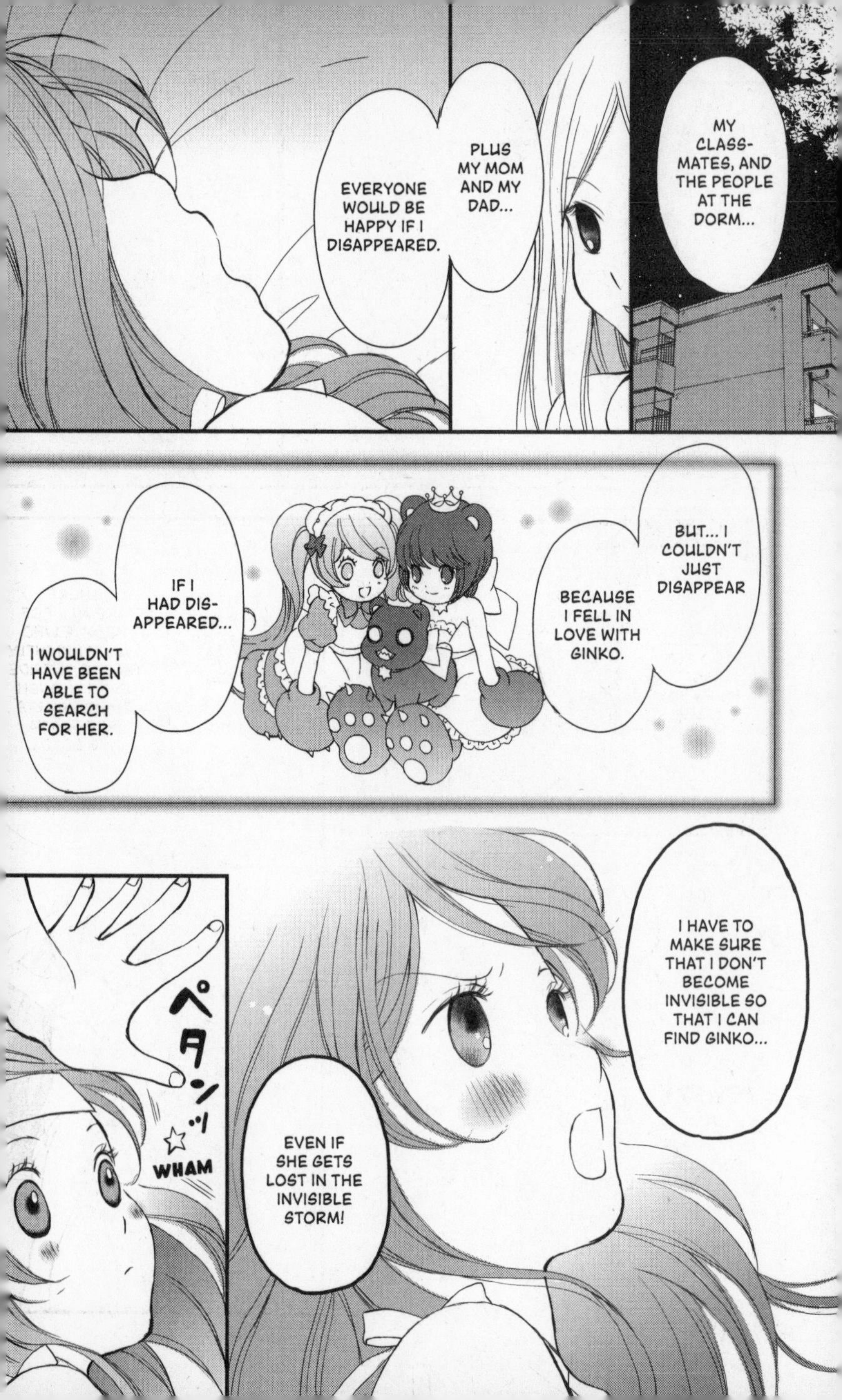
MY CLASSMATES, AND THE PEOPLE AT THE DORM...
PLUS MY MOM AND MY DAD...
EVERYONE WOULD BE HAPPY IF I DISAPPEARED.
BUT... I COULDN'T JUST DISAPPEAR
BECAUSE I FELL IN LOVE WITH GINKO.
IF I HAD DISAPPEARED...
I WOULDN'T HAVE BEEN ABLE TO SEARCH FOR HER.
I HAVE TO MAKE SURE THAT I DON'T BECOME INVISIBLE SO THAT I CAN FIND GINKO...
EVEN IF SHE GETS LOST IN THE INVISIBLE STORM!
ペタンッ
WHAM

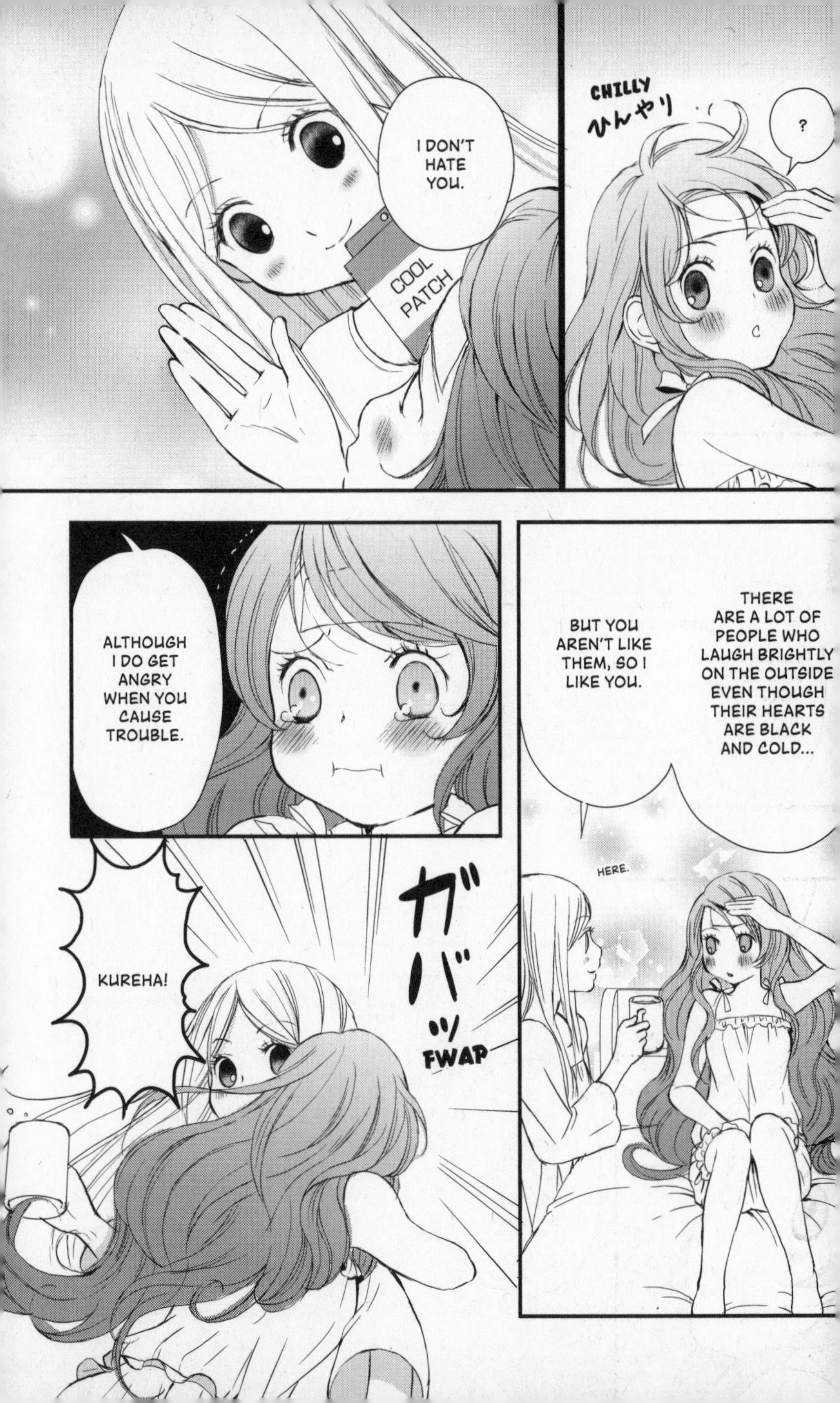
CHILLY
ひんやり
?
I DON'T HATE YOU.
COOL PATCH
THERE ARE A LOT OF PEOPLE WHO LAUGH BRIGHTLY ON THE OUTSIDE EVEN THOUGH THEIR HEARTS ARE BLACK AND COLD...
BUT YOU AREN'T LIKE THEM, SO I LIKE YOU.
HERE.
ALTHOUGH I DO GET ANGRY WHEN YOU CAUSE TROUBLE.
ガバッ
FWAP
KUREHA!

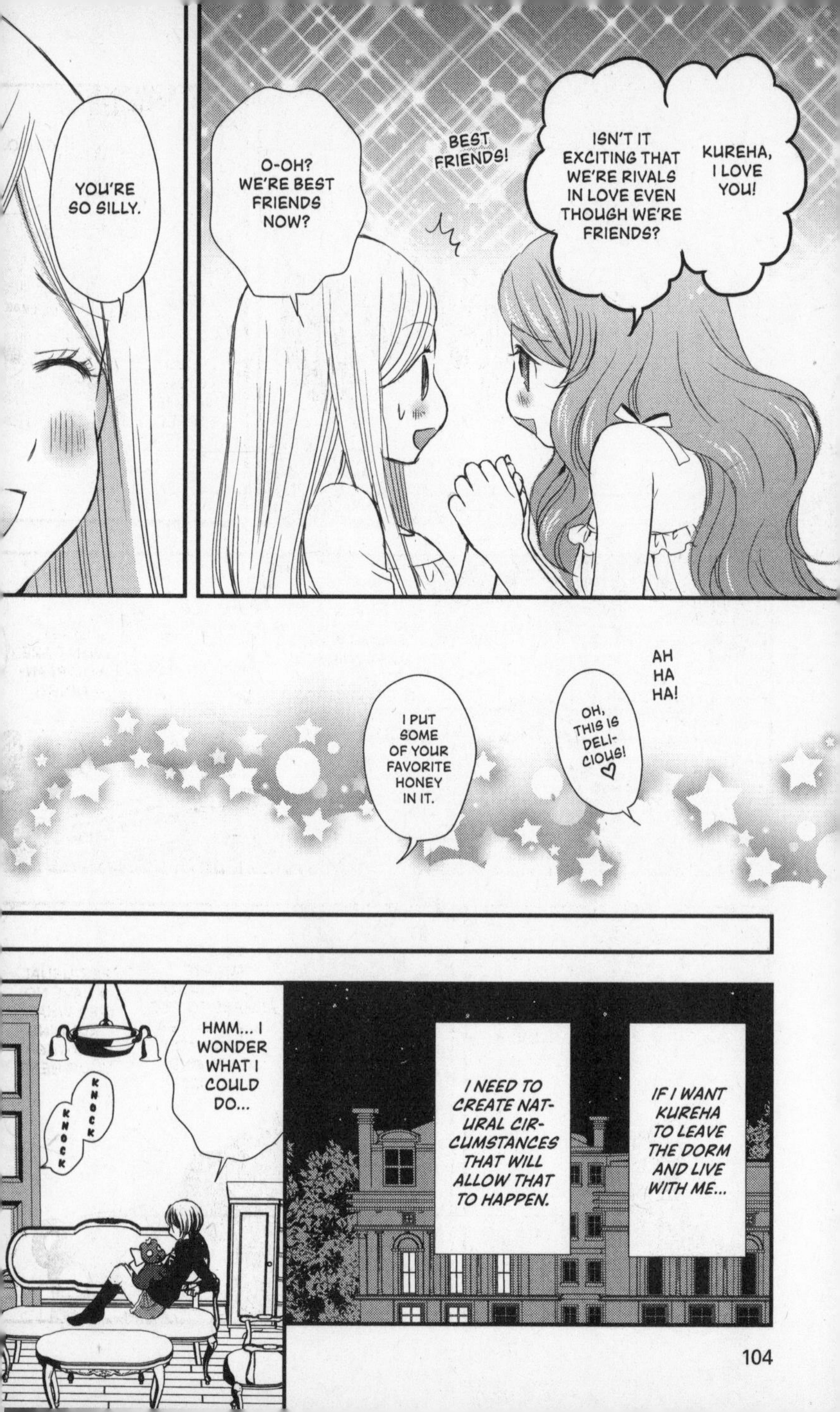
KUREHA, I LOVE YOU!
ISN'T IT EXCITING THAT WE'RE RIVALS IN LOVE EVEN THOUGH WE'RE FRIENDS?
BEST FRIENDS!
O-OH? WE'RE BEST FRIENDS NOW?
YOU'RE SO SILLY.
AH HA HA!
OH, THIS IS DELI-CIOUS! ♥
I PUT SOME OF YOUR FAVORITE HONEY IN IT.
IF I WANT KUREHA TO LEAVE THE DORM AND LIVE WITH ME...
I NEED TO CREATE NAT-URAL CIR-CUMSTANCES THAT WILL ALLOW THAT TO HAPPEN.
HMM... I WONDER WHAT I COULD DO...
KNOCK KNOCK

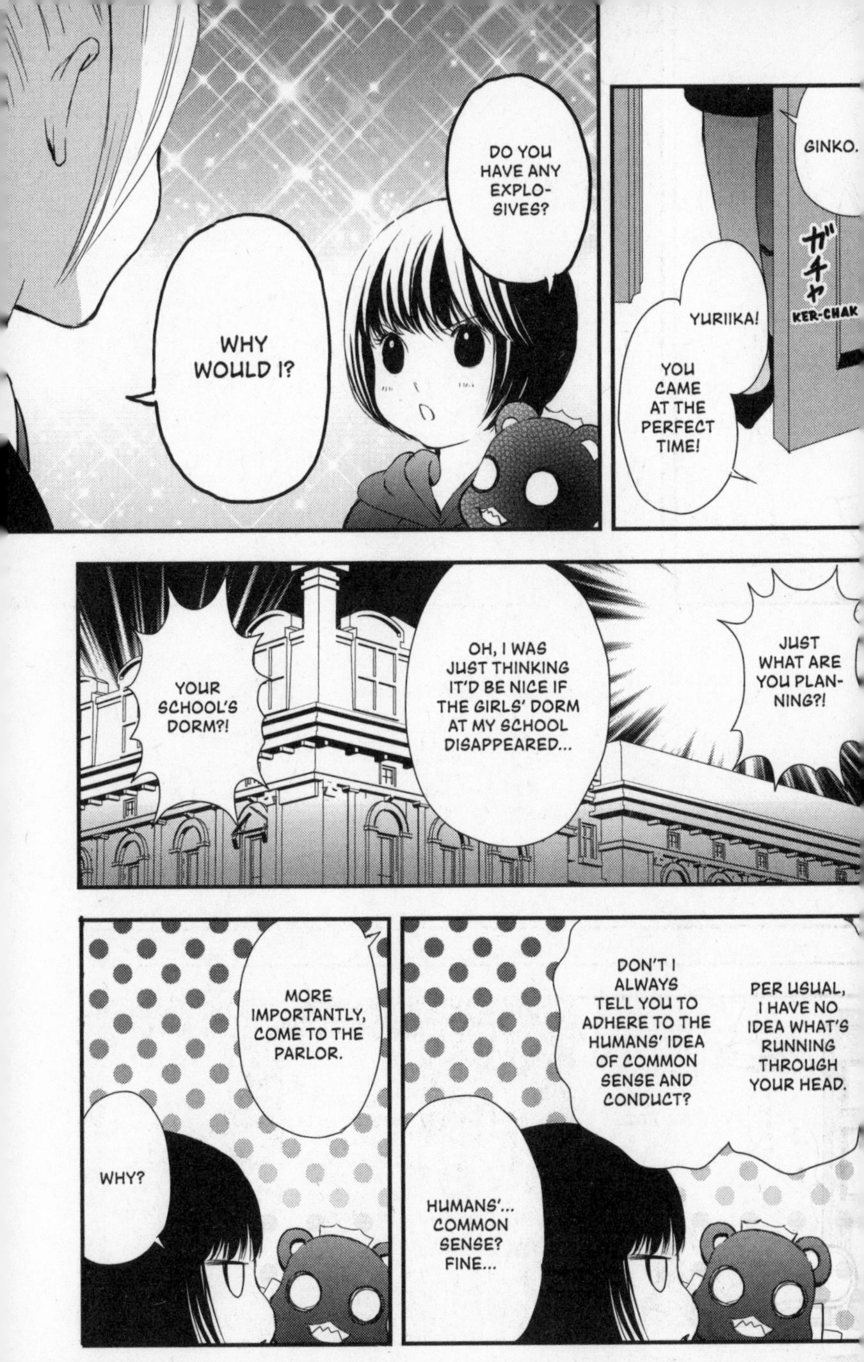

GINKO.
ガチャ
KER-CHAK
YURIIKA!
YOU CAME AT THE PERFECT TIME!
DO YOU HAVE ANY EXPLO-SIVES?
WHY WOULD I?
JUST WHAT ARE YOU PLAN-NING?!
OH, I WAS JUST THINKING IT'D BE NICE IF THE GIRLS' DORM AT MY SCHOOL DISAPPEARED...
YOUR SCHOOL'S DORM?!
PER USUAL, I HAVE NO IDEA WHAT'S RUNNING THROUGH YOUR HEAD.
DON'T I ALWAYS TELL YOU TO ADHERE TO THE HUMANS' IDEA OF COMMON SENSE AND CONDUCT?
HUMANS'... COMMON SENSE? FINE...
MORE IMPORTANTLY, COME TO THE PARLOR.
WHY?

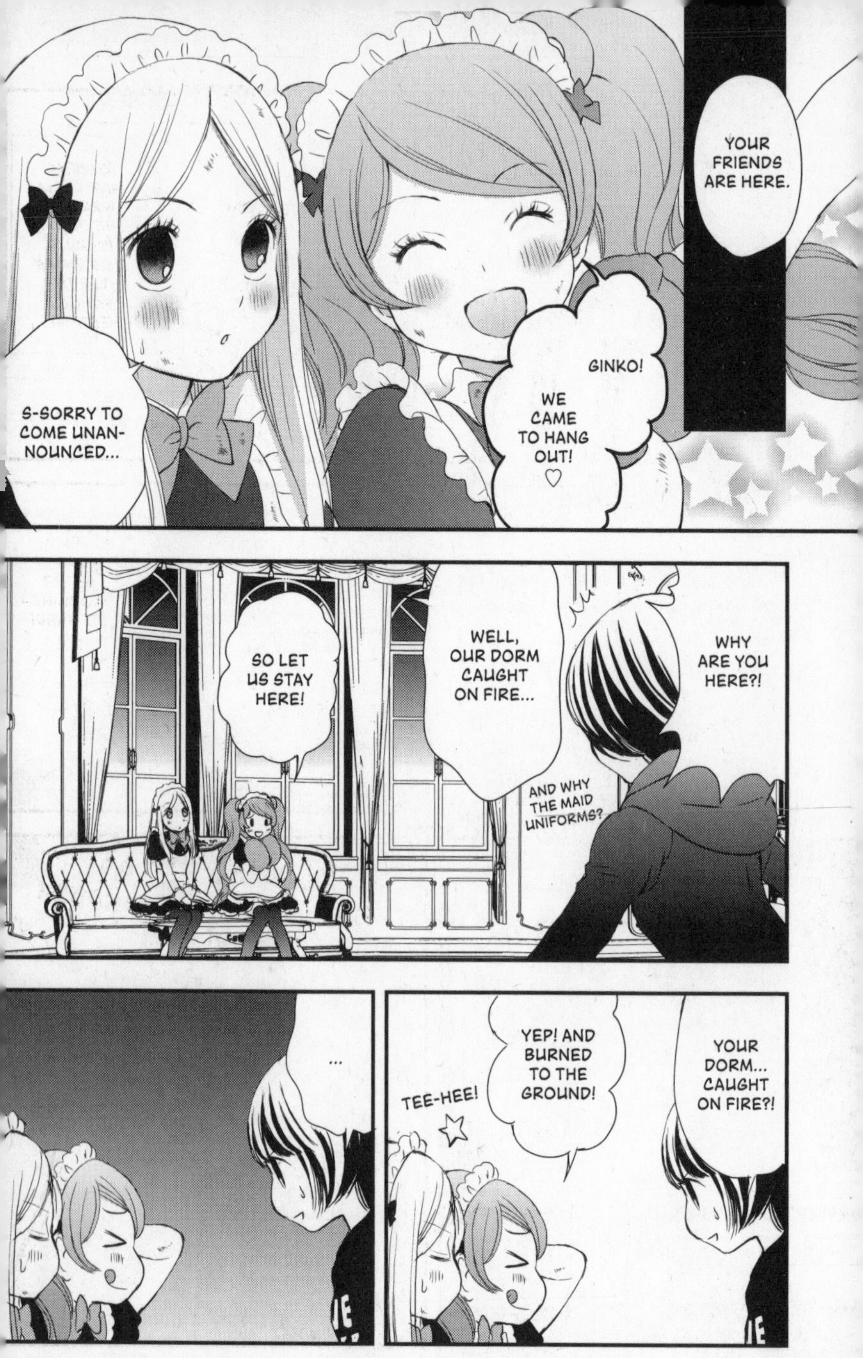
YOUR FRIENDS ARE HERE.
GINKO!
WE CAME TO HANG OUT! ♡
S-SORRY TO COME UNAN-NOUNCED...
WHY ARE YOU HERE?!
AND WHY THE MAID UNIFORMS?
WELL, OUR DORM CAUGHT ON FIRE...
SO LET US STAY HERE!
YOUR DORM... CAUGHT ON FIRE?!
YEP! AND BURNED TO THE GROUND!
TEE-HEE!
...

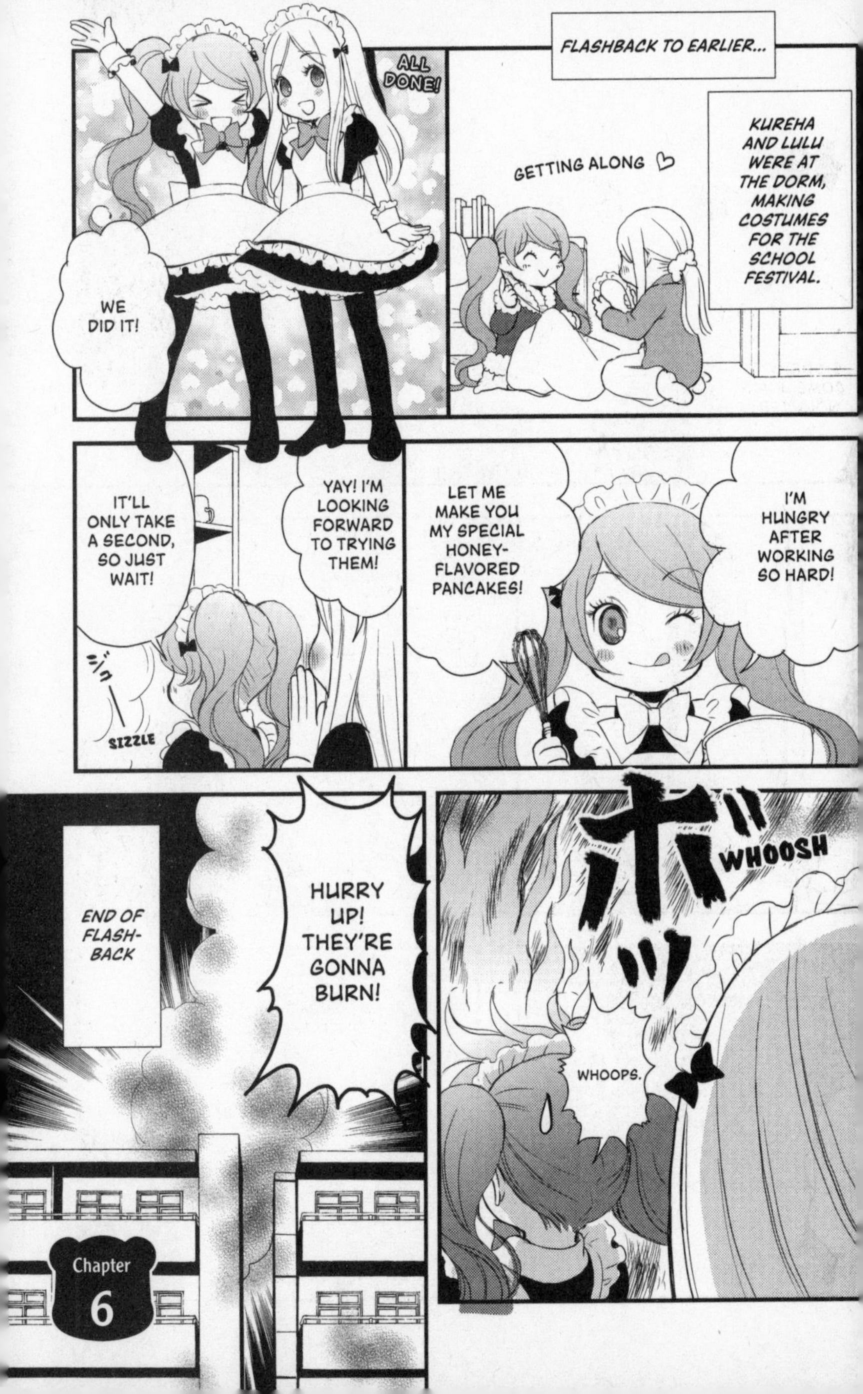
FLASHBACK TO EARLIER...
KUREHA AND LULU WERE AT THE DORM, MAKING COSTUMES FOR THE SCHOOL FESTIVAL.
GETTING ALONG ♡
ALL DONE!
WE DID IT!
I'M HUNGRY AFTER WORKING SO HARD!
LET ME MAKE YOU MY SPECIAL HONEY-FLAVORED PANCAKES!
YAY! I'M LOOKING FORWARD TO TRYING THEM!
IT'LL ONLY TAKE A SECOND, SO JUST WAIT!
SIZZLE
ボッ
WHOOSH
WHOOPS.
HURRY UP! THEY'RE GONNA BURN!
END OF FLASH-BACK
Chapter 6

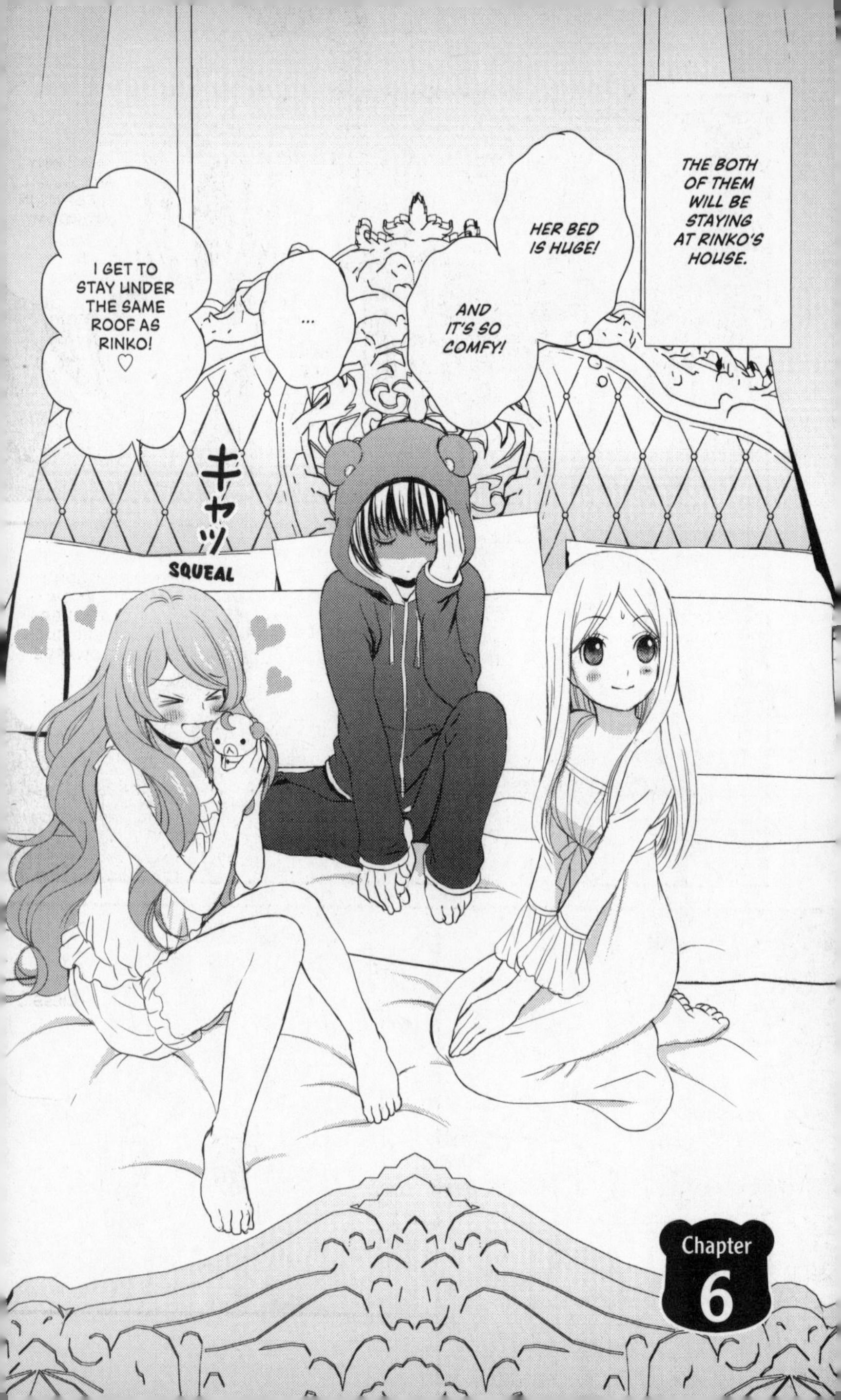
THE BOTH OF THEM WILL BE STAYING AT RINKO'S HOUSE.
HER BED IS HUGE!
AND IT'S SO COMFY!
...
I GET TO STAY UNDER THE SAME ROOF AS RINKO! ♡
キャッ
SQUEAL
Chapter 6

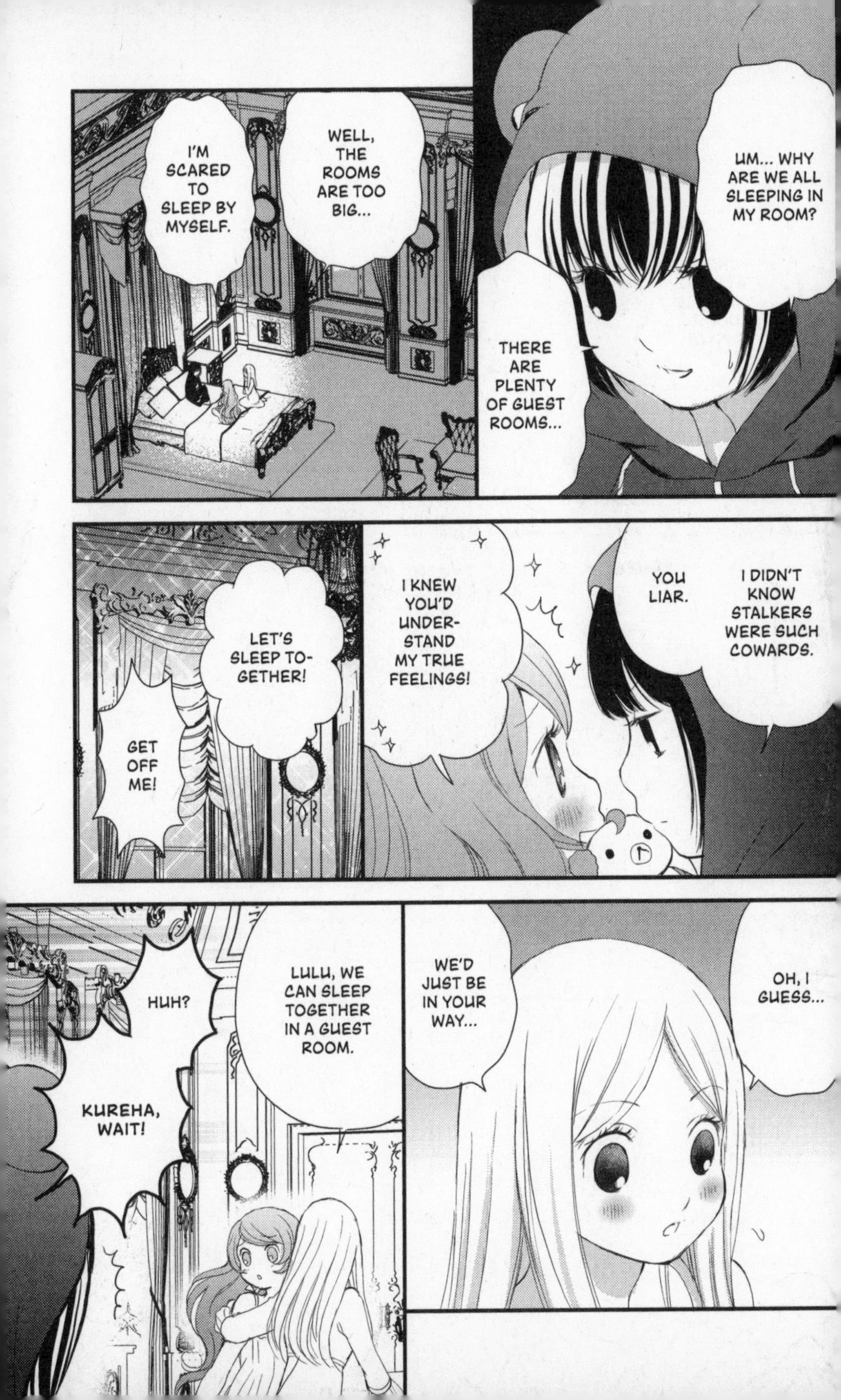
UM... WHY ARE WE ALL SLEEPING IN MY ROOM?
THERE ARE PLENTY OF GUEST ROOMS...
WELL, THE ROOMS ARE TOO BIG...
I'M SCARED TO SLEEP BY MYSELF.
I DIDN'T KNOW STALKERS WERE SUCH COWARDS.
YOU LIAR.
I KNEW YOU'D UNDER-STAND MY TRUE FEELINGS!
LET'S SLEEP TO-GETHER!
GET OFF ME!
OH, I GUESS...
WE'D JUST BE IN YOUR WAY...
LULU, WE CAN SLEEP TOGETHER IN A GUEST ROOM.
HUH?
KUREHA, WAIT!

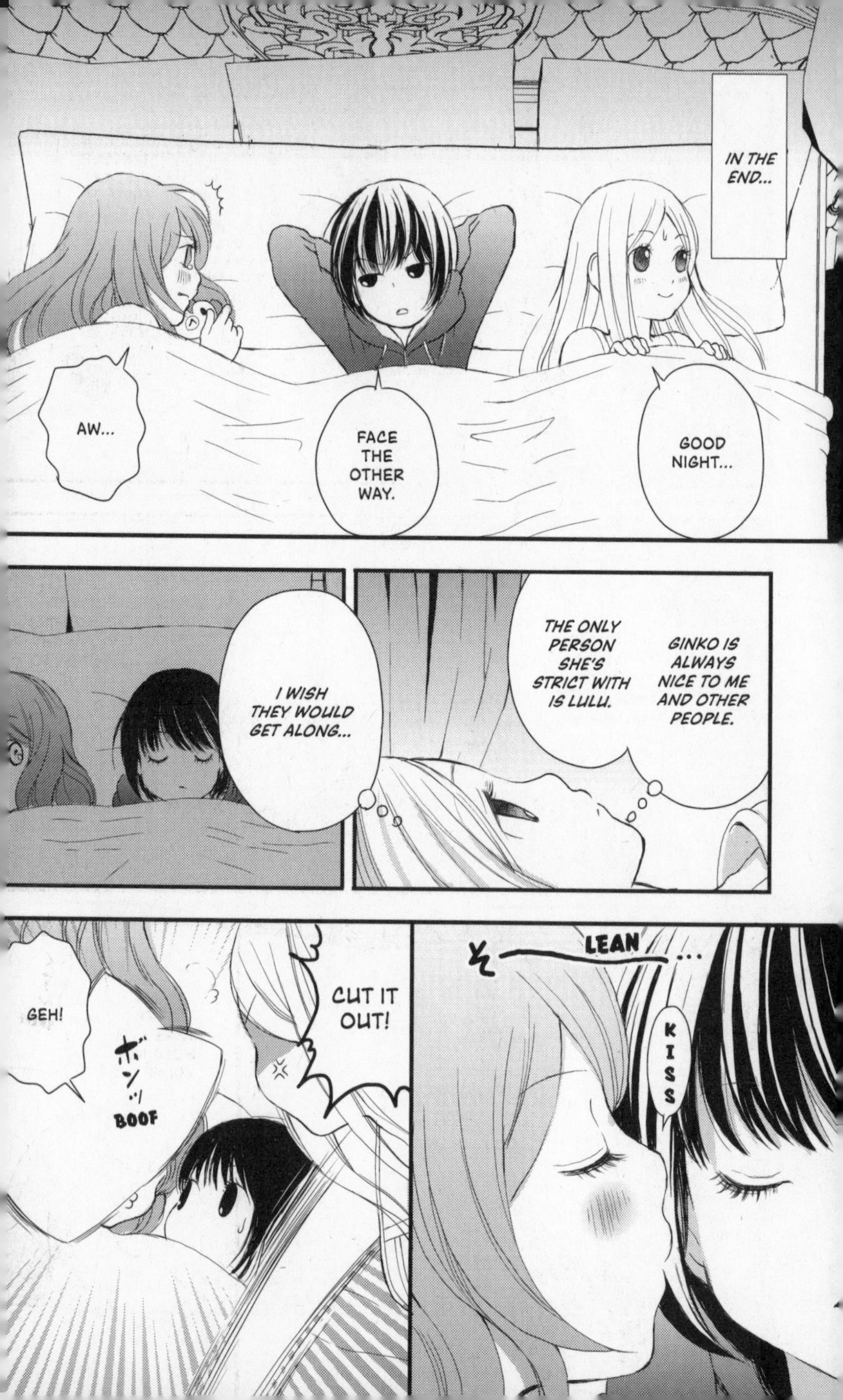

IN THE END...
GOOD NIGHT...
FACE THE OTHER WAY.
AW...
GINKO IS ALWAYS NICE TO ME AND OTHER PEOPLE.
THE ONLY PERSON SHE'S STRICT WITH IS LULU.
I WISH THEY WOULD GET ALONG...
LEAN...
KISS
CUT IT OUT!
GEH!
ボンッ
BOOF

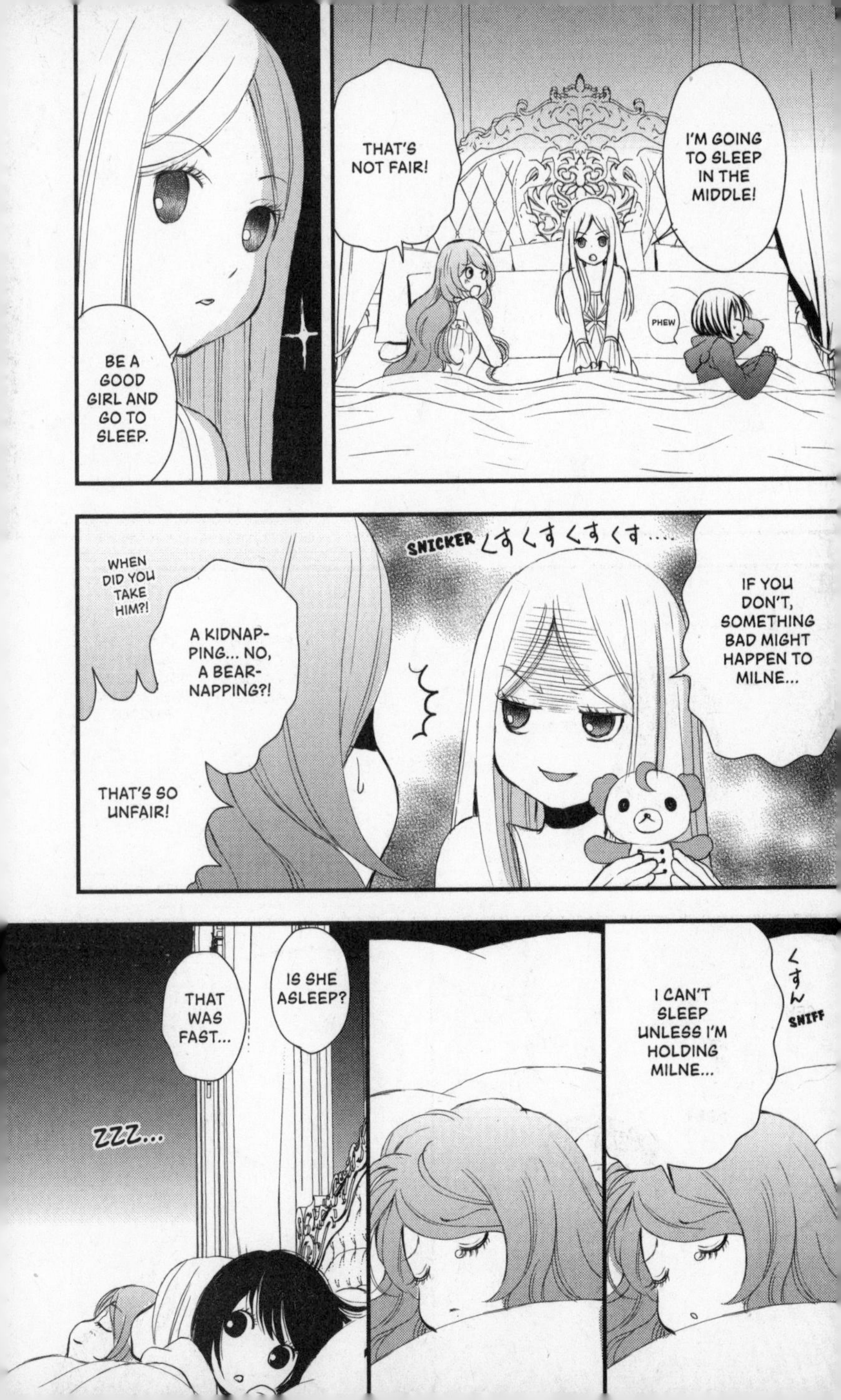
I'M GOING TO SLEEP IN THE MIDDLE!
PHEW
THAT'S NOT FAIR!
BE A GOOD GIRL AND GO TO SLEEP.
IF YOU DON'T, SOMETHING BAD MIGHT HAPPEN TO MILNE...
SNICKER くすくすくすくす....
A KIDNAP-PING... NO, A BEAR-NAPPING?!
WHEN DID YOU TAKE HIM?!
THAT'S SO UNFAIR!
くすん SNIFF
I CAN'T SLEEP UNLESS I'M HOLDING MILNE...
IS SHE ASLEEP?
THAT WAS FAST...
ZZZ...

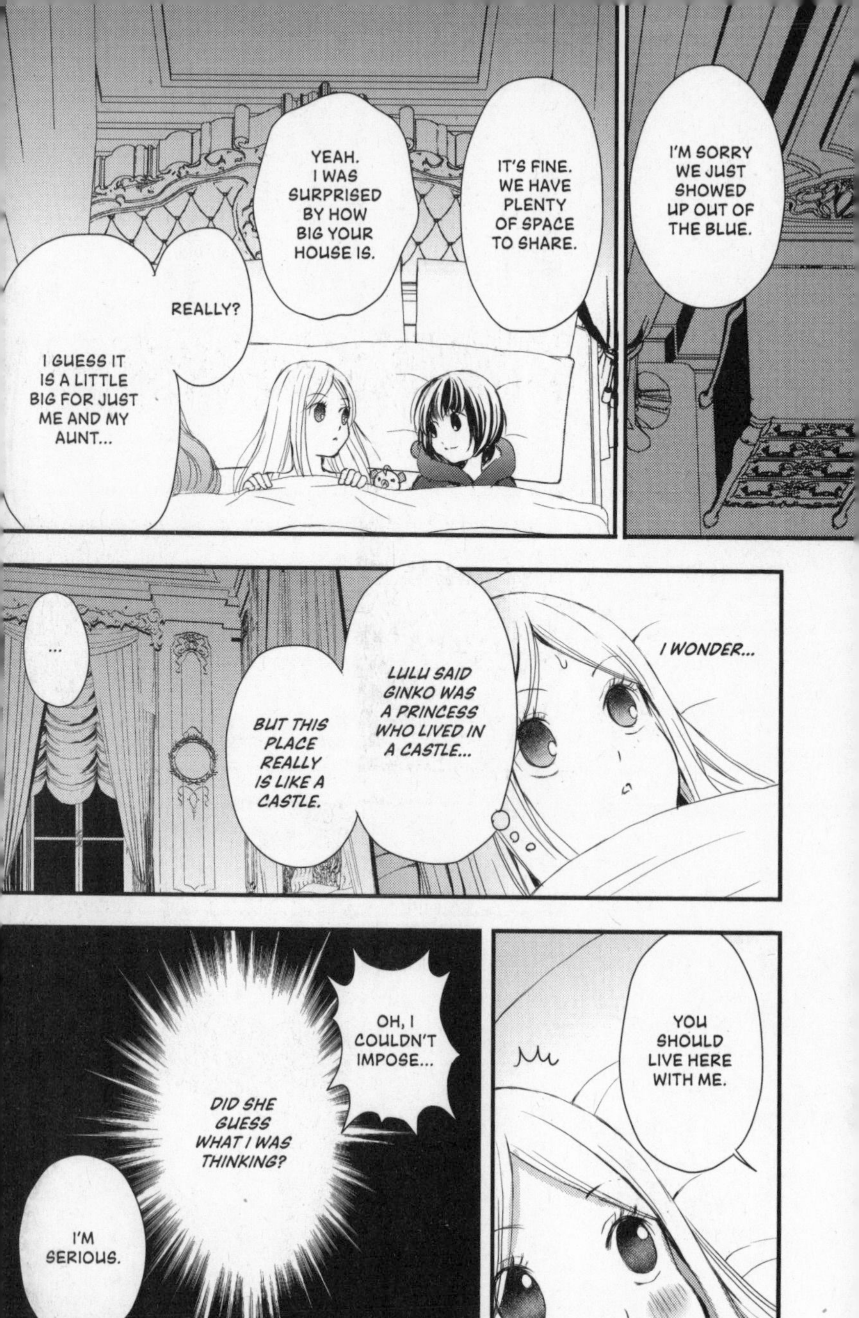
I'M SORRY WE JUST SHOWED UP OUT OF THE BLUE.
IT'S FINE. WE HAVE PLENTY OF SPACE TO SHARE.
YEAH. I WAS SURPRISED BY HOW BIG YOUR HOUSE IS.
REALLY?
I GUESS IT IS A LITTLE BIG FOR JUST ME AND MY AUNT...
I WONDER...
LULU SAID GINKO WAS A PRINCESS WHO LIVED IN A CASTLE...
BUT THIS PLACE REALLY IS LIKE A CASTLE.
...
YOU SHOULD LIVE HERE WITH ME.
OH, I COULDN'T IMPOSE...
DID SHE GUESS WHAT I WAS THINKING?
I'M SERIOUS.

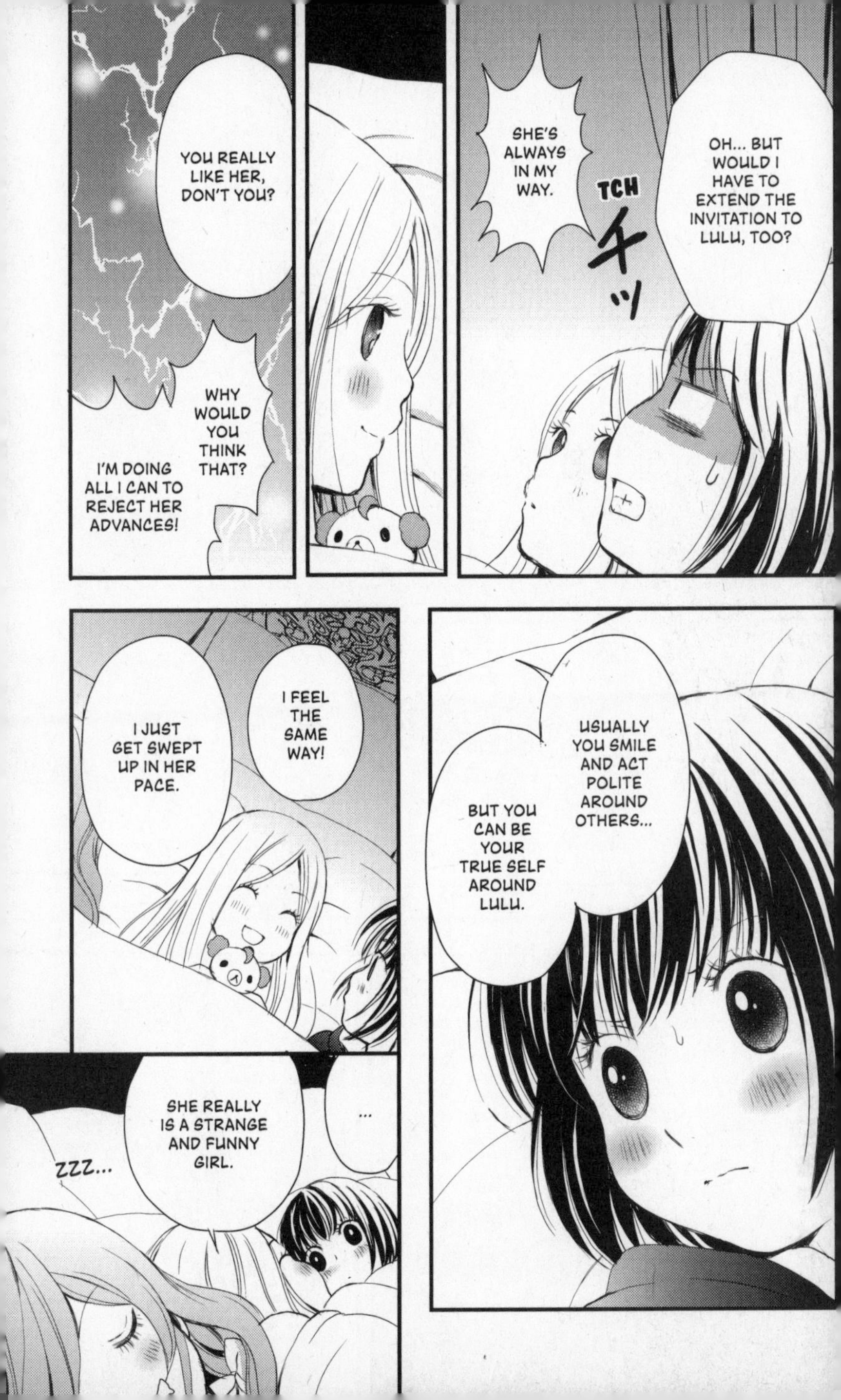
OH... BUT WOULD I HAVE TO EXTEND THE INVITATION TO LULU, TOO?
SHE'S ALWAYS IN MY WAY.
TCH
チッ
YOU REALLY LIKE HER, DON'T YOU?
WHY WOULD YOU THINK THAT?
I'M DOING ALL I CAN TO REJECT HER ADVANCES!
USUALLY YOU SMILE AND ACT POLITE AROUND OTHERS...
BUT YOU CAN BE YOUR TRUE SELF AROUND LULU.
I FEEL THE SAME WAY!
I JUST GET SWEPT UP IN HER PACE.
...
SHE REALLY IS A STRANGE AND FUNNY GIRL.
ZZZ...

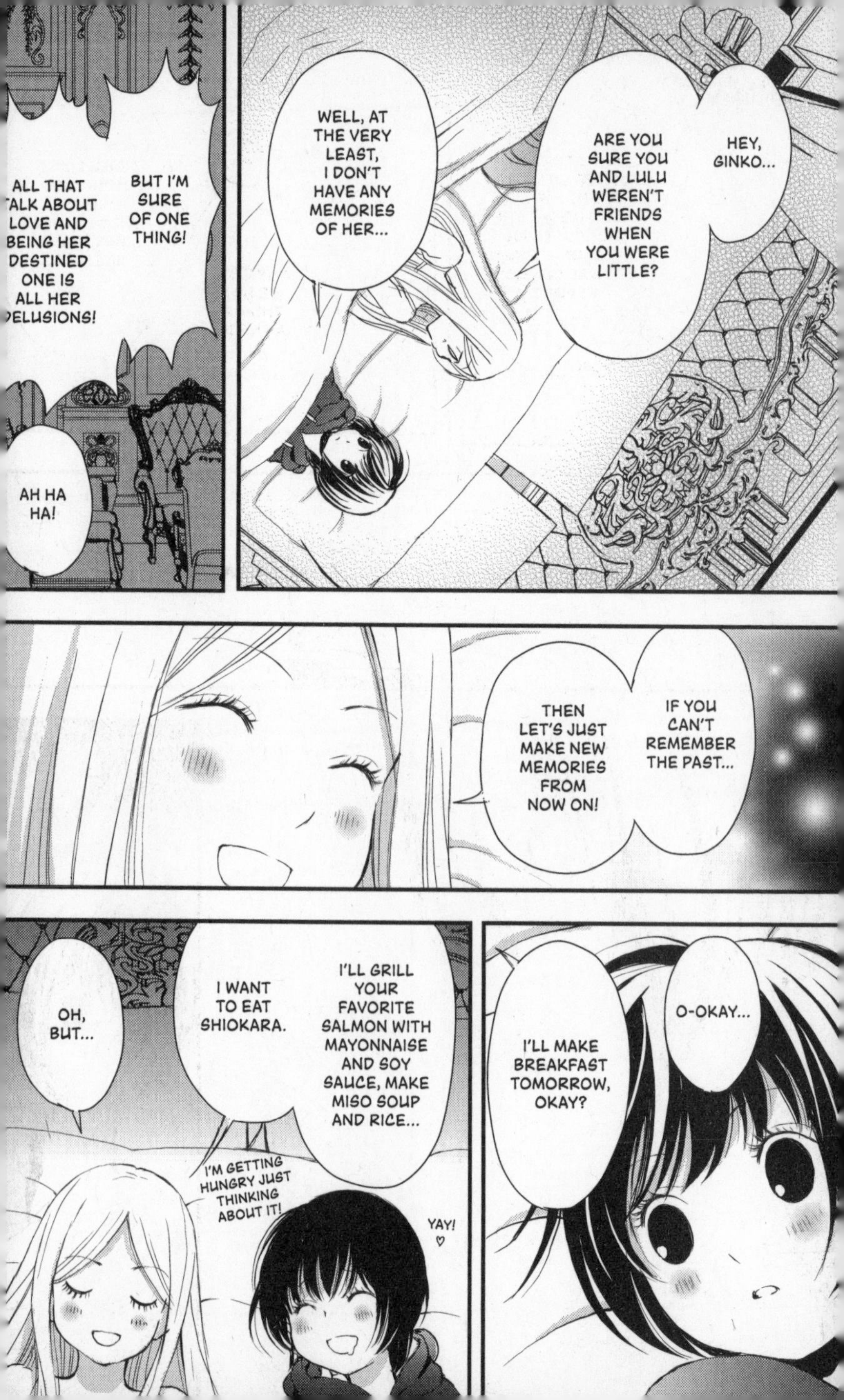
HEY, GINKO...
ARE YOU SURE YOU AND LULU WEREN'T FRIENDS WHEN YOU WERE LITTLE?
WELL, AT THE VERY LEAST, I DON'T HAVE ANY MEMORIES OF HER...
BUT I'M SURE OF ONE THING!
ALL THAT TALK ABOUT LOVE AND BEING HER DESTINED ONE IS ALL HER DELUSIONS!
AH HA HA!
IF YOU CAN'T REMEMBER THE PAST...
THEN LET'S JUST MAKE NEW MEMORIES FROM NOW ON!
O-OKAY...
I'LL MAKE BREAKFAST TOMORROW, OKAY?
I'LL GRILL YOUR FAVORITE SALMON WITH MAYONNAISE AND SOY SAUCE, MAKE MISO SOUP AND RICE...
I WANT TO EAT SHIOKARA.
OH, BUT...
YAY! ♡
I'M GETTING HUNGRY JUST THINKING ABOUT IT!

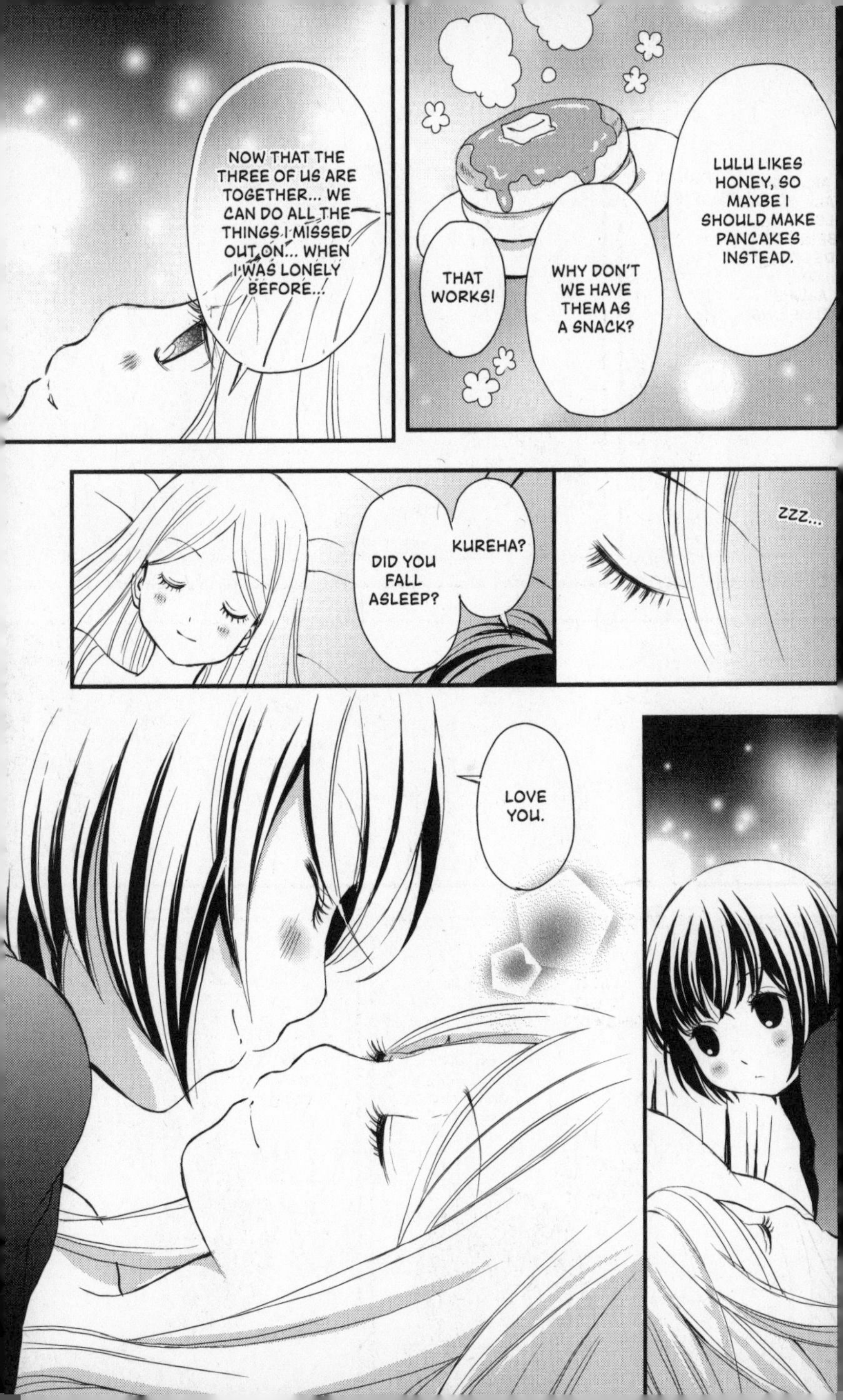
LULU LIKES HONEY, SO MAYBE I SHOULD MAKE PANCAKES INSTEAD.
WHY DON'T WE HAVE THEM AS A SNACK?
THAT WORKS!
NOW THAT THE THREE OF US ARE TOGETHER... WE CAN DO ALL THE THINGS I MISSED OUT ON... WHEN I WAS LONELY BEFORE...
ZZZ...
KUREHA?
DID YOU FALL ASLEEP?
LOVE YOU.

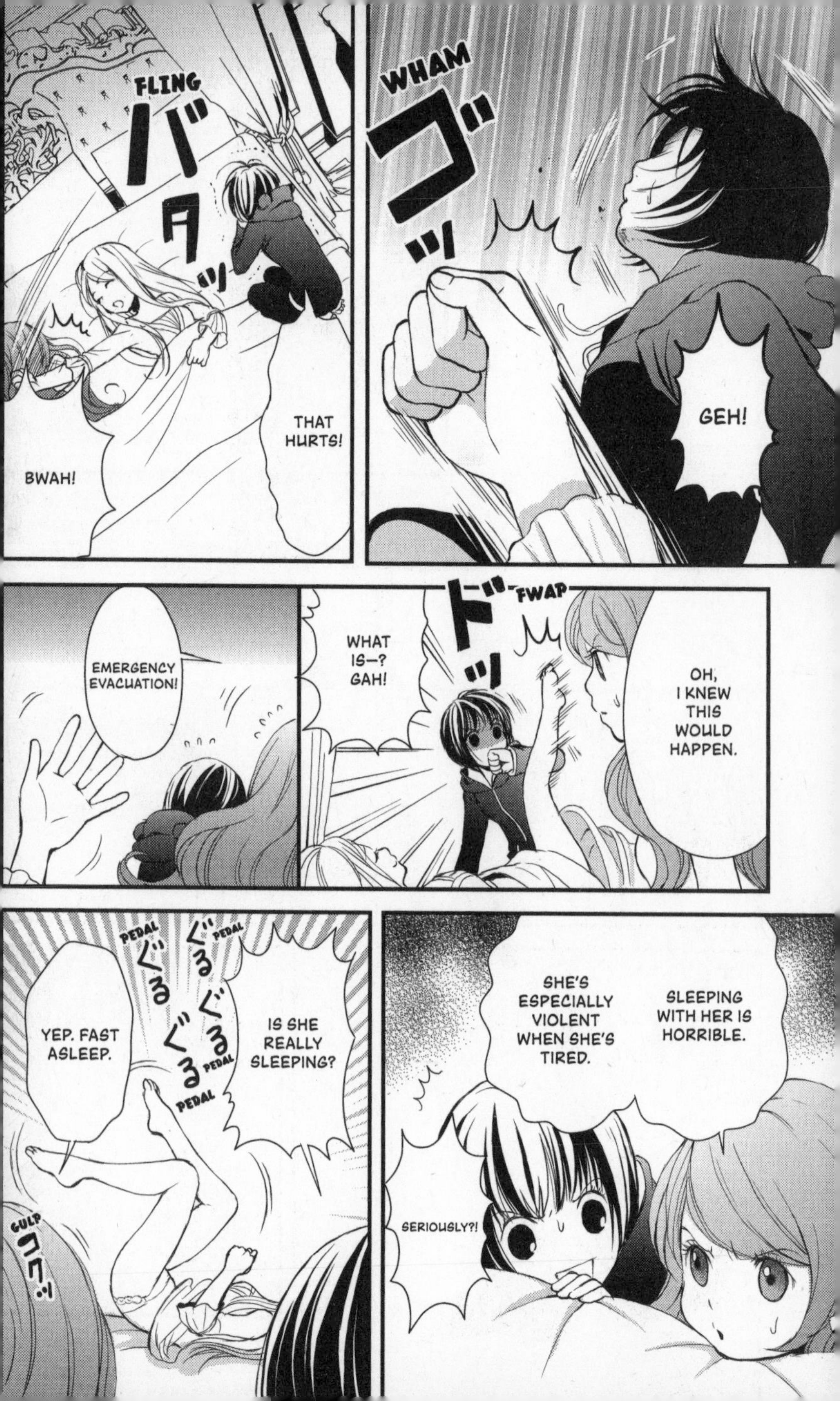
WHAM
ゴッ
GEH!
FLING
バタッ
THAT HURTS!
BWAH!
OH, I KNEW THIS WOULD HAPPEN.
ドッ
FWAP
WHAT IS—? GAH!
EMERGENCY EVACUATION!
SLEEPING WITH HER IS HORRIBLE.
SHE'S ESPECIALLY VIOLENT WHEN SHE'S TIRED.
SERIOUSLY?!
IS SHE REALLY SLEEPING?
PEDAL ぐるぐる PEDAL
ぐるぐる PEDAL PEDAL
YEP. FAST ASLEEP.
GULP
ゴクッ

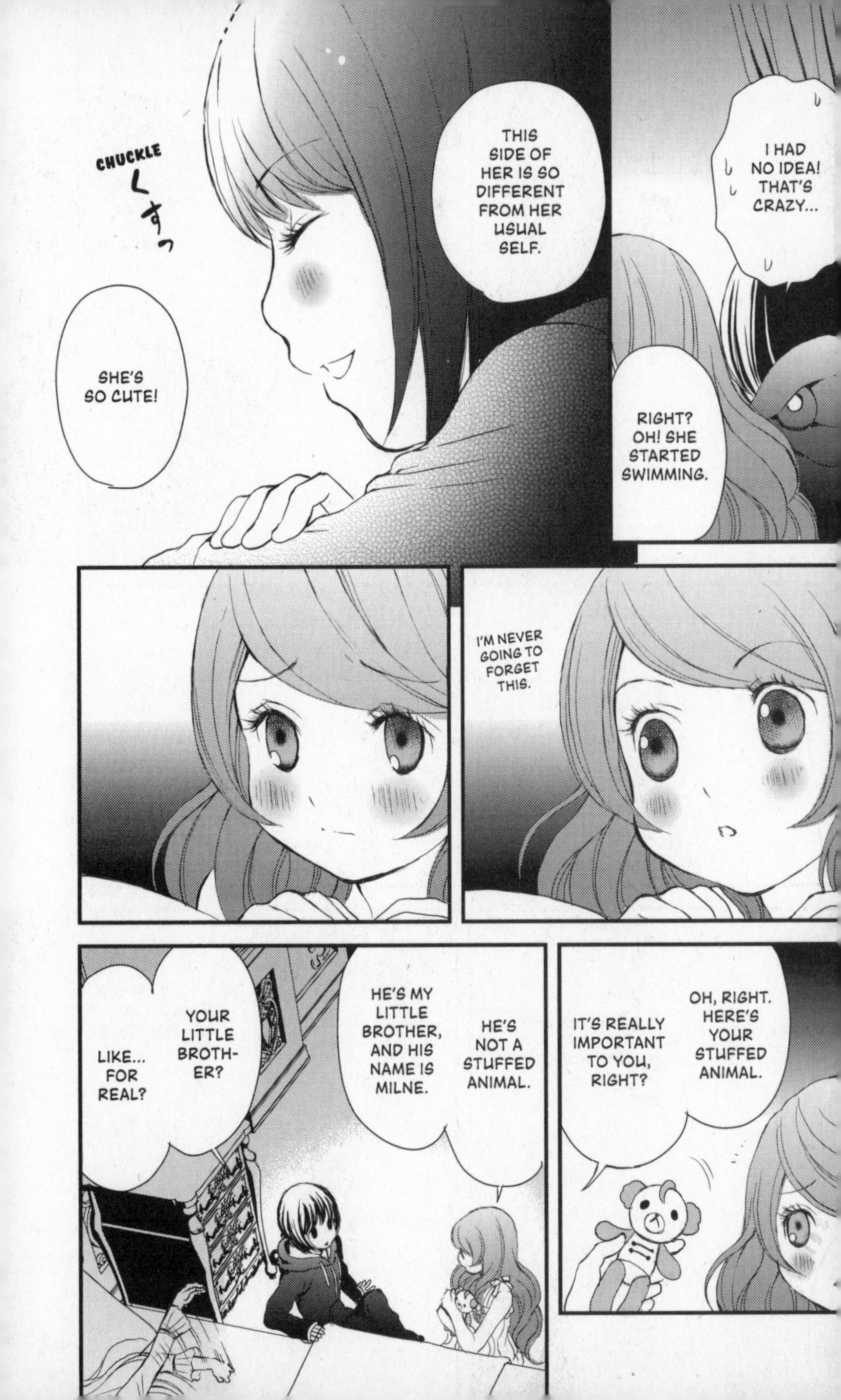
I HAD NO IDEA! THAT'S CRAZY...
RIGHT? OH! SHE STARTED SWIMMING.
THIS SIDE OF HER IS SO DIFFERENT FROM HER USUAL SELF.
CHUCKLE くすっ
SHE'S SO CUTE!
I'M NEVER GOING TO FORGET THIS.
OH, RIGHT. HERE'S YOUR STUFFED ANIMAL.
IT'S REALLY IMPORTANT TO YOU, RIGHT?
HE'S NOT A STUFFED ANIMAL.
HE'S MY LITTLE BROTHER, AND HIS NAME IS MILNE.
YOUR LITTLE BROTH-ER?
LIKE... FOR REAL?

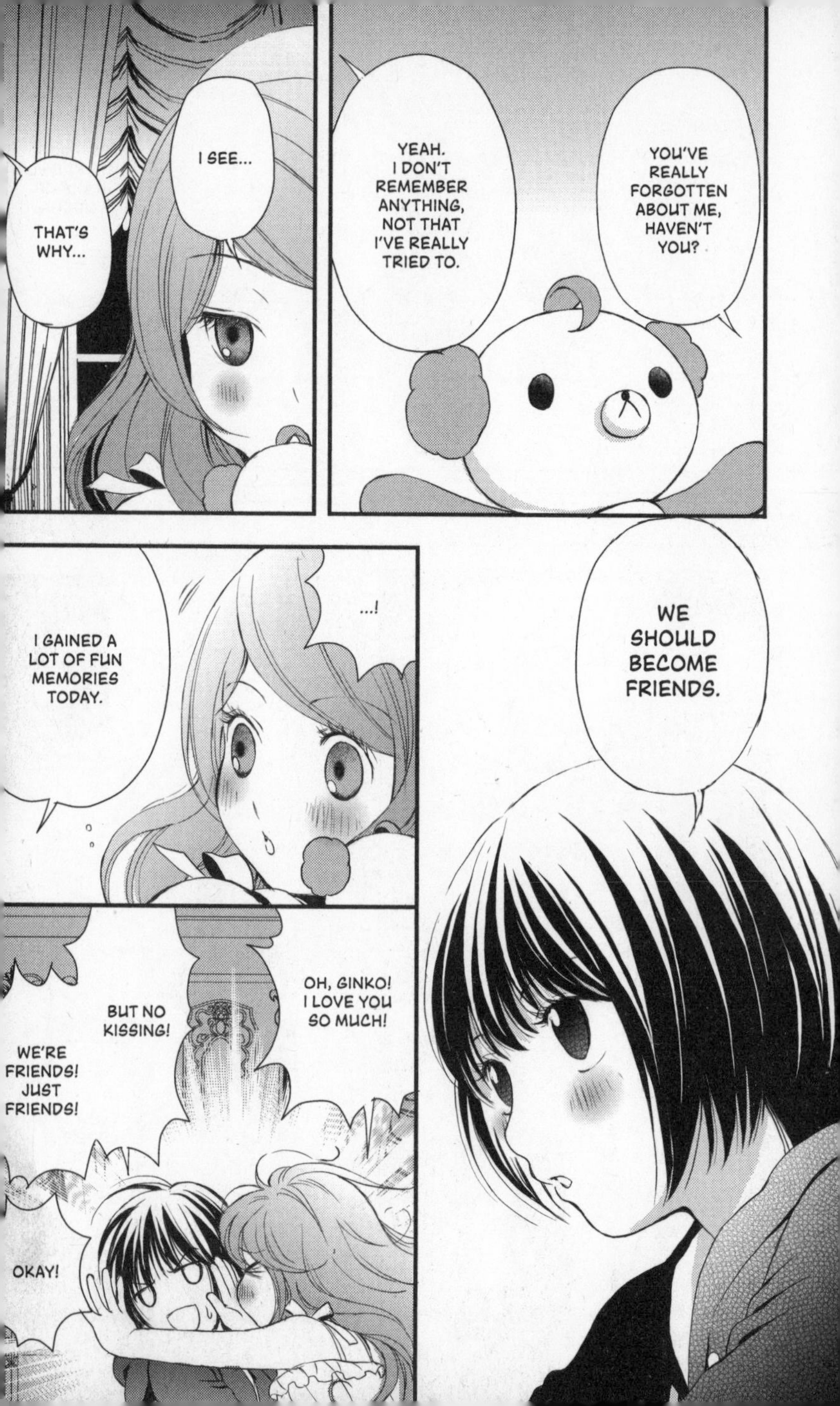
YOU'VE REALLY FORGOTTEN ABOUT ME, HAVEN'T YOU?
YEAH. I DON'T REMEMBER ANYTHING, NOT THAT I'VE REALLY TRIED TO.
I SEE...
THAT'S WHY...
WE SHOULD BECOME FRIENDS.
...!
I GAINED A LOT OF FUN MEMORIES TODAY.
OH, GINKO! I LOVE YOU SO MUCH!
BUT NO KISSING!
WE'RE FRIENDS! JUST FRIENDS!
OKAY!

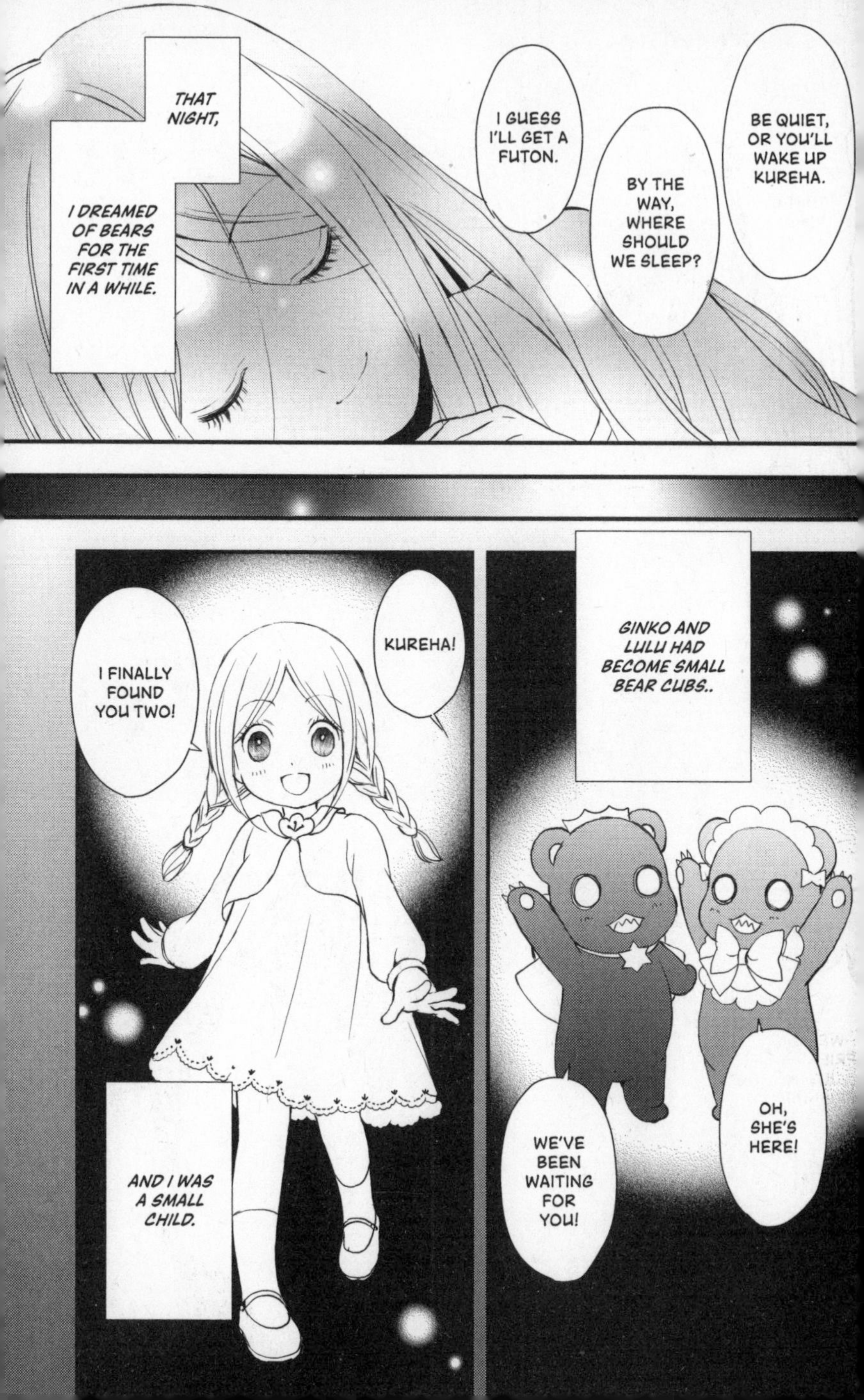
BE QUIET, OR YOU'LL WAKE UP KUREHA.
BY THE WAY, WHERE SHOULD WE SLEEP?
I GUESS I'LL GET A FUTON.
THAT NIGHT,
I DREAMED OF BEARS FOR THE FIRST TIME IN A WHILE.
GINKO AND LULU HAD BECOME SMALL BEAR CUBS..
OH, SHE'S HERE!
WE'VE BEEN WAITING FOR YOU!
KUREHA!
I FINALLY FOUND YOU TWO!
AND I WAS A SMALL CHILD.

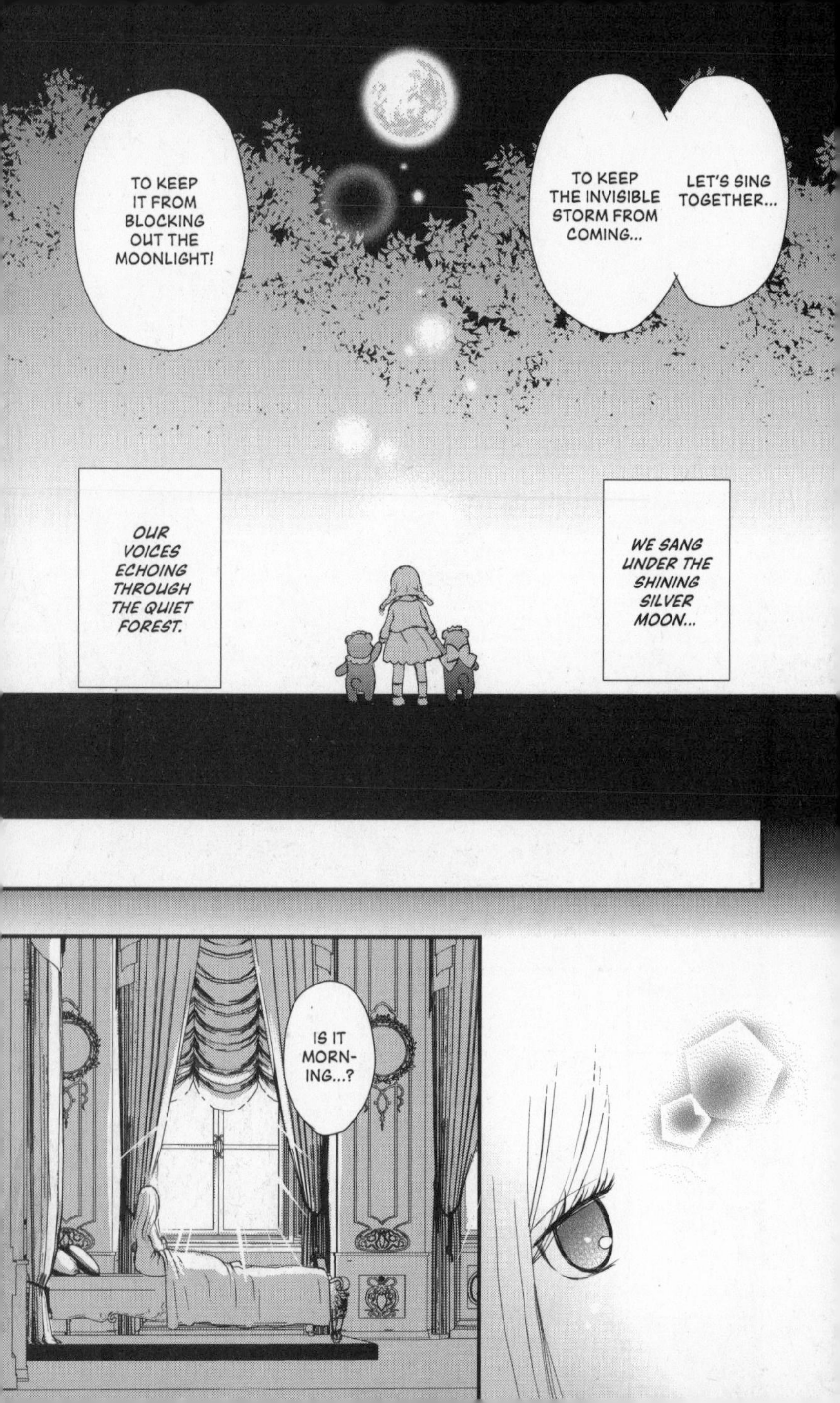
LET'S SING TOGETHER...
TO KEEP THE INVISIBLE STORM FROM COMING...
TO KEEP IT FROM BLOCKING OUT THE MOONLIGHT!
WE SANG UNDER THE SHINING SILVER MOON...
OUR VOICES ECHOING THROUGH THE QUIET FOREST.
IS IT MORN-ING...?

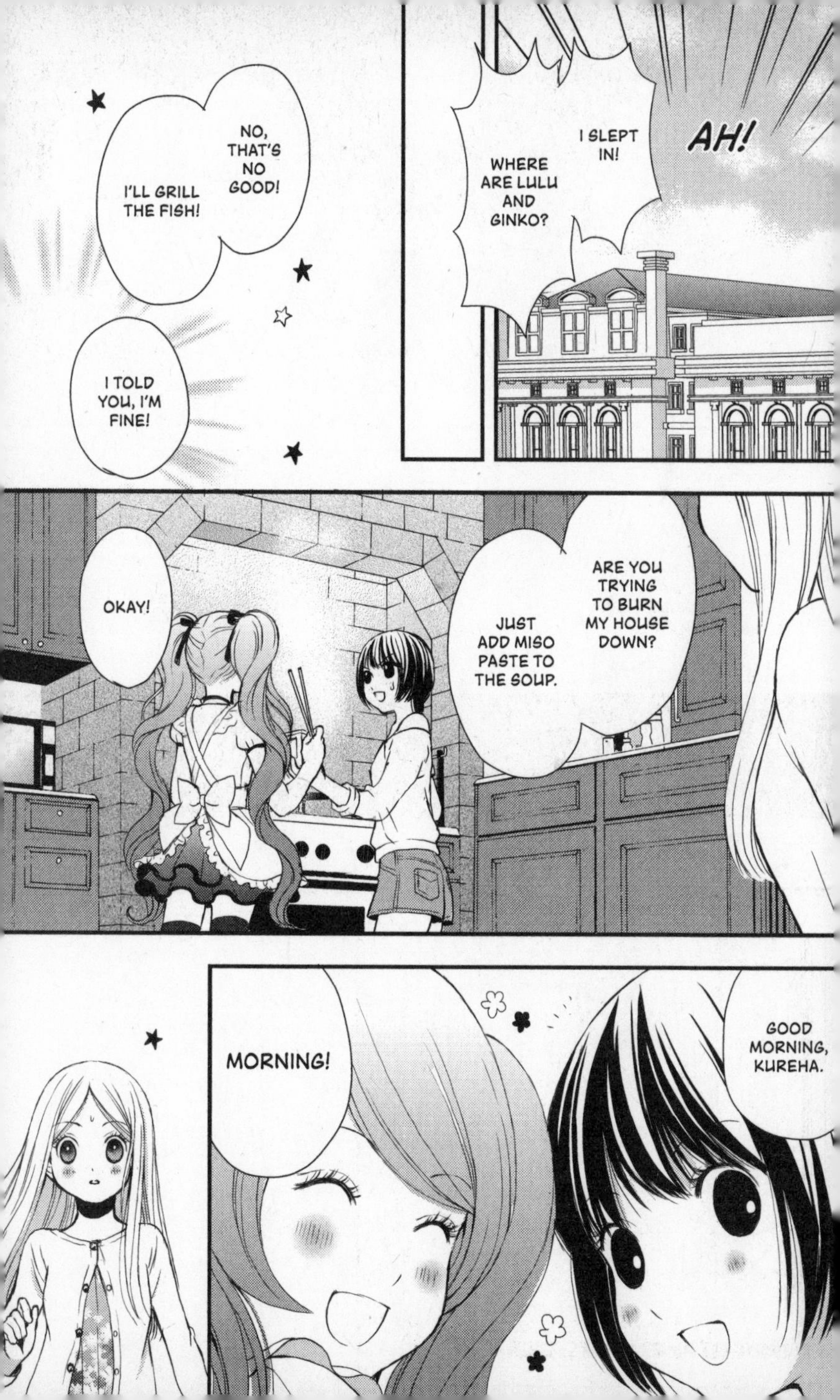
AH!
I SLEPT IN!
WHERE ARE LULU AND GINKO?
NO, THAT'S NO GOOD!
I'LL GRILL THE FISH!
I TOLD YOU, I'M FINE!
ARE YOU TRYING TO BURN MY HOUSE DOWN?
JUST ADD MISO PASTE TO THE SOUP.
OKAY!
GOOD MORNING, KUREHA.
MORNING!

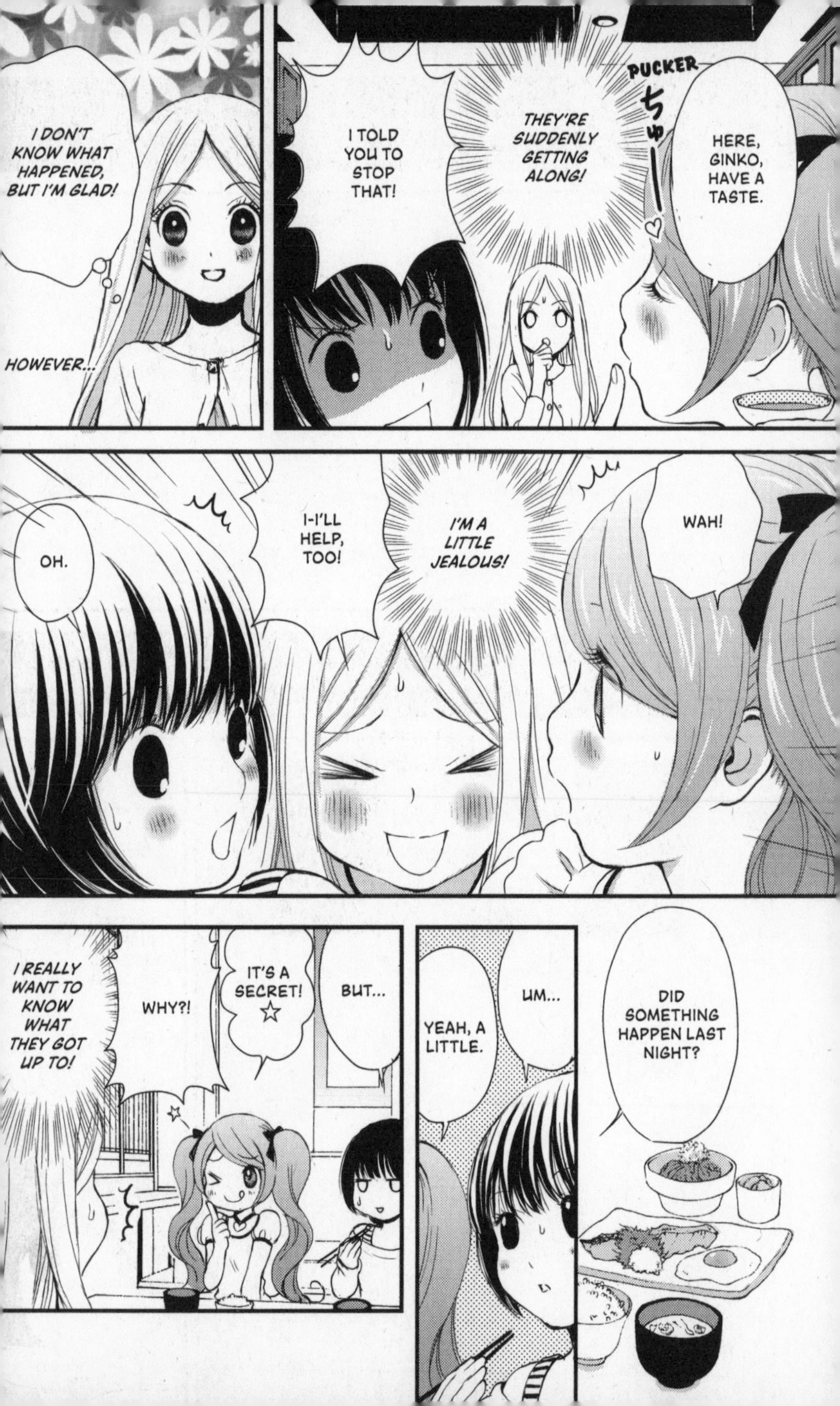
PUCKER
ちゅー
HERE, GINKO, HAVE A TASTE.
THEY'RE SUDDENLY GETTING ALONG!
I TOLD YOU TO STOP THAT!
I DON'T KNOW WHAT HAPPENED, BUT I'M GLAD!
HOWEVER...
WAH!
I'M A LITTLE JEALOUS!
I-I'LL HELP, TOO!
OH.
DID SOMETHING HAPPEN LAST NIGHT?
UM...
YEAH, A LITTLE.
BUT...
IT'S A SECRET! ☆
WHY?!
I REALLY WANT TO KNOW WHAT THEY GOT UP TO!

# Chapter 7

*BEARS ARE THE ARCHE OF EVERYTHING.*

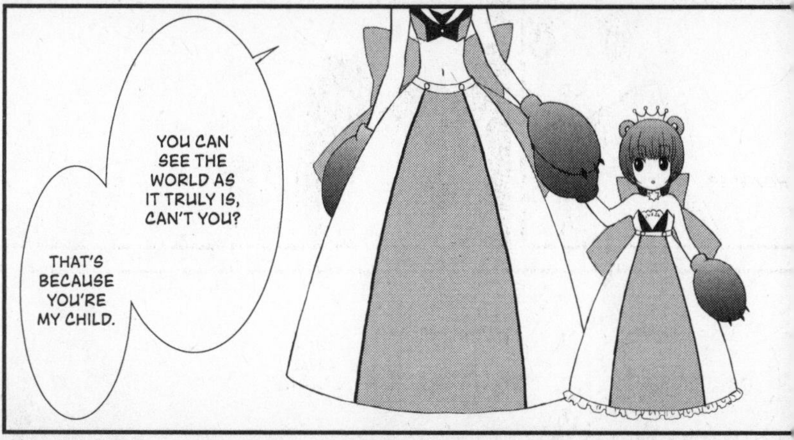
YOU CAN SEE THE WORLD AS IT TRULY IS, CAN'T YOU?
THAT'S BECAUSE YOU'RE MY CHILD.

*ARCHE AND TELOS. BEARS ARE THE BEGINNING AND END OF EVERYTHING.*

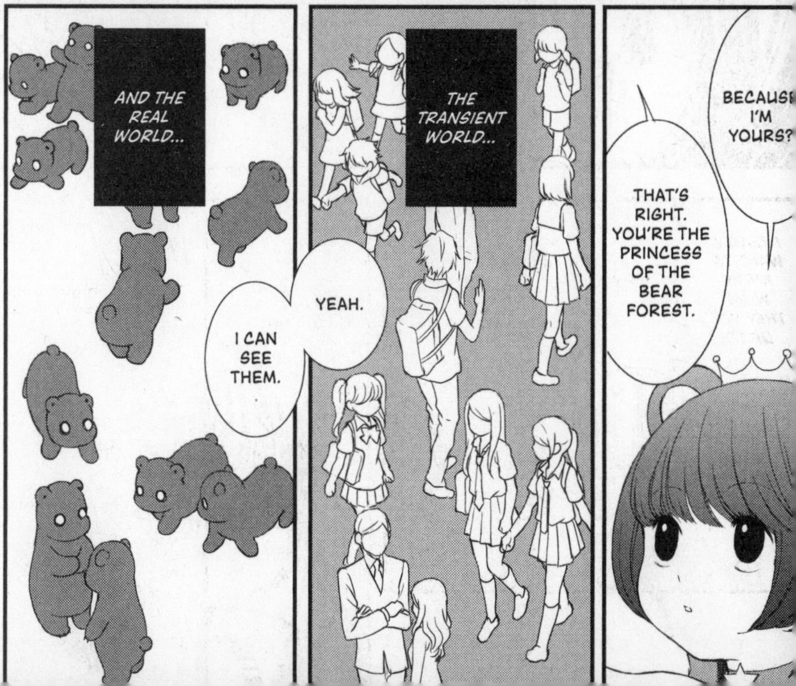
BECAUSE I'M YOURS?
THAT'S RIGHT. YOU'RE THE PRINCESS OF THE BEAR FOREST.
THE TRANSIENT WORLD...
YEAH.
I CAN SEE THEM.
AND THE REAL WORLD...

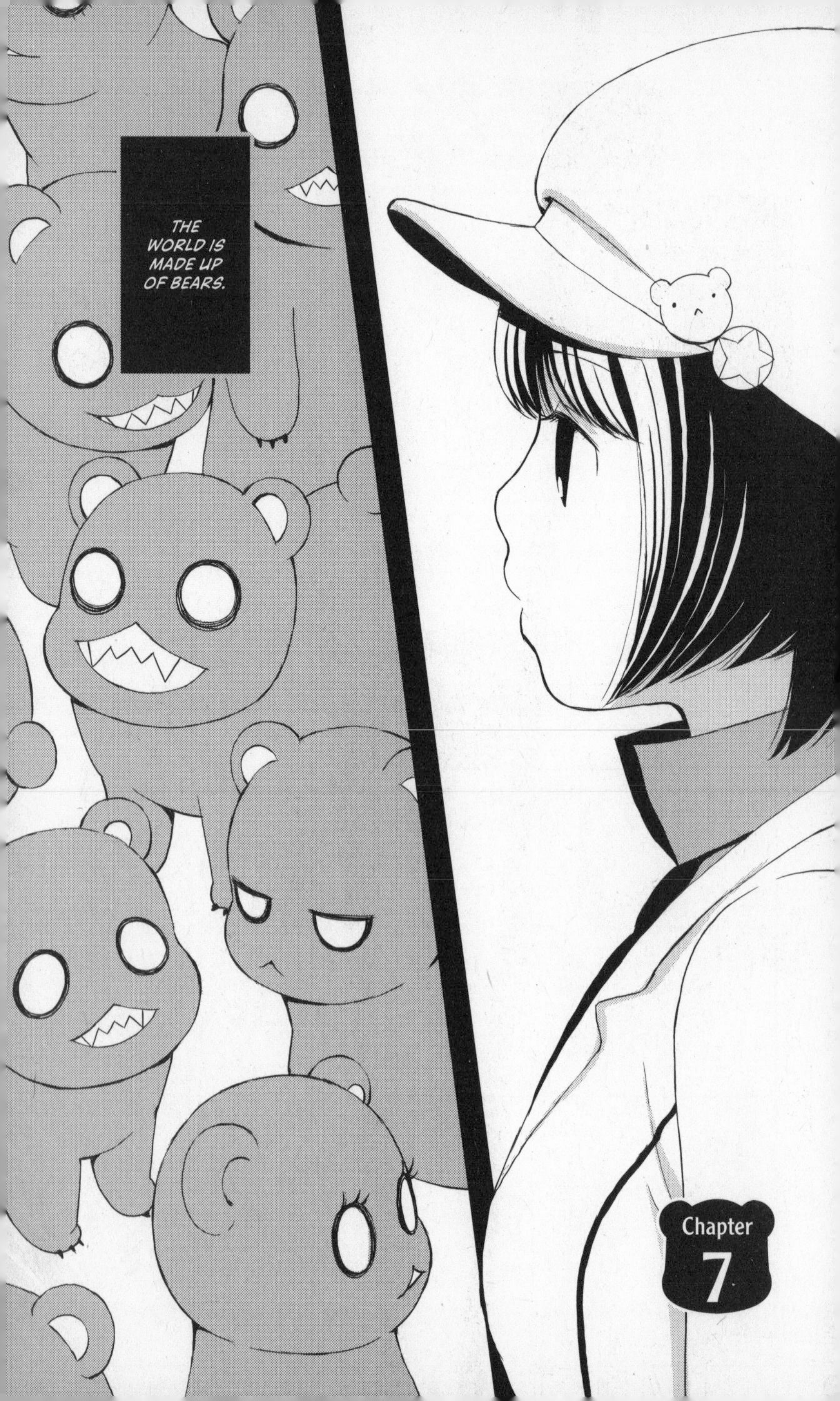
THE WORLD IS MADE UP OF BEARS.
Chapter 7

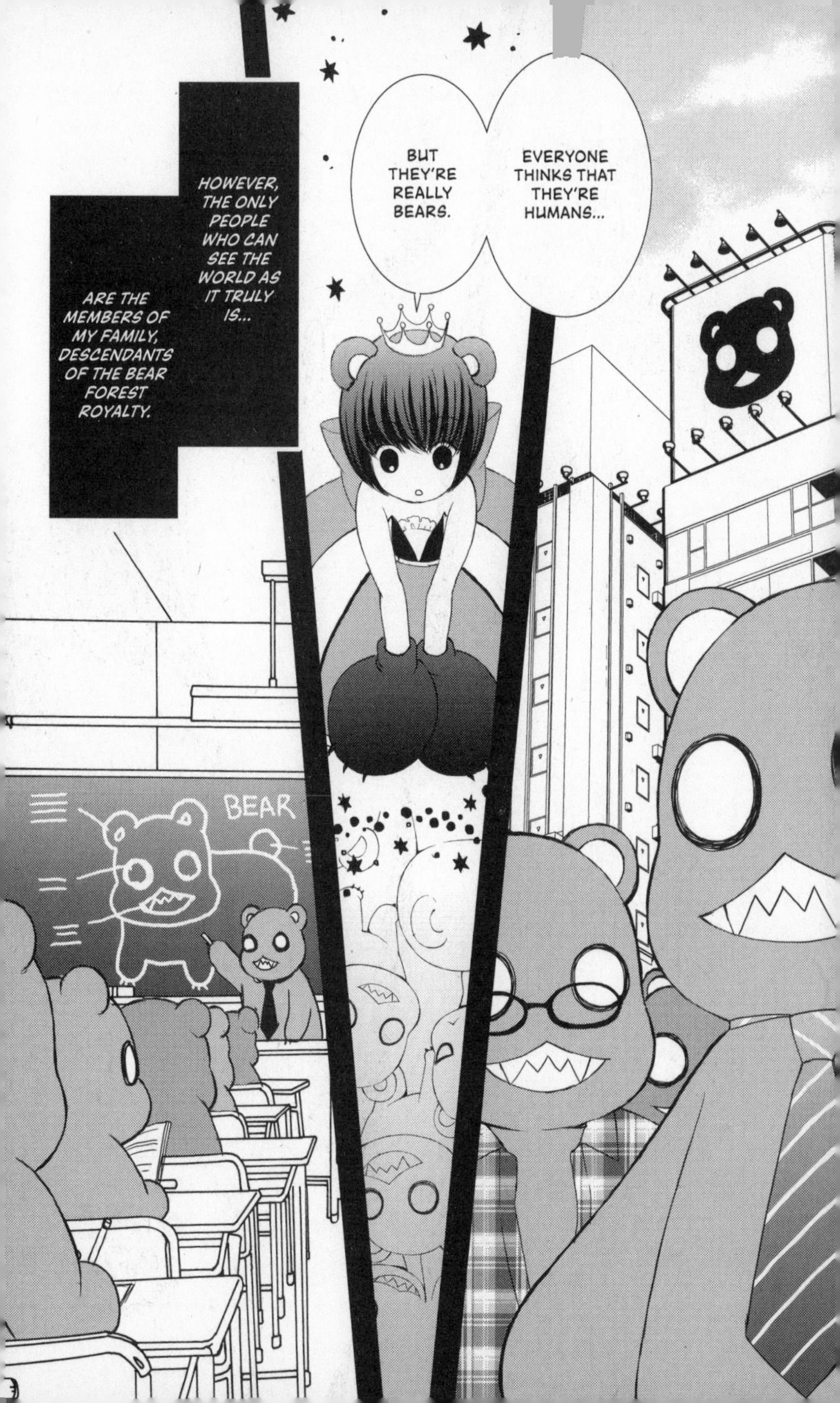

EVERYONE THINKS THAT THEY'RE HUMANS...
BUT THEY'RE REALLY BEARS.
HOWEVER, THE ONLY PEOPLE WHO CAN SEE THE WORLD AS IT TRULY IS...
ARE THE MEMBERS OF MY FAMILY, DESCENDANTS OF THE BEAR FOREST ROYALTY.
BEAR

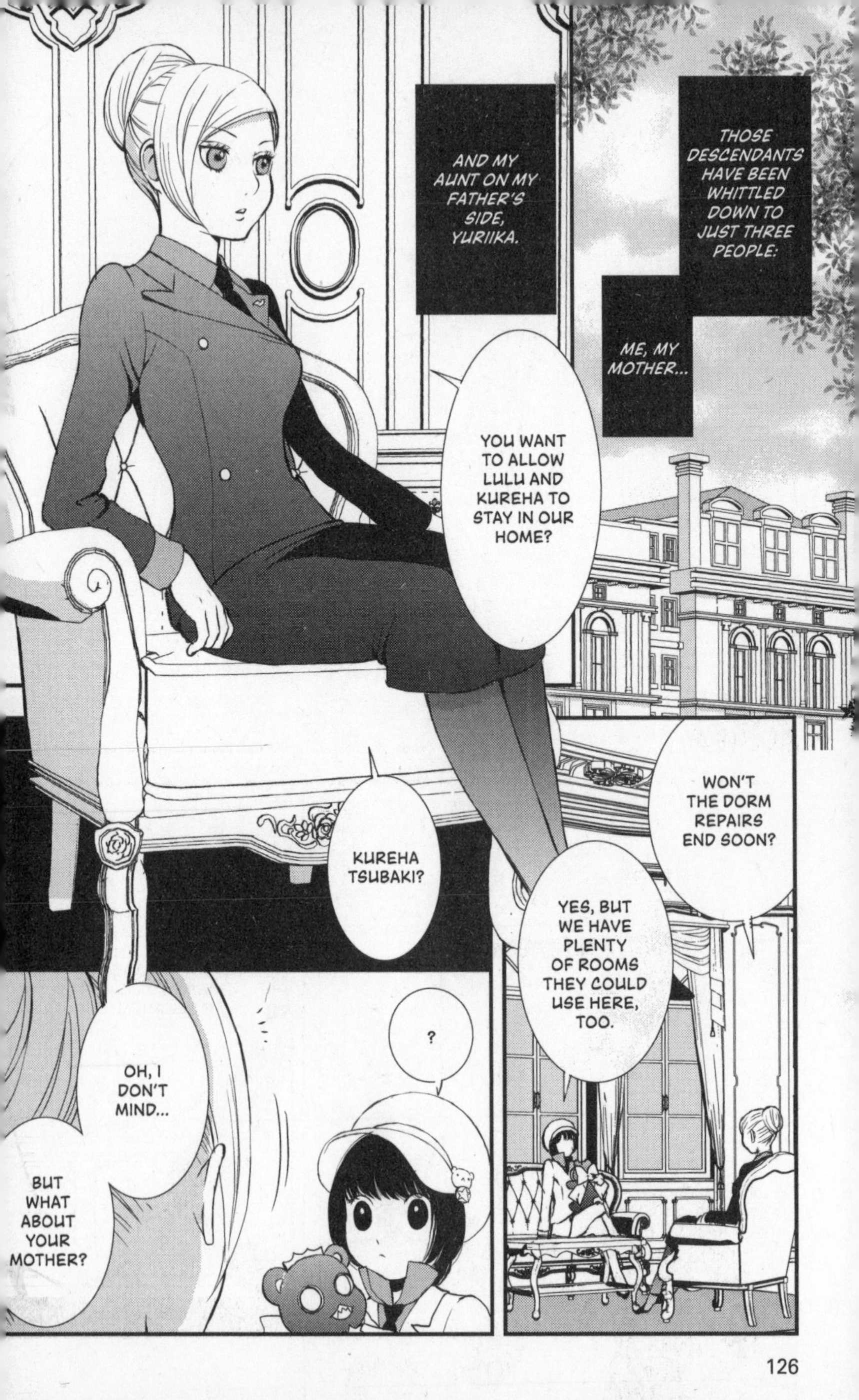
THOSE DESCENDANTS HAVE BEEN WHITTLED DOWN TO JUST THREE PEOPLE:
ME, MY MOTHER...
AND MY AUNT ON MY FATHER'S SIDE, YURIIKA.
YOU WANT TO ALLOW LULU AND KUREHA TO STAY IN OUR HOME?
WON'T THE DORM REPAIRS END SOON?
YES, BUT WE HAVE PLENTY OF ROOMS THEY COULD USE HERE, TOO.
KUREHA TSUBAKI?
?
OH, I DON'T MIND...
BUT WHAT ABOUT YOUR MOTHER?

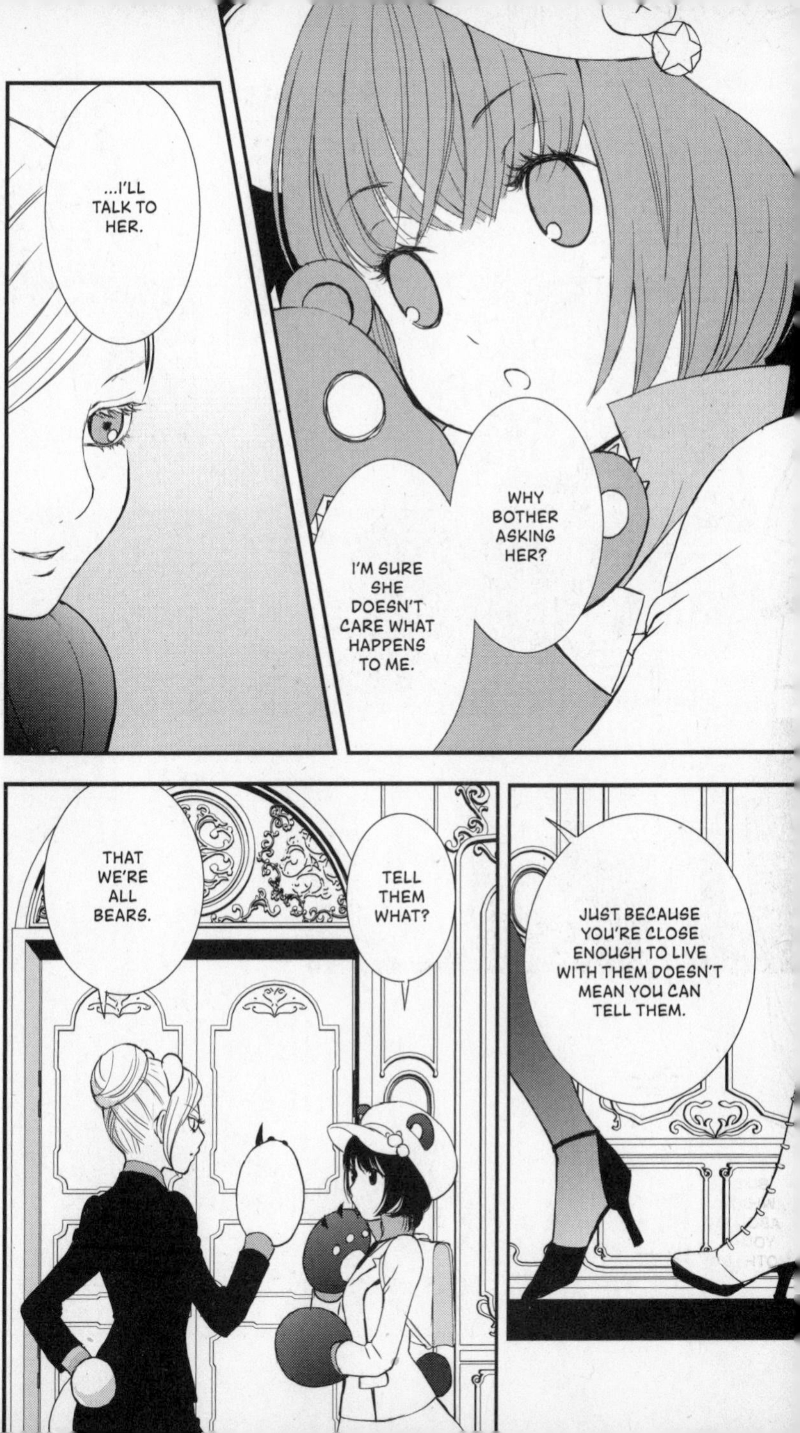
WHY BOTHER ASKING HER?
I'M SURE SHE DOESN'T CARE WHAT HAPPENS TO ME.
...I'LL TALK TO HER.
JUST BECAUSE YOU'RE CLOSE ENOUGH TO LIVE WITH THEM DOESN'T MEAN YOU CAN TELL THEM.
TELL THEM WHAT?
THAT WE'RE ALL BEARS.

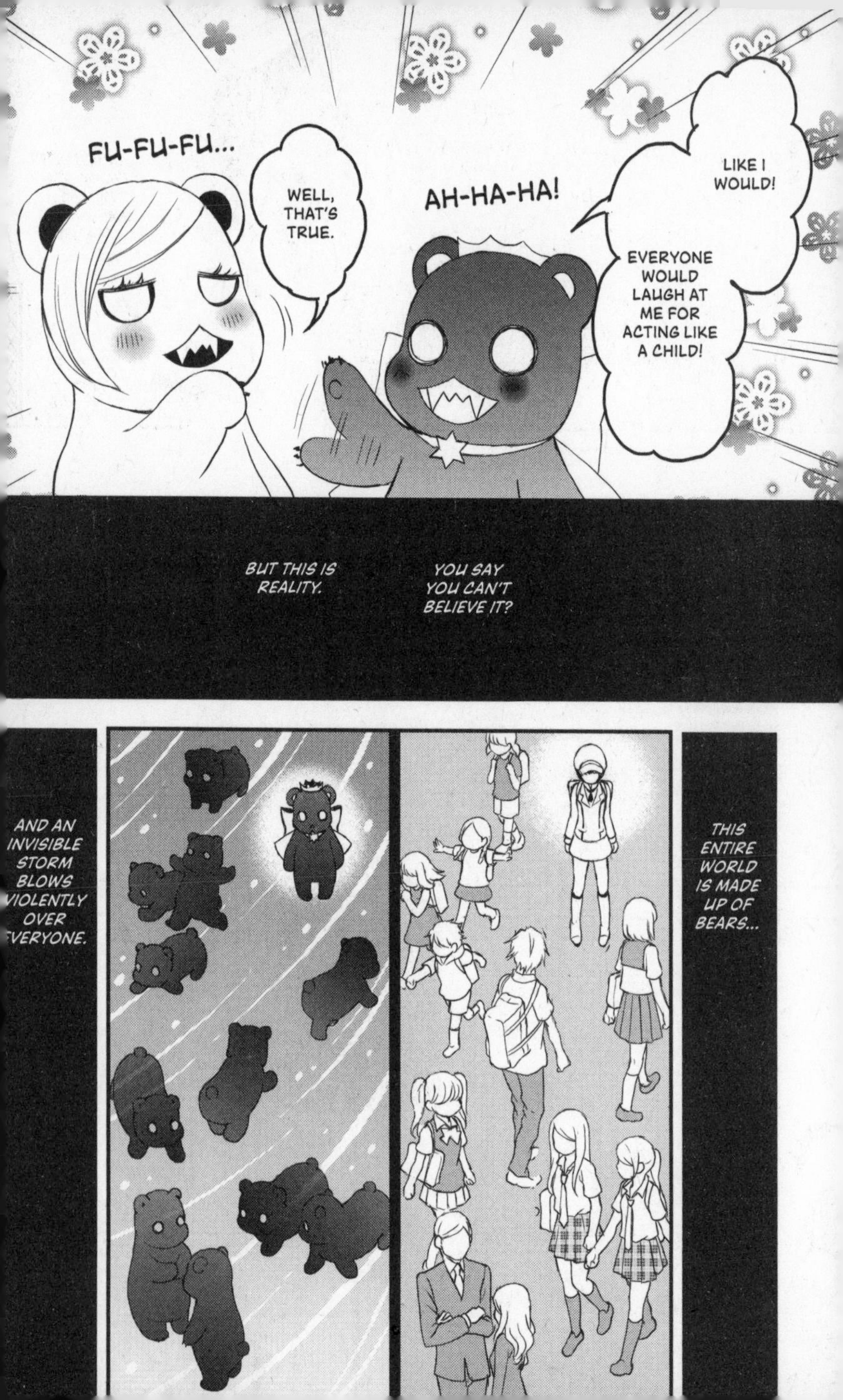
AH-HA-HA!
LIKE I WOULD!
EVERYONE WOULD LAUGH AT ME FOR ACTING LIKE A CHILD!
FU-FU-FU...
WELL, THAT'S TRUE.
YOU SAY YOU CAN'T BELIEVE IT?
BUT THIS IS REALITY.
THIS ENTIRE WORLD IS MADE UP OF BEARS...
AND AN INVISIBLE STORM BLOWS VIOLENTLY OVER EVERYONE.

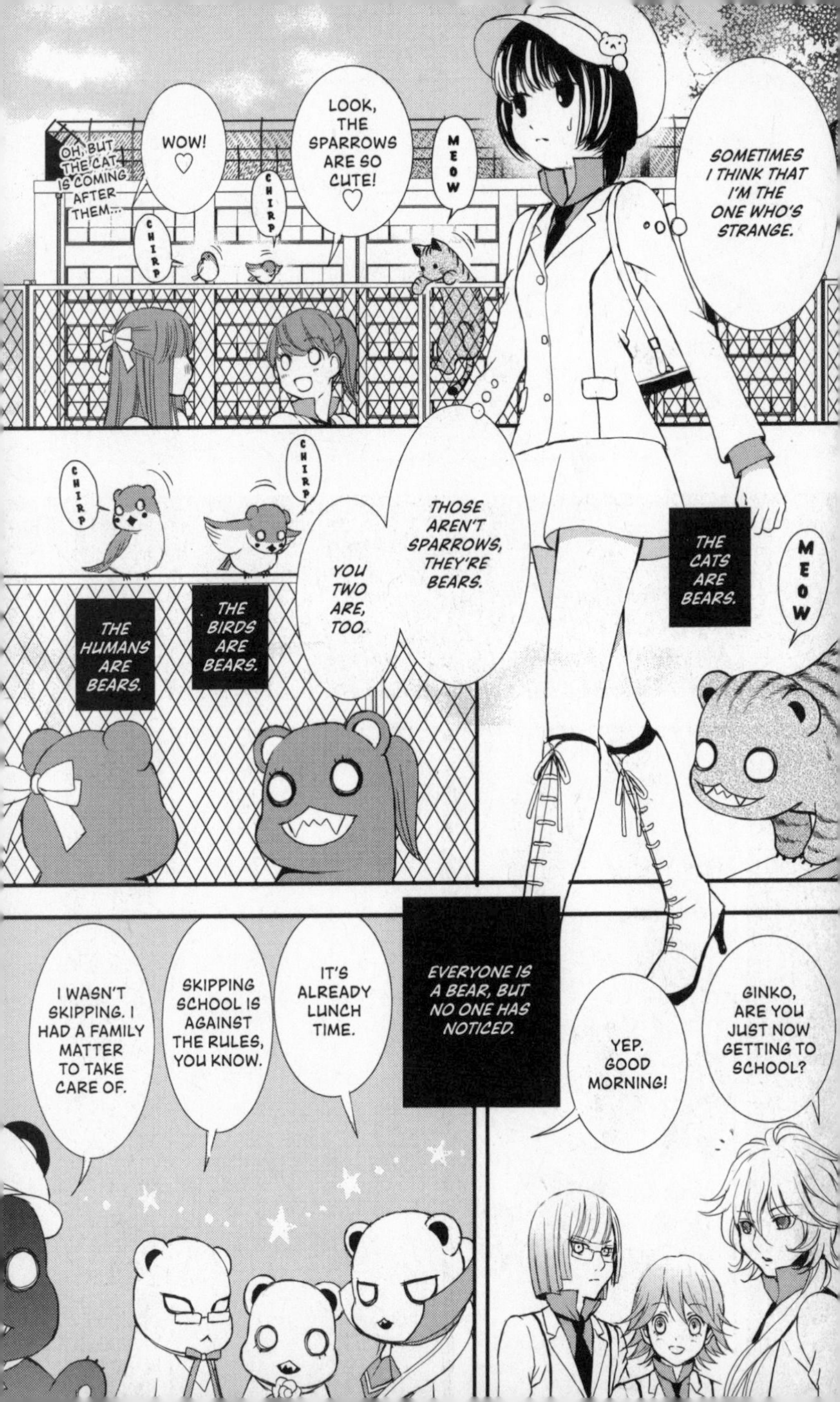
SOMETIMES I THINK THAT I'M THE ONE WHO'S STRANGE.
MEOW
LOOK, THE SPARROWS ARE SO CUTE! ♡
CHIRP
WOW! ♡
CHIRP
OH, BUT THE CAT IS COMING AFTER THEM...
THE CATS ARE BEARS.
MEOW
THOSE AREN'T SPARROWS, THEY'RE BEARS.
YOU TWO ARE, TOO.
CHIRP
CHIRP
THE BIRDS ARE BEARS.
THE HUMANS ARE BEARS.
EVERYONE IS A BEAR, BUT NO ONE HAS NOTICED.
GINKO, ARE YOU JUST NOW GETTING TO SCHOOL?
YEP. GOOD MORNING!
IT'S ALREADY LUNCH TIME.
SKIPPING SCHOOL IS AGAINST THE RULES, YOU KNOW.
I WASN'T SKIPPING. I HAD A FAMILY MATTER TO TAKE CARE OF.

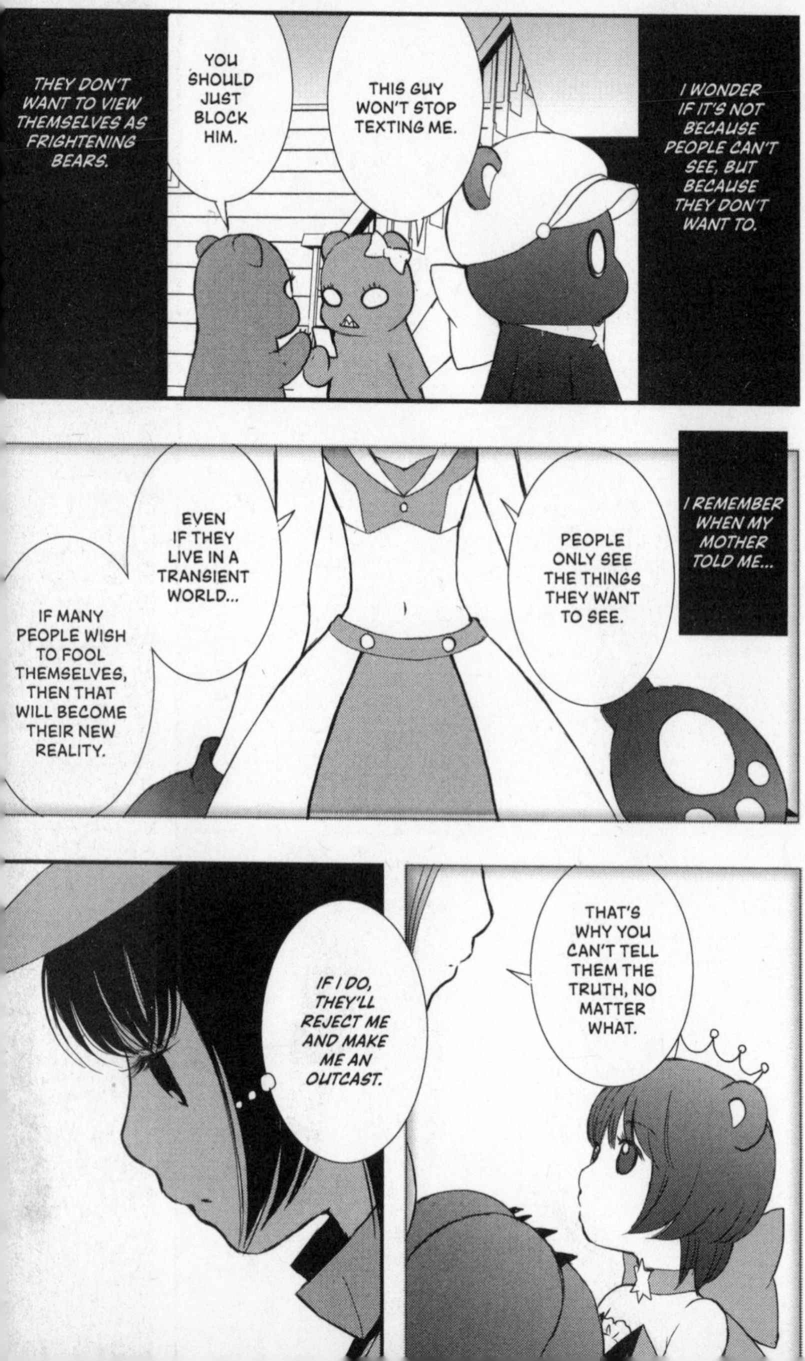

I WONDER IF IT'S NOT BECAUSE PEOPLE CAN'T SEE, BUT BECAUSE THEY DON'T WANT TO.
THIS GUY WON'T STOP TEXTING ME.
YOU SHOULD JUST BLOCK HIM.
THEY DON'T WANT TO VIEW THEMSELVES AS FRIGHTENING BEARS.
I REMEMBER WHEN MY MOTHER TOLD ME...
PEOPLE ONLY SEE THE THINGS THEY WANT TO SEE.
EVEN IF THEY LIVE IN A TRANSIENT WORLD...
IF MANY PEOPLE WISH TO FOOL THEMSELVES, THEN THAT WILL BECOME THEIR NEW REALITY.
THAT'S WHY YOU CAN'T TELL THEM THE TRUTH, NO MATTER WHAT.
IF I DO, THEY'LL REJECT ME AND MAKE ME AN OUTCAST.

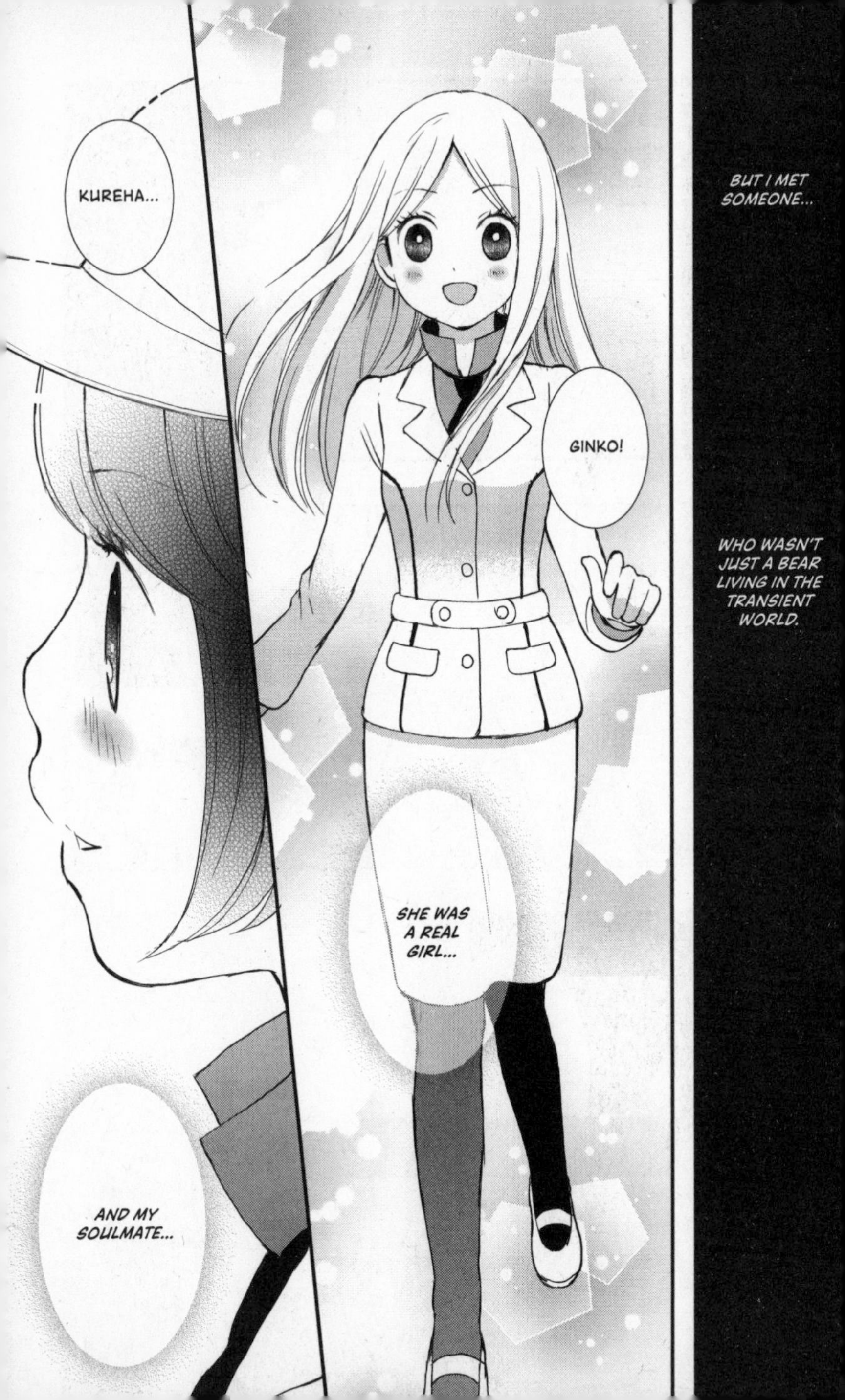
BUT I MET SOMEONE...
WHO WASN'T JUST A BEAR LIVING IN THE TRANSIENT WORLD.
GINKO!
SHE WAS A REAL GIRL...
KUREHA...
AND MY SOULMATE...

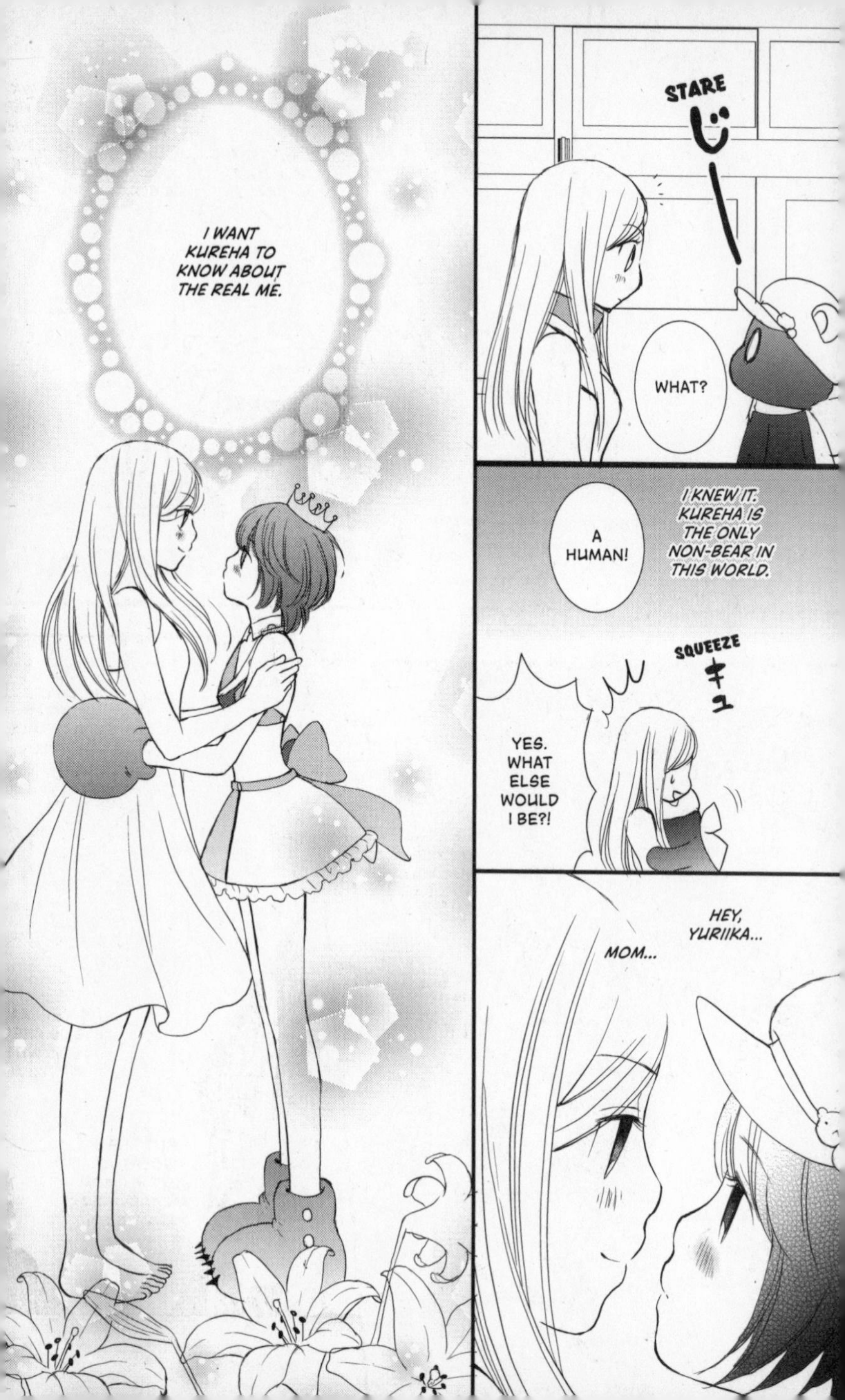
STARE
じー
WHAT?
I KNEW IT. KUREHA IS THE ONLY NON-BEAR IN THIS WORLD.
A HUMAN!
SQUEEZE
キュ
YES. WHAT ELSE WOULD I BE?!
HEY, YURIIKA...
MOM...
I WANT KUREHA TO KNOW ABOUT THE REAL ME.

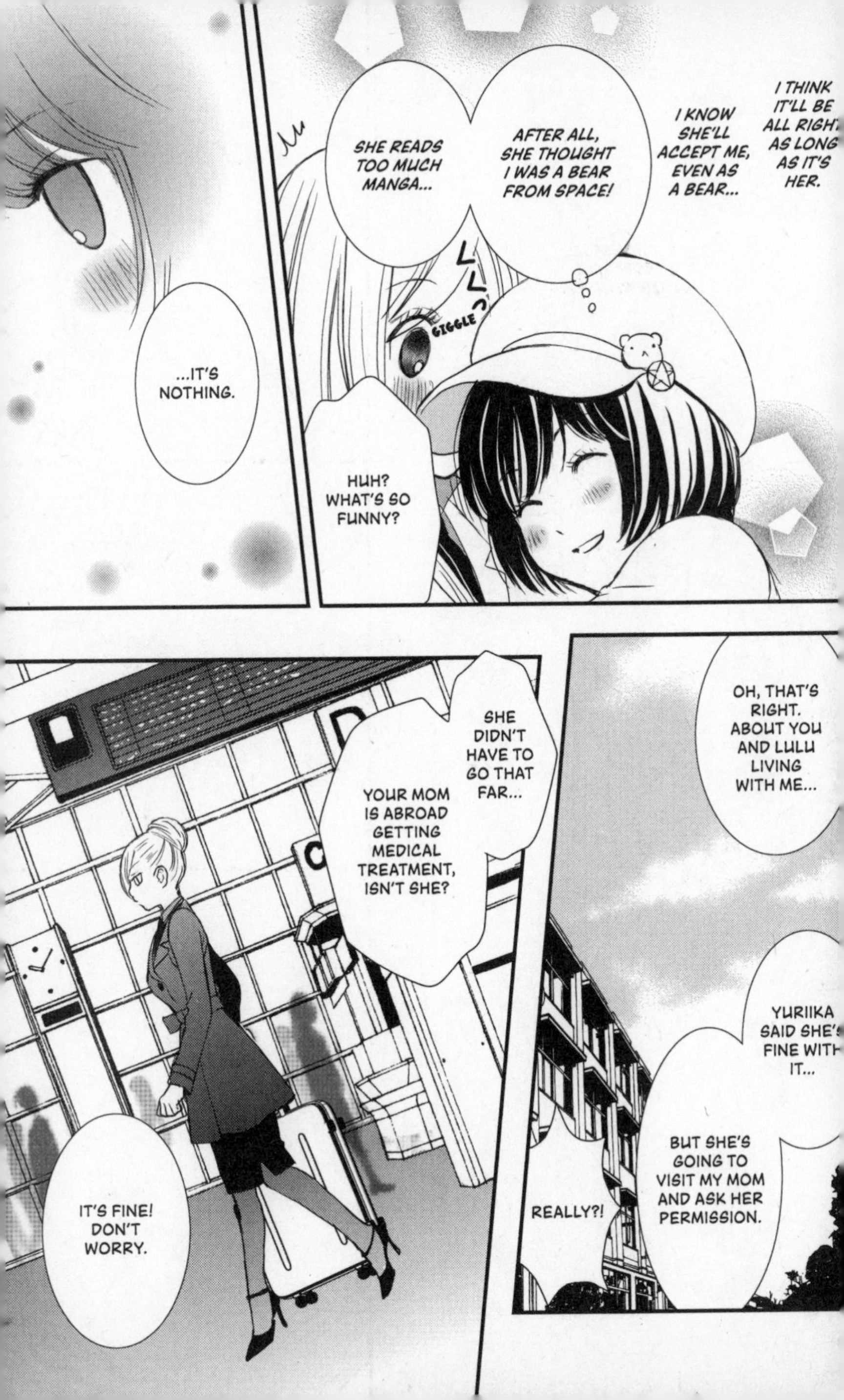
I THINK IT'LL BE ALL RIGH AS LONG AS IT'S HER.
I KNOW SHE'LL ACCEPT ME, EVEN AS A BEAR...
AFTER ALL, SHE THOUGHT I WAS A BEAR FROM SPACE!
SHE READS TOO MUCH MANGA...
GIGGLE
HUH? WHAT'S SO FUNNY?
...IT'S NOTHING.
OH, THAT'S RIGHT. ABOUT YOU AND LULU LIVING WITH ME...
YURIIKA SAID SHE' FINE WITH IT...
BUT SHE'S GOING TO VISIT MY MOM AND ASK HER PERMISSION.
REALLY?!
SHE DIDN'T HAVE TO GO THAT FAR...
YOUR MOM IS ABROAD GETTING MEDICAL TREATMENT, ISN'T SHE?
IT'S FINE! DON'T WORRY.

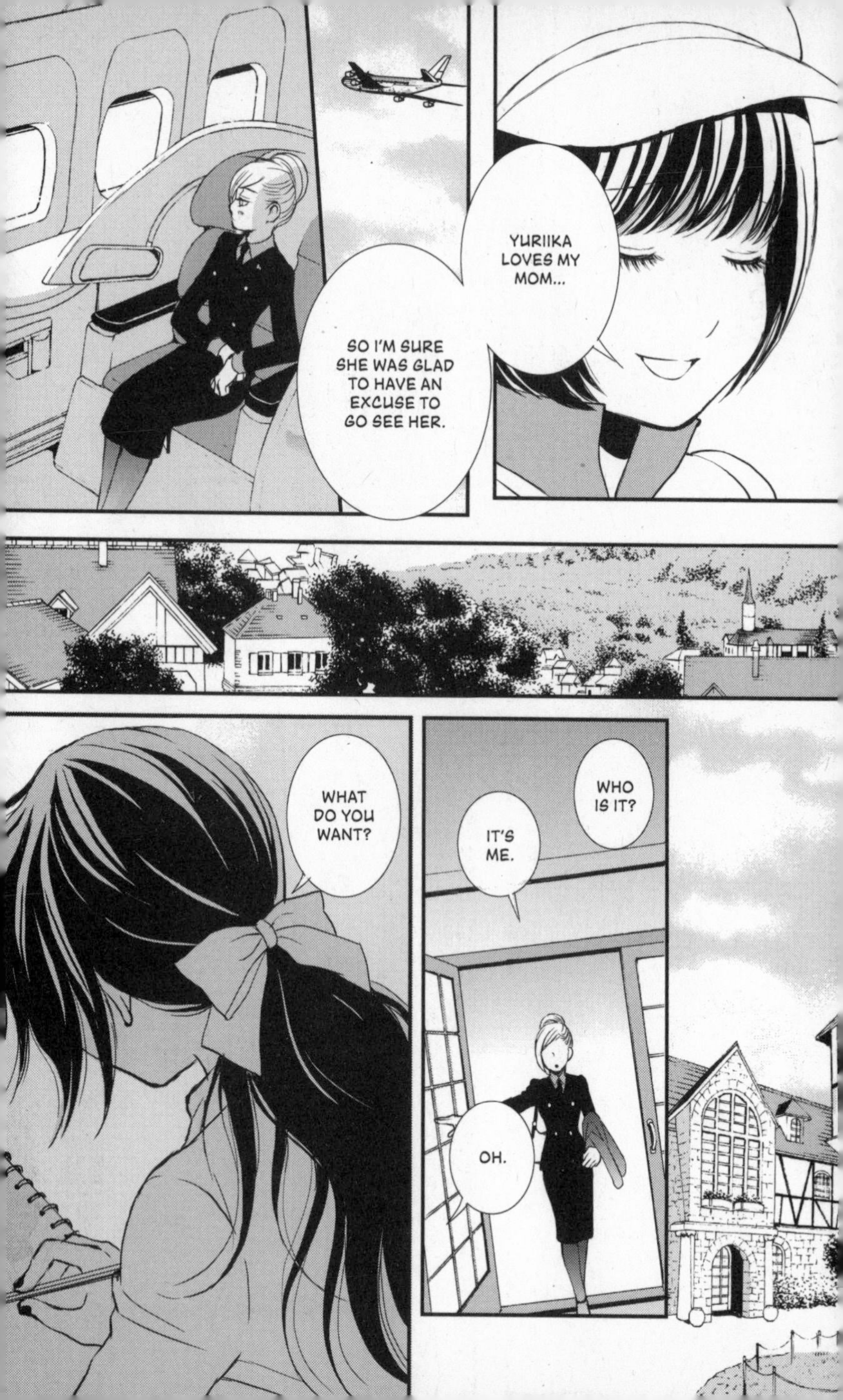
YURIIKA LOVES MY MOM...
SO I'M SURE SHE WAS GLAD TO HAVE AN EXCUSE TO GO SEE HER.
WHO IS IT?
IT'S ME.
OH.
WHAT DO YOU WANT?

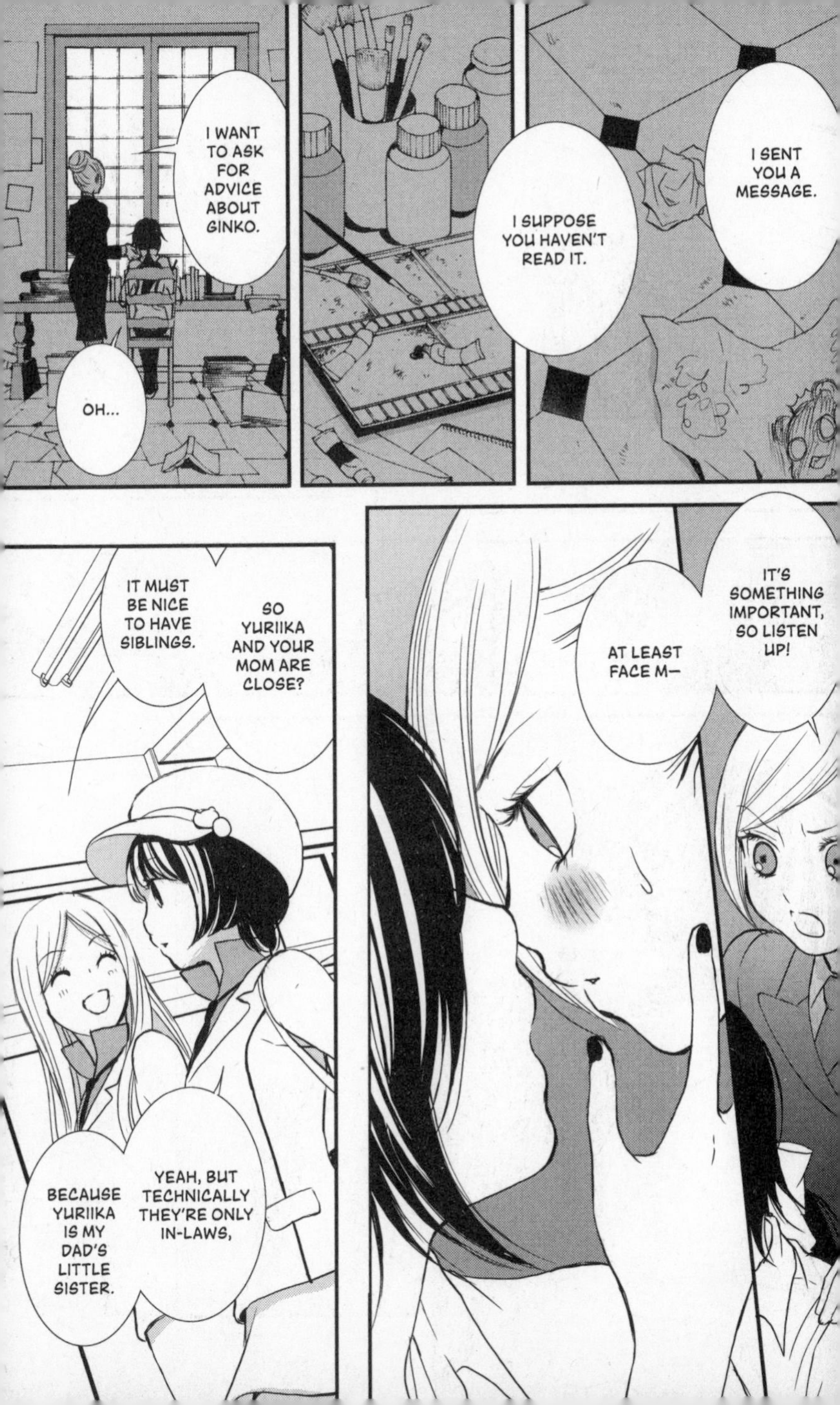
I SENT YOU A MESSAGE.
I SUPPOSE YOU HAVEN'T READ IT.
I WANT TO ASK FOR ADVICE ABOUT GINKO.
OH...
IT'S SOMETHING IMPORTANT, SO LISTEN UP!
AT LEAST FACE M—
SO YURIIKA AND YOUR MOM ARE CLOSE?
IT MUST BE NICE TO HAVE SIBLINGS.
YEAH, BUT TECHNICALLY THEY'RE ONLY IN-LAWS,
BECAUSE YURIIKA IS MY DAD'S LITTLE SISTER.

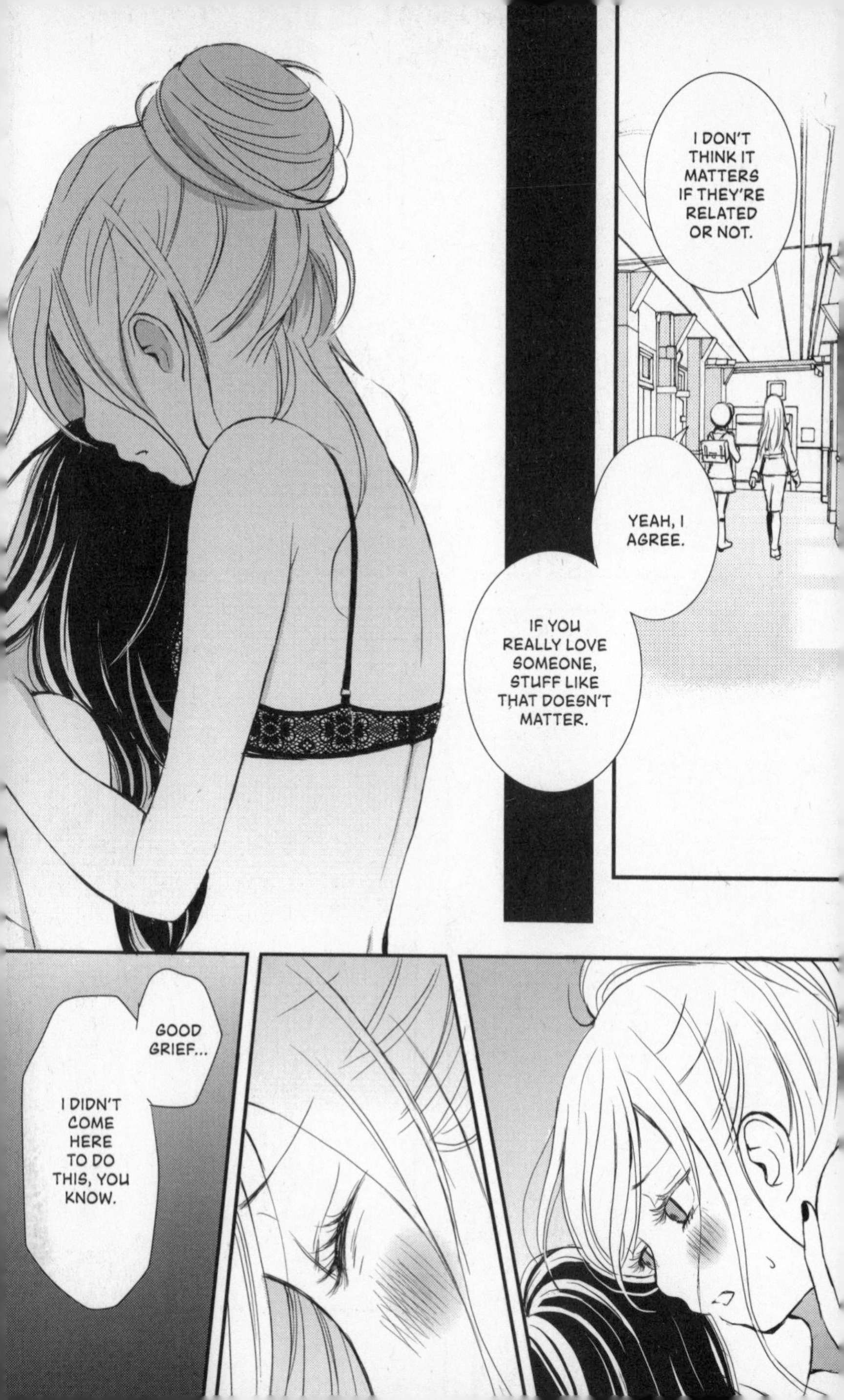
I DON'T THINK IT MATTERS IF THEY'RE RELATED OR NOT.
YEAH, I AGREE.
IF YOU REALLY LOVE SOMEONE, STUFF LIKE THAT DOESN'T MATTER.
GOOD GRIEF...
I DIDN'T COME HERE TO DO THIS, YOU KNOW.

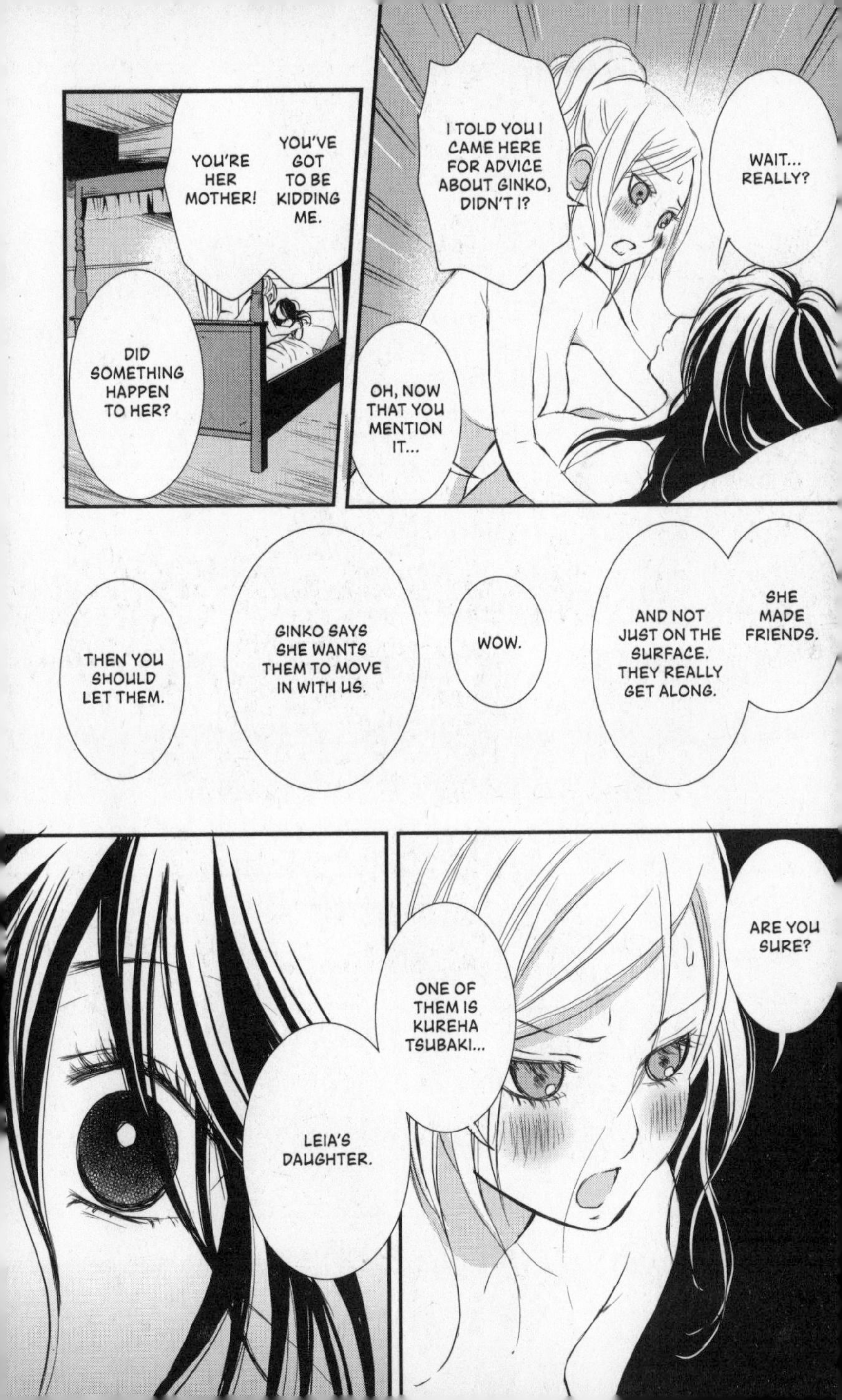
WAIT... REALLY?
I TOLD YOU I CAME HERE FOR ADVICE ABOUT GINKO, DIDN'T I?
OH, NOW THAT YOU MENTION IT...
YOU'VE GOT TO BE KIDDING ME.
YOU'RE HER MOTHER!
DID SOMETHING HAPPEN TO HER?
SHE MADE FRIENDS.
AND NOT JUST ON THE SURFACE. THEY REALLY GET ALONG.
WOW.
GINKO SAYS SHE WANTS THEM TO MOVE IN WITH US.
THEN YOU SHOULD LET THEM.
ARE YOU SURE?
ONE OF THEM IS KUREHA TSUBAKI...
LEIA'S DAUGHTER.

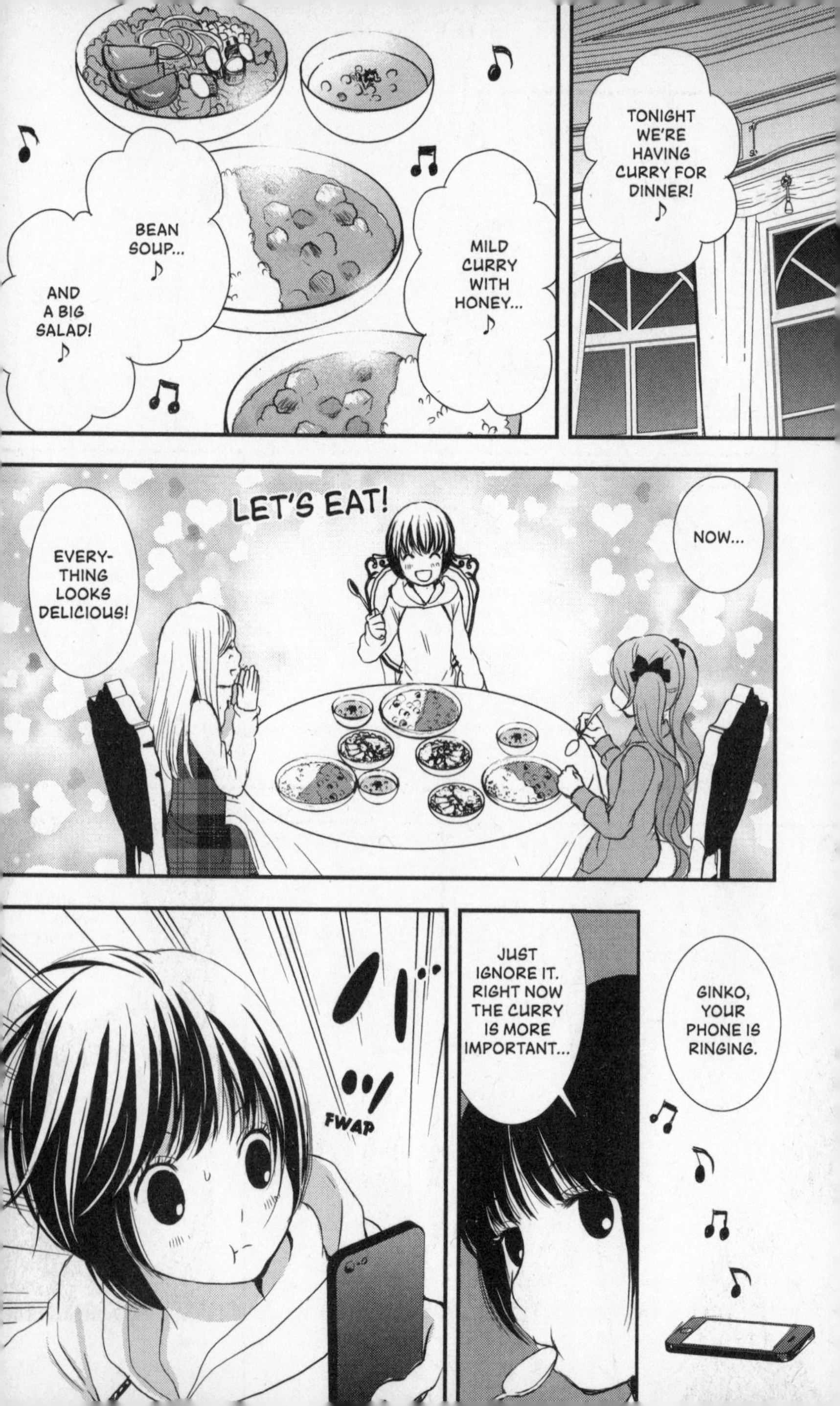
TONIGHT WE'RE HAVING CURRY FOR DINNER! ♪
MILD CURRY WITH HONEY... ♪
BEAN SOUP... ♪
AND A BIG SALAD! ♪
NOW...
LET'S EAT!
EVERY-THING LOOKS DELICIOUS!
GINKO, YOUR PHONE IS RINGING.
JUST IGNORE IT. RIGHT NOW THE CURRY IS MORE IMPORTANT...
FWAP

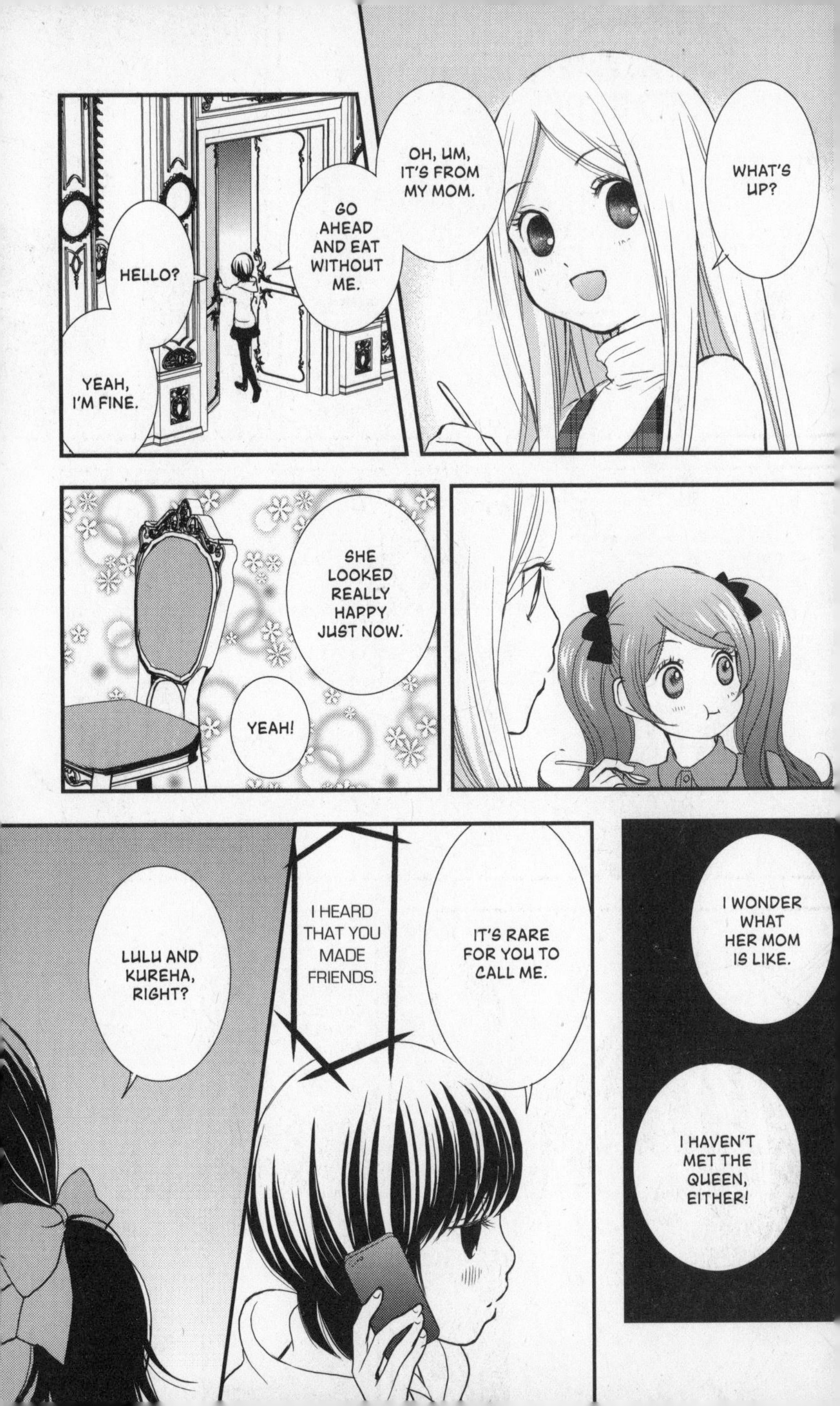
WHAT'S UP?
OH, UM, IT'S FROM MY MOM.
GO AHEAD AND EAT WITHOUT ME.
HELLO?
YEAH, I'M FINE.
SHE LOOKED REALLY HAPPY JUST NOW.
YEAH!
I WONDER WHAT HER MOM IS LIKE.
I HAVEN'T MET THE QUEEN, EITHER!
IT'S RARE FOR YOU TO CALL ME.
I HEARD THAT YOU MADE FRIENDS.
LULU AND KUREHA, RIGHT?

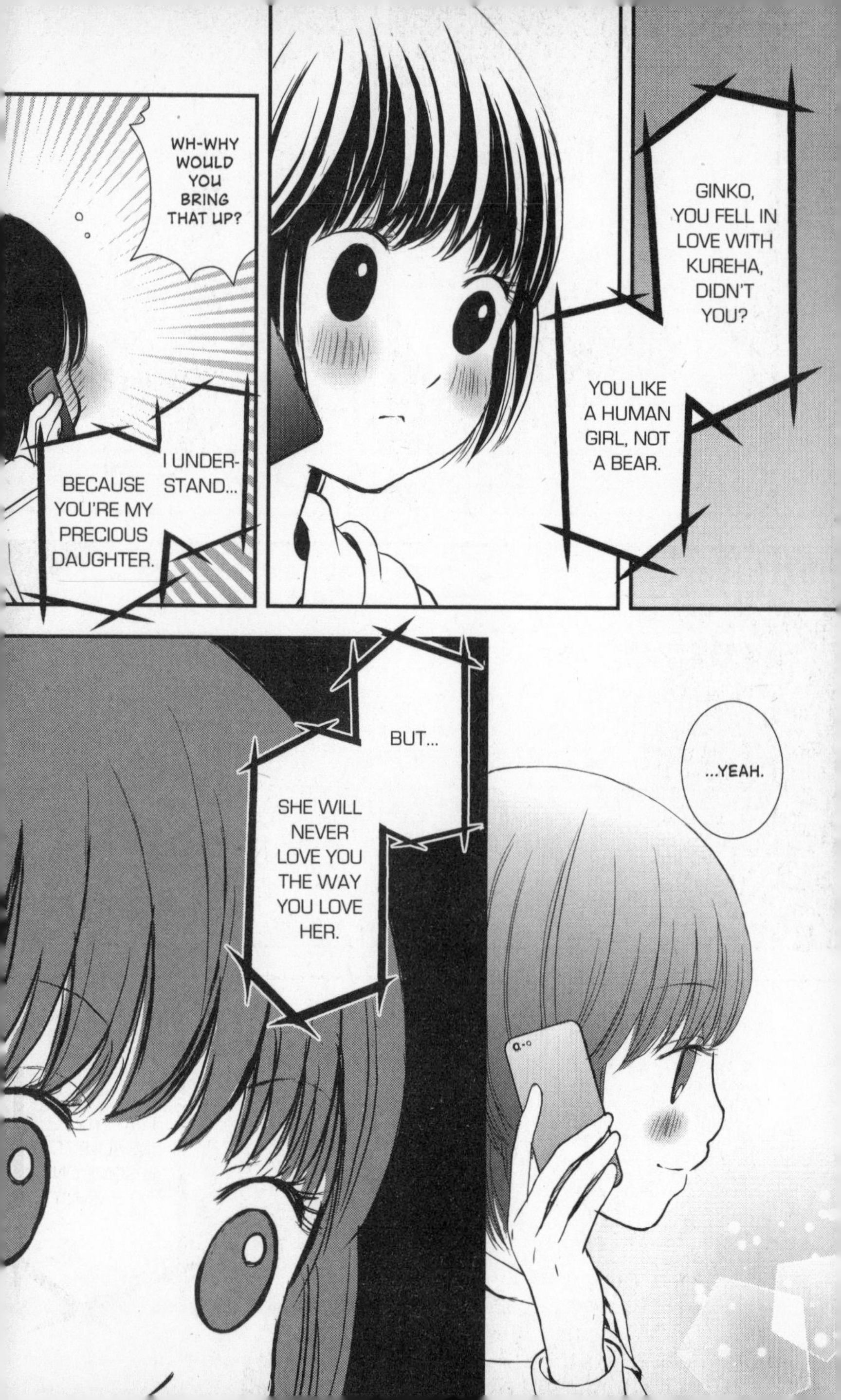
GINKO, YOU FELL IN LOVE WITH KUREHA, DIDN'T YOU?
YOU LIKE A HUMAN GIRL, NOT A BEAR.
WH-WHY WOULD YOU BRING THAT UP?
I UNDER-STAND...
BECAUSE YOU'RE MY PRECIOUS DAUGHTER.
...YEAH.
BUT...
SHE WILL NEVER LOVE YOU THE WAY YOU LOVE HER.

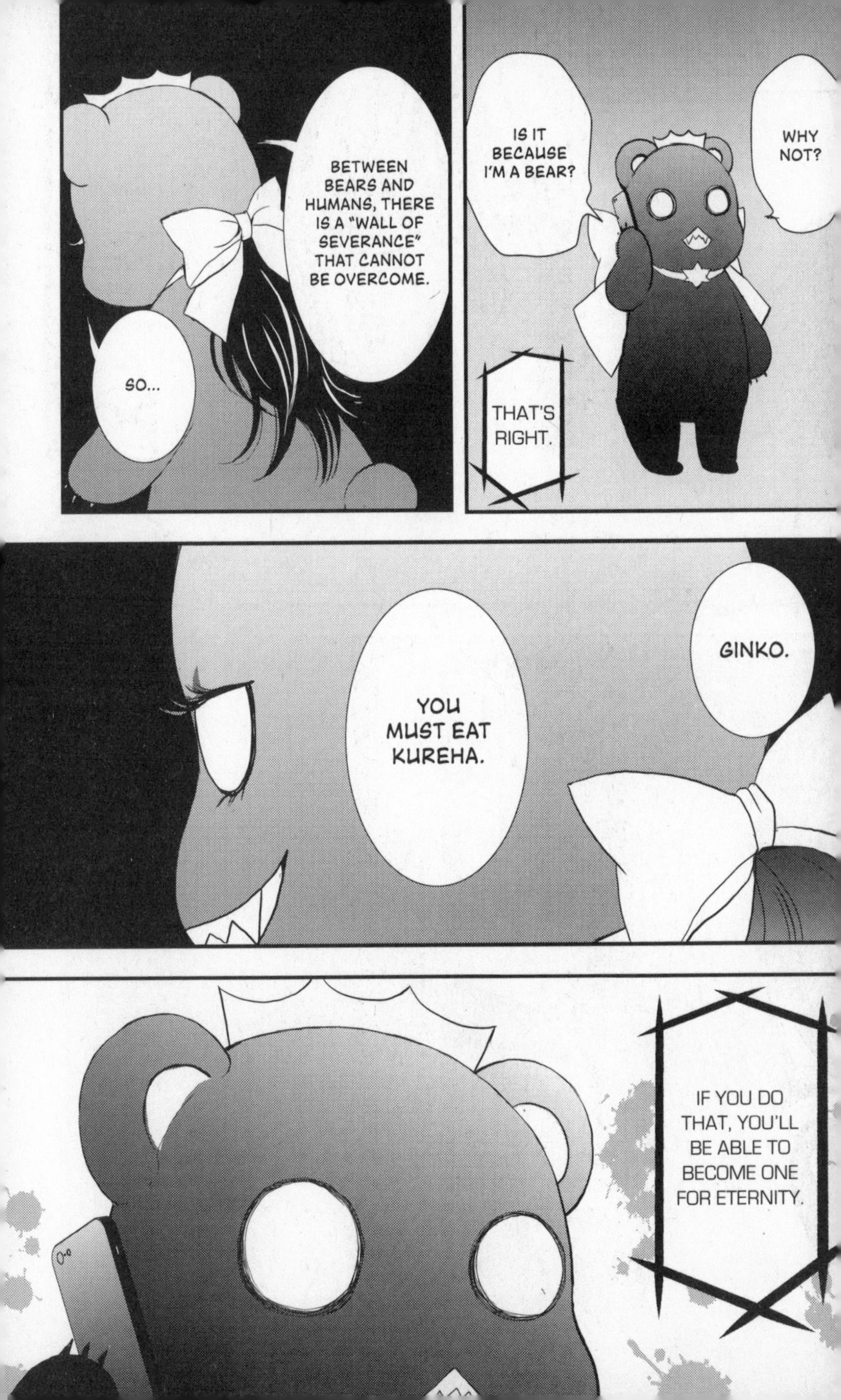
WHY NOT?
IS IT BECAUSE I'M A BEAR?
THAT'S RIGHT.
BETWEEN BEARS AND HUMANS, THERE IS A "WALL OF SEVERANCE" THAT CANNOT BE OVERCOME.
SO...
GINKO.
YOU MUST EAT KUREHA.
IF YOU DO THAT, YOU'LL BE ABLE TO BECOME ONE FOR ETERNITY.

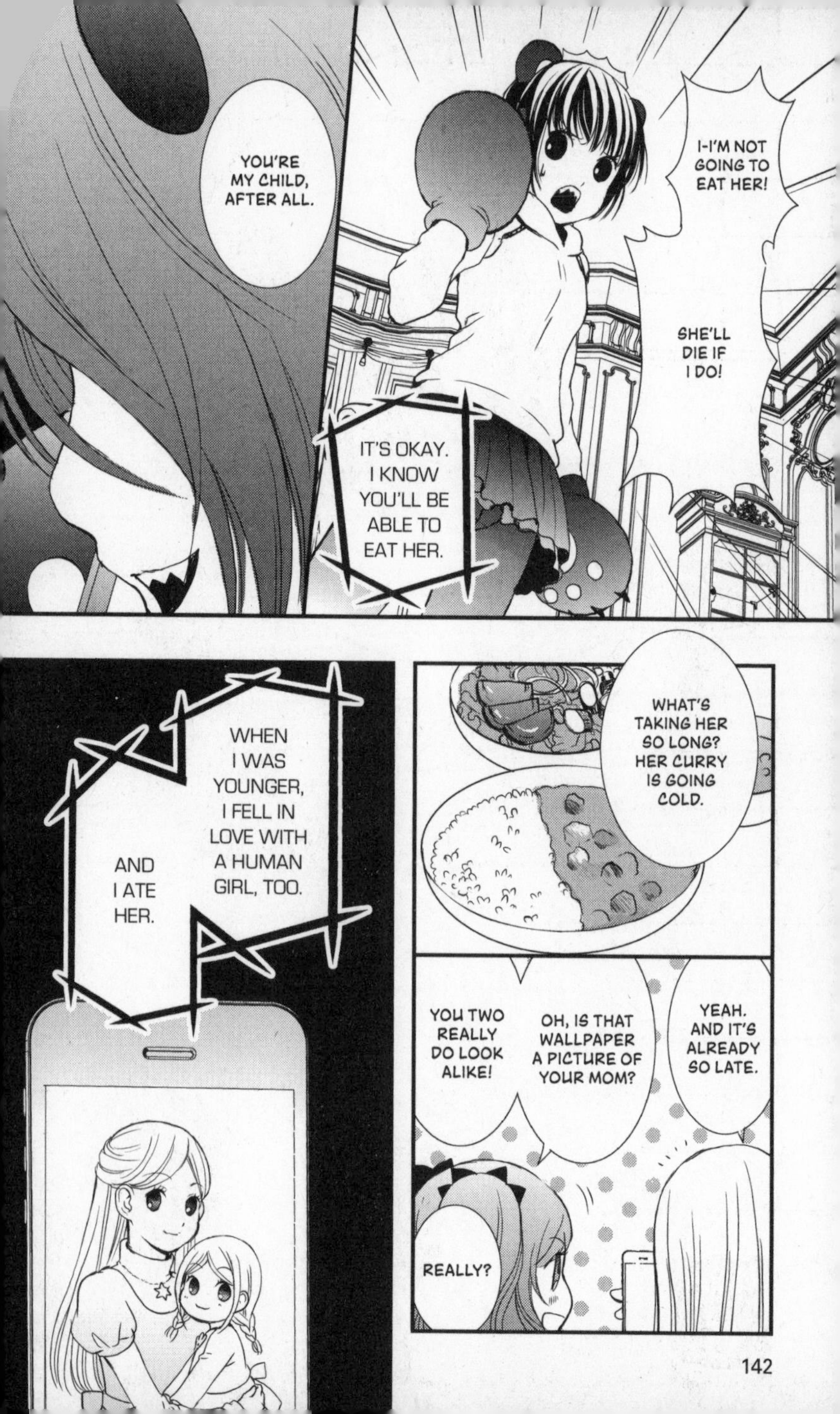
I-I'M NOT GOING TO EAT HER!
SHE'LL DIE IF I DO!
IT'S OKAY. I KNOW YOU'LL BE ABLE TO EAT HER.
YOU'RE MY CHILD, AFTER ALL.
WHAT'S TAKING HER SO LONG? HER CURRY IS GOING COLD.
YEAH. AND IT'S ALREADY SO LATE.
OH, IS THAT WALLPAPER A PICTURE OF YOUR MOM?
YOU TWO REALLY DO LOOK ALIKE!
REALLY?
WHEN I WAS YOUNGER, I FELL IN LOVE WITH A HUMAN GIRL, TOO.
AND I ATE HER.

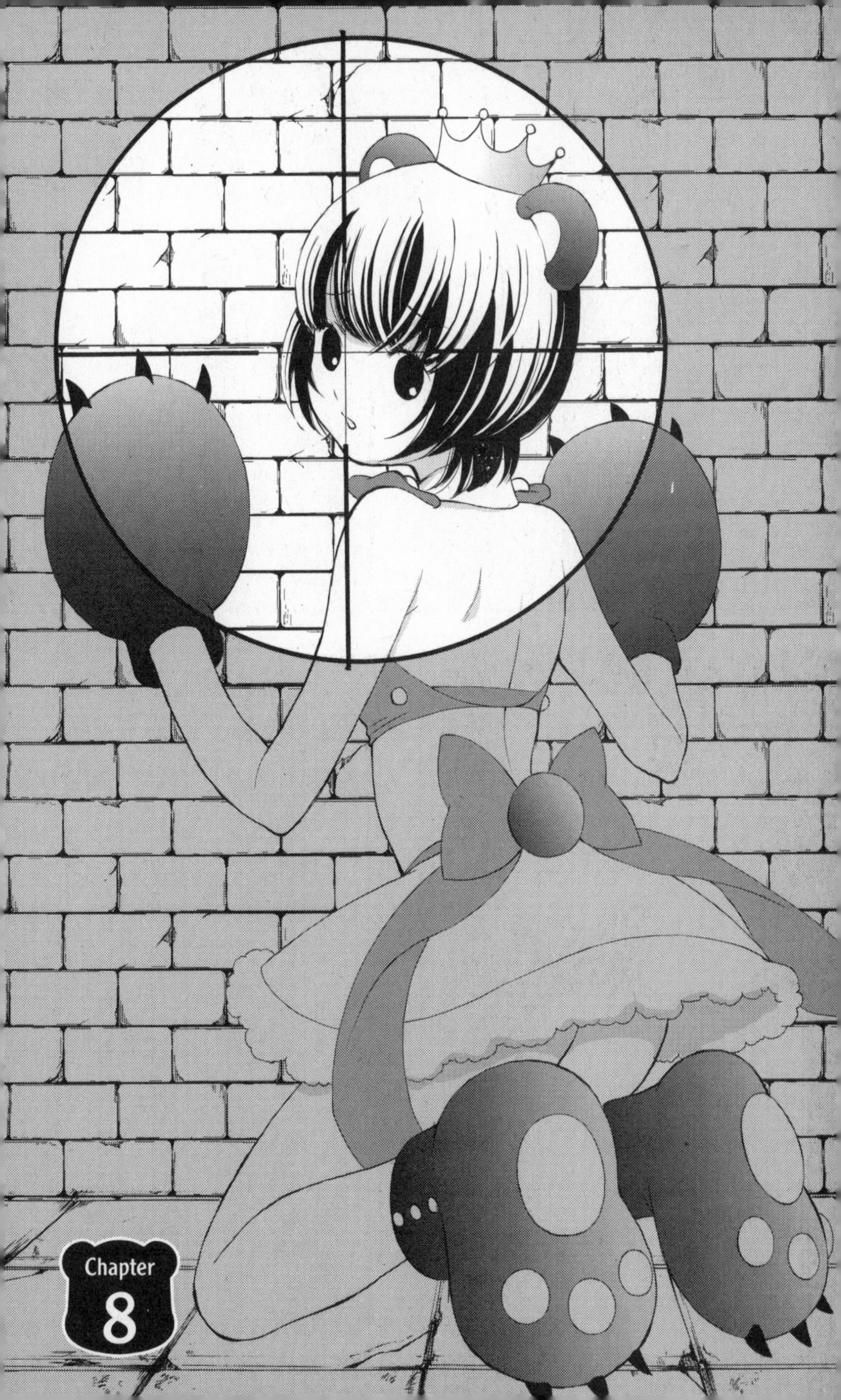
Chapter
8

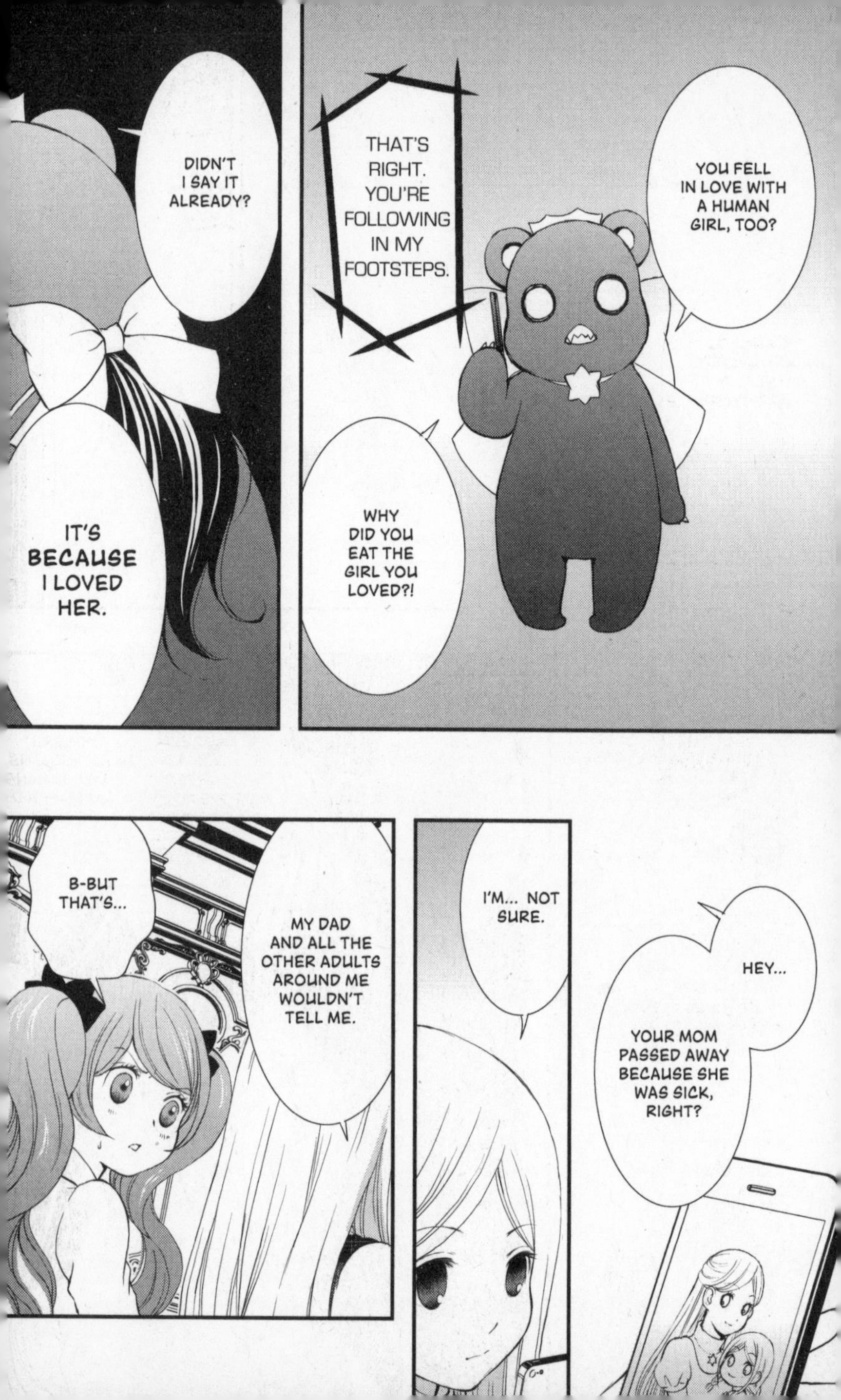
YOU FELL IN LOVE WITH A HUMAN GIRL, TOO?
THAT'S RIGHT. YOU'RE FOLLOWING IN MY FOOTSTEPS.
WHY DID YOU EAT THE GIRL YOU LOVED?!
DIDN'T I SAY IT ALREADY?
IT'S BECAUSE I LOVED HER.
HEY...
YOUR MOM PASSED AWAY BECAUSE SHE WAS SICK, RIGHT?
I'M... NOT SURE.
MY DAD AND ALL THE OTHER ADULTS AROUND ME WOULDN'T TELL ME.
B-BUT THAT'S...

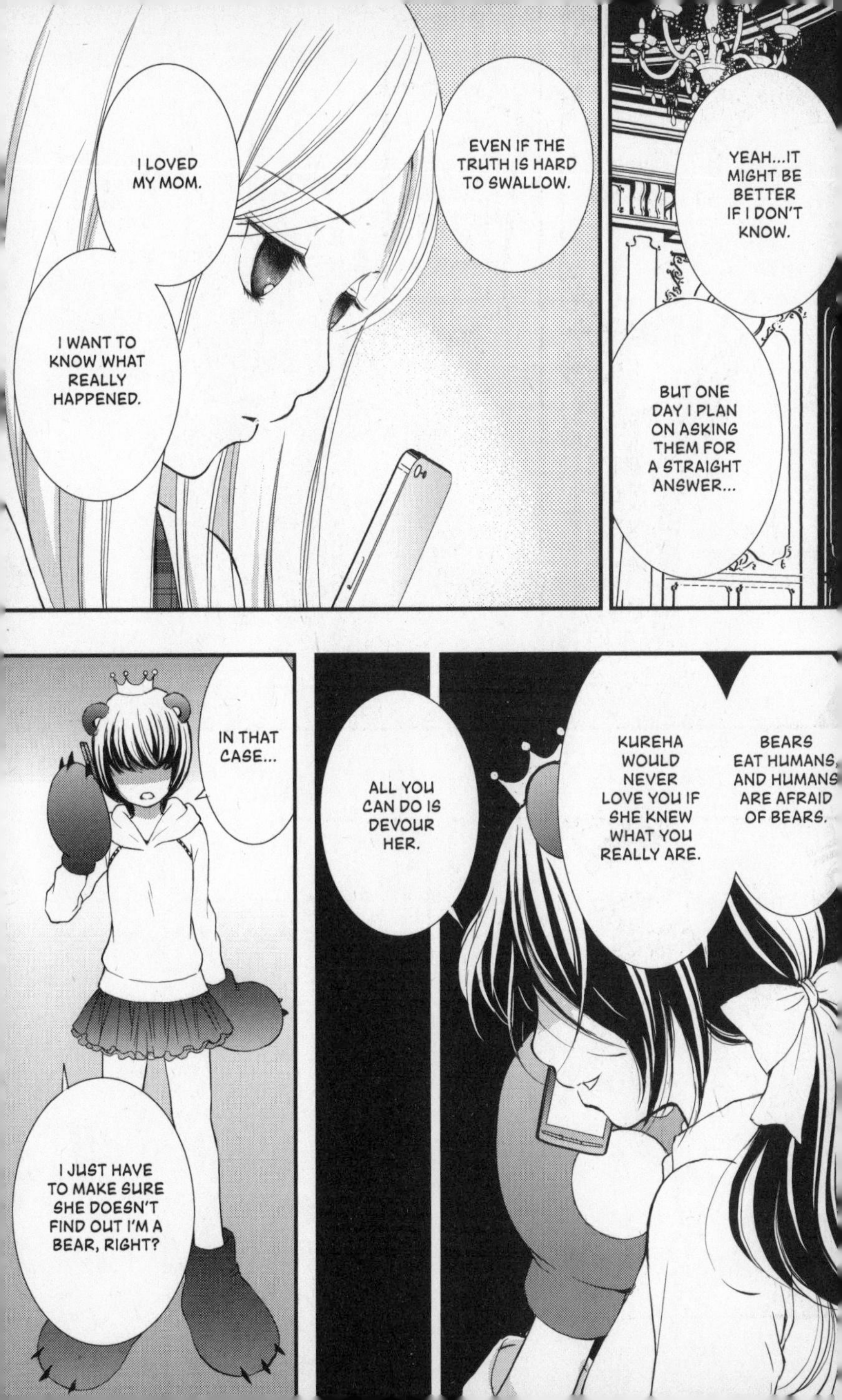
YEAH...IT MIGHT BE BETTER IF I DON'T KNOW.
BUT ONE DAY I PLAN ON ASKING THEM FOR A STRAIGHT ANSWER...
EVEN IF THE TRUTH IS HARD TO SWALLOW.
I LOVED MY MOM.
I WANT TO KNOW WHAT REALLY HAPPENED.
BEARS EAT HUMANS, AND HUMANS ARE AFRAID OF BEARS.
KUREHA WOULD NEVER LOVE YOU IF SHE KNEW WHAT YOU REALLY ARE.
ALL YOU CAN DO IS DEVOUR HER.
IN THAT CASE...
I JUST HAVE TO MAKE SURE SHE DOESN'T FIND OUT I'M A BEAR, RIGHT?

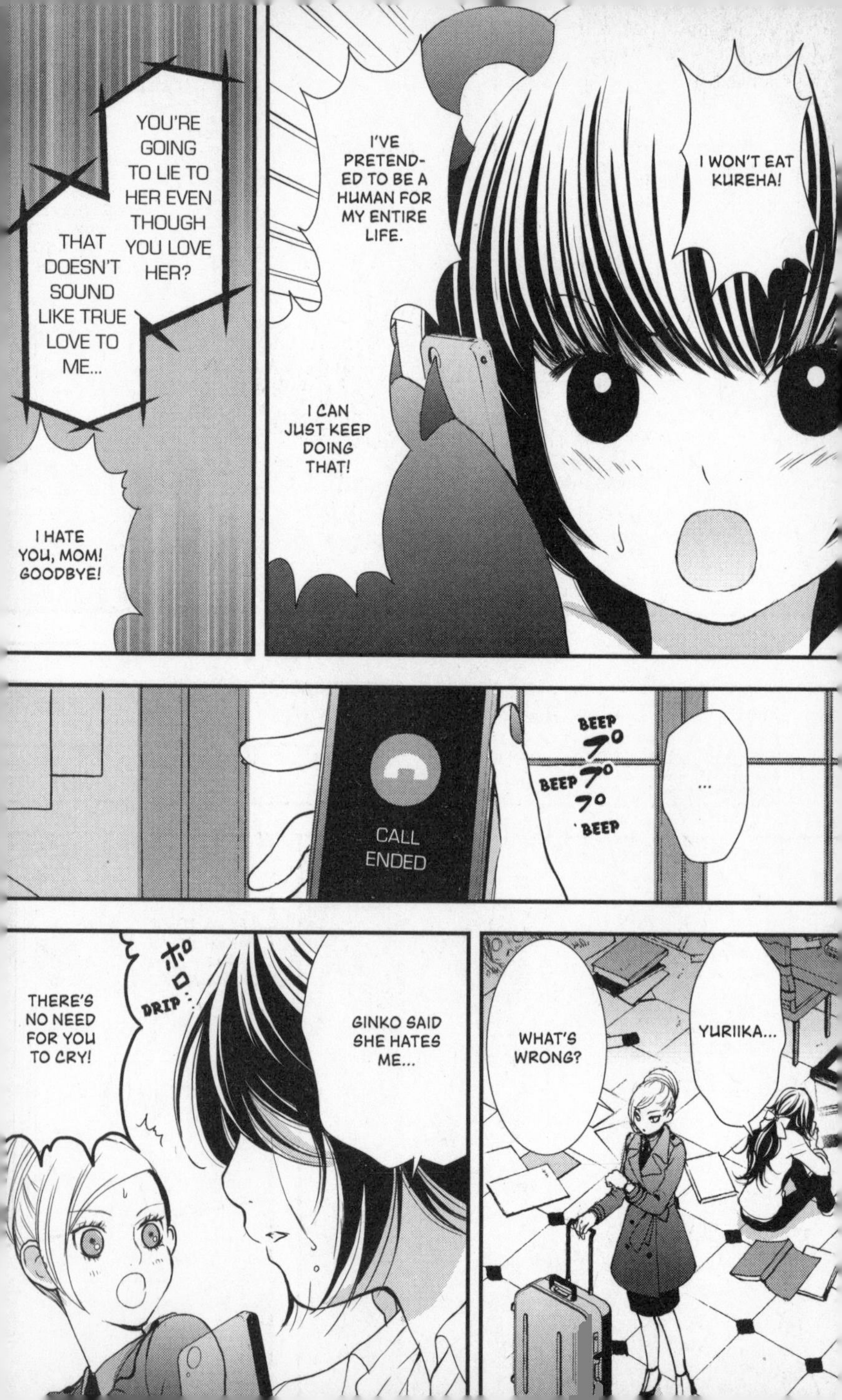
I WON'T EAT KUREHA!
I'VE PRETENDED TO BE A HUMAN FOR MY ENTIRE LIFE.
I CAN JUST KEEP DOING THAT!
YOU'RE GOING TO LIE TO HER EVEN THOUGH YOU LOVE HER?
THAT DOESN'T SOUND LIKE TRUE LOVE TO ME...
I HATE YOU, MOM! GOODBYE!
...
BEEP
BEEP
BEEP
CALL ENDED
YURIIKA...
WHAT'S WRONG?
GINKO SAID SHE HATES ME...
DRIP
THERE'S NO NEED FOR YOU TO CRY!

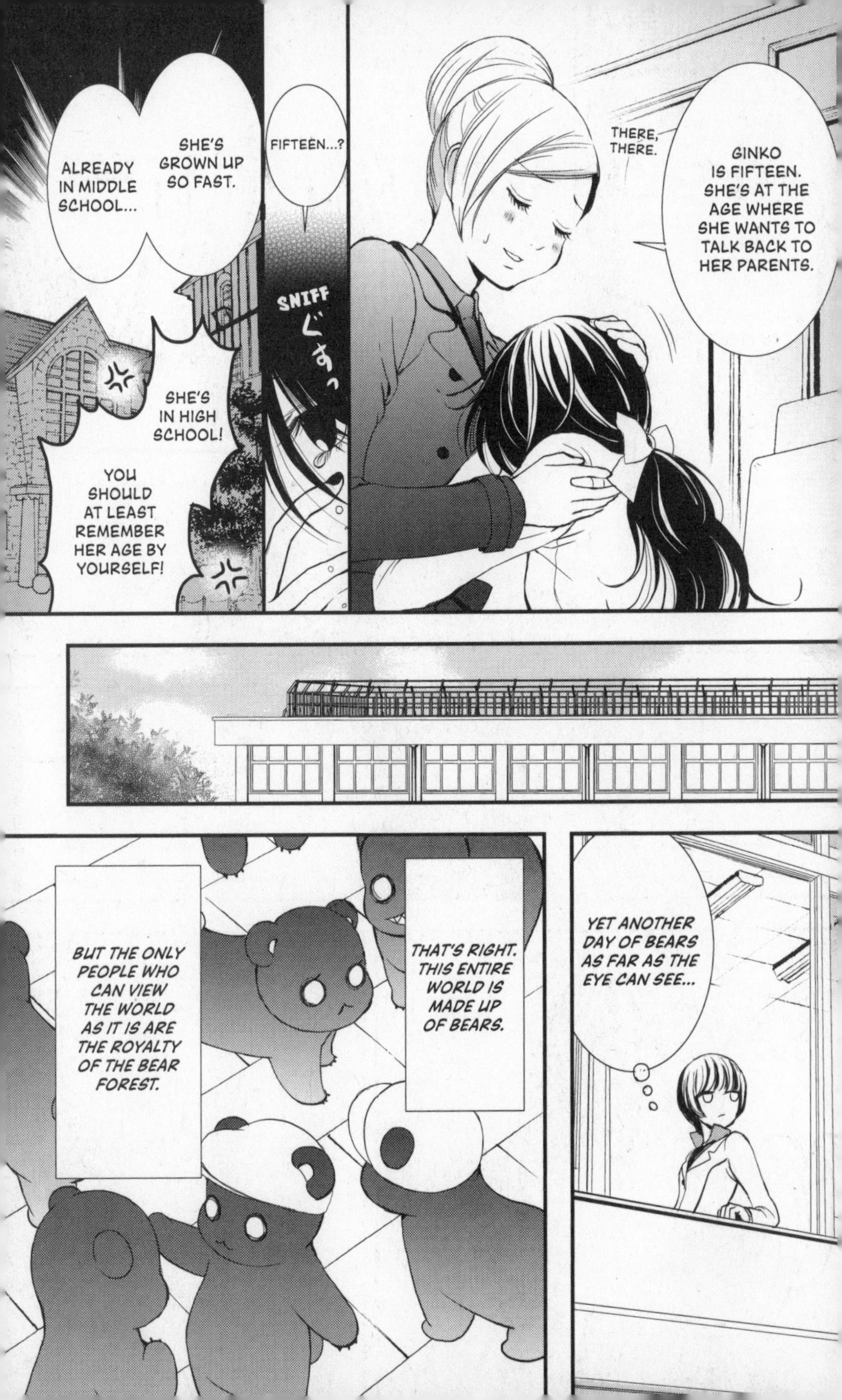
GINKO IS FIFTEEN. SHE'S AT THE AGE WHERE SHE WANTS TO TALK BACK TO HER PARENTS.
THERE, THERE.
FIFTEEN...?
SNIFF
ぐすっ
SHE'S GROWN UP SO FAST.
ALREADY IN MIDDLE SCHOOL...
SHE'S IN HIGH SCHOOL!
YOU SHOULD AT LEAST REMEMBER HER AGE BY YOURSELF!
YET ANOTHER DAY OF BEARS AS FAR AS THE EYE CAN SEE...
THAT'S RIGHT. THIS ENTIRE WORLD IS MADE UP OF BEARS.
BUT THE ONLY PEOPLE WHO CAN VIEW THE WORLD AS IT IS ARE THE ROYALTY OF THE BEAR FOREST.

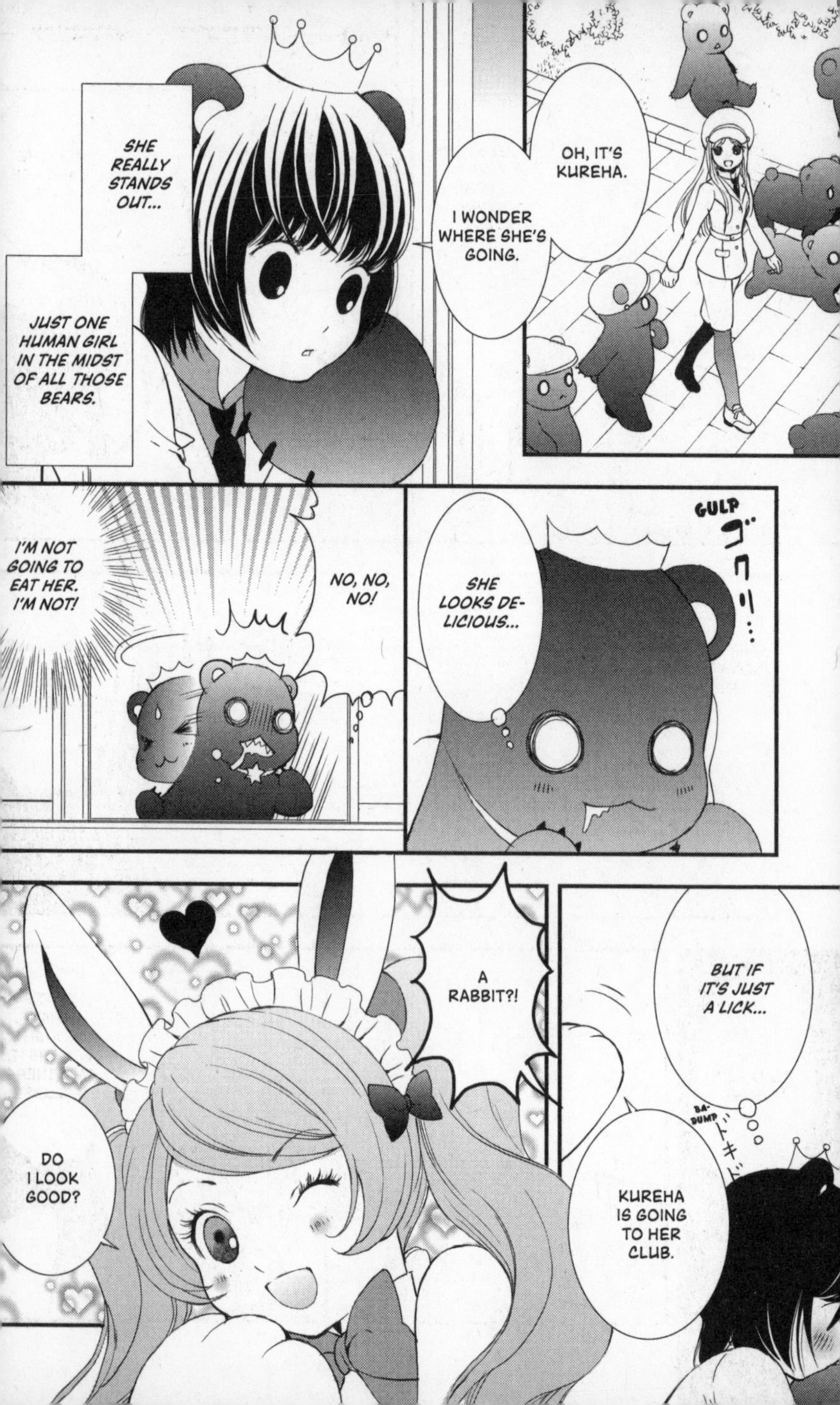
OH, IT'S KUREHA.
I WONDER WHERE SHE'S GOING.
SHE REALLY STANDS OUT...
JUST ONE HUMAN GIRL IN THE MIDST OF ALL THOSE BEARS.
GULP
SHE LOOKS DE-LICIOUS...
NO, NO, NO!
I'M NOT GOING TO EAT HER. I'M NOT!
BUT IF IT'S JUST A LICK...
BA-DUMP
KUREHA IS GOING TO HER CLUB.
A RABBIT?!
DO I LOOK GOOD?

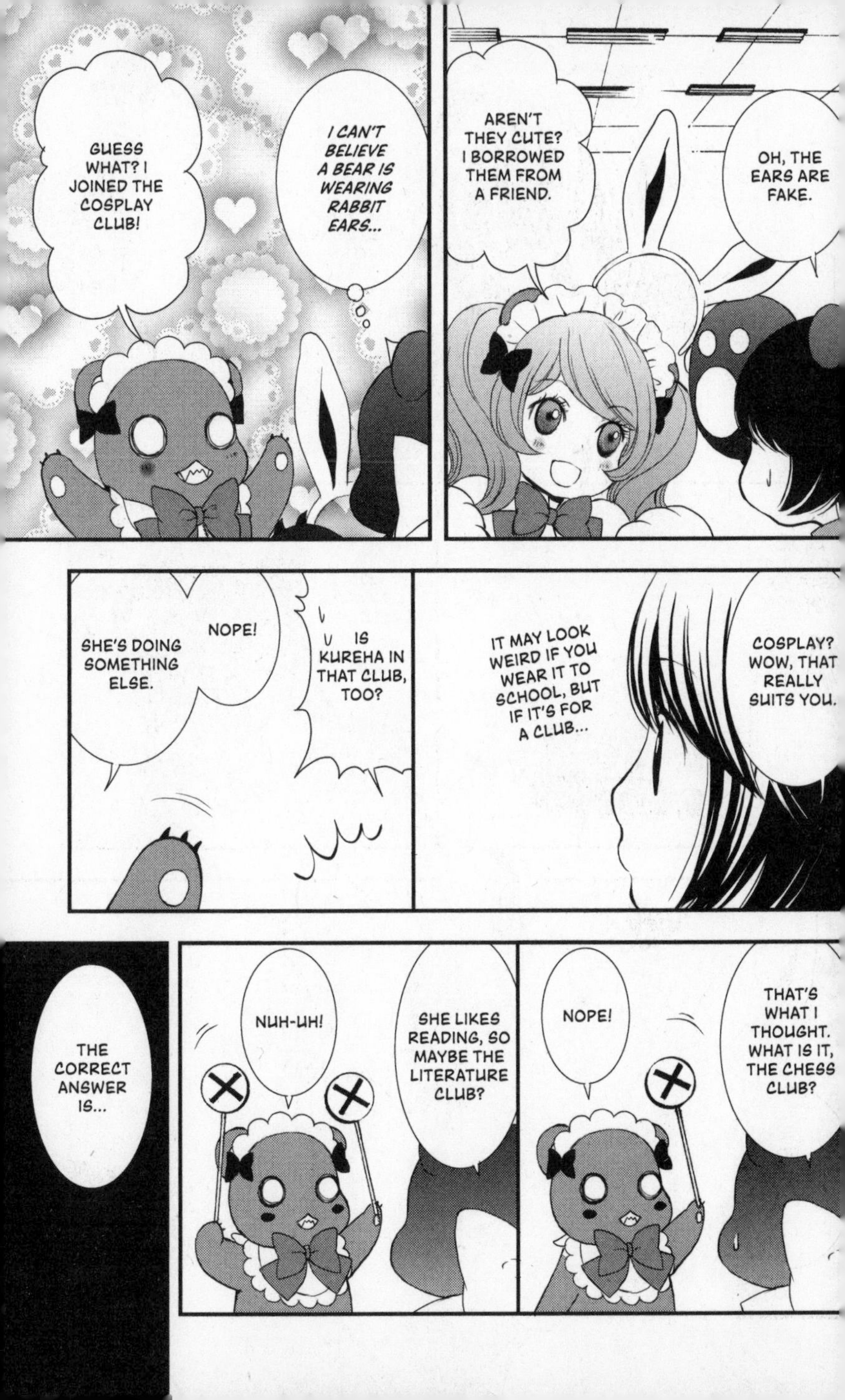
OH, THE EARS ARE FAKE.
AREN'T THEY CUTE? I BORROWED THEM FROM A FRIEND.
GUESS WHAT? I JOINED THE COSPLAY CLUB!
I CAN'T BELIEVE A BEAR IS WEARING RABBIT EARS...
COSPLAY? WOW, THAT REALLY SUITS YOU.
IT MAY LOOK WEIRD IF YOU WEAR IT TO SCHOOL, BUT IF IT'S FOR A CLUB...
IS KUREHA IN THAT CLUB, TOO?
NOPE!
SHE'S DOING SOMETHING ELSE.
THAT'S WHAT I THOUGHT. WHAT IS IT, THE CHESS CLUB?
NOPE!
SHE LIKES READING, SO MAYBE THE LITERATURE CLUB?
NUH-UH!
THE CORRECT ANSWER IS...

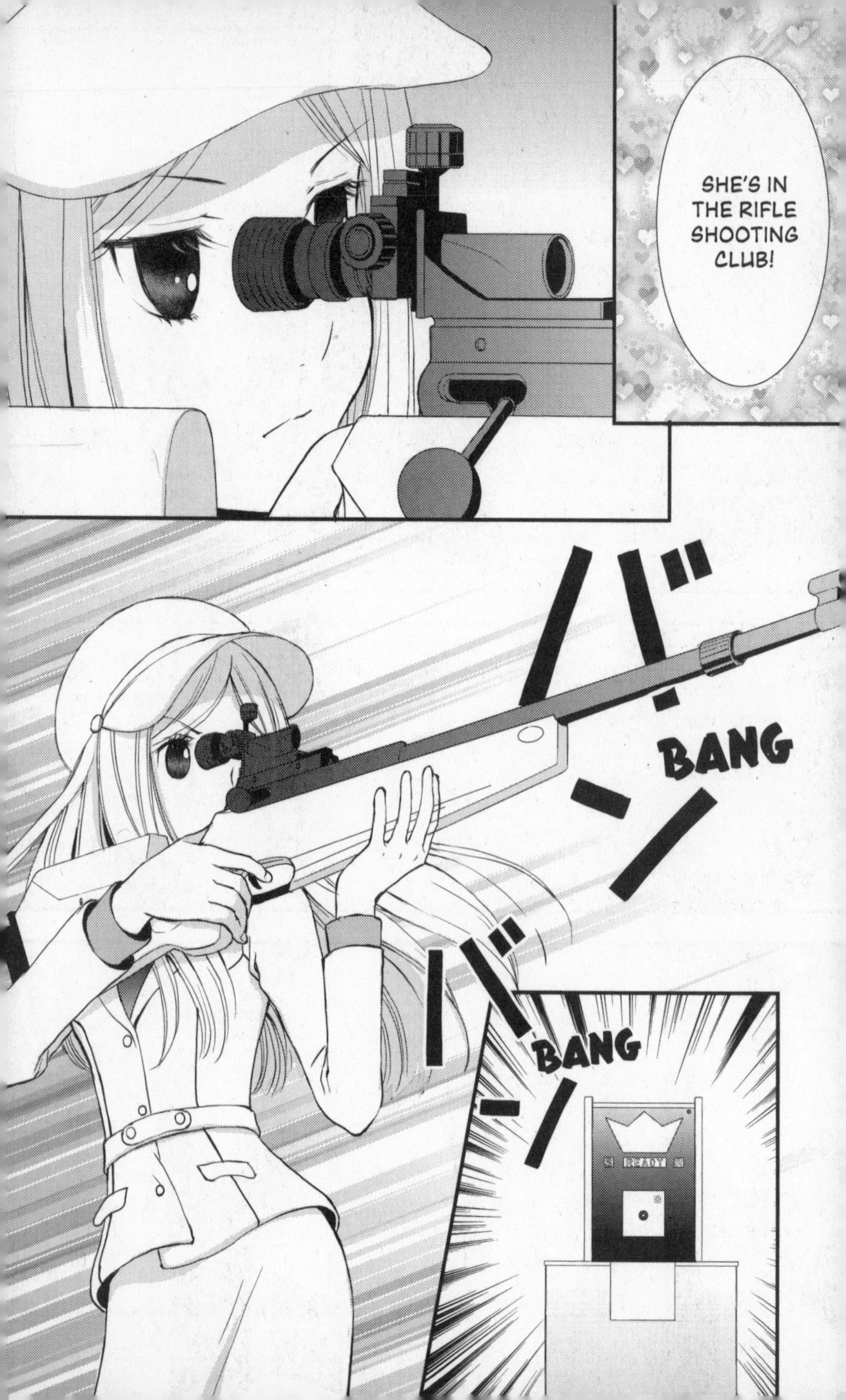
SHE'S IN THE RIFLE SHOOTING CLUB!
バーン
BANG
バーン
BANG
READY

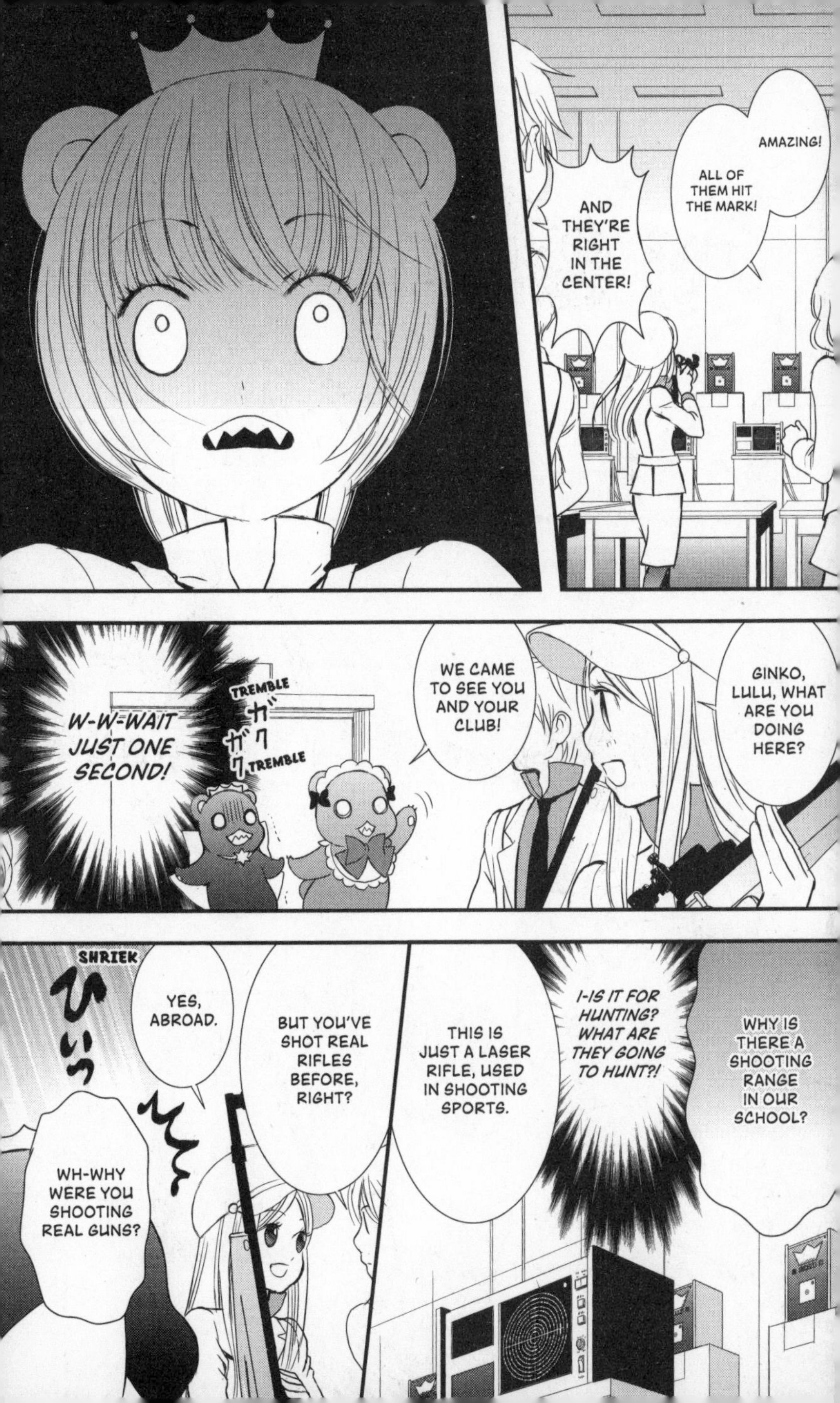
AMAZING!
ALL OF THEM HIT THE MARK!
AND THEY'RE RIGHT IN THE CENTER!
GINKO, LULU, WHAT ARE YOU DOING HERE?
WE CAME TO SEE YOU AND YOUR CLUB!
TREMBLE
ガク
ガク
TREMBLE
W-W-WAIT JUST ONE SECOND!
WHY IS THERE A SHOOTING RANGE IN OUR SCHOOL?
I-IS IT FOR HUNTING? WHAT ARE THEY GOING TO HUNT?!
THIS IS JUST A LASER RIFLE, USED IN SHOOTING SPORTS.
BUT YOU'VE SHOT REAL RIFLES BEFORE, RIGHT?
YES, ABROAD.
SHRIEK
WH-WHY WERE YOU SHOOTING REAL GUNS?

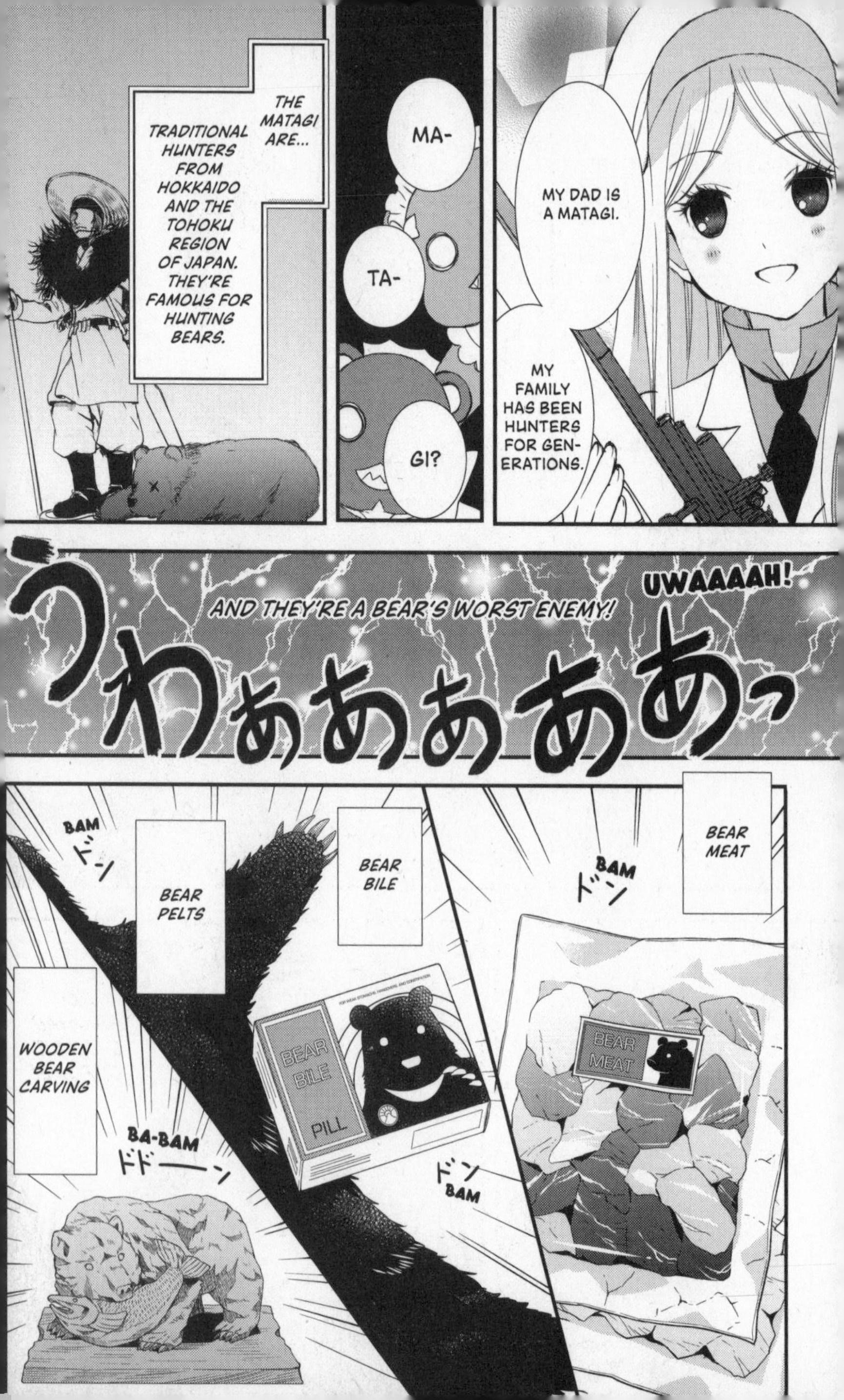
MY DAD IS A MATAGI.
MY FAMILY HAS BEEN HUNTERS FOR GENERATIONS.
MA-
TA-
GI?
THE MATAGI ARE...
TRADITIONAL HUNTERS FROM HOKKAIDO AND THE TOHOKU REGION OF JAPAN. THEY'RE FAMOUS FOR HUNTING BEARS.
UWAAAAH!
うわぁあああっ
AND THEY'RE A BEAR'S WORST ENEMY!
BEAR MEAT
BAM
ドン
BEAR MEAT
BEAR BILE
BEAR BILE PILL
ドン
BAM
BEAR PELTS
BAM
ドン
WOODEN BEAR CARVING
BA-BAM
ドドーン

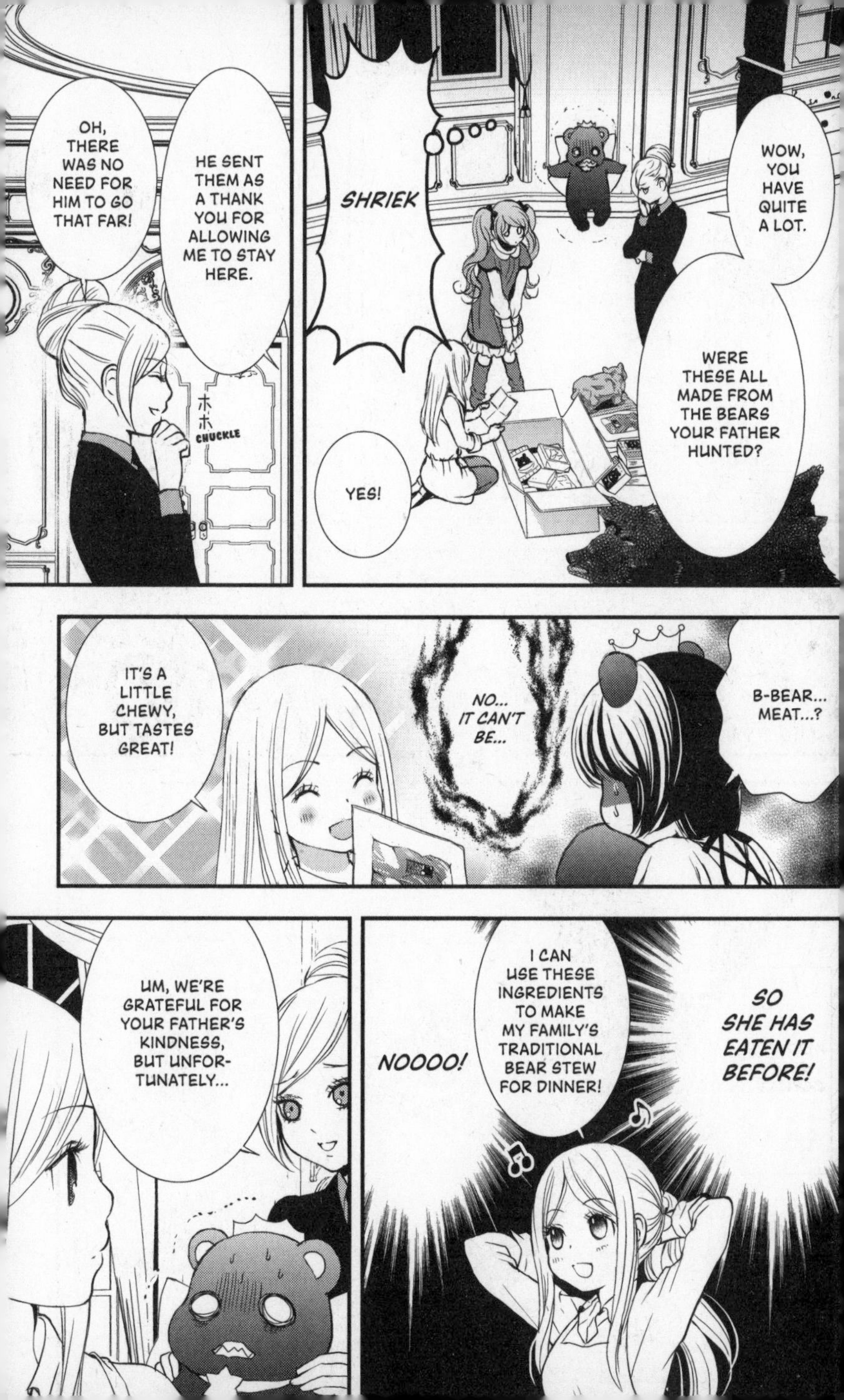
WOW, YOU HAVE QUITE A LOT.
OOOO
SHRIEK
WERE THESE ALL MADE FROM THE BEARS YOUR FATHER HUNTED?
YES!
HE SENT THEM AS A THANK YOU FOR ALLOWING ME TO STAY HERE.
OH, THERE WAS NO NEED FOR HIM TO GO THAT FAR!
ホホ
CHUCKLE
B-BEAR... MEAT...?
NO... IT CAN'T BE...
IT'S A LITTLE CHEWY, BUT TASTES GREAT!
SO SHE HAS EATEN IT BEFORE!
I CAN USE THESE INGREDIENTS TO MAKE MY FAMILY'S TRADITIONAL BEAR STEW FOR DINNER!
NOOOO!
UM, WE'RE GRATEFUL FOR YOUR FATHER'S KINDNESS, BUT UNFOR-TUNATELY...

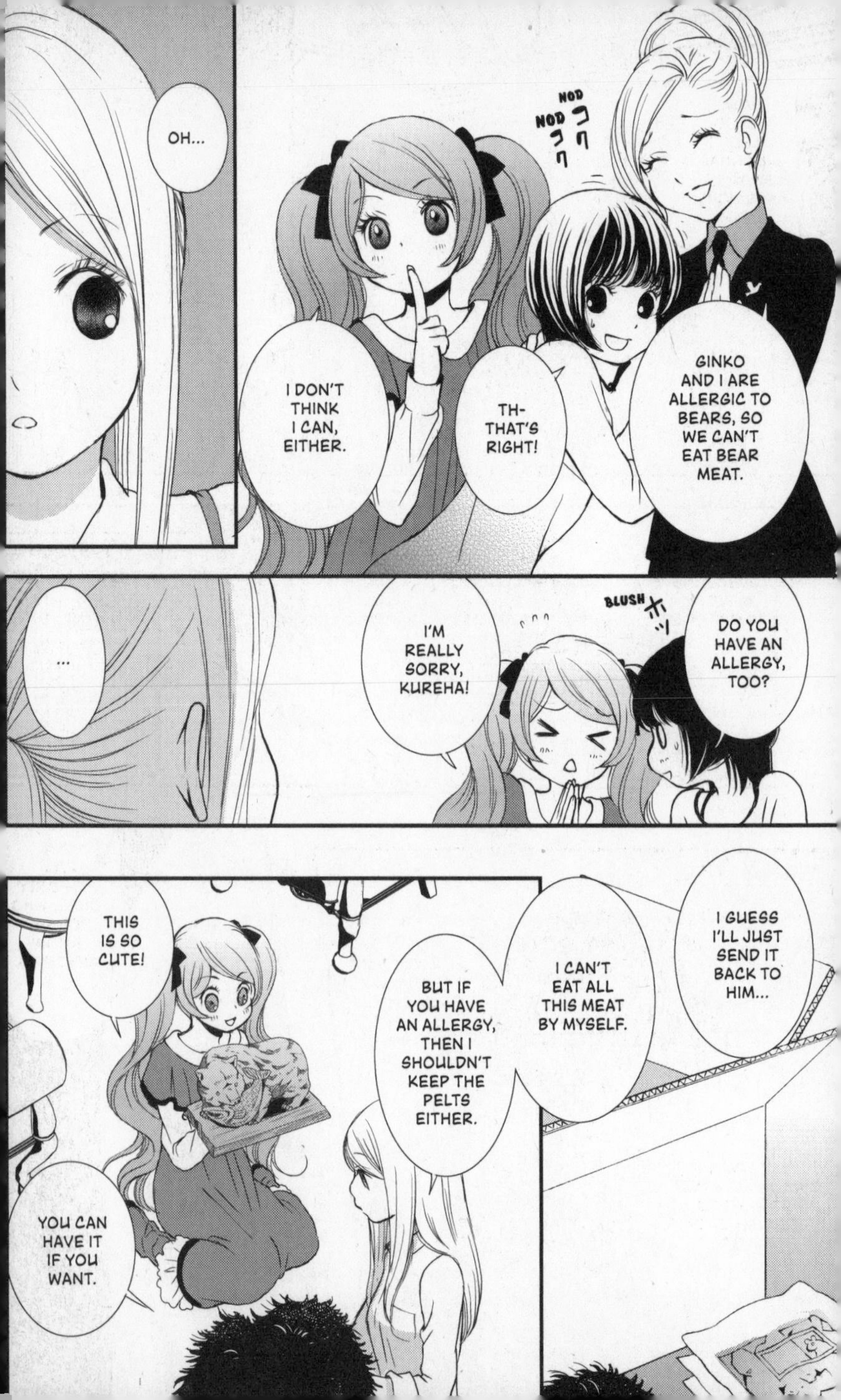
NOD NOD
コク コク
GINKO AND I ARE ALLERGIC TO BEARS, SO WE CAN'T EAT BEAR MEAT.
TH-THAT'S RIGHT!
I DON'T THINK I CAN, EITHER.
OH...
BLUSH
ホッ
DO YOU HAVE AN ALLERGY, TOO?
I'M REALLY SORRY, KUREHA!
...
I GUESS I'LL JUST SEND IT BACK TO HIM...
I CAN'T EAT ALL THIS MEAT BY MYSELF.
BUT IF YOU HAVE AN ALLERGY, THEN I SHOULDN'T KEEP THE PELTS EITHER.
THIS IS SO CUTE!
YOU CAN HAVE IT IF YOU WANT.

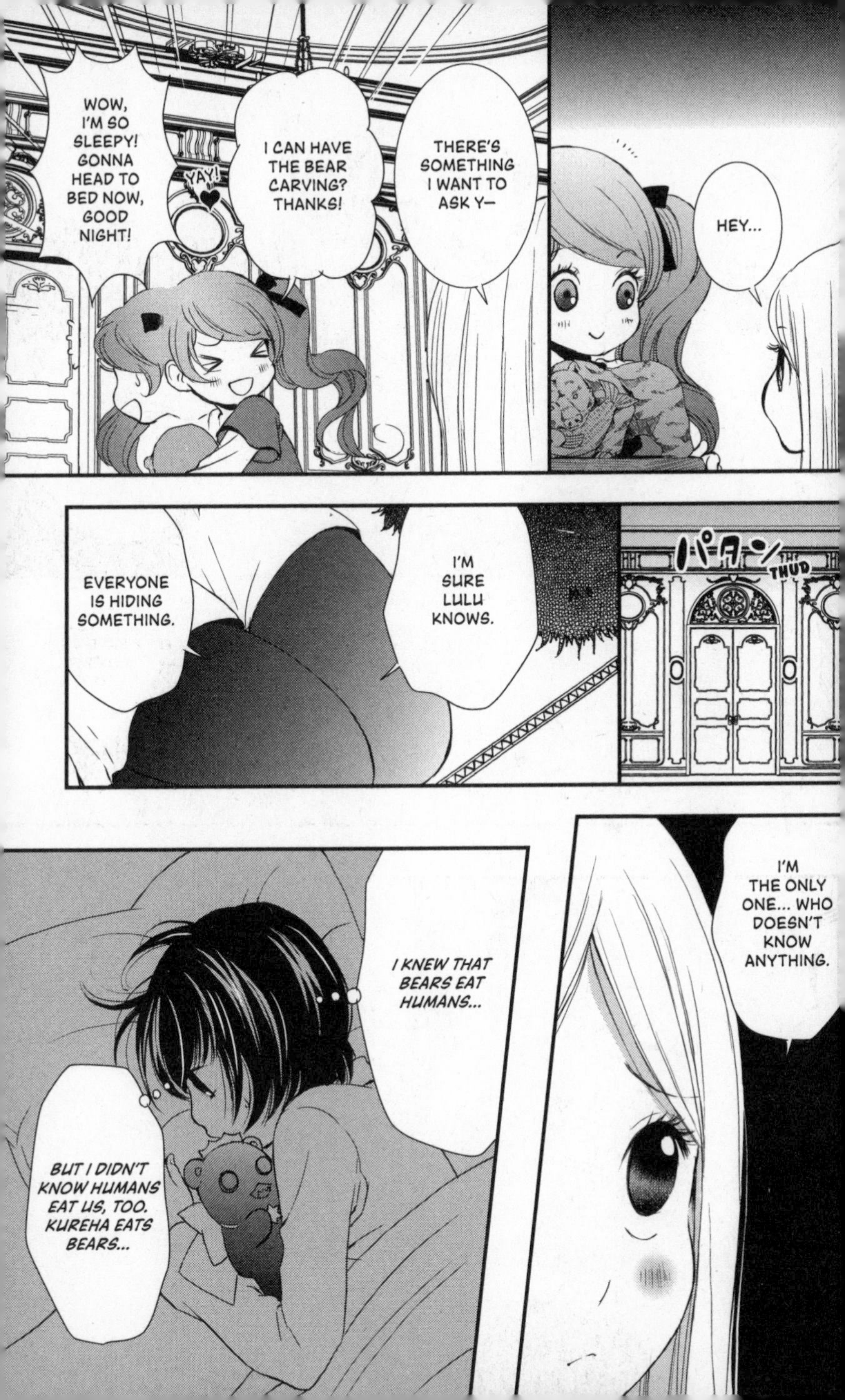
HEY...
THERE'S SOMETHING I WANT TO ASK Y—
I CAN HAVE THE BEAR CARVING? THANKS!
YAY! ♥
WOW, I'M SO SLEEPY! GONNA HEAD TO BED NOW, GOOD NIGHT!
パタン
THUD
I'M SURE LULU KNOWS.
EVERYONE IS HIDING SOMETHING.
I'M THE ONLY ONE... WHO DOESN'T KNOW ANYTHING.
I KNEW THAT BEARS EAT HUMANS...
BUT I DIDN'T KNOW HUMANS EAT US, TOO. KUREHA EATS BEARS...

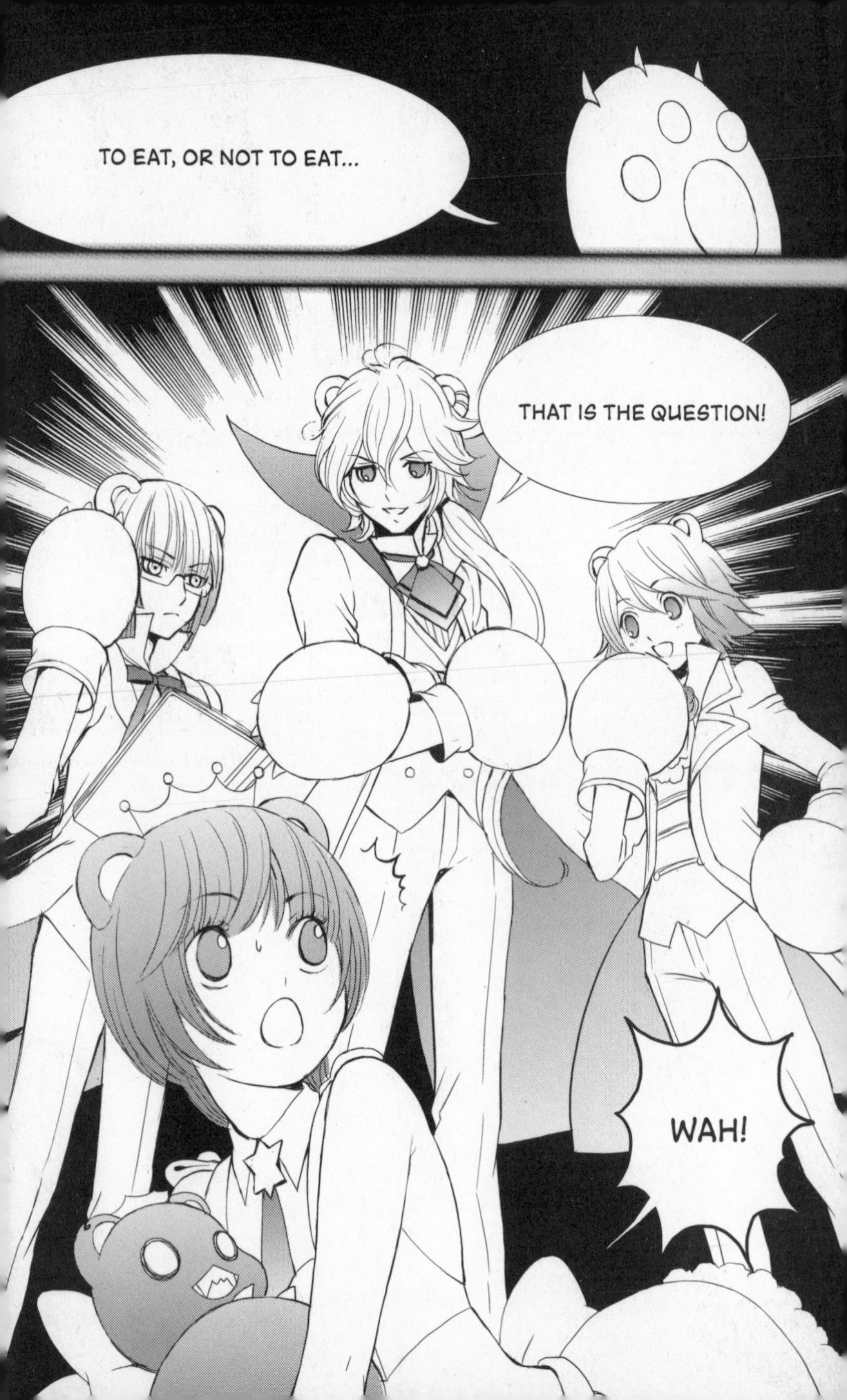
TO EAT, OR NOT TO EAT...
THAT IS THE QUESTION!
WAH!

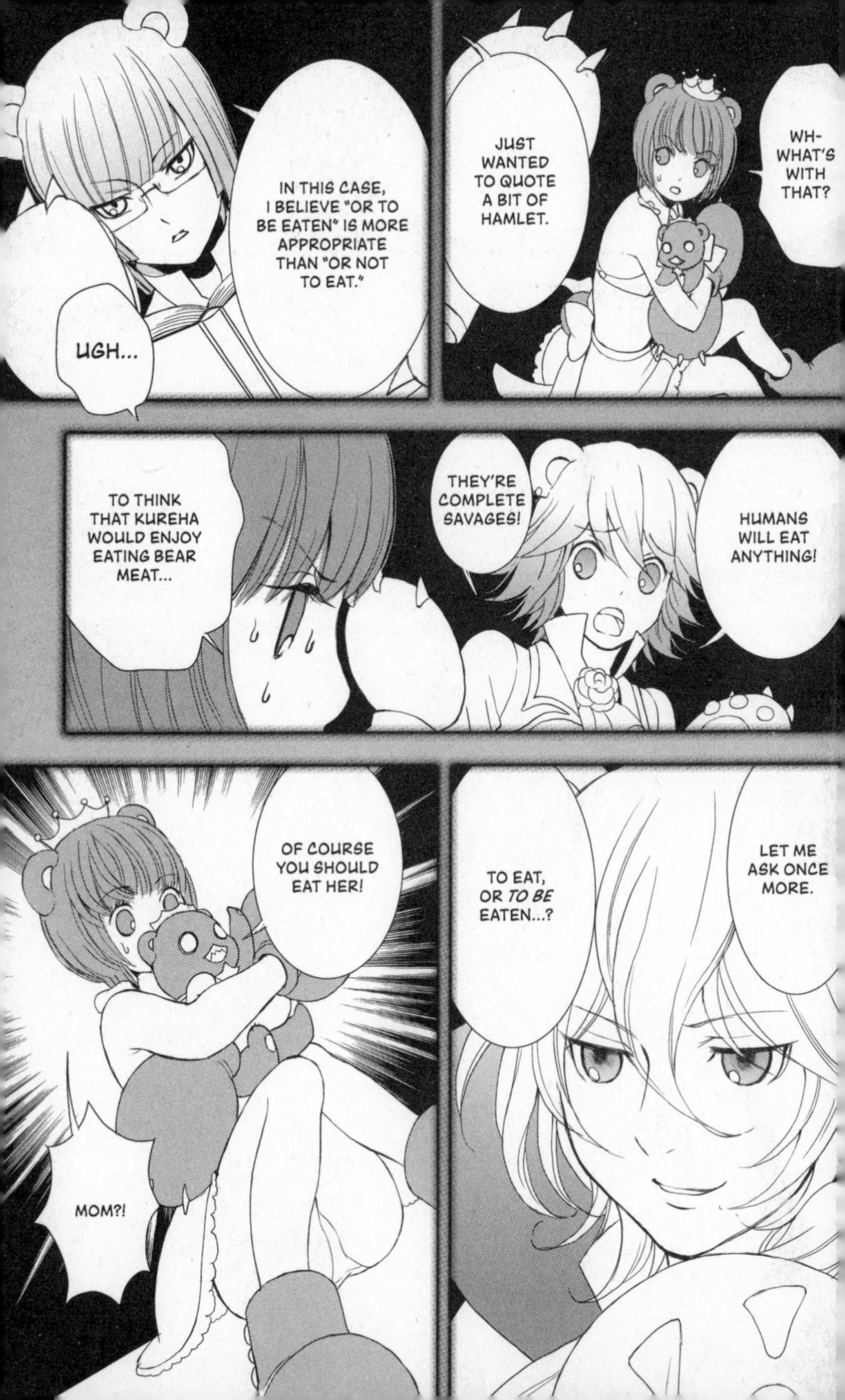
WH- WHAT'S WITH THAT?
JUST WANTED TO QUOTE A BIT OF HAMLET.
IN THIS CASE, I BELIEVE "OR TO BE EATEN" IS MORE APPROPRIATE THAN "OR NOT TO EAT."
UGH...
HUMANS WILL EAT ANYTHING!
THEY'RE COMPLETE SAVAGES!
TO THINK THAT KUREHA WOULD ENJOY EATING BEAR MEAT...
LET ME ASK ONCE MORE.
TO EAT, OR *TO BE* EATEN...?
OF COURSE YOU SHOULD EAT HER!
MOM?!

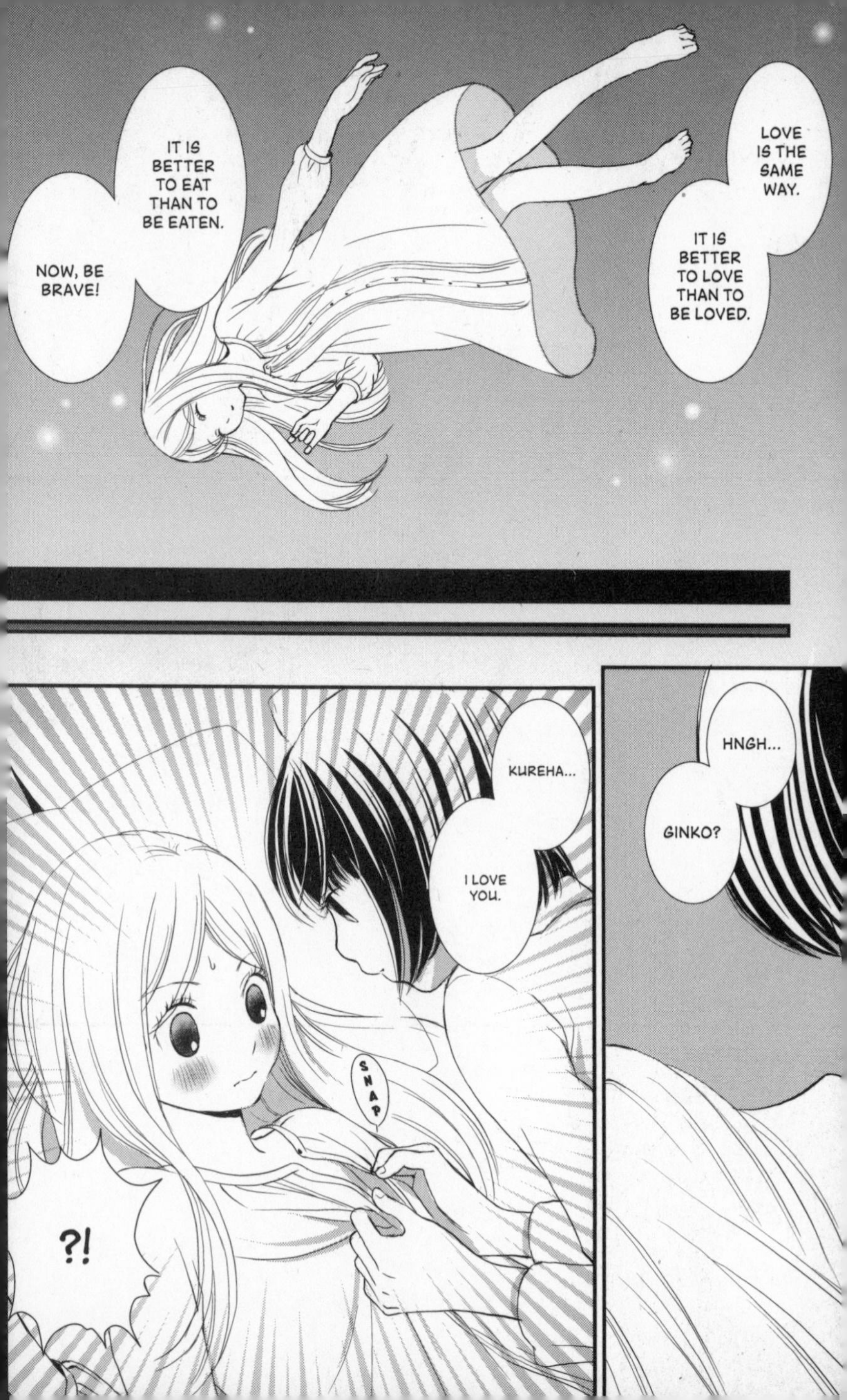
LOVE IS THE SAME WAY.
IT IS BETTER TO LOVE THAN TO BE LOVED.
IT IS BETTER TO EAT THAN TO BE EATEN.
NOW, BE BRAVE!
HNGH...
GINKO?
KUREHA...
I LOVE YOU.
SNAP
?!

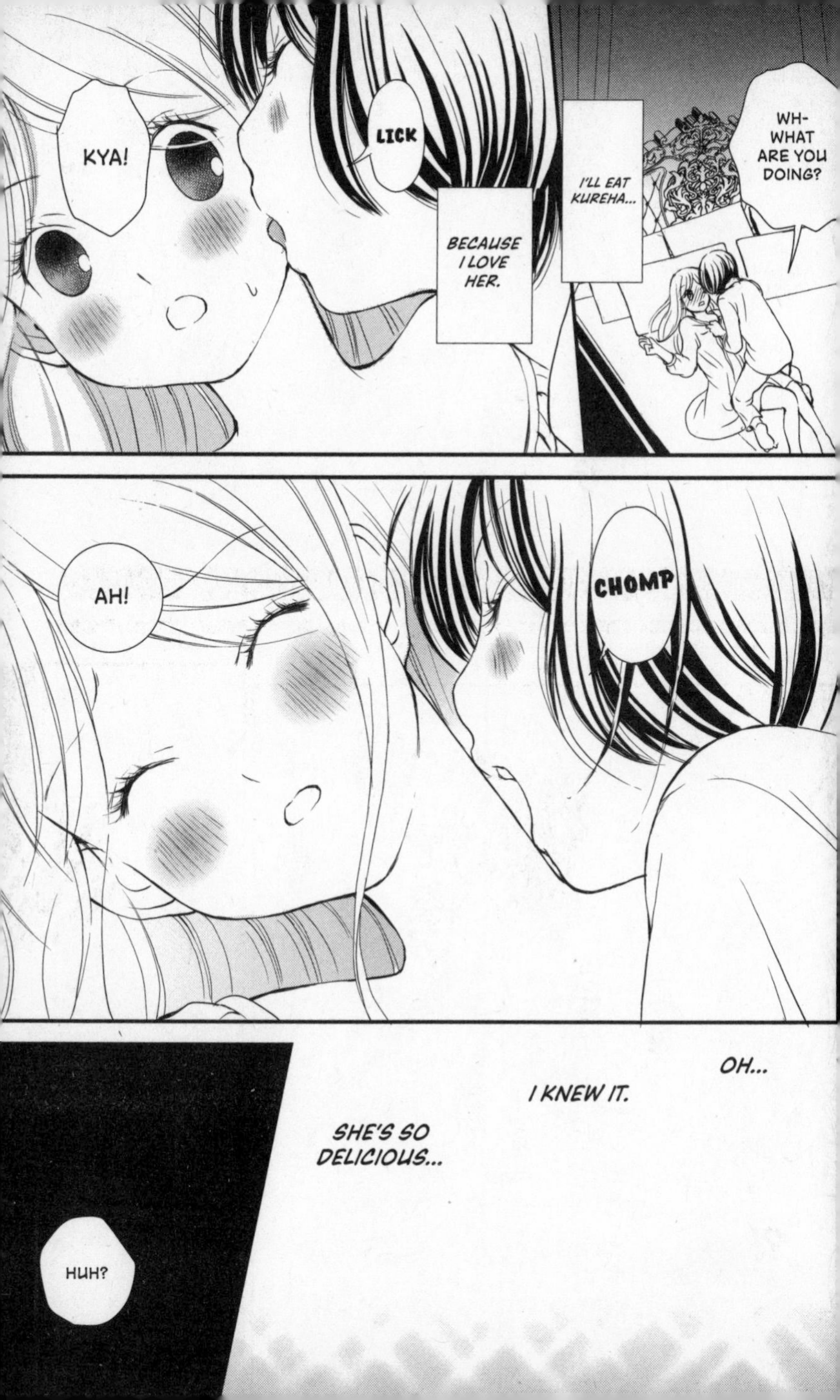
WH-
WHAT
ARE YOU
DOING?
I'LL EAT KUREHA...
BECAUSE I LOVE HER.
LICK
KYA!
CHOMP
AH!
OH...
I KNEW IT.
SHE'S SO DELICIOUS...
HUH?

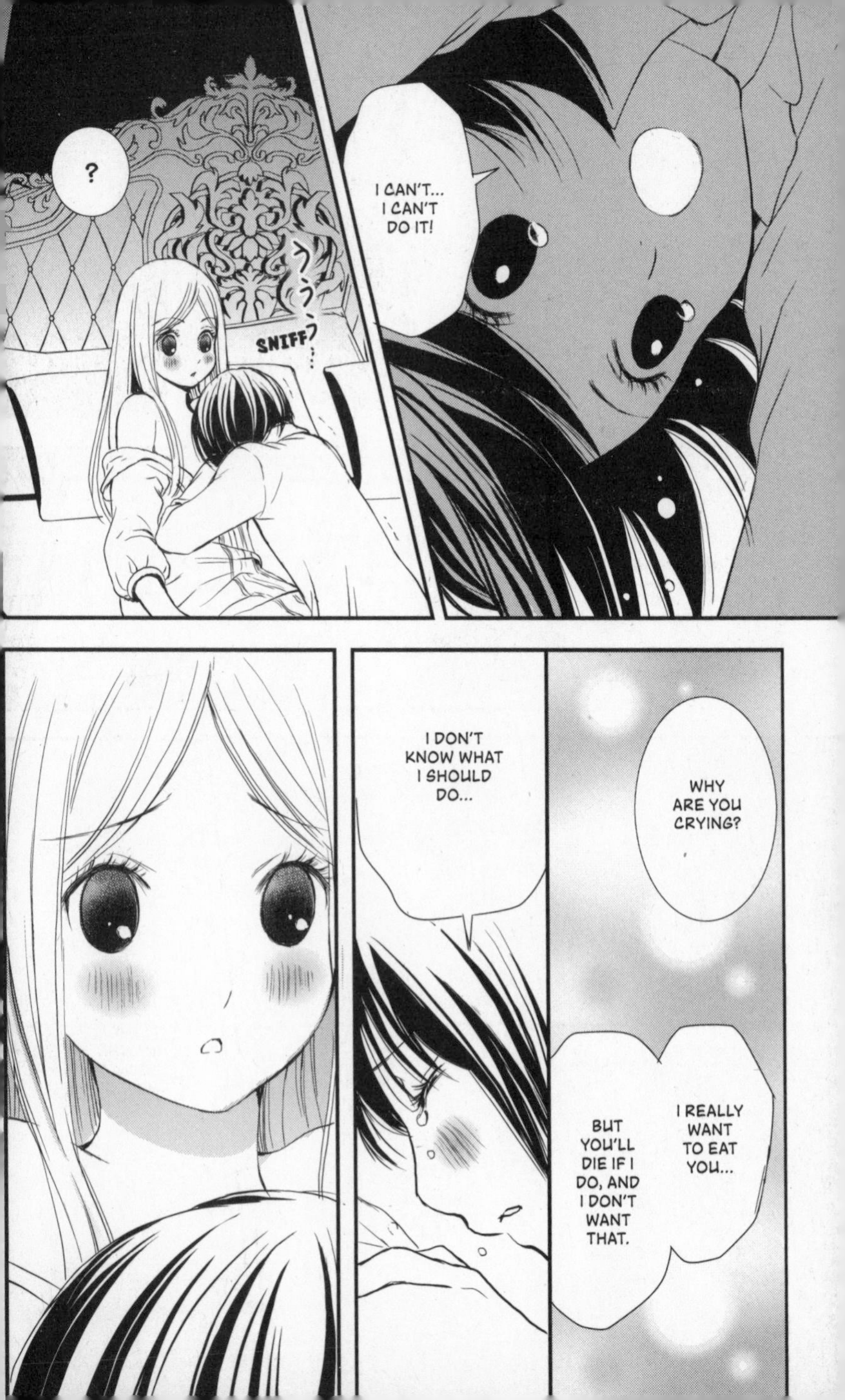
I CAN'T... I CAN'T DO IT!
?
SNIFF
WHY ARE YOU CRYING?
I REALLY WANT TO EAT YOU...
BUT YOU'LL DIE IF I DO, AND I DON'T WANT THAT.
I DON'T KNOW WHAT I SHOULD DO...

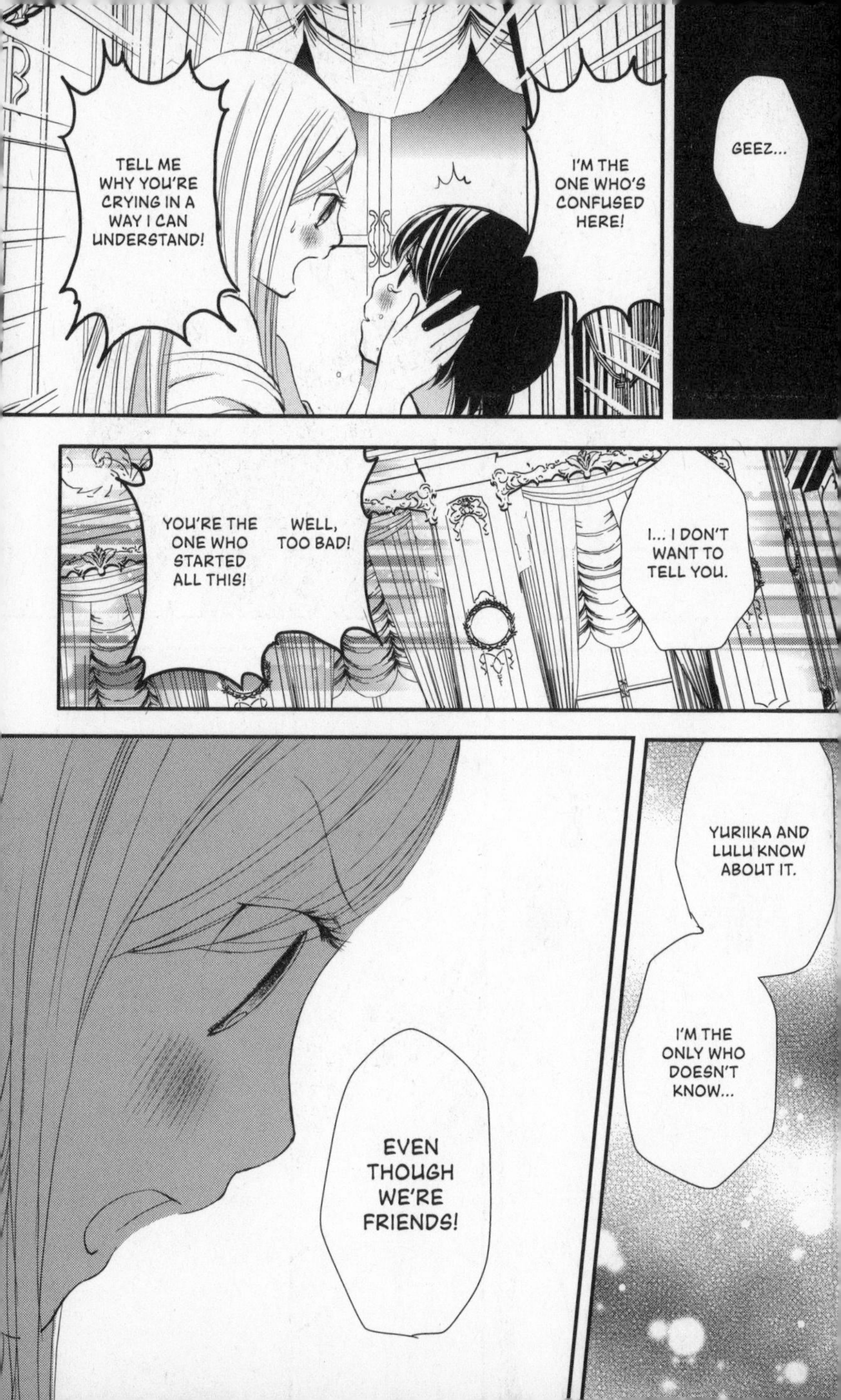
GEEZ...
I'M THE ONE WHO'S CONFUSED HERE!
TELL ME WHY YOU'RE CRYING IN A WAY I CAN UNDERSTAND!
I... I DON'T WANT TO TELL YOU.
WELL, TOO BAD!
YOU'RE THE ONE WHO STARTED ALL THIS!
YURIIKA AND LULU KNOW ABOUT IT.
I'M THE ONLY WHO DOESN'T KNOW...
EVEN THOUGH WE'RE FRIENDS!

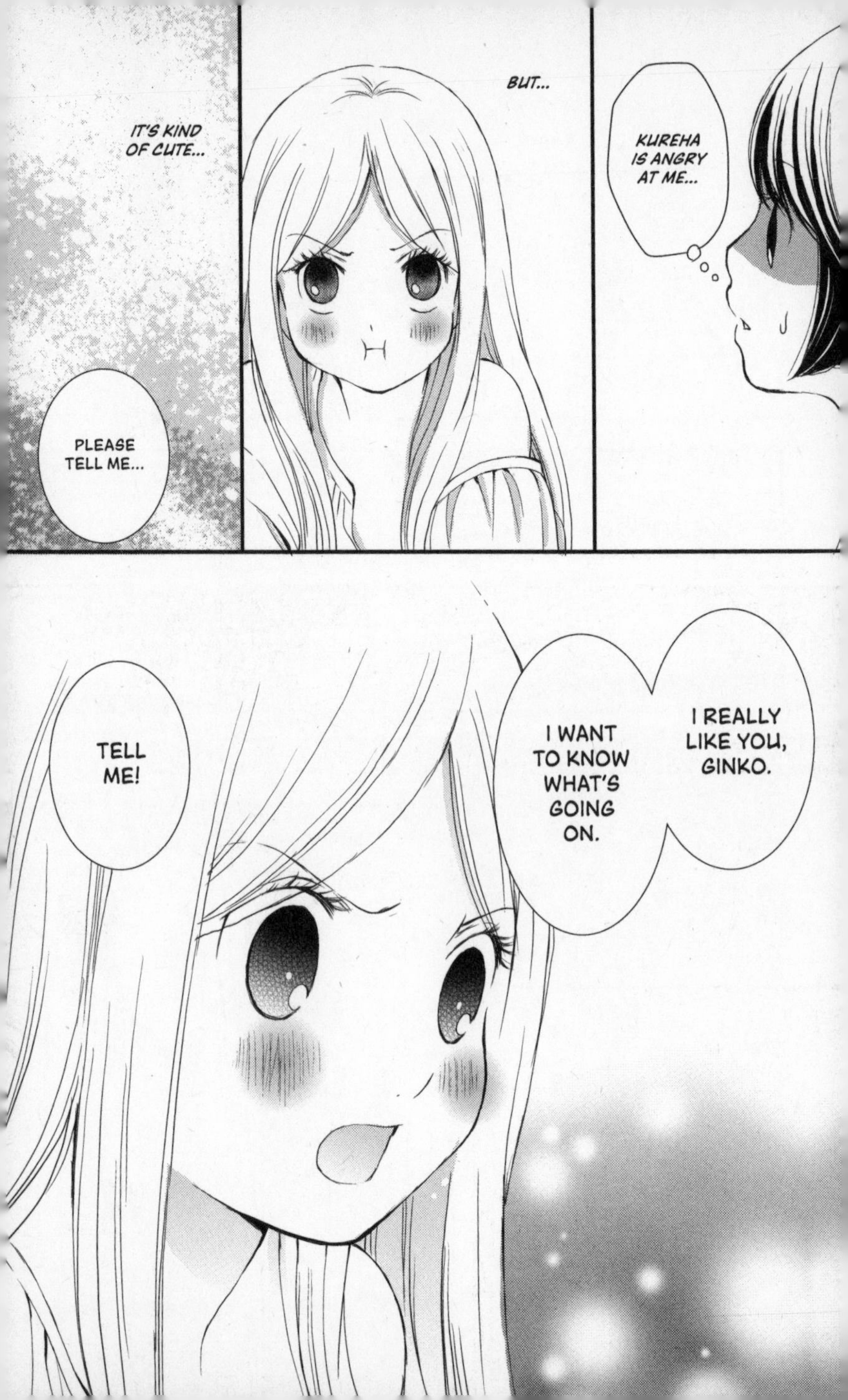
KUREHA IS ANGRY AT ME...
BUT...
IT'S KIND OF CUTE...
PLEASE TELL ME...
I REALLY LIKE YOU, GINKO.
I WANT TO KNOW WHAT'S GOING ON.
TELL ME!

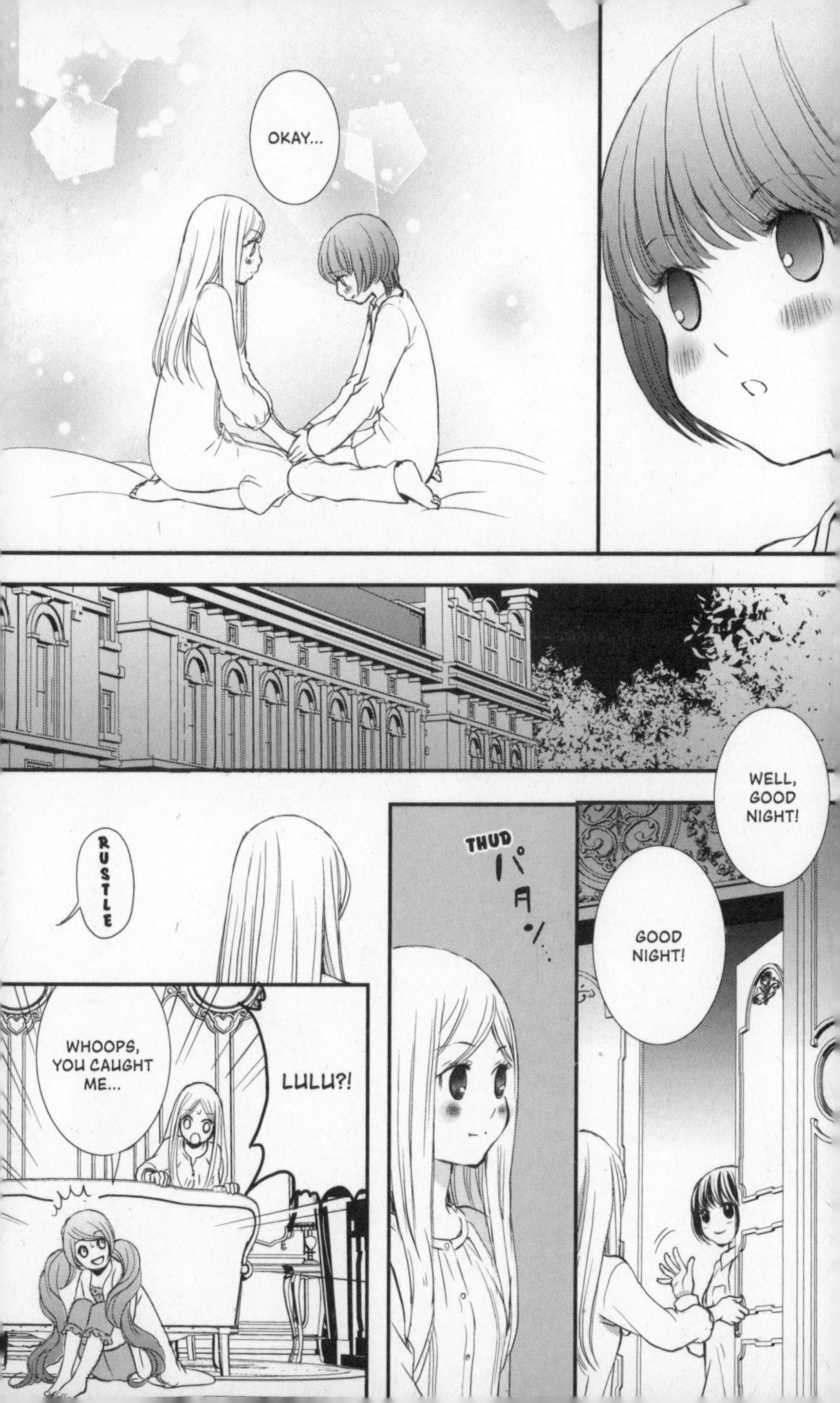
OKAY...
WELL, GOOD NIGHT!
GOOD NIGHT!
THUD
RUSTLE
LULU?!
WHOOPS, YOU CAUGHT ME...

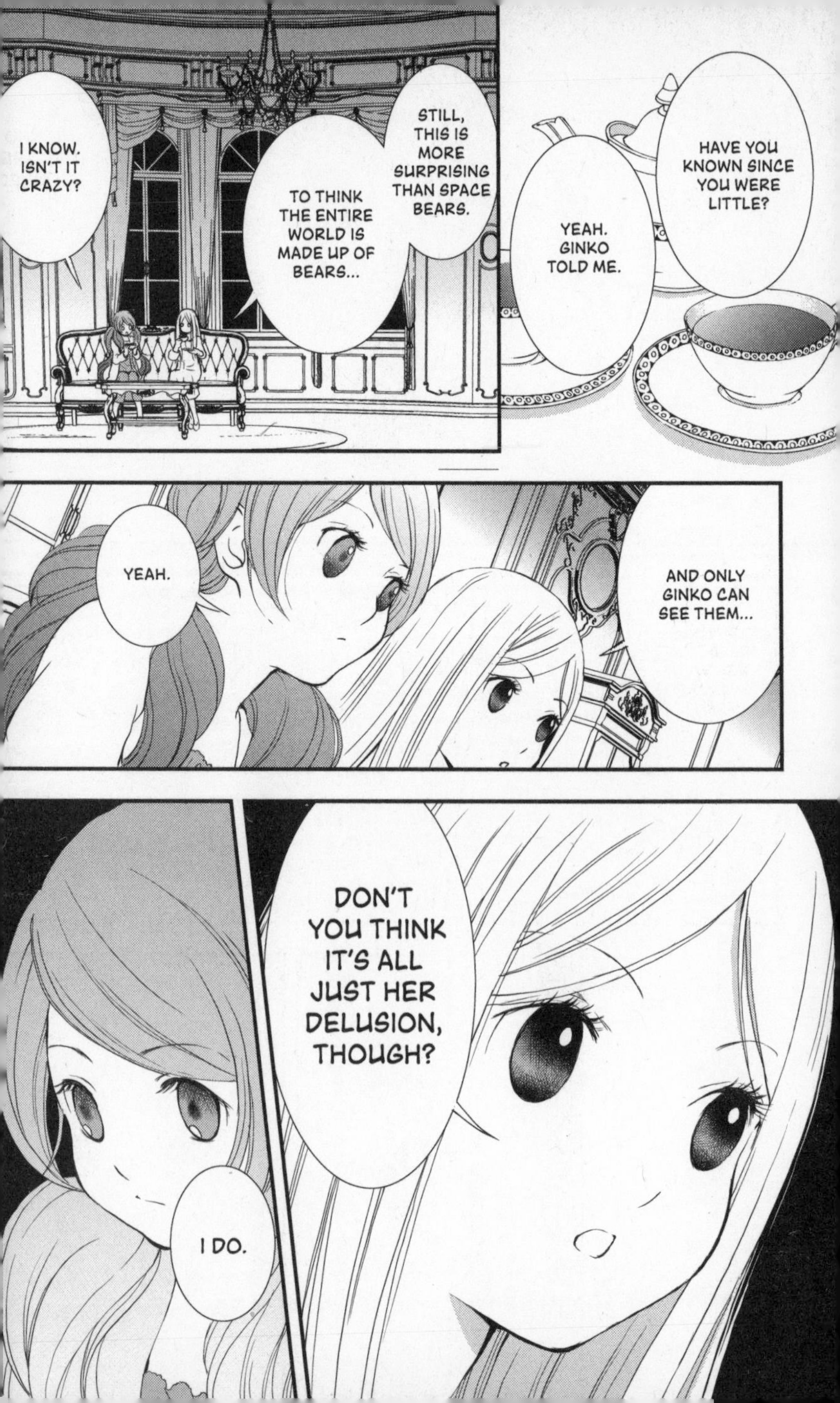
HAVE YOU KNOWN SINCE YOU WERE LITTLE?
YEAH. GINKO TOLD ME.
STILL, THIS IS MORE SURPRISING THAN SPACE BEARS.
TO THINK THE ENTIRE WORLD IS MADE UP OF BEARS...
I KNOW. ISN'T IT CRAZY?
AND ONLY GINKO CAN SEE THEM...
YEAH.
DON'T YOU THINK IT'S ALL JUST HER DELUSION, THOUGH?
I DO.

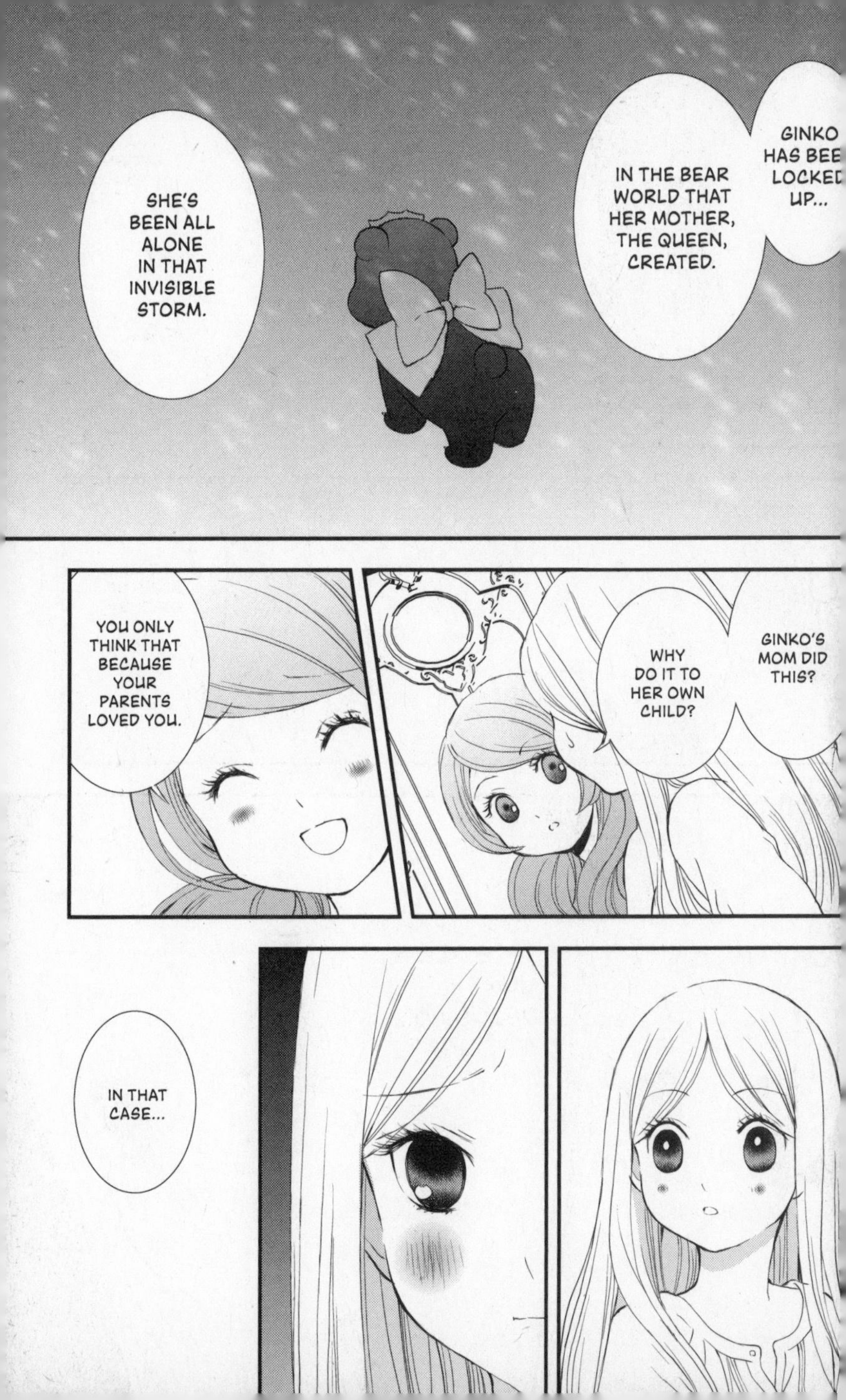
GINKO HAS BEE LOCKED UP...
IN THE BEAR WORLD THAT HER MOTHER, THE QUEEN, CREATED.
SHE'S BEEN ALL ALONE IN THAT INVISIBLE STORM.
GINKO'S MOM DID THIS?
WHY DO IT TO HER OWN CHILD?
YOU ONLY THINK THAT BECAUSE YOUR PARENTS LOVED YOU.
IN THAT CASE...

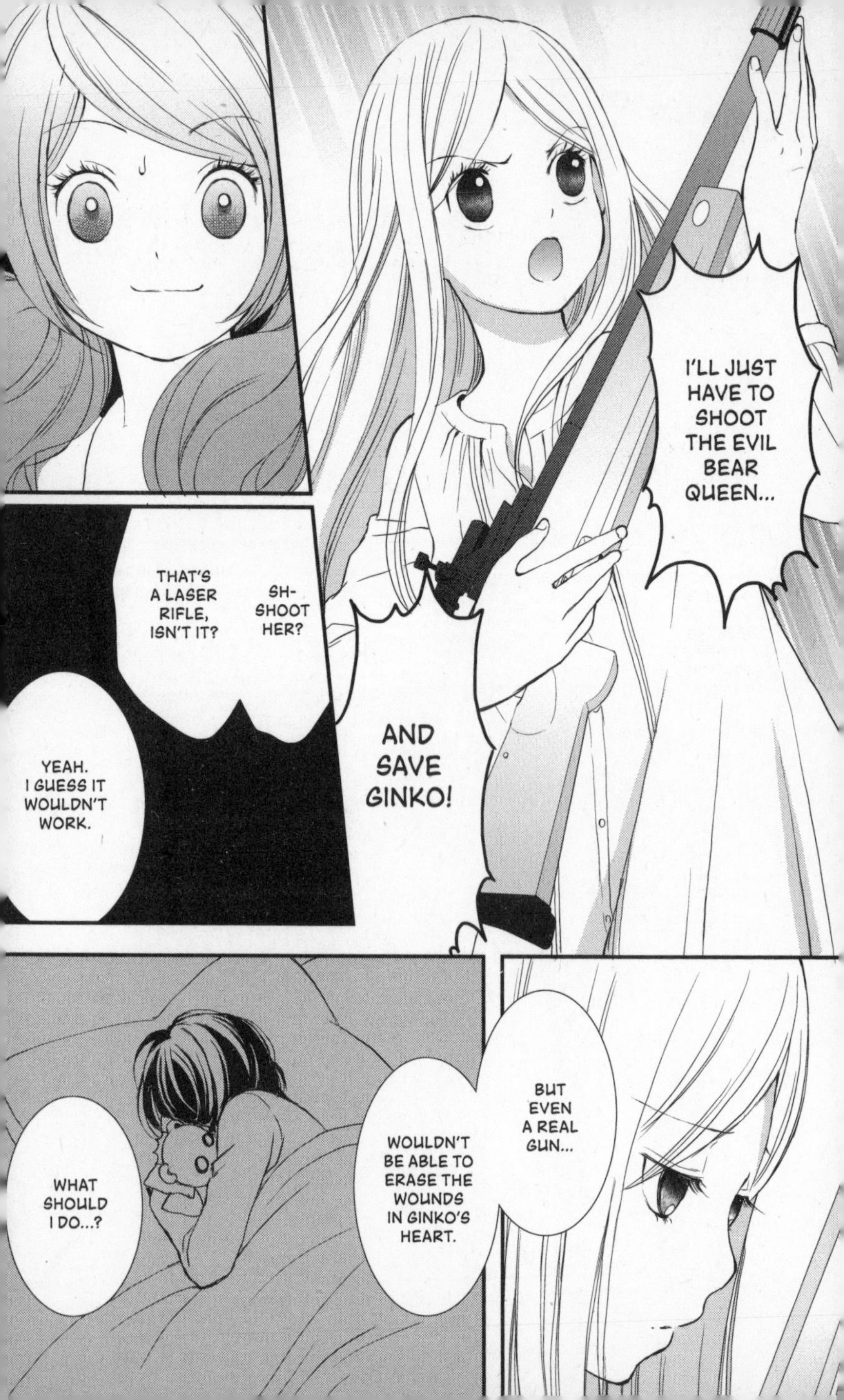
I'LL JUST HAVE TO SHOOT THE EVIL BEAR QUEEN...
AND SAVE GINKO!
SH-SHOOT HER?
THAT'S A LASER RIFLE, ISN'T IT?
YEAH. I GUESS IT WOULDN'T WORK.
BUT EVEN A REAL GUN...
WOULDN'T BE ABLE TO ERASE THE WOUNDS IN GINKO'S HEART.
WHAT SHOULD I DO...?

## Bonus Chapter

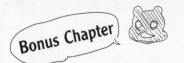

# (Not) Yuri Bear Storm!

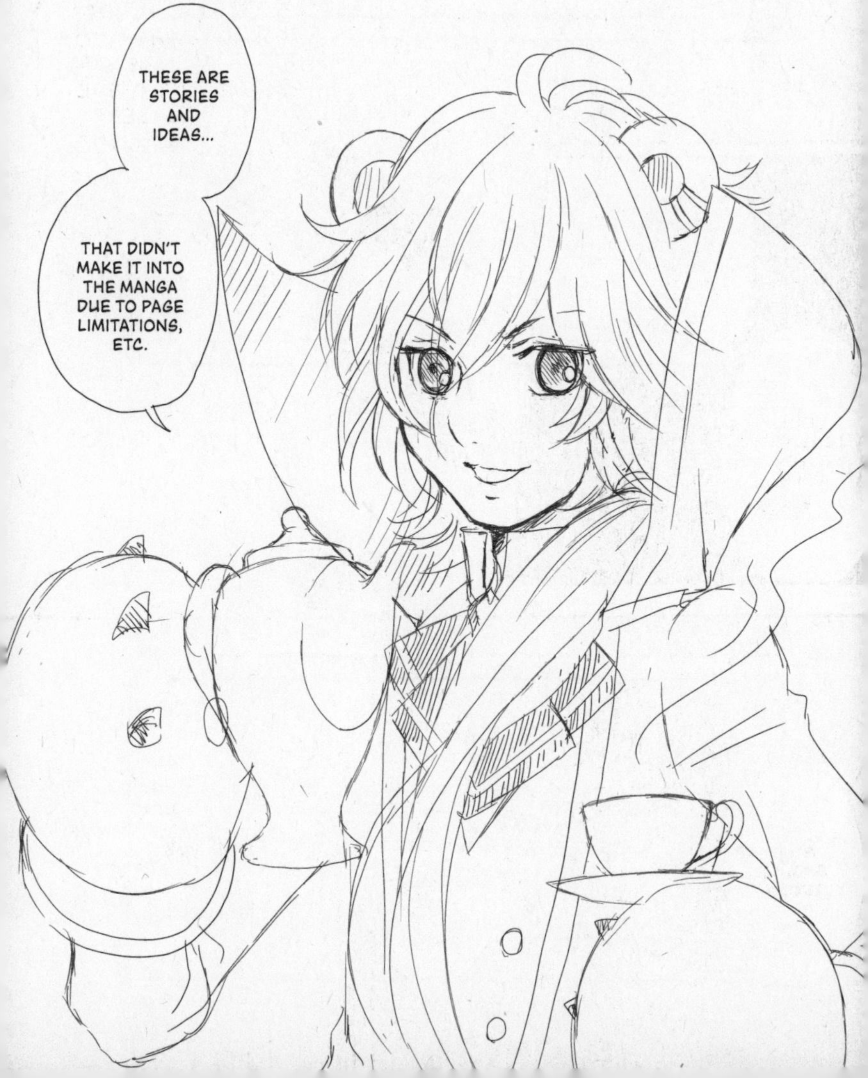
THESE ARE STORIES AND IDEAS...
THAT DIDN'T MAKE IT INTO THE MANGA DUE TO PAGE LIMITATIONS, ETC.

## Chapter 2: Cut Scene

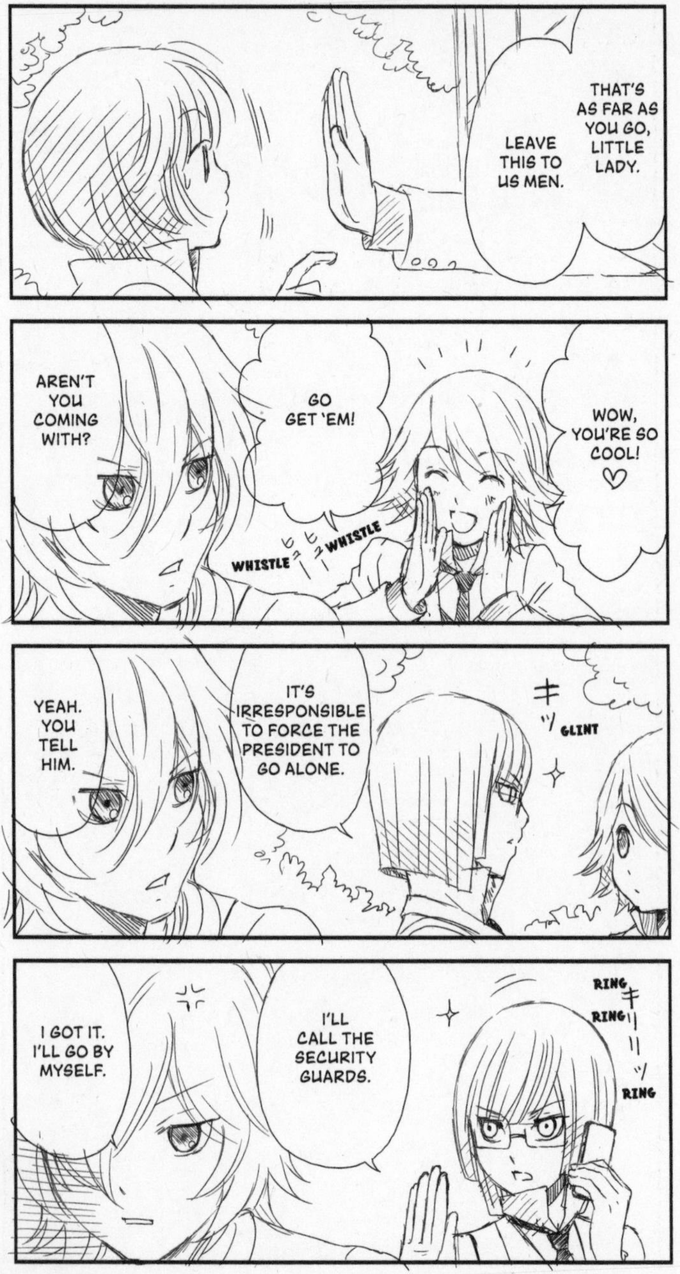
THAT'S AS FAR AS YOU GO, LITTLE LADY.
LEAVE THIS TO US MEN.
WOW, YOU'RE SO COOL! ♡
GO GET 'EM!
AREN'T YOU COMING WITH?
WHISTLE
WHISTLE
GLINT
IT'S IRRESPONSIBLE TO FORCE THE PRESIDENT TO GO ALONE.
YEAH. YOU TELL HIM.
RING
RING
RING
I'LL CALL THE SECURITY GUARDS.
I GOT IT. I'LL GO BY MYSELF.

## Chapter 5: An Idea I Thought of Later

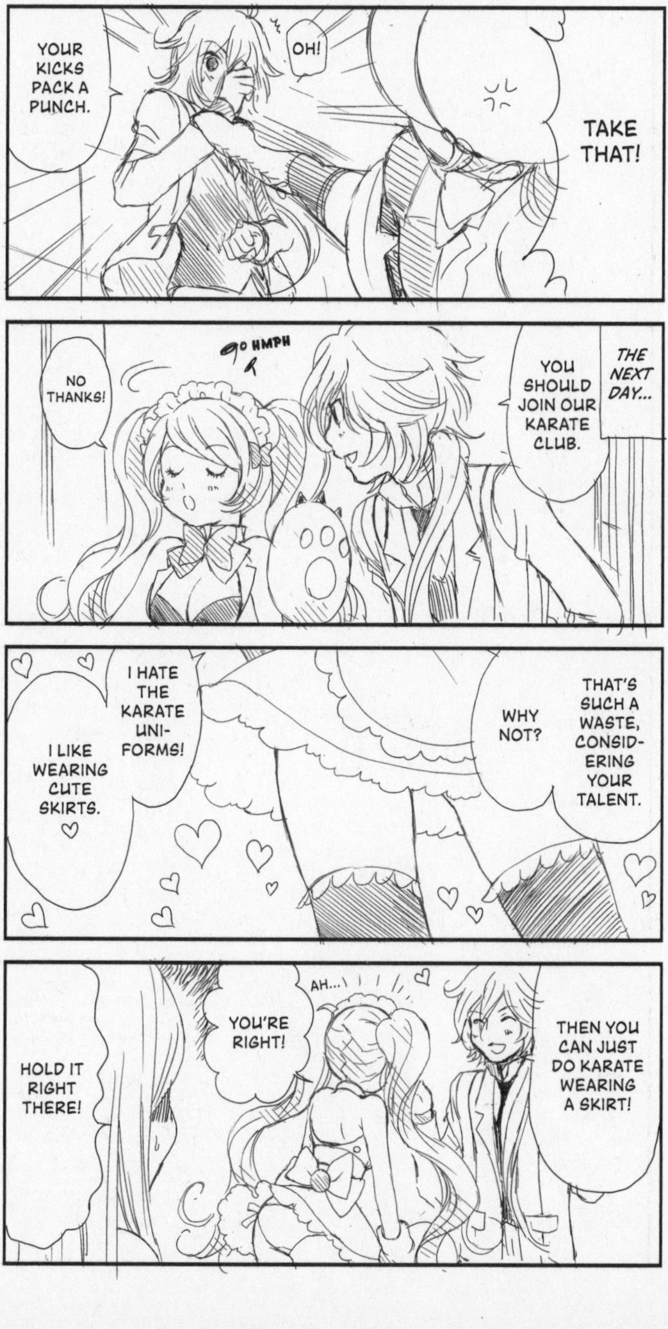
TAKE THAT!
OH!
YOUR KICKS PACK A PUNCH.
THE NEXT DAY...
YOU SHOULD JOIN OUR KARATE CLUB.
HMPH
NO THANKS!
THAT'S SUCH A WASTE, CONSIDERING YOUR TALENT.
WHY NOT?
I HATE THE KARATE UNIFORMS!
I LIKE WEARING CUTE SKIRTS.
THEN YOU CAN JUST DO KARATE WEARING A SKIRT!
AH...
YOU'RE RIGHT!
HOLD IT RIGHT THERE!

## Chapter 8: Cut Scene (The Next Morning)

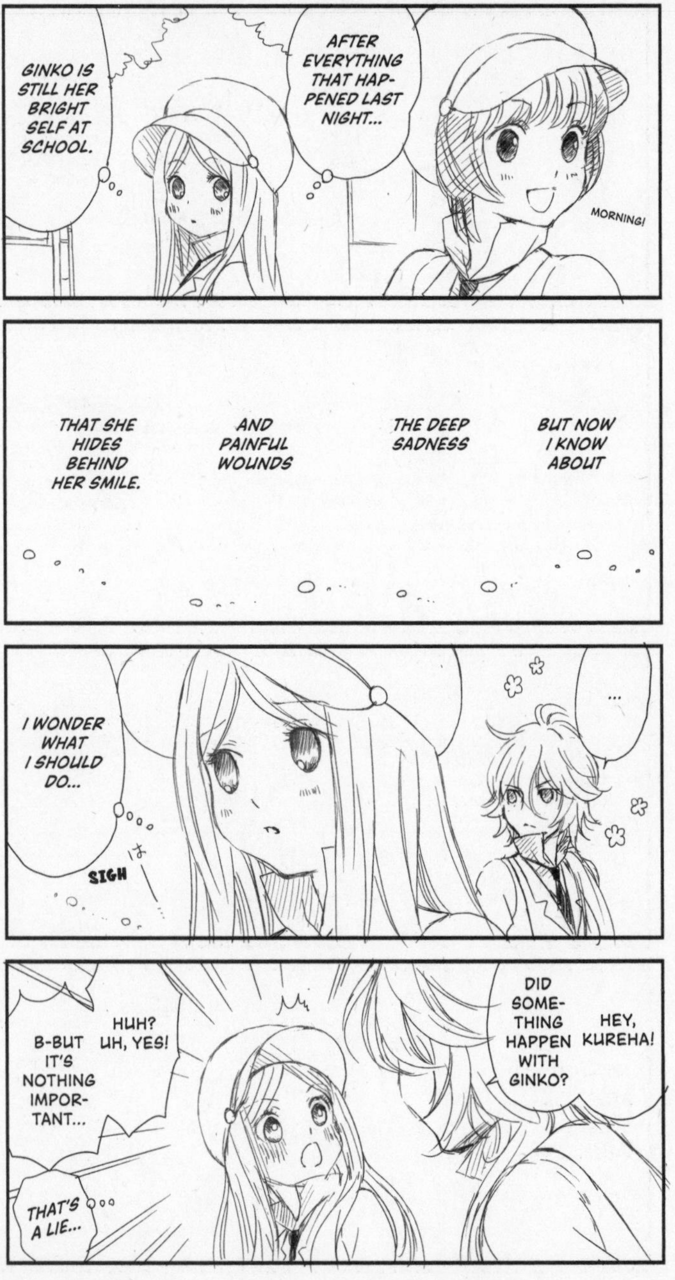
MORNING!
AFTER EVERYTHING THAT HAPPENED LAST NIGHT...
GINKO IS STILL HER BRIGHT SELF AT SCHOOL.
BUT NOW I KNOW ABOUT
THE DEEP SADNESS
AND PAINFUL WOUNDS
THAT SHE HIDES BEHIND HER SMILE.
...
I WONDER WHAT I SHOULD DO...
は
SIGH
HEY, KUREHA!
DID SOMETHING HAPPEN WITH GINKO?
HUH? UH, YES!
B-BUT IT'S NOTHING IMPORTANT...
THAT'S A LIE...

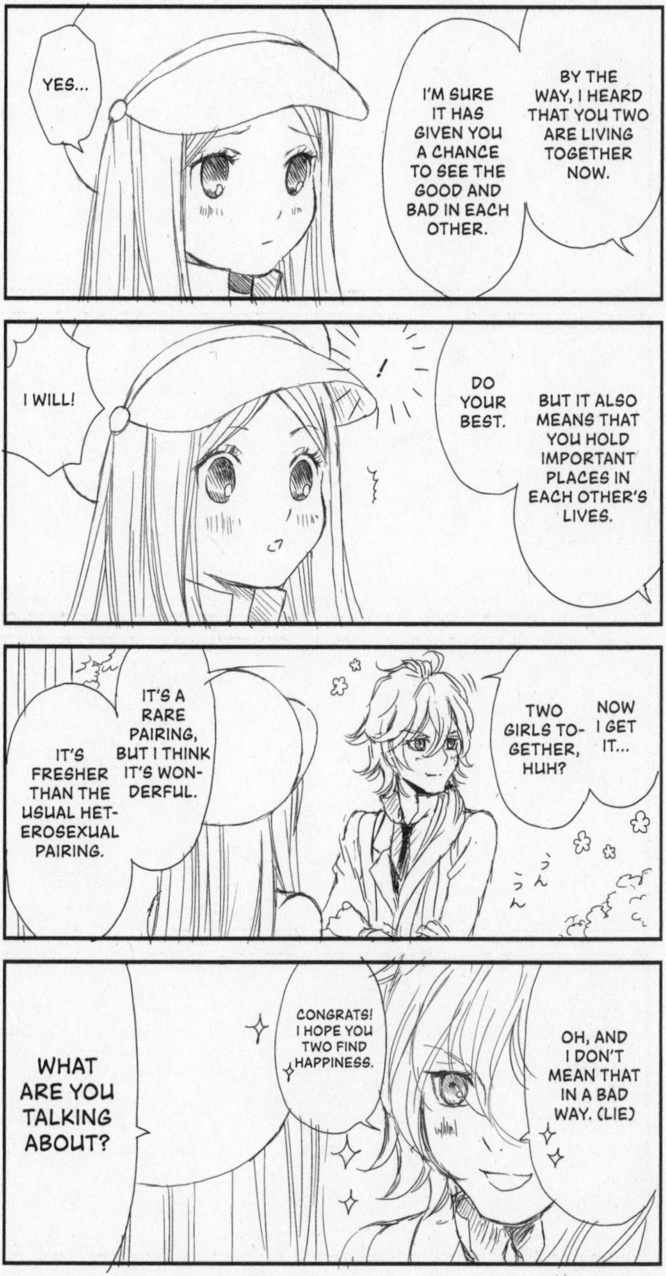
BY THE WAY, I HEARD THAT YOU TWO ARE LIVING TOGETHER NOW.
I'M SURE IT HAS GIVEN YOU A CHANCE TO SEE THE GOOD AND BAD IN EACH OTHER.
YES...
BUT IT ALSO MEANS THAT YOU HOLD IMPORTANT PLACES IN EACH OTHER'S LIVES.
DO YOUR BEST.
!
I WILL!
NOW I GET IT...
TWO GIRLS TOGETHER, HUH?
うん うん
IT'S A RARE PAIRING, BUT I THINK IT'S WONDERFUL.
IT'S FRESHER THAN THE USUAL HETEROSEXUAL PAIRING.
OH, AND I DON'T MEAN THAT IN A BAD WAY. (LIE)
CONGRATS! I HOPE YOU TWO FIND HAPPINESS.
WHAT ARE YOU TALKING ABOUT?

**A scene that almost made it in but was cut due to page limitations...**

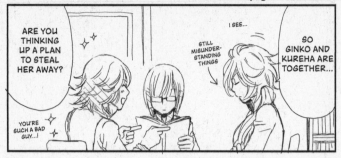

SO GINKO AND KUREHA ARE TOGETHER...
I SEE...
STILL MISUNDERSTANDING THINGS
ARE YOU THINKING UP A PLAN TO STEAL HER AWAY?
YOU'RE SUCH A BAD GUY...!
OF COURSE NOT.
ALTHOUGH THINGS WOULD BE DIFFERENT IF HER PARTNER WAS A MAN.
I WOULD NEVER DO ANYTHING TO MAKE A WOMAN CRY.
I KNOW!
MAYBE ONE DAY THEY'LL LET YOU IN AND THE THREE OF YOU CAN HAVE FUN TOGETHER.
YOU SHOULDN'T SAY THAT TO A LESBIAN COUPLE, EVEN AS A JOKE.
THEY'LL TELL YOU TO WATCH PORN INSTEAD...
OR THAT THEY'VE BEEN TOLD THAT A MILLION TIMES, OR THEY'LL JUST GET PISSED AND ASK IF YOU REALLY THINK THAT'S FUNNY.
YOU HAVE TO BE CAREFUL.
JUST HOW MANY LESBIAN COUPLES HAVE YOU PISSED OFF?

END

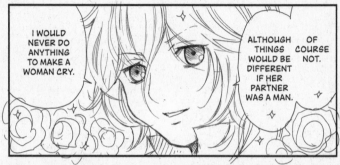

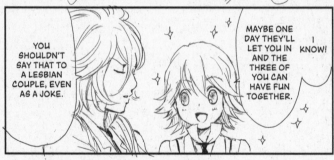

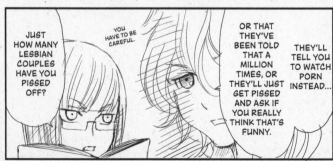

**YURIKUMA ARASHI**

# Yuri Bear Storm

E N D

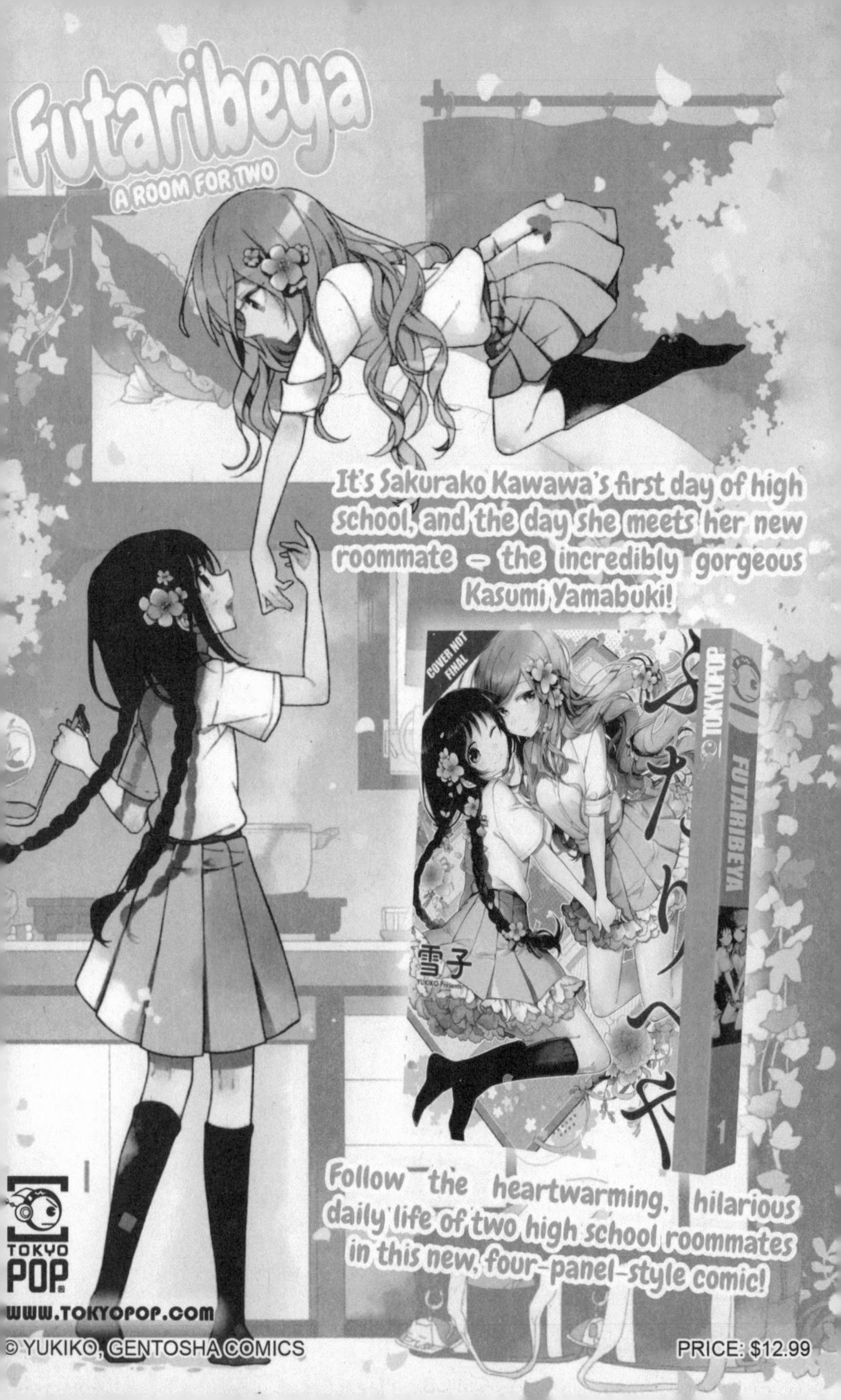
Futaribeya
A ROOM FOR TWO
It's Sakurako Kawawa's first day of high school, and the day she meets her new roommate – the incredibly gorgeous Kasumi Yamabuki!
COVER NOT FINAL
TOKYOPOP
FUTARIBEYA
雪子
YUKIKO Presents
1
Follow the heartwarming, hilarious daily life of two high school roommates in this new, four-panel-style comic!
TOKYO POP
WWW.TOKYOPOP.COM
© YUKIKO, GENTOSHA COMICS
PRICE: $12.99

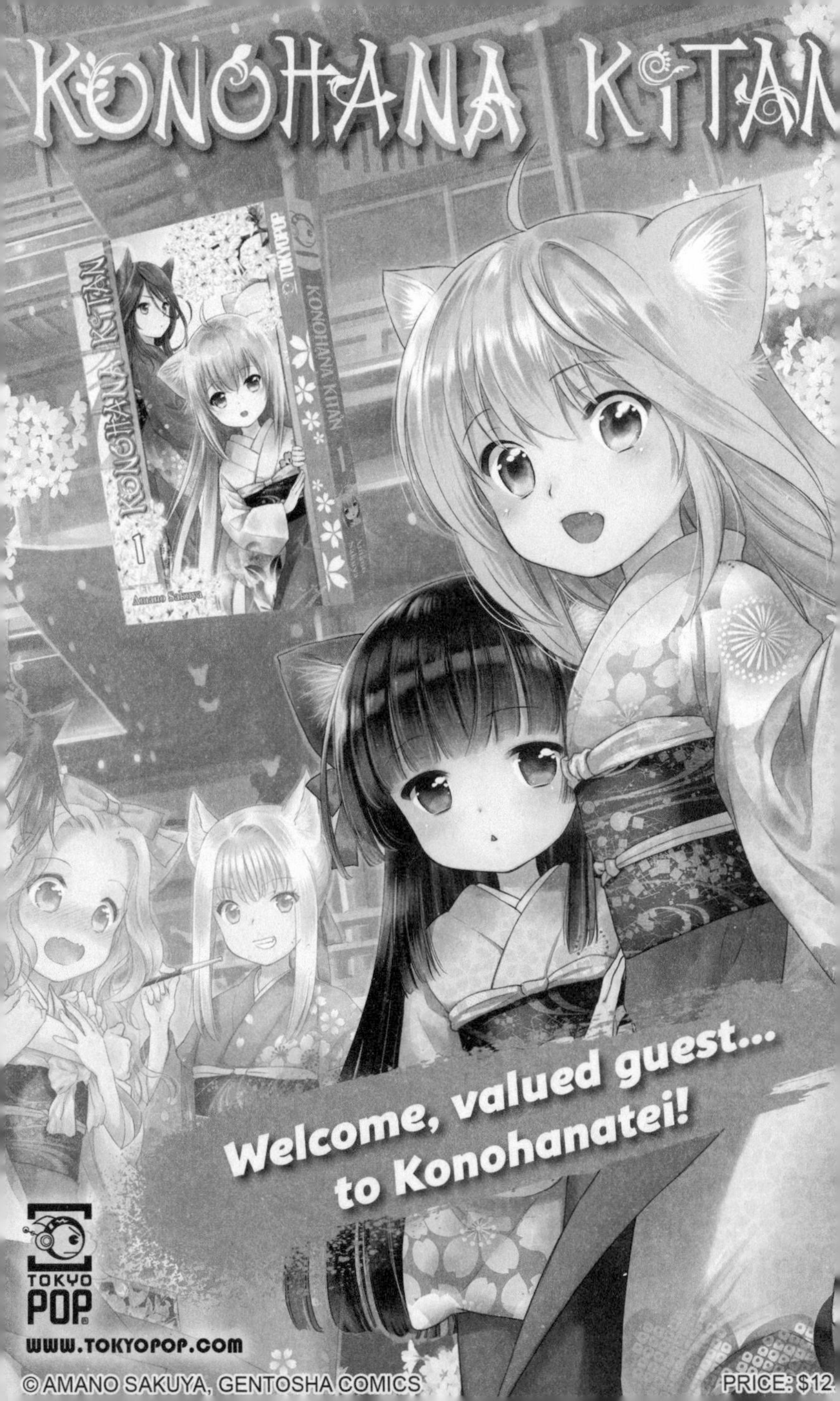
KONOHANA KITAN
KONOHANA KITAN
1
Amano Sakuya
KONOHANA KITAN
TOKYOPOP
Welcome, valued guest...
to Konohanatei!
TOKYO POP
WWW.TOKYOPOP.COM
© AMANO SAKUYA, GENTOSHA COMICS
PRICE: $12

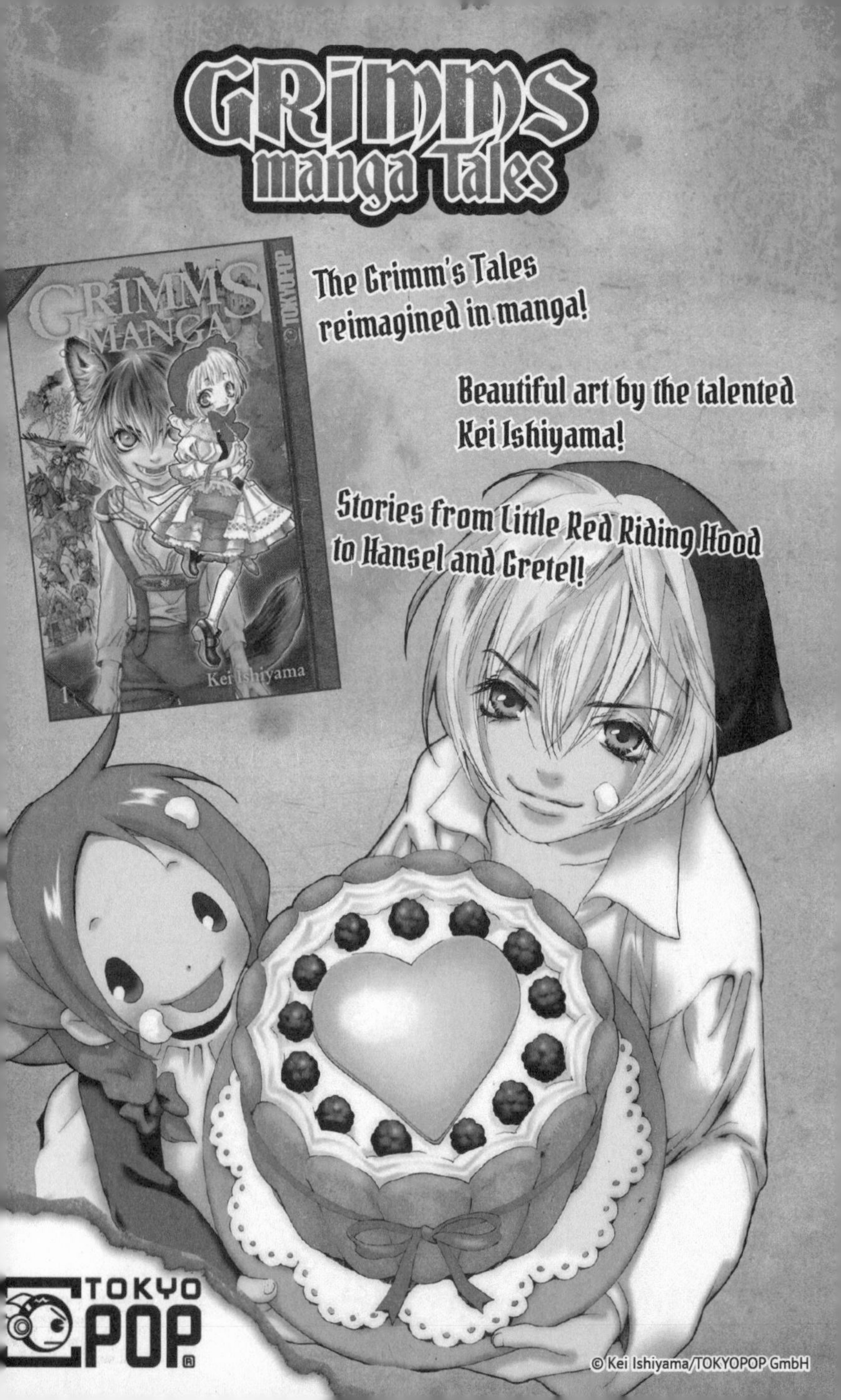
GRIMMS
manga Tales
GRIMMS MANGA
TOKYOPOP
Kei Ishiyama
1
The Grimm's Tales
reimagined in manga!
Beautiful art by the talented
Kei Ishiyama!
Stories from Little Red Riding Hood
to Hansel and Gretel!
TOKYO POP
© Kei Ishiyama/TOKYOPOP GmbH

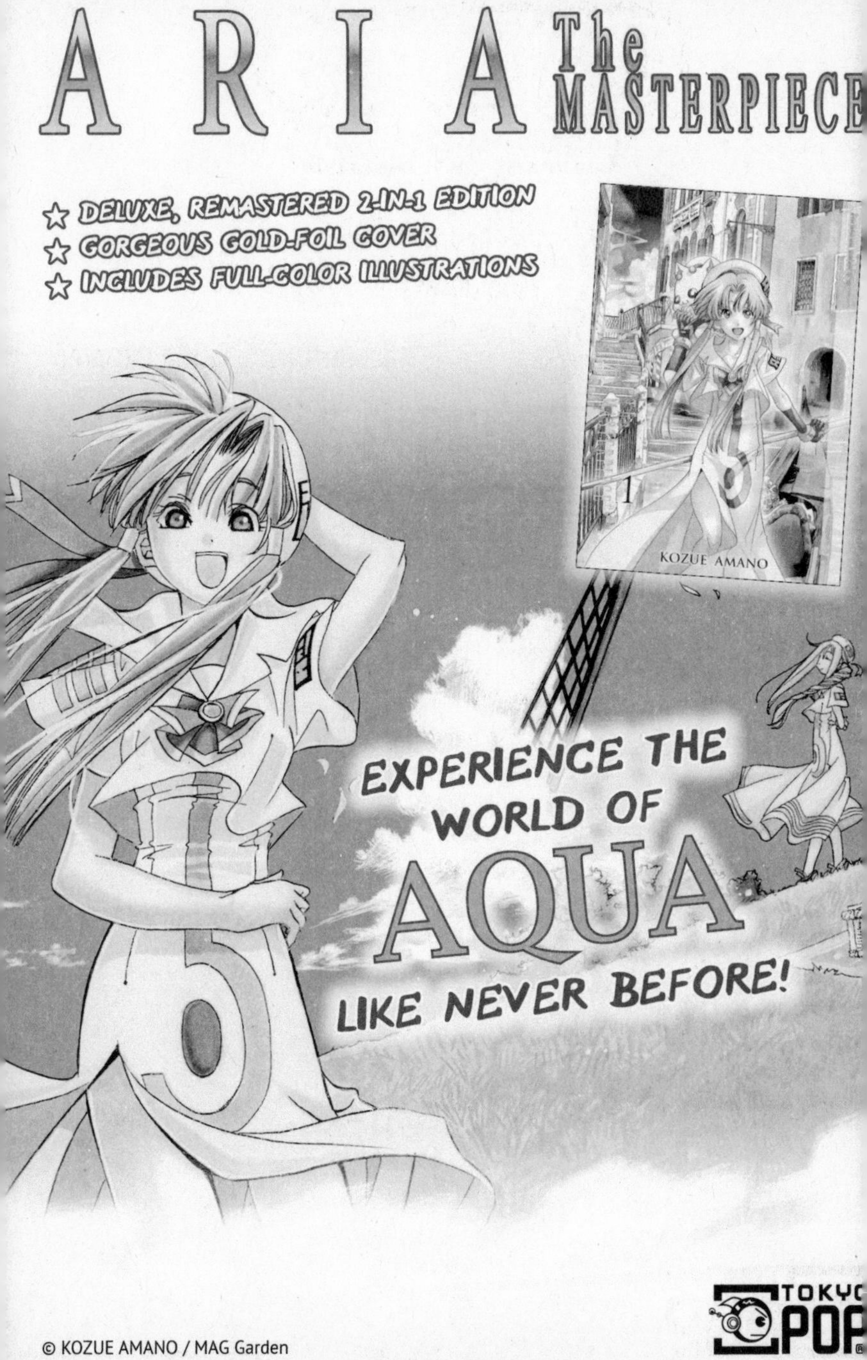
ARIA The MASTERPIECE
☆ DELUXE, REMASTERED 2-IN-1 EDITION
☆ GORGEOUS GOLD-FOIL COVER
☆ INCLUDES FULL-COLOR ILLUSTRATIONS
1
KOZUE AMANO
EXPERIENCE THE WORLD OF
AQUA
LIKE NEVER BEFORE!
TOKYOPOP

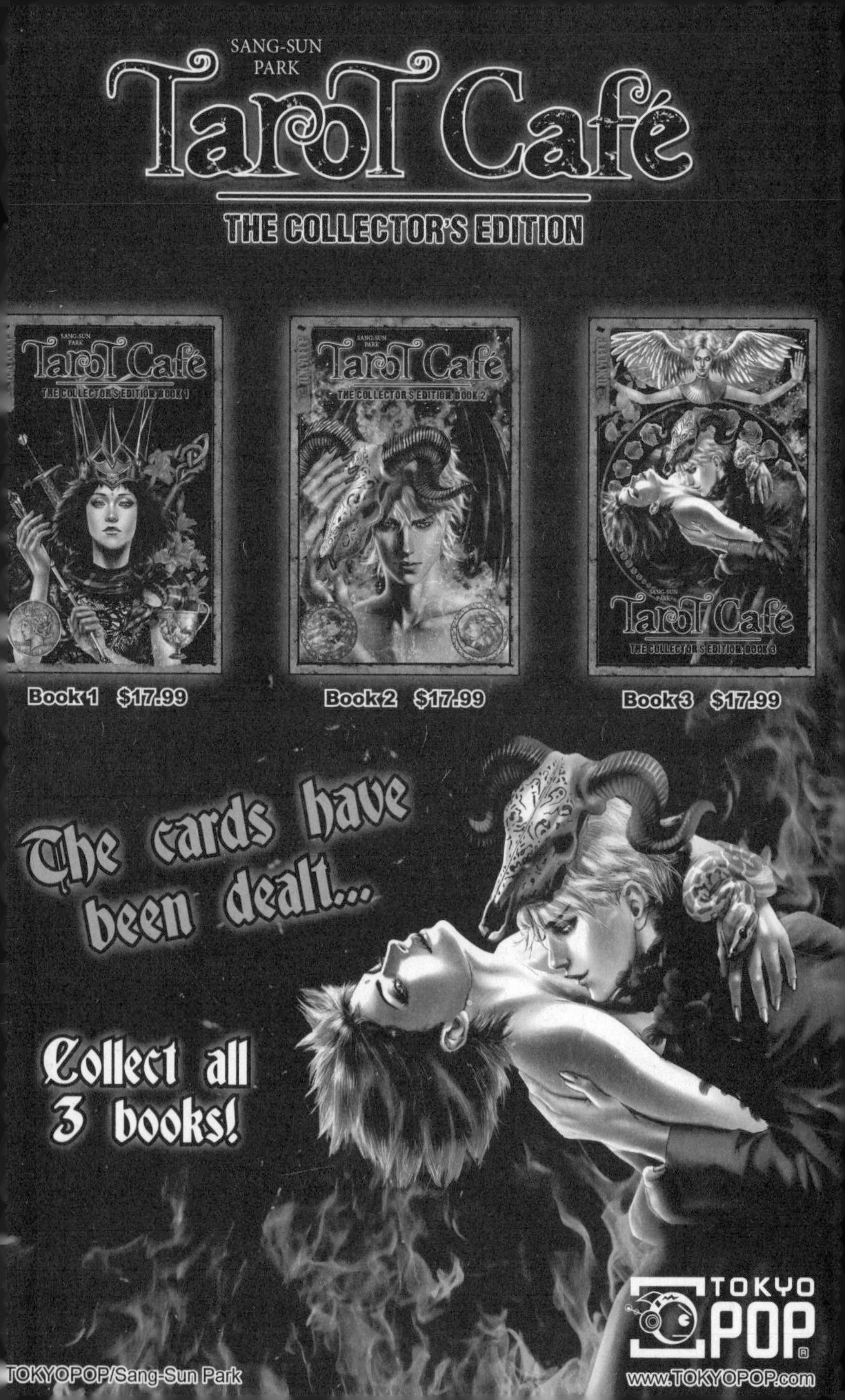
SANG-SUN PARK
Tarot Café
THE COLLECTOR'S EDITION
Book 1 $17.99
Book 2 $17.99
Book 3 $17.99
The cards have been dealt...
Collect all 3 books!
TOKYOPOP
TOKYOPOP/Sang-Sun Park
www.TOKYOPOP.com

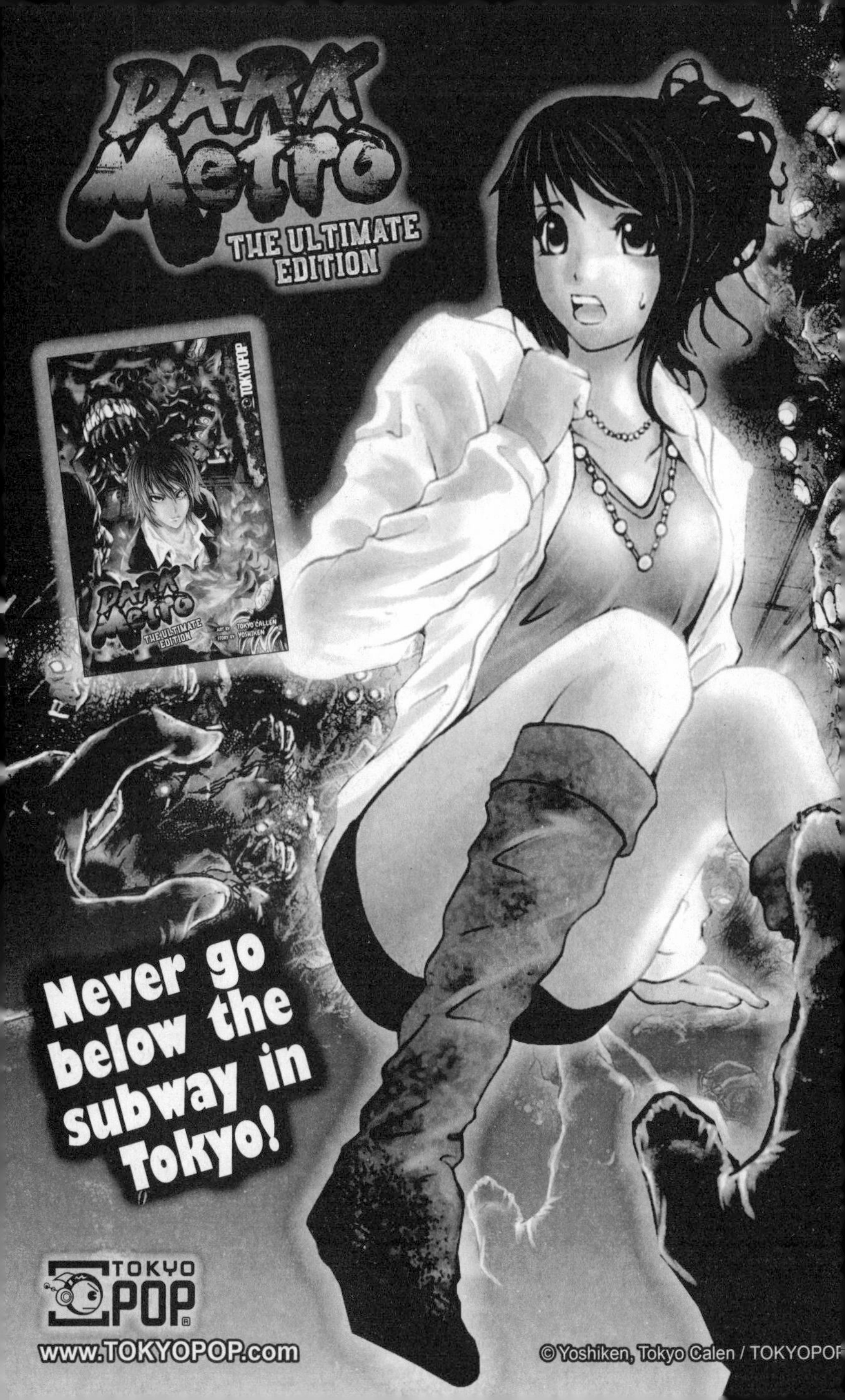
DARK Metro
THE ULTIMATE EDITION
Never go below the subway in Tokyo!
TOKYOPOP
www.TOKYOPOP.com
© Yoshiken, Tokyo Calen / TOKYOPOP

TOKYOPOP
PRESENTS

TOKYOPOP GmbH / *Goldfisch* - NANA YAA / *Kamo* - BAN ZARBO / *Undead Messiah* - GIN ZARBO / *Ocean of Secrets* - SOPHIE-CHAN /
*ord Princess Amaltea* - NATALIA BATISTA

TOKYO
POP

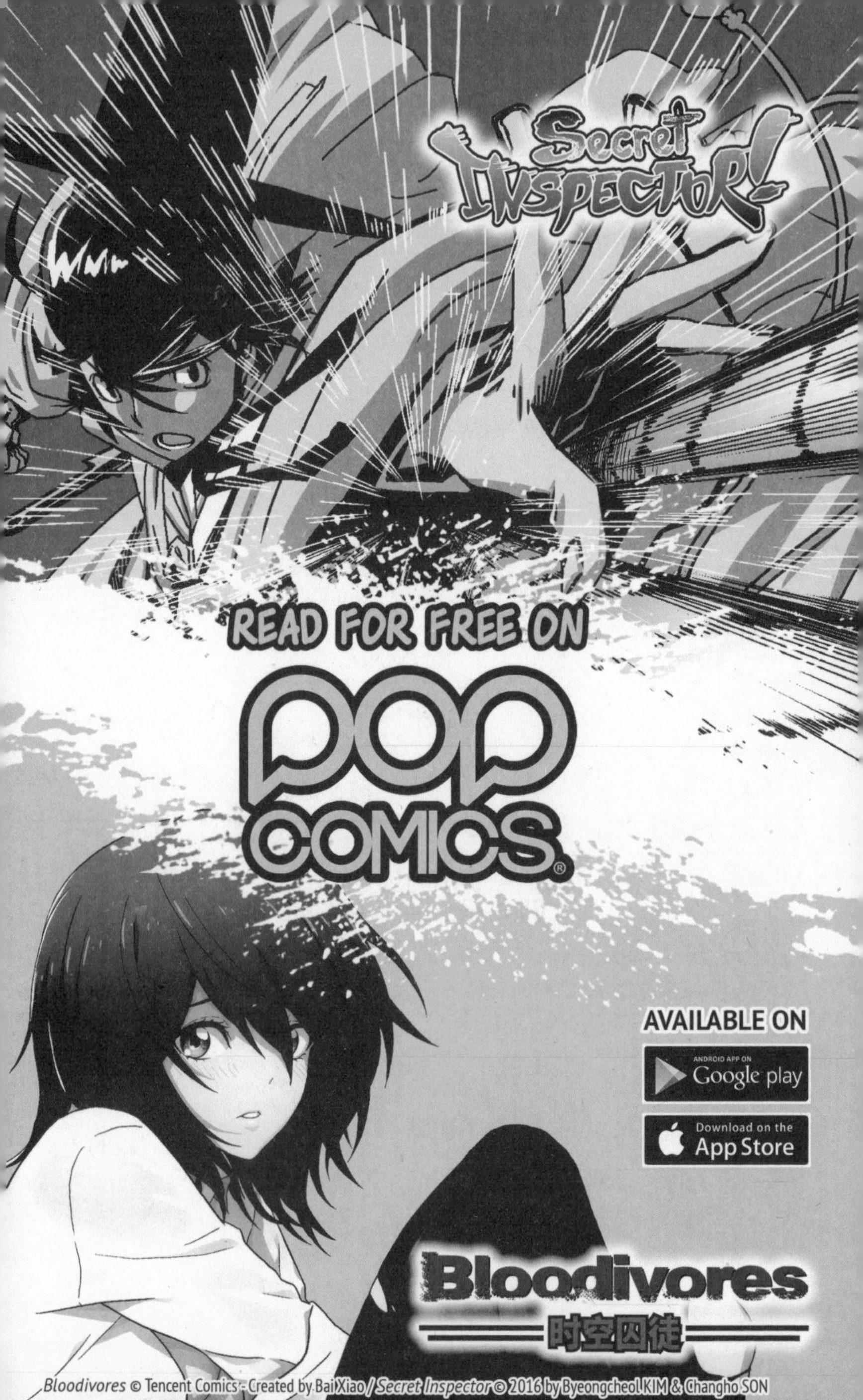

Secret INSPECTOR!
READ FOR FREE ON
POP COMICS®
AVAILABLE ON
ANDROID APP ON
Google play
Download on the
App Store
Bloodivores
时空囚徒